EUROPEAN PINE IMPORTS

Importers & Exporters of Quality Antique Pine Furniture

NOW YOU CAN FIND IT ALL IN ENGLAND

STOP PRESS

Planned opening in Berkshire in late Spring 95

FREE DELIVERY THROUGHOUT THE UK ON ORDERS OVER £3,000

Scaled down charges on orders below this amount.
Many of our dealers buy one or two pieces, others buy more.

All our customers are made welcome.

Small section of our warehouse

A superb dresser beautifully made and heavily carved, a real one off!

NEW WAREHOUSE!
We now have a further 15,000 sq ft of space filled with imported furniture

Why travel abroad. when all you need is right here?... and at better prices too!

European Pine Imports' Average Price Guide

Knock down robes, 2 & 3 door ....£180 - £230	Czech 2 door robes.......£160 - £180
Blanket boxes, flat & dome ....£35 - £70	Pot cupboards..............£30 - £50
Czech single door robes ....£130 - £150	Static robes..................£70 - £280
	Chest of drawers ....£65 - £240
	Beds..............................£35 - £65
	Kitchen dressers ....£150 - £220

Bookcases, desks, kitchenalia, hand carts, small items in pine, baskets, sledges, skis, etc, always in stock

DEBBIE, left, responsible for the day to day running of European Pine Imports.
You can phone her for container updates on:

01642 584351 or 0860 710951 mobile

Fax **01642 584351** **European & UK mobile: 0802 226240**

OPEN 7 DAYS A WEEK BY APPOINTMENT

JIDE

pine & country furniture

MILLER'S

MILLER'S PINE & COUNTRY FURNITURE BUYER'S GUIDE

Compiled and designed by
Miller's Publications Ltd
The Cellars, High Street
Tenterden, Kent TN30 6BN
Tel: 01580 766411

Project Editor: Jo Wood
Editorial Assistants: Caroline Bugeja, Rosemary Cooke,
Carol Gillings, Lalage Johnstone
Production Assistants: Elaine Burrell, Gillian Charles
Advertising Executive: Melinda Williams
Index compiled by: DD Editorial Services, Beccles
Design: Philip Hannath, Kari Reeves
Advertisement Designer: Simon Cook
Jacket Design: Colin Goody
Additional photography: Ian Booth, David Copsey, Roddy Paine, Robin Saker

First published in Great Britain in 1995
by Miller's, a division of Mitchell Beazley,
imprints of Octopus Publishing Group Ltd,
2–4 Heron Quays, London E14 4JP

A CIP catalogue record for this book is
available from the British Library

ISBN 1-84000-374-X

Bromide output by Perfect Image, Hurst Green, East Sussex
Illustrations by G. H. Graphics, St. Leonard's-on-Sea, East Sussex
Colour origination by Scantrans, Singapore
Film output by CK Litho, Whitstable, Kent
Printed and bound by Toppan Printing Co (HK) Ltd, China

MILLER'S

pine & country furniture

JO WOOD PROJECT EDITOR

ACKNOWLEDGEMENTS

Miller's Publications would like to acknowledge the great assistance given by our consultants:

PINE FURNITURE

Graham Price became interested in country furniture after renovating a Sussex farmhouse in 1976 and furnishing it with pine. He became a regular buyer of pine at local auctions which led to dealing on a part-time basis. In 1980 he acquired premises in Bexhill and in 1982 established an export antiques warehouse near Eastbourne. Up Country was established in Tunbridge Wells in 1987. Since 1982, Graham has travelled widely and bought country furniture throughout the UK, Ireland, France, Scandinavia, Holland and Central Europe. He has contributed articles on country furniture to magazines and has been involved in antiques and restoration programmes for television in the US.
Up Country, The Old Corn Stores, 68 St John's Road, Tunbridge Wells, Kent TN4 9PE

Ann Lingard began collecting needlework tools and samplers and then moved on to pine and country furniture. She has run her shop in Rye, Sussex for over 25 years and sells to top dealers all over the world, particularly in the US and Japan. Ann writes articles for many antiques publications.
Rope Walk Antiques, Rope Walk, Rye, Sussex TN31 7NA

COUNTRY FURNITURE

Robert Young left Sotheby's in 1975 to start his own business. In 1978 he opened a shop in Battersea specializing in country furniture and folk art. He has written many articles for the *Antique Collector* and *Antique Collector's Club* magazine, as well as lecturing at Sotheby's and the Women's institute. Robert co-wrote *Treen for the Table* with Dr Jonathan Levi in 1998 and in 1999 wrote *Folk Art* published by Mitchell Beazley. He is Chairman of vetting Country Furniture and Folk Art at the Fine Art and Antiques Fair at Olympia, London and also vets the San Francisco Fall Antiques Show, Grosvenor House Antiques Fair, Antiques for Everyone in Birmingham and the Chelsea Antiques Fairs.
Robert Young Antiques, 68 Battersea Bridge Road, London SW11 3AG

Derek Green of Cedar Antiques has been trading in Hartley Wintney for many years, specializing in country furniture and associated items. His wife Sally joined the company, adding a new design and furniture-finding service.
Cedar Antiques, High Street, Hartley Wintney, Hampshire RG27 8NY

Patrick Robbins began dealing in the late 1960s, and as his interest in oak and country furniture grew he began to specialize. Patrick has contributed many articles to antiques publications.

Richard Bebb has been dealing in Welsh furniture and folk art for over 25 years and is the author of *Welsh Country Furniture*. He also contributes regularly to many antiques magazines.
Country Antiques, Castle Mill, Kidwelly, Dyfed, Wales SA17 4UU

KITCHENWARE

Annie Marchant began dealing in kitchen antiques many years ago at Bermondsey Market and Covent Garden in London. Since then she has progressed to the large fairs specializing in kitchen, laundry and dairy antiques. Her own passion is for dairy antiques and breadboards, which she has collected for many years.
Wenderton Antiques. Tel: 01227 720295

Christina Bishop has had a stall in the Portobello Road Antiques Market and has dealt in kitchenware for many years. Christina was born and brought up in Lancashire and her enthusiasm for kitchenware stems from an interest in social and domestic history as well as a passion for baking. She is the author of *Miller's Collecting Kitchenware*.
Christina Bishop Kitchenware, Westway, Portobello Road Market, London W11

CONTENTS

MILLER'S

KEY TO ILLUSTRATIONS

Each illustration and descriptive caption is accompanied by a letter code. By referring to the following list of contributors, auctioneers (denoted by *) and dealers (•), the source of any item may be immediately determined. In no way does this constitute or imply a contract or binding offer on the part of any of our contributors to supply or sell the goods illustrated, or similar articles, at the prices stated. Advertisers are denoted by †.

A/ALD * Aldridges, Newark House, 26–45 Cheltenham Street, Bath, Somerset BA2 3EX Tel: 01225 462830
AF • Albert Forsythe, The Old Rectory, 24 Carnteel Road, Aughmacloy, Co Tyrone, Northern Ireland BT69 2DU Tel: 01662 557522
AG * Anderson & Garland (Auctioneers), Marlborough House, Marlborough Crescent, Newcastle-upon-Tyne, Tyne & Wear NE1 4EE Tel: 0191 232 6278
AGr * Andrew Grant, St Mark's House, St Mark's Close, Worcester WR5 3DJ Tel: 01905 357547
AH * Andrew Hartley, Victoria Hall Salerooms, Little Lane, Ilkley, Yorks LS29 8EA Tel: 01943 816363 Email: ahartley.finearts@talk21.com
AHL • Adrian Hornsey Ltd, Langdons, Sidmouth Road, Clyst St Mary, Exeter EX5 1DR Tel: 01392 877395
AI • Antiques & Interiors, Romney Bay House, Coast Road, Littlestone, New Romney, Kent TN28 8QY Tel: 01797 364747
AL •† Ann Lingard, Ropewalk Antiques, Ropewalk, Rye, East Sussex TN31 7NA Tel: 01797 223486
AnD •† Antique & Design, The Old Oast, Hollow Lane, Canterbury, Kent CT1 3SA Tel: 01227 762871
AP * G E Sworder incorporating Andrew Pickford, The Hertford Saleroom, 42 St Andrew Street, Hertford SG14 1JA Tel: 01992 583508/501421
AP • Angela Page Antiques, 15 Cumberland Walk, Tunbridge Wells, Kent TN1 1VT Tel: 01892 522217
B * Boardman Fine Art Auctioneers, Station Road Corner, Haverhill, Suffolk CB9 0EY Tel: 01440 730414
Bea * Bearnes, Avenue Road, Torquay, Devon TQ2 5TG Tel: 01803 296277
BEL • Bell Antiques, 68A Harold Street, Grimsby, Humberside DN35 0HH Tel: 01472 695110
Ber • Berry Antiques, Berry House, 11–13 Stone Street, Cranbrook, Kent TN17 3HF Tel: 01580 712345
BH/ BOA/ HOA •† Bob Hoare Antiques, Unit Q, Phoenix Place, North Street, Lewes, East Sussex BN7 2DQ Tel: 01273 480557
Bon * Bonhams & Brooks, Montpelier Street, Knightsbridge, London SW7 1HH Tel: 020 7393 3900
BR • Bed of Roses, 12 Prestbury Road, Cheltenham, Gloucestershire GL52 2PW Tel: 01242 231918
Byl •† Bygones of Ireland Ltd, Lodge Road, Westport, County Mayo, Republic of Ireland Tel: (098) 26132/25701
C * Christie, Manson & Wood Ltd, 8 King Street, St James's, London SW1Y 6QT Tel: 020 7839 9060
CAL/ Ced • Cedar Antiques Ltd, High Street, Hartley Wintney, Hampshire RG27 8NY Tel: 01252 843252
CCA • Combe Cottage Antiques, Castle Combe, Chippenham, Wiltshire SN14 7HU Tel: 01249 782250
CDC * Capes Dunn & Co, The Auction Galleries, 38 Charles Street, Off Princess Street, Greater Manchester M1 7DB Tel: 0161 273 6060/1911
CEMB • Christina Bishop Kitchenware 1890s–1960s. Viewing by appointment only Tel: 020 7221 4688
CGC * Cheffins Grain & Comins, 2 Clifton Road, Cambridge CB2 4BW Tel: 01223 358731
CNY * Christie, Manson & Woods International Inc., 502 Park Avenue, (including Christie's East), New York 10022 USA Tel: 001 212 546 1000
CoA • Country Antiques (Wales), Castle Mill, Kidwelly, Carmarthenshire, Wales SA17 4UU Tel: 01554 890534
COT •† Christopher Peters Antiques, 19 Broad Street, Brinklow, Nr Rugby, Warwickshire CV23 0LS Tel: 01788 832673
Cou • Country Homes, 61 Long Street, Tetbury, Gloucestershire GL8 8AA Tel: 01666 502342
CSK * Christie's South Kensington Ltd, 85 Old Brompton Road, London SW7 3LD Tel: 020 7581 7611
CUL • Cullompton, Old Tannery Antiques, The Old Tannery, Exeter Road, Cullompton, Devon EX15 1DT Tel: 01884 38476/266429
DA * Dee, Atkinson & Harrison, The Exchange Saleroom, Driffield, Yorkshire YO25 7LJ Tel: 01377 253151 Email: exchange@dee-atkinson-harrison Website: www.dee-atkinson-harrison.co.uk
DDM * Dickinson Davy & Markham, Wrawby Street, Brigg, Humberside DN20 8JJ Tel: 01652 653666
DDS • Dorking Desk Shop, 41 West Street, Dorking, Surrey RH4 1BU Tel: 01306 883327
DEL • Ann Delores, Bartlett Street Antique Centre, 5–10 Bartlett Street, Bath, Somerset BA1 2QZ Tel: 01225 310457
DEN/ GD * Denham's, The Auction Galleries, Warnham, Horsham, West Sussex RH12 3RZ Tel: 01403 255699/253837 Email: denhams@lineone.net
DFA •† Delvin Farm Antiques, Gormonston, Co Meath, Republic of Ireland Tel: 00 353 1 841 2285
DM * Diamond Mills & Co, 117 Hamilton Road, Felixstowe, Suffolk IP11 7BL Tel: 01394 282281
DMA • David Masters Antiques, Elm Tree Farm, High Halden, Ashford, Kent TN26 3BP Tel: 01233 850551
DMe • Ireland's Own Antiques, Alpine House, Carlow Road, Abbeyleix, Co Laois, Republic of Ireland Tel: 00 353 502 31348
DN/ DWB * Dreweatt Neate, Donnington Priory, Donnington, Newbury, Berkshire RG13 2JE Tel: 01635 553553
EL * Eldred's, Robert C Eldred Co Inc, 1475 Route 6A, East Dennis, Massachusetts 0796 USA 02641 Tel: 00 1 508 385 3116
ERA •† English Rose Antiques, 7 Church Street, Coggeshall, Essex CO6 1TU Tel: 01376 562683 Mobile 07770 880790
FAG • Fagins Antiques, The Old Whiteways, Cider Factory, Hele, Exeter, Devon EX5 4PW Tel: 01392 882062
FHA • Flower House Antiques, 90 High Street, Tenterden, Kent TN30 6HT Tel: 01580 763764
FOX • Foxhole Antiques, Swan & Foxhole, Albert House, Stone Street, Cranbrook, Kent Tel: 01580 712720
FP • For Pine, 340 Berkhampstead Road, Chesham, Buckinghamshire HP5 3HF Tel: 01494 776119
FRM * Frank R Marshall & Co, Marshall House, Church Hill, Knutsford, Cheshire WA16 6DH Tel: 01565 653284
GA(W) * Phillips of Winchester, The Red House, Hyde Street, Winchester, Hampshire SO23 7DX Tel: 01962 862515
GD •† Gilbert & Dale Antiques, The Old Chapel, Church Street, Ilchester, Nr Yeovil, Somerset BA22 8ZA Tel: 01935 840464
GPA •† Graham Price Antiques Ltd, Apple Store, Chaucer Industrial Estate, Dittons Road, Polegate, East Sussex BN26 6JF Tel: 01323 487167
HeR •† Heritage Restorations, Maes Y Glydfa, Llanfair Caereinion, Welshpool, Powys, Wales SY21 0HD Tel: 01938 810384 Website: www.heritagerestorations.co.uk
HON •† Honan's Antiques, Crowe Street, Gort, Co. Galway, Republic of Ireland Tel: 00 353 916 31407
HSS * Phillips, 20 The Square, Retford, Nottinghamshire DN22 6BX Tel: 01777 708633
IW • Islwyn Watkins, Offa's Dyke Antique Centre, 4 High Street, Knighton, Powys, Wales LD7 1AT Tel: 01547 520145
JAC • John & Anne Clegg, 12 Old Street, Ludlow, Shropshire SY8 1NP Tel: 01584 873176
JBL • Judi Bland, Durham House Antique Centre, Sheep Street, Stow-on-the-Wold,

Gloucestershire GL54 1AA
Tel: 01451 870404/01276 857576

JD * Lewes Auction Rooms (Julian Dawson), 56 High Street, Lewes, E Sussex BN7 1XE Tel: 01273 478221 www.lewesauctions.com

JH * Jacobs & Hunt, 26 Lavant Street, Petersfield, Hampshire GU32 3EF Tel: 01730 233933

JHW • John Howkins, 1 Dereham Rd, Norwich NR2 4HX Tel: 01603 627832

JMW * Trembath Welch, The Old Town Hall, Great Dunmow, Essex CM6 1AU Tel: 01371 873014

KEY • Key Antiques.

L * Lawrence Fine Art Auctioneers, South Street, Crewkerne, Somerset TA18 8AB Tel: 01460 73041

LAM • Penny Lampard, 28 High Street, Headcorn, Kent TN27 9NE Tel: 01622 890682

LAM * Lambrays, incorporating R J Hamm ASVA, Polmorla Walk, The Platt, Wadebridge, Cornwall PL27 7AE Tel: 0120 881 3593

LAY * David Lay ASVA, Auction House, Alverton, Penzance, Cornwall TR18 4RE Tel: 01736 361414

LHA * Lesley Hindman Auctioneers, 215 West Ohio Street, Chicago, Illinois USA 60610 Tel: 001 312 670 0010

LIB • Libra Antiques Tel: 01580 860569

LRG * Lots Road Galleries, 71–73 Lots Road, Chelsea, London SW10 0RN Tel: 020 7351 7771

M * Morphets of Harrogate, 6 Albert Street, Harrogate, Yorkshire HG1 1JL Tel: 01423 530030

MAT * Christopher Matthews, 23 Mount Street, Harrogate, Yorkshire HG2 8DQ Tel: 01423 871756

MCA * Mervyn Carey, Twysden Cottage, Benenden, Cranbrook, Kent TN17 4LD Tel: 01580 240283

MGM * Bonhams & Brooks West Country, Devon Fine Art Auction House, Dowell Street, Honiton, Devon EX14 8LX Tel: 01404 41872

MIL • Milverton Antiques. No longer trading

N * Neales, 192–194 Mansfield Road, Nottingham, NG1 3HU Tel: 0115 962 4141

NWE •† North Wiltshire Exporters, Farm Hill House, Brinkworth, Nr Chippenham, Wilts SN15 5AJ Tel: 01666 510876

OB • Oola Boola, 166 Tower Bridge Rd, London SE1 3LS Tel: 020 7403 0794/020 8693 5050 Mobile 0956 261252

OCP • Old Court Pine (Alain & Alicia Chawner).

OL * Outhwaite & Litherland, Kingsway Galleries, Fontenoy Street, Liverpool, Merseyside L3 2BE Tel: 0151 236 6561

OMH • The Old Mint House, High Street, Pevensey, East Sussex BN24 5LF Tel: 01323 762337 E-mail: minthouse@mistral.co.uk

OPH • The Old Pine House, 16 Warwick Street, Royal Leamington Spa, Warwickshire CV32 5LL Tel: 01926 470477

OSc • Simon & Penny Rumble, Causeway End Farm House, Chittering, Cambridgeshire CB5 9PW Tel: 01223 861831

P * Phillips, Blenstock House, 7 Blenheim Street, New Bond Street, London W1Y 0AS Tel: 020 7629 6602

P(L) * Phillips Leeds, 17a East Parade, Leeds, Yorkshire LS1 2BH Tel: 0113 2448011

P(M) * Phillips, 114 Washway Road, Sale, Greater Manchester M33 7RF Tel: 0161 962 9237

P(S)/PWC * Phillips, 49 London Road, Sevenoaks, Kent TN13 1AR Tel: 01732 740310

PC •† The Pine Cellars, 39 Jewry Street, Winchester, Hampshire SO23 8RY Tel: 01962 777546

PC Private Collection

PC/PCh* Peter Cheney, Western Road Auction Rooms, Western Road, Littlehampton, West Sussex BN17 5NP Tel: 01903 722264/713418

PEN • Pennard House Antiques, 3–4 Piccadilly, London Road, Bath, Somerset BA1 6PL Tel: 01225 313791/ 01749 860260

Ph • Robert Phelps Ltd, 133–135 St Margaret's Road, East Twickenham, Middlesex TW1 1RG Tel: 020 8892 1778/7129

PHA • Paul Hopwell, 30 High Street, West Haddon, Northamptonshire NN6 7AP Tel: 01788 510636

POT •† The Pot Board, 30 King Street, Carmarthen, Wales SA31 1BS Tel: 01834 842699/01267 236623 Email: Gill@potboard.co.uk Website: www.potboard.co.uk

PS * Phillips North West, New House, 150 Christleton Road, Chester CH3 5TD Tel: 01244 313936

R * Rendells, Stonepark, Ashburton, Devon TQ13 7RH Tel: 01364 653017 Website: www.rendells.co.uk

RA • Roberts Antiques, Lancashire Tel: 01253 827798

RBB * Brightwells Ltd, Ryelands Road, Leominster, Herefordshire HR6 8NZ Tel: 01568 611122 Email: fineart@rbbm.co.uk Website: www.rbbm.co.uk

RdeR • Rogers de Rin, 76 Royal Hospital Road, London SW3 4HN Tel: 020 7352 9007

RIT * Ritchie Inc, D & J Auctioneers & Appraisers of Antiques & Fine Arts, 288 King Street East, Toronto, Ontario, Canada M5A 1K4 Tel: (416) 364 1864

RK • Richard Kimbell, Riverside, Market Harborough, Leicestershire LE16 7PT Tel: 01858 433444

RP • Robert Pugh, Avon Tel: 01225 314713

RYA •† Robert Young Antiques, 68 Battersea Bridge Road, London SW11 3AG Tel: 020 7228 7847

S * Sotheby's, 34–35 New Bond Street, London W1A 2AA Tel: 020 7293 5000

S(NY) * Sotheby's, 1334 York Avenue, New York, USA NY 10021 Tel: 212 606 7000

S(S) * Sotheby's Sussex, Summers Place, Billingshurst, West Sussex RH14 9AD Tel: 01403 833500

SA/SAn • Somerville Antiques & Country Furniture Ltd. Retired

SHA • Shambles, 22 North Street, Ashburton, Devon TQ13 7QD Tel: 01364 653848

SK(B) * Skinner Inc, 357 Main Street, Bolton, USA MA 01740 Tel: 00 1 978 779 6241

SPa • Sparks Antiques. No longer trading

SSP • Stanley Stripped Pine.

SV • Sutton Valence Antiques, North Street, Sutton Valence, Kent Tel: 01622 675332

SWN • Swan Antiques, Stone Street, Cranbrook, Kent TN17 3HF Tel: 01580 712720

TaB • Tartan Bow, Suffolk Tel: 01379 783057 (open Fridays 10–5pm, other days by appt)

TEN * Tennants, The Auction Centre, Harmby Road, Leyburn, Yorks DL8 5SG Tel: 01969 623780

TM * Thomas Mawer & Son, The Lincoln Saleroom, 63 Monks Road, Lincoln LN2 5HP Tel: 01522 524984

TPC •† The Pine Cellars, 39 Jewry Street, Winchester, Hampshire SO23 8RY Tel: 01962 777546/867014

TRU • The Trumpet, West End, Minchinhampton, Gloucestershire GL6 9JA Tel: 01453 883027

UC •† Graham Price, Up Country, The Old Corn Stores, 68 St John's Road, Tunbridge Wells, Kent TN4 9PE Tel: 01892 523341

UP • Utopia Antiques Ltd, Yew Tree Barn (on A590), Newton-in-Cartnel, Grange-over-Sands, Cumbria LA11 6JP Tel: 015395 30065

W * Walter's, No 1 Mint Lane, Lincoln LN1 1UD Tel: 01522 525454

WAC • Worcester Antiques Centre, Reindeer Court, Mealcheapen Street, Worcester WR1 4DF Tel: 01905 610680

WaH •† The Warehouse, 29–30 Queens Gardens, Worthington Street, Dover, Kent CT17 9AH Tel: 01304 242006

WAT •† Crudwell Furniture Strippers, The Workshop, Oddpenny Farm, Crudwell, Wiltshire SN16 9SJ Tel: 01285 770970

WEL • Wells Reclamation & Co, Coxley, Nr Wells, Somerset BA5 1RQ Tel: 01749 677087

WHA • Wych House Antiques, Wych Hill, Woking, Surrey GU22 0EU Tel: 01483 764636

WHL * W H Lane & Son, Jubilee House, Queen Street, Penzance, Cornwall TR18 2DF Tel: 01736 361447 Email: graham.bazlet@excite.com

WIL * Peter Wilson, Victoria Gallery, Market Street, Nantwich, Cheshire CW5 5DG Tel: 01270 623878

WL * Wintertons Ltd, Lichfield Auction Centre, Wood End Lane, Fradley, Lichfield, Staffordshire WS13 8NF Tel: 01543 263256

WRe • Walcot Reclamations, 108 Walcot Street, Bath, Somerset BA1 5BG Tel: 01225 444404

WV •† Westville House Antiques, Littleton, Nr Somerton, Somerset TA11 6NP Tel: 01458 273376

WW * Woolley & Wallis, Salisbury Salerooms, 51–61 Castle Street, Salisbury, Wiltshire SP1 3SU Tel: 01722 424500

INTRODUCTION

In recent years there has been a distinct move away from the emphasis on luxury and extravagance which dominated the 1980s. The growth in popularity of pine and country furniture is an indication of our changing tastes, that have become increasingly focused on simplicity, versatility and practicality.

Country furniture was designed to be plain, solid and functional, and was made for use in ordinary houses and cottages rather than stately homes, mansions or palaces. The oldest pieces that are available to buy today date from the early 17th century. The fact that furniture in this style continued to be made and used in the 18th and 19th centuries, principally in rural areas, has led to the somewhat misleading term 'country furniture'. The most commonly-used wood was oak, but pieces were also made in chestnut, beech, walnut, elm, ash, yew and the fruitwoods. Craftsmen used designs that reflected the natural properties of the materials available, such as the suppleness of beech, and the wonderful rich colours of the fruitwoods.

There is a wide variety of styles and forms that exist in British country furniture – Welsh-made pieces are particularly characteristic, and even have their own names. Country furniture was also produced in the United States and in the rest of Europe, and French Provincial Furniture in particular has become more readily available.

Although sometimes not as old as some oak and country furniture, pine has also become increasingly popular. Solid wood has a universal appeal, and the warm, golden colour of pine is easy to work with when decorating a room, a flat or a whole house. The functional nature of the designs means that pieces will not go out of fashion, and also gives them a great deal of versatility – a pine side table will look equally good in a living room, bedroom or bathroom.

Pine furniture exists in many different types: antique, old Continental, 'antique' and reproduction, and may be painted or unpainted. Depending on your tastes or your budget, these can be mixed and matched; the timelessness of pine furniture means that an antique table can sit quite comfortably with a set of 20th century pine chairs.

When buying country furniture, bear in mind that for 17th and 18th century pieces, the colour and patina (the glow the wood develops over the years from an accumulation of wax, polish and dirt) account for around fifty per cent of the value. This is particularly true of oak which will not withstand cleaning and French polishing like mahogany. Other important factors include the condition, the quality of the carving or decoration, and the existence of carved dates and inscriptions.

Pine is likely to be found in almost any condition, and the original quality may also be variable; some pieces were skillfully made, while others were hastily nailed together. If a piece of pine furniture has not already been stripped down to the natural wood, then it may be covered with paint, or black or brown varnish – to find out what the bottom layer is, remove part of the paint or varnish in a concealed place, with the edge of a coin for example, taking care not to damage the wood itself. If you want to buy a piece you can strip down, look for plain wood, and avoid pine which has a red stain – this will have been caused by the pigment of an old paint or brown stain. However, if you are after a piece that you can repaint then this will not matter, and you may be able to buy at a lower price.

If you are buying stripped pine, check that the arms and legs are secure as the chemical process of stripping the wood can loosen joints. The softness of pine also means that parts such as feet and cornices may have been replaced on older pieces. Check that the workmanship is good, and the colours match.

There is a wide variety of items available in both pine and country furniture suitable to furnish any room. For kitchens there are tables, chairs, dressers, serving tables, benches and settles (wooden settees with high backs). Originally designed to divide the cooking area from the dining space, dressers are an attractive addition to any kitchen and allow you to display crockery and other items. Depending on their age, country chairs, especially matching sets, can become expensive. It is possible, however, to buy single, non-matching chairs for relatively modest amounts, particularly those from the 19th century and these can look very effective. Even in a small kitchen, shelves or wall cabinets provide space for storage or display without making the room feel cluttered.

If you decide to give your living room a country theme, side tables, bureaux, Windsor and other armchairs, stools and small tables can all help towards the effect. Again, if you have a limited budget, you could concentrate on small and non-matching pieces and build up the look slowly. Chests are always good value and can serve as low tables.

Small pieces of pine or country furniture can also transform the feel of a bedroom; a box can sit at the foot of a bed (and provide useful storage for bedding) and old shelves and chests of drawers are also an attractive addition. Other accessories can help to build up the look, such as folk-style decorations, old prints, baskets, candlesticks and country fabrics particularly patchwork.

Whether you are buying from an auction, dealer, secondhand shop or a warehouse, always buy the best you can afford, and take comfort in the knowledge that your fruitwood stool from c1800, your three-legged elm cricket table, or your pine pot cupboard from c1870 are likely to maintain, if not increase, their value in the present market.

PINE FURNITURE

Over the past few years, the pine trade has become established in its own right with pine furniture a popular choice for houses both old and modern. Pine itself falls into several categories: antique, old, Continental, 'antique' and reproduction. A variety of size, design and finish ensures that there is something for everyone within this thriving market.

It is helpful to bear a few pointers in mind when buying a piece of pine furniture, as style, availability, condition and age all have a bearing on the price and value of a piece. In addition, the modern-day requirements of individuals, interior designers and fashion trends, tend to dictate and have an effect on price and availability of styles.

An example of the above is seen in the present-day demand for turned leg pine dining tables, measuring between 72 and 96in (182.5 and 243.5cm) long and 36in (91.5cm) wide. Such pieces are greatly sought after as most tables of these dimensions were made in mahogany. On the other hand, the honest straight leg pine kitchen table is readily available – a factor reflected in its lower price. Sometimes the straight legs are removed on such tables and replaced with turned legs, partly to be fashionable and partly to add height under the apron of the table.

The proportion and condition of a piece are important to its value and price. For example, a wardrobe that is not deep enough to take a coat hanger, or a table of the right height with insufficient leg-room, or one that is not tall enough, is not a practical piece of furniture. Some people like pine to look pristine and in mint condition, others prefer the worn and slightly battered look – whatever your preference, do ensure that the piece is in a sufficiently good condition to stand up to its proper use. If in doubt, ask the dealer or auction house for guidance, they should be happy to advise you.

Much old pine has been painted, and a great deal comes to the trade with as many as twelve coats of paint (on top of the original), which should be removed. There are two basic ways of doing this. It can be done painstakingly by hand with a sharp knife or razor blade, in order to retain as much of the original paint as possible, or it must be dipped and washed off well. However, it is usually these coats of paint which have, over the years, protected the soft wood underneath. When the paint has all gone, one hopes that the beautiful original wood will be revealed; on the other hand, you may find that the piece has been made up from different, mismatching pine or, worse, not from pine at all!

Once the wood is quite dry, it can be gently sanded and finished with a wax polish. It will soon mellow to its own unique colour and, if kept polished, will take on a glowing appearance. Be wary of any pine that needs repairing: it is difficult to match woods for invisible restoration, particularly as it may have mellowed with the passing years. Pieces which have been used in a workshop and have oily patches are also problematic areas – oil is very difficult to remove, and produces a sticky finish when waxed.

The price of antique pine has continued to increase in value in line with, and sometimes ahead of, other woods. Many pieces which were widely available ten years ago are now relatively difficult to find: linen presses, good dressers, press tables, pot cupboards and chairs are prime examples. Although this may be a relatively expensive collecting area, there is nearly always something interesting, unusual and useful to be found. More everyday furniture, such as tables, chests of drawers and boxes, are still in plentiful supply.

The diverse origins of pine furniture, and numerous types of pine trees, all contribute to its varied repertoire. Pine, or deal as it was known in early times, was partly home-grown, with some imported from Scandinavia and North America. This accounts for its wide variety of colour and grain. Pitch pine, another variety, is a dark, grainy wood and, although very hard, is not as popular since its unique colour does not mix well with other woods.

Apart from Maples, Heal's, Shoolbreds of London and Gillows of Lancaster, there are few well-known makers of pine furniture in Britain. Some furniture was made in country workshops, giving us engaging primitive pieces; some was made for 'the big house' by estate carpenters and joiners, who produced free-standing furniture, one-off pieces, and built-in panelling and shutters. Fine cabinet-makers also used pine as a carcass for exotic and expensive woods.

British pine furniture can largely be divided into regional types: for example, in the south of England one can find conventional chests of drawers, tall closed and open dressers, and potboard bases; Wales has superbly conventional dressers, and many unusual chests of drawers; Scotland boasts a great deal of quality pine, including huge chests of drawers with twisted panels and various drawer arrangements, wall racks and wall shelves, and low Scottish dressers. Irish pine has its own primitive charm, with one-piece dressers, primitive chairs and substantial food cupboards.

With such a diverse and versatile wood as pine, there will be something to appeal to everyone. The wide range available means the piece that you choose, as well as being pleasing to the eye, should serve a long and useful life.

Ann Lingard

An Irish pine dresser, with glazed doors to top, 2 drawers and cupboards to base, 19thC, 54in (137cm) wide.
£1,400–1,700 *TPC*

A Winchester pine haberdashery chest, with glazed sliding doors above 12 graduated drawers, on bun feet, c1860, 72in (183cm) wide.
£1,400–1,700 *TPC*

A Continental pine dresser, with glazed doors to top, on turned supports, over carved, piano fronted two-drawer, two-door base, 19thC, 50in (127cm) wide.
£1,200–1,500 *TPC*

A pine dresser with pierced and fretted frieze above an open delft plate rack and 4 spice drawers, on a base with a central cupboard flanked by 3 drawers each side, on bun feet, 19thC, 52in (132cm) wide.
£1,500–1,800 *TPC*

A pine dresser, with open delft plate rack and spice drawers, on base with 2 drawers above a pair of double panelled doors, 19thC, 52in (132cm) wide.
£1,300–1,600 *TPC*

r. A pine open potboard dresser with 2 drawers, on square legs, 19thC, 48in (122cm) wide.
£1,100–1,300 *TPC*

l. A country pine dresser, with open delft plate rack, on unusual base with centre cupboard flanked by stepped and graduated drawers, early 19thC, 90in (229cm) wide.
£2,100–2,500 *TPC*

r. A pine farmhouse dresser, with stepped delft plate rack above a three-drawer, three-door base, 19thC, 78in (198cm) high.
£2,200–2,700 *TPC*

An Irish pine dresser, c1840, 55in (139.5cm) wide.
£1,700–2,000 *UP*

A West Country cottage glazed pine dresser, with cupboards below and applied split mouldings, 19thC, 48in (122cm) wide.
£2,500–3,000 *CC*

A pine free-standing base, c1860, 46in (116.5cm) wide.
£750–950 *AL*

An Irish pine dresser, c1840, 68in (172.5cm) wide.
£1,800–2,200 *UP*

A German pine breakfront dresser, 19thC, 59in (149.5cm) wide.
£1,700–2,100 *PC*

An Irish one-piece pine dresser, with a plate rack, c1860, 54in (135cm) wide.
£1,300–1,600 *PIN*

A Cornish pine dresser, 18thC, 58in (147cm) wide.
£2,200–2,650 *PH*

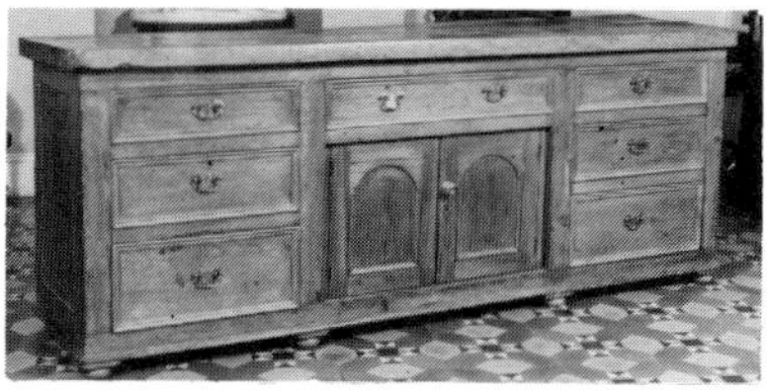

A North Wales pine dresser base, with a thick sycamore top, 90in (228.5cm) wide.
£2,000–2,400 *PH*

A miniature pine dresser base, c1840, 25in (63.5cm) wide.
£600–750 *AS*

A long potboard dresser base, c1830, 134in (340cm) wide.
£2,200–2,600 *PH*

A North Country enclosed dresser, 19thC.
£1,700–2,100 *JMW*

A pine base unit, c1870, 60in (152cm) wide.
£900–1,100 *SSD*

A pine dresser, 48in (122cm) wi
£1,600–1,900 *LAM*

A pine half-glazed Welsh dresser, early 19thC, 72in (182.5cm) wide.
£1,700–2,000 *TPC*

An early Victorian Irish pine dresser, 54½in (138cm) wide.
£1,800–2,200 *WAT*

A Victorian pine Welsh dresser, with 3 drawers, c1860, 48in (122cm) wide.
£1,400–1,700 *CUL*

An Irish pine dresser, with fretted top and fiddle front, c1860, 58in (147cm) wide.
£2,100–2,500 *HON*

l. A late Georgian pine potboard dresser, 93in (236cm) wide.
£2,500–3,000 *WAT*

l. A pine dresser, with 3 central drawers flanked by 2 cupboards to base, late 19thC, 43in (109cm) wide.
£1,400–1,700
CUL

A pine dresser, c1850, 88in (223.5cm) wide.
£2,400–2,900 *Sca*

An Irish pine dresser, c1880, 63in (160cm) wide.
£1,800–2,200 *UP*

An Irish pine dresser, c1860, 52in (132cm) wide.
£1,800–2,200 *UP*

A pine dresser, 19thC, 60in (152cm) wide.
£1,400–1,700 *PH*

A George III pine dresser, with moulded cornice above a plate rack, the lower section with 3 frieze drawers above a pair of fielded arched panelled cupboard doors, on square section feet, 54in (137cm) wide.
£2,800–3,300 *Bon*

A Yorkshire serpentine front pine dresser, 54in (137cm) wide.
£1,800–2,200 *SSD*

A Dutch pine dresser, with green textured glass doors, 19thC, 41in (104cm) wide.
£900–1,100 *CI*

An Irish pine dresser, c1880, 62in (157cm) wide.
£1,800–2,200 *CPA*

A pine display dresser, c1880, 76in (193cm) wide.
£1,300–1,600 *SPA*

A pine dresser base, c1830, 60in (152cm) wide.
£900–1,100 *SPA*

A pine dresser base, c1875, 60in (152cm) wide.
£1,200–1,500 *SPA*

A Flemish pine dresser base, c1890, 34in (86cm) wide.
£650–800 *AnD*

A pine dresser, with glazed doors, 3 drawers and cupboards to base, late 19thC, 66in (167.5cm) wide.
£1,200–1,500 *CUL*

A Cornish glazed dresser, 19thC, 48in (122cm) wide.
£1,150–1,400 *WV*

A pine dresser, with 3 frieze drawers and 3 cupboards, 19thC, 60in (152cm) wide.
£1,800–2,250 *WV*

l. A pine dresser, early 19thC, 72in (183cm) wide.
£1,800–2,250 *WV*

A Georgian pine dresser base, 72in (182.5cm) wide.
£2,400–2,900 *PEN*

A pine dresser, 19thC, 120in (304.5cm) wide.
£3,300–4,000 *WV*

A Devonshire pine dresser, with glazed top, 51in (129.5cm) wide.
£1,700–2,100 *PH*

A pine dresser, c1890.
£1,300–1,600 *CPA*

An Irish pine dresser, c1880, 37in (94cm) wide.
£1,700–2,100 *UP*

A pine dresser, 18thC, 58in (147cm) wide.
£2,700–3,200 *VV*

A pine dresser, c1870.
£1,700–2,100 *CPA*

A glazed two-piece pine dresser, c1850.
£1,600–1,900 *CPA*

A pine dresser, c1880.
£1,700–2,100 *CPA*

A glazed two-piece pine dresser, unrestored, c1860.
£900–1,100 *CPA*

A pine dresser, c1840, 42in (106.5cm) wide.
£1,300–1,600 *AL*

l. A Victorian Irish pine dresser, 49in (124.5cm) wide.
£1,700–2,100 *Ad*

r. An Irish pine one-piece dresser, with original feet and cornice, c1840.
£1,700–2,100 *GPA*

An Irish pine dresser, c1860, 52in (132cm) wide.
£1,700–2,100 *LC*

A pine dresser base, with 7 drawers and central cupboard, c1860, 71in (180cm) wide.
£1,300–1,600 *ASP*

A pine dresser base, c1880, 85in (216cm) wide.
£1,000–1,200 *OCP*

An Irish pine dresser, c1870, 47in (119cm) wide.
£1,700–2,100 *ASP*

r. A Victorian dresser base, with 9 drawers and one door, c1870, 85in (216cm) wide.
£1,500–1,750 *ASP*

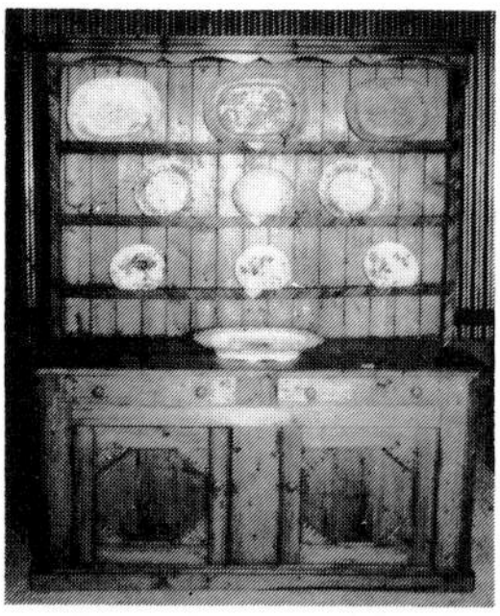

An Irish pine dresser, with rope-twist shelves, c1840, 66in (167.5cm) wide.
£1,700–2,100 *LC*

A pine dresser base, c1840, 39in (99cm) wide.
£1,000–1,200 *SSD*

A North Wales pine dresser, with a potboard, c1780, 78in (198cm) wide.
£3,200–3,900 *HG*

A French pine dresser, c1900, 74in (188cm) wide.
£1,600–1,900 *AD*

A Lincolnshire pine chiffonier, with a carved backboard, 60in (152cm) wide.
£1,600–2,000 *PC*

A pine dresser, with a shaped top, c1800.
£1,600–2,000 *AL*

An early pine base, 52½in (131cm) wide.
£1,000–1,250 *AL*

r. An Austrian dresser, 40in (101.5cm) wide.
£1,200–1,500
RK

A pine breakfront Welsh dresser, Anglesey, c1830 80in (203cm) wide.
£3,700–4,500 *HG*

An Irish country pine dresser, 54in (137cm) wide.
£1,700–2,100 *RK*

A Victorian pine buffet, on 5 legs, fitted with 7 drawers, 71in (180cm) wide.
£1,200–1,500 *AL*

A Scottish dresser, 51in (129.5cm) wide.
£1,600–1,900 *RK*

A French dresser, c1860.
£1,000–1,250 *TPF*

A Shetland Islands dresser, with iron handles, c1880, 51in (130cm) wide.
£1,400–1,700 *AL*

A Bavarian pine kitchen dresser, handles replaced, 49in (124.5cm) wide.
£1,150–1,400 *CHA*

A Scottish pine dresser base, with inlay to drawers, c1860, 43in (109cm) wide.
£1,200–1,450 *HOA*

A Victorian pine dresser, with 4 small and 4 large drawers and a central cupboard, c1860, 60in (152cm) wide.
£1,500–1,750 *COT*

A Polish pine kitchen dresser, with drawers and glazed doors, c1840, 39½in (100cm) wide.
£900–1,100 *POT*

A mid-Victorian pine potboard dresser, c1870, 60in (152cm) wide.
£2,500–3,000 *POT*

l. An early Victorian pine single drawer dog kennel dresser, with wide boarded rack, c1850, 56in (142cm) wide.
£1,800–2,250 *POT*

A pine dresser base, c1850, 42in (106.5cm) wide.
£800–1,000 *GD*

A Polish pine country dresser base, with one drawer and 2 panelled doors, c1870, 51in (129.5cm) wide.
£800–1,000 *ASP*

A fiddle-front dresser, c1780, 54in (135cm) wide. **£1,700–2,100** *UP*

A two-piece pine dresser, c1780, 90in (229cm) wide. **£3,300–4,000** *UP*

A George III pine dresser, the later raised open shelved back with a moulded cornice, c1790, 66in (168cm) wide. **£4,100–4,900** *SS*

A scratch carved pine dresser, c1780. **£1,700–2,100** *UP*

A pitch pine glazed top dresser, 44in (110cm) wide. **£1,150–1,400** *SV*

A pine potboard dresser, with a new base, 83½in (212cm) wide. **£2,000–2,400** *AL*

l. An Irish pine dresser, 18thC, 54in (135cm) wide. **£1,700–2,100** *PCL*

A pine dresser, with new drawers and back boarding, 19thC, 84½in (216cm) wide. **£2,200–2,700** *AL*

An Irish pine dresser, c1880, 50in (125cm) wide. **£1,600–2,000** *UP*

An Irish pine dresser, c1840, 48in (122cm) wide. **£1,700–2,100** *AL*

A Lancashire pine dresser, with 3 bowfront drawers, c1860, 59in (147.5cm) wide. **£1,600–1,900** *Sca*

A Yorkshire serpentine front dresser, c1850, 54in (135cm) wide. **£1,600–2,000** *SSD*

Continental Pine

The majority of Continental pine furniture is relatively recent, and mainly from Eastern Europe. The styles and construction of Continental pine furniture, such as knock-down wardrobes and small glazed kitchen dressers, is very suitable for today's smaller houses.

r. A pine dresser, with boarded back, 19thC, 60in (152cm) wide.
£1,700–2,100 *WV*

A pine dresser, with original decorative frieze, wide backboards, c1840, 61in (155cm) wide.
£1,600–1,900 *OCP*

A pine dresser, with plate rack, c1890, 57in (144.5cm) wide.
£1,700–2,100 *OCP*

A pine dresser, the open base with stretchers, early 19thC, 78in (198cm) wide.
£2,500–3,000 *WV*

A pine chicken coop dresser, c1860, 59in (149.5cm) wide.
£2,100–2,500 *OCP*

A pine dresser, with spice drawers, c1870, 58in (147cm) wide.
£2,100–2,500 *OCP*

An Irish pine dresser, with fretwork top, 2 drawers and 2 panelled doors to base, c1880, 48in (122cm) wide.
£1,700–2,000 *SA*

A Continental pine kitchen dresser, with glazed doors to top and 2 panelled doors to base, c1870, 92in (233.5cm) high.
£1,150–1,400 *ASP*

An Irish pine cottage dresser, Co. Galway, c1840.
£1,700–2,100 *HON*

A Scottish pitch pine dresser base, with 7 drawers and shaped back, c1870, 80in (203cm) wide.
£1,700–2,000 *LRG*

A late Victorian pine dresser, 53in (134.5cm) wide.
£1,700–2,100 *W*

A West Country pine dresser, c1790, 88½in (225cm) wide.
£2,400–2,900 *BH*

A Lincolnshire pine low dresser base, c1870, 52in (132cm) wide.
£1,000–1,250 *UC*

A Cornish pine dresser, late 19thC, 53in (134.5cm) wide.
£1,700–2,100 *Ad*

A Scottish pine dresser, with spice drawers, c1850, 70in (177.5cm) high.
£1,150–1,400 *BH*

A Victorian pine china cabinet, with unusual relief on cornice, 46in (116.5cm) wide.
£1,700–2,100 *OA*

A pine dresser base, c1840, 44in (111.5cm) wide.
£900–1,100 *AL*

An Edwardian pine Welsh breakfront dresser, with stained glass cupboard doors above, 59in (149.5cm) wide.
£2,400–2,900 *OA*

A Victorian pine breakfront dresser, with astragal-glazed doors.
£5,000–6,000 *WEL*

A pine glazed two-piece dresser, c1840.
£1,600–1,900 *CPA*

A pine dresser, Co. Longford, c1850, 47in (119cm) wide.
£1,600–1,950 *DMe*

An Irish pine dresser, with a single drawer, c1855, 37in (94cm) wide.
£1,600–1,950 *DMe*

A goose dresser, with 2 drawers and open base, County Laois, c1780, 60in (152cm) wide.
£2,400–2,850 *DMe*

r. A pine dresser, with 6 spice drawers, c1840, 83in (210.5cm) wide.
£2,100–2,500 *DME*

l. A pine dresser, Co. Kildare, c1845, 45in (114cm) wide.
£1,400–1,650
DMe

l. A pine dresser, with herring-bone panels. Co. Tipperary, c1850, 40in (101.5cm) wide.
£1,300–1,650 *DMe*

A pine glazed dresser, c1860, 52in (132cm) wide.
£2,400–2,900 *Far*

An Irish cottage dresser, c1850, 48in (122cm) wide.
£2,100–2,500 *BR*

An Irish dresser, 18thC, 54in (137cm) wide.
£2,400–2,900 *Ad*

A Victorian pine dresser, c1870s, 75in (190.5cm) wide.
£2,400–2,900 *OA*

A mid-Victorian dresser, 76in (193cm) wide.
£2,500–3,000 *Ad*

A Lincolnshire pine dresser, c1880, 60in (152cm) wide.
£2,300–2,800 *W*

l. A Georgian astragal-glazed pine dresser, 58in (147cm) wide.
£3,300–4,000 *Ad*

An Irish pine dresser, 53in (137cm) wide.
£1,800–2,200 *Ad*

A pine breakfront dresser, 56in (142cm) wide.
£1,800–2,200 *Far*

An Irish dresser, 18thC, 56in (142cm) wide.
£2,000–2,400 *Ad*

An early Victorian pine dresser, with ornate fretwork, Co. Laois, c1840, 63in (160cm) wide.
£1,700–2,100 *DMe*

A pine dresser, c1860, 56in (142cm) wide.
£1,900–2,300 *DFA*

A pine dresser, restored, c1890, 50in (127cm) wide.
£1,500–1,850 *DFA*

An Irish pine open rack dresser, with reeded sides and top, the base with 2 drawers and 2 cupboard doors, c1850, 59in (149.5cm) wide.
£1,700–2,100 *HON*

An Irish pine fiddle-front dresser, with fretwork top and 2 drawers, c1840, 58in (147cm) wide.
£1,700–2,100 *HON*

A pine dresser, with 2 glazed doors to top, 2 drawers and 2 cupboard doors to base, c1880, 41in (104cm) wide.
£1,150–1,400 *Byl*

An Irish pine dresser, c1880, 52in (132cm) wide.
£1,400–1,700 *Byl*

A pine dresser, with 2 panelled doors, c1865, 48in (122cm) wide.
£1,700–2,100 *Byl*

An Irish pine dresser, with 3 shelves, 2 drawers and 2 panelled cupboard doors, c1860, 53in (134.5cm) wide.
£1,700–2,100 *Byl*

An Irish pine dresser in 2 sections, c1840, 48in (122cm) wide.
£1,700–2,100 *AL*

An Irish pine fiddle front dresser, c1840, 57in (145cm) wide.
£1,850–2,250 *UP*

A pine dresser, the doors with leaded glass, c1890, 68in (172.5cm) wide.
£2,100–2,500 *W*

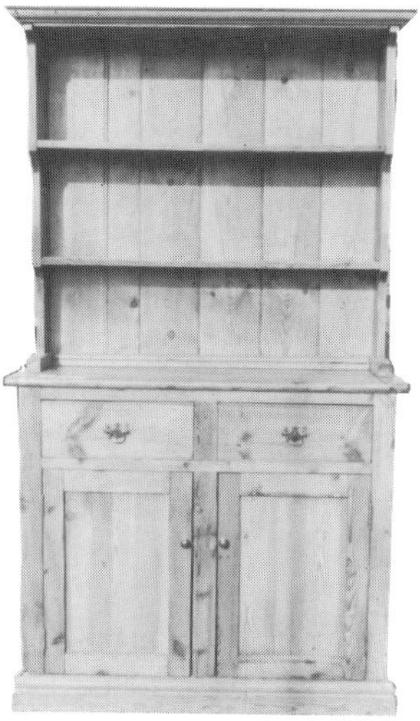

A Scottish dresser, c1880, 49in (125cm) wide.
£1,100–1,350 *RK*

An early Victorian pine dresser base, with original handles, c1840, 58in (147cm) wide.
£1,500–1,800 *Sca*

A Welsh pine dresser, with 2 glazed cupboards, original handles and hooks, c1790, 62in (157cm) high.
£2,100–2,500 *Sca*

A dresser base, c1840, 73in (185cm) wide.
£1,350–1,650 *AL*

r. A mixed wood Irish dresser, c1800, 52in (133cm) high.
£1,700–2,100 *UP*

A Welsh glazed dresser, c1880, 39in (99cm) wide.
£1,350–1,650 *RK*

A late Victorian Cornish dresser, c1870, 78in (198cm) high.
£2,100–2,500 *Ad*

A narrow cottage spice dresser, c1860, 34in (85cm) wide.
£1,000–1,250 *PIN*

An Irish pine fiddle-front dresser, with 3 drawers, c1840, 78in (198cm) high.
£1,700–2,100 *LC*

An Irish pine dresser, with 3 shelves and 2 cupboard doors, c1880, 48in (122cm) wide.
£1,150–1,400 *Byl*

An Irish pine dresser, with 2 drawers and 2 cupboard doors to base, c1880, 43in (109cm) wide.
£1,150–1,400 *Byl*

An Irish pine dresser, with 3 drawers and 2 cupboard doors to base, c1860, 50in (127cm) wide.
£1,500–1,800 *Byl*

A pine dresser, the top with glazed doors, the base with 2 drawers and 2 cupboard doors, c1870, 50in (127cm) wide.
£1,300–1,600 *Byl*

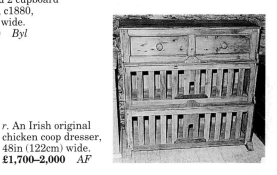

r. An Irish original chicken coop dresser, 48in (122cm) wide.
£1,700–2,000 *AF*

l. An Irish fiddle-front pine dresser, with fretwork top and 3 drawers to base, c1800, 60in (152cm) wide.
£2,650–3,200 *SA*

An Irish pine dresser, with fretwork top, 2 drawers and 2 doors, with moulded panels to base, c1870, 52in (132cm) wide.
£1,700–2,100 *SA*

An Irish pine dresser, with fretwork top, 2 drawers and 2 decorated doors to base, c1870, 43in (109cm) wide.
£1,700–2,100 *SA*

An Irish pine dresser, with 2 drawers, and 2 panelled doors to base, feet replaced, c1850, 56in (142cm) wide.
£1,700–2,100 *SA*

A pine two-piece dresser, with 18thC top, 57in (144.5cm) wide.
£1,700–2,000 *OCP*

An Irish pine fiddle-front dresser, with 2 drawers, c1865, 55in (139.5cm) wide.
£1,700–2,100 *Byl*

A pine cottage dresser, with carving on cornice, 2 drawers and 2 decorated doors, c1870, 42in (106.5cm) wide.
£1,500–1,800 *SA*

A pine dresser, with 2 glazed doors to top, 2 drawers and 2 panelled doors to base, c1880, 48in (122cm) wide.
£1,300–1,600 *Byl*

An Irish pine dresser, with 2 cupboard doors and shoe feet, c1860, 50in (127cm) wide.
£1,700–2,100 *Byl*

Make the most of Miller's

In *Miller's Pine & Country Buyer's Guide* we do NOT just reprint saleroom estimates. Our consultants work from realised prices and then calculate a price range for similar items, avoiding uncharacteristic 'one off' high or low results.

A pine refectory table, with twin-plank top, plain moulded friezes and square chamfered legs, joined by flattened stretchers, 19thC, 160in (406cm) long.
£1,600–1,900 *C*

A pine drop-leaf table, c1880, 34in (86cm) long.
£250–300 *AL*

A pine side table, c1880, 36in (91.5cm) wide.
£225–275 *AnD*

A Victorian pine table, with 4 frieze drawers, c1860, 63in (160cm) wide.
£650–800 *COT*

A Victorian pine side table, with 2 drawers, bamboo style legs, some repairs, 35in (89cm) wide.
£300–400 *HNG*

A pine side table, with single plank top, single drawer and porcelain handles, turned legs, late 19thC, 22in (56cm) wide.
£350–450 *HNG*

r. A German pine breakfast table, with twin pedestals and heavily carved feet, c1850, 39in (99cm) wide.
£550–700 *HNG*

A Regency pine tilt-top table, on central reeded base, with 3 legs and original wood casters, 19thC, 46in (117cm) diam.
£800–1,000 *CI*

A pine serving table, c1830, 96in (244cm) long.
£1,000–1,200 *SPA*

A pine kitchen table, cut down for use as a coffee table, c1880, 39in (99cm) wide.
£450–550 *SPA*

A pine serving table, c1900, 36in (91.5cm) high.
£500–600 *MofC*

A pine kitchen table, c1875, 72in (183cm) long.
£1,200–1,500 *SPA*

A Victorian pine side table, with 2 drawers, 46½in (118cm) wide.
£700–850 *AL*

l. A farmhouse table, c1870, 66in (167.5cm) wide.
£1,000–1,200 *SPA*

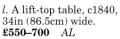

A pine and elm tilt-top pedestal table, c1840, 36in (91.5cm) wide.
£900–1,100 *SSD*

l. A lift-top table, c1840, 34in (86.5cm) wide.
£550–700 *AL*

A drop-leaf table, with drawer under, c1840, 60in (152.5cm) wide.
£500–600 *AL*

A cricket table, c1840, 34in (86.5cm) wide.
£600–750 *AL*

l. A Regency bowfronted side table, 36in (91.5cm) high. **£500–600** *AL*

A pitch pine desk, with side flap and two porcelain inkwells, 19thC, 36in (91.5cm) wide.
£400–500 *AL*

A pine cricket table, 24in (61cm) diam.
£500–600 *GD*

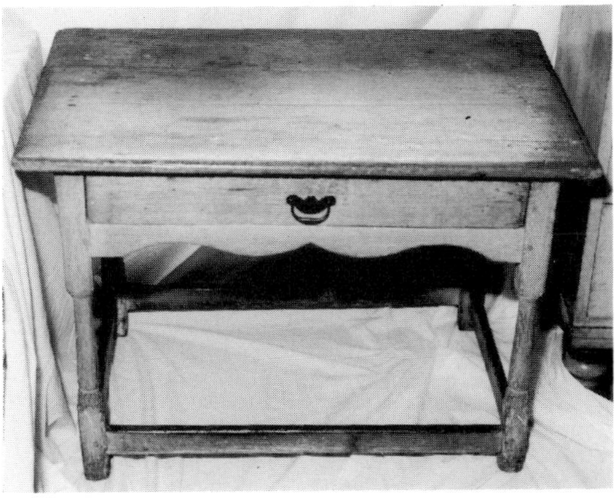

A country pine side table, stretchers restored, c1750, 30in (76cm) wide.
£700–850 *PEN*

A Continental pine candle stand, c1870, 13in (33cm) diam.
£250–300 *PEN*

A farmhouse table, with elm single plank top, 2 drawers and original brass handles, square tapered feet, 72in (183cm) long.
£1,150–1,400 *HGN*

A Georgian pine kitchen table, with original brass bail handles, on square tapered legs, 28in (71cm) wide.
£400–500 *ERA*

r. A Continental table, with cupboard below, c1820, 37½in (95.5cm) wide.
£350–400 *GD*

A pine trestle refectory table, 1830s, 109in (277cm) long.
£1,000–1,250 *GD*

An early Victorian pine flap-over tea table, with gateleg, hardwood legs, c1850, 36in (91.5cm) wide.
£450–550 *POT*

A Victorian pine kitchen table, with drawer, c1860, 60in (152.5cm) wide.
£750–950 *GD*

A Victorian pine occasional table, on turned fruitwood base, top damaged, 30in (76cm) wide.
£300–350 *POT*

A pine cider table, with cross frame, c1910, 25in (63.5cm) wide.
£250–350 *ASP*

A Victorian pine stretchered table, with 2 drawers, c1850, 48in (122cm) long.
£500–600 *GD*

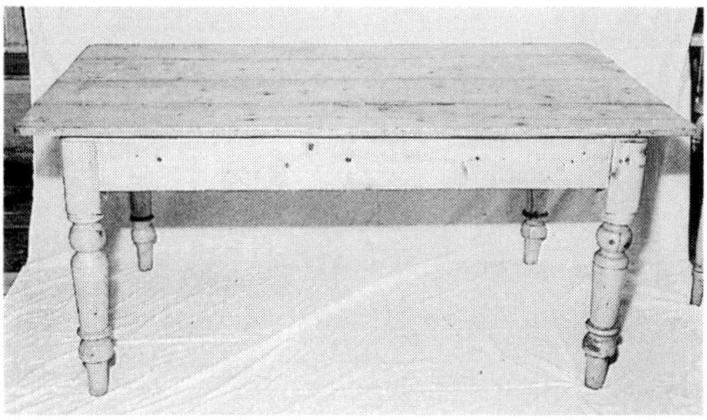

A Victorian pine kitchen table, on turned legs, c1880, 68in (172.5cm) long.
£750–950 *POT*

An early Victorian pine side table, with simulated bamboo legs, c1840, 34in (86.5cm) wide.
£350–450 *POT*

A cricket table, mid-19thC, 32½in (82.5cm) diam.
£600–750 *POT*

A pine table, with beech legs, on original casters, c1905, 38in (96.5cm) wide.
£500–600 *POT*

An early Victorian pine side table, on tapered square legs, c1850, 34in (86.5cm) wide.
£250–350 *POT*

A pine table, with one drop-leaf and 2 drawers, c1890, 36in (91.5cm) wide.
£350–400 *AL*

A pine cupboard, with one long drawer above a cupboard with pigeonholes, c1870, 38in (96.5cm) wide.
£650–800 *AL*

A pine cupboard, with 2 panelled doors, c1870, 57in (144.8cm) wide.
£350–400 *AL*

A pine table, with turned legs, cut down, c1890, 39in (99cm) wide.
£350–400 *FAG*

A pine combination chest of drawers, with a cupboard at the top, c1860, 42in (106.5cm) wide.
£1,150–1,400 *AL*

A pine table, with one drawer, the legs cut down, c1890, 35in (89cm) wide.
£350–400 *AL*

A pine washstand, with a marble top, a drawer, and a shelf beneath, c1880, 30in (76cm) wide.
£400–500 *AL*

A side table, with one small drawer, c1880, 38in (96.5cm) wide.
£350–400 *AL*

A pine side table, with 2 drawers and a drop leaf, c1870, 42in (106.5cm) wide.
£350–450 *AL*

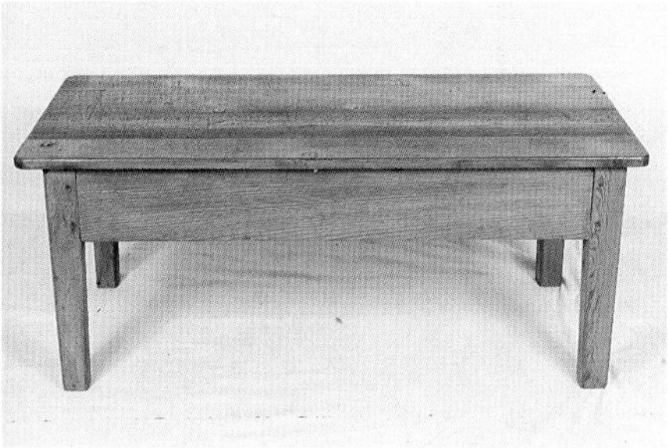

A pine table, cut down, c1870, 46in (117cm) wide.
£300–375 *AL*

A pine box, with 2 drawers, the interior with a candle box, the inside of the lid panelled, c1880, 42in (106.5cm) wide.
£350–450 *AL*

A pine box, the interior fitted with a tray, c1860, 37in (94cm) wide.
£250–300 *AL*

A set of pine shelves, c1890, 30in (76cm) wide.
£300–350 *AL*

A pine cricket table, with 3 legs and a shelf beneath, c1860, 28½in (72.5cm) wide.
£600–750 *AL*

A pine chest of drawers, with 2 drawers above a deep bottom drawer, c1870, 26in (66cm) wide.
£375–450 *AL*

A Continental pine pot cupboard, c1910, 17in (43cm) wide.
£200–250 *FAG*

A pine hanging cupboard, c1880, 16in (40.5cm) wide.
£250–300 *COP*

A pine pot cupboard, with a wooden knob, 15in (38cm) wide.
£275–350 *AL*

A pine chest of 6 small drawers, c1860, 23½in (59.5cm) wide.
£300–375 *FAG*

A pine pot cupboard, with brass handle, c1890, 14½in (37cm) wide.
£200–250 *AL*

A pine plate rack, c1880, 16in (40.5cm) wide.
£150–200 *FAG*

A pine chiffonier, with 3 drawers and one cupboard, and a shaped back, c1865, 42½in (108cm) wide.
£900–1,100 *DMA*

A Dutch pine dresser base, c1840, 46in (117cm) wide.
£750–950 *DMA*

A Louis Philippe style pine sideboard, of European origin, c1890, 42in (106.5cm) wide.
£750–950 *AnD*

A pine side table, with 3 drawers, c1860, 45in (114.5cm) long.
£750–950 *DMA*

A pine D-end breakfront sideboard, 19thC, 62in (157.5cm) wide.
£1,300–1,600 *TPC*

A set of pine wall shelves, c1890, 18½in (47cm) wide.
£110–135 *AL*

A pine swing mirror, c1880, 27in (68.5cm) wide.
£250–300 *AL*

A pine stool, c1890, 12in (30.5cm) wide.
£75–95 *AL*

A set of pine wall shelves, c1880, 36in (91.5cm) wide.
£120–150 *AL*

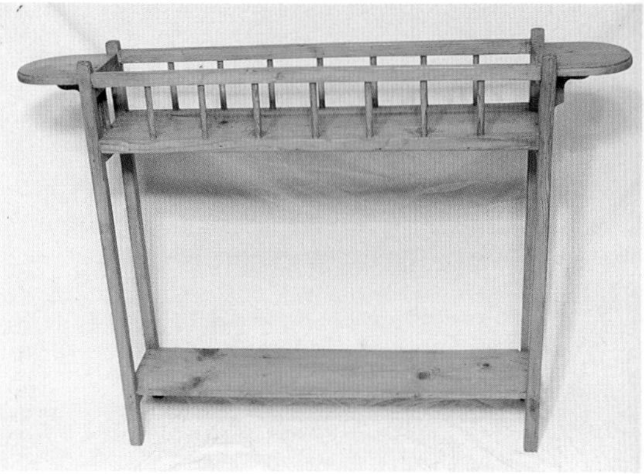

A Continental pine plant stand, c1920, 45in (114.5cm) wide.
£150–200 *AL*

A set of pine steps, c1890, 17½in (44.5cm) wide.
£75–90 *AL*

A pine cricket table, with a shelf, c1860, 25in (63.5cm) wide.
£550–650 *AL*

A pine table, with straight legs and one drawer, c1890, 36in (91.5cm) wide.
£250–300 *AL*

A set of pine steps, c1890, 16in (40.5cm) wide.
£70–85 *AL*

A set of pine shelves, by Liberty & Co, c1890, 20½in (52cm) wide.
£150–180 *AL*

A pine stool, c1890, 17in (43cm) wide.
£75–90 *AL*

An early Victorian pine cupboard, with 2 glazed doors, above a base with 2 long drawers and 2 cupboards, c1850, 48in (122cm) wide.
£2,500–3,000 *DMA*

A Cornish pitch pine display cupboard on chest, the top with 2 astragal glazed Gothic-style doors, 48in (122cm) wide.
£2,200–2,700 *TPC*

A Bavarian pine cupboard, with one panelled door, c1880, 36in (91.5cm) wide.
£700–850 *AnD*

A Bavarian pine bread cupboard, once with wire panels to the front, 70in (180.5cm) wide.
£750–900 *AnD*

A Continental pine vitrine, c1880, with a later top, 42in (106.5cm) wide.
£900–1,100 *AnD*

An early Victorian cupboard, with 2 doors 2 drawers, c1850, 48in (122cm) wide.
£600–750 *DMA*

A pine panelled cupboard, with 2 doors, wooden knobs, 19thC, 72in (183cm) wide.
£1,200–1,500 *TPC*

A Dutch pine cupboard, with internal shelves and drawers, c1840, 48in (122cm) wide.
£1,000–1,200 *AnD*

A Continental pine cupboard, with 2 doors glazed at the top, c1865, 48in (122cm) wide.
£800–1,000 *AnD*

A pine side table, with 2 drawers, on turned legs, 19thC, 36in (91.5cm) wide.
£350–400 *TPC*

A pine table, with up-stand back, the drawer with pottery knobs, on turned legs, c1880, 37in (94cm) wide.
£350–400 *AL*

A pine table, with turned legs, c1880, 47in (119.5cm) wide.
£400–500 *AL*

A pine table, with one end drawer, on turned legs, c1890, 42½in (108cm) wide.
£400–500 *AL*

A pine cricket table, c1850, 24in (61cm) wide.
£550–650 *AL*

A pine table, with turned legs, c1880, 40½in (103cm) wide.
£350–400 *AL*

A pine table, with straight legs, c1890, 36in (91.5cm) wide.
£300–350 *AL*

A pine table, with one end drawer, on straight legs, c1890, 42in (106.5cm) wide.
£375–450 *AL*

A pine table, with a centre drawer, on tapering legs with stretchers, 18thC, 42in (106.5cm) wide.
£375–450 *TPC*

A pine glazed bookcase, c1840, 43in (109cm) wide.
£1,000–1,250 *DMA*

A mid-European pine bookcase, with 2 glazed doors, and a drawer under, 1890, 36in (91.5cm) wide.
£850–1,000 *DMA*

A pine bookcase, the glazed doors with cotton reel turning at the sides, 2 drawers and 2 doors below, c1840, 48in (122cm) wide.
£1,300–1,600 *DMA*

A Czechoslovakian pine bureau/bookcase, with an inlaid walnut interior, c1875, 48in (122cm) wide.
£1,300–1,600 *AnD*

A pine glazed bookcase, with reeded column supports, and one long drawer, c1870, 40in (101.5cm) wide.
£850–1,000 *COP*

A pine glazed bookcase, with 2 short and 2 long drawers to base, with applied moulding, c1860, 48in (122cm) wide.
£1,350–1,600 *MIL*

A Victorian Irish pine dresser, with glazed top, turned columns, 2 drawers and 2 doors, the panels carved, handles replaced, c1880, 49in (124.5cm) wide.
£1,600–1,900 *OPH*

A Victorian pine glazed bookcase, c1860, 36in (91.5cm) wide.
£700–850 *AnD*

An Eastern European pine kitchen cabinet, with glass upper doors, 2 drawers and 2 cupboard doors, c1870, 39in (99cm) wide.
£800–1,000 *NEW*

A pine armoire, with two doors, c1850.
£800–950 *COP*

A pine dresser base, with one long drawer, above 2 cupboard doors, c1870, 42in (106.5cm) wide.
£500–650 *COP*

A pine corner cupboard, 19thC, 38in (96.5cm) wide.
£1,400–1,700 *FOX*

A pine dressing table, c1880, 54in (137cm) wide.
£550–650 *COP*

A pine cupboard, with 4 doors.
£1,000–1,200 *COP*

A pine dresser, with 2 glazed cupboard doors above turned columns, 2 drawers and 2 cupboards beneath, c1880, 45in (114.5cm) wide.
£950–1,150 *COP*

A pine armoire, with 2 doors, c1880, 48in (122cm) wide.
£750–900 *COP*

A Czechoslovakian food cupboard, c1860, 40in (101.5cm) wide.
£900–1,100 *COP*

A pine sideboard, with a shelf between 2 cupboards, c1880, 54in (137cm) wide.
£1,150–1,350 *AL*

A pine corner cupboard, with 4 doors and one drawer, c1865.
£2,200–2,600 *COP*

A pine chest of drawers, with 2 short and 3 long drawers, on bracket feet, c1820, 21in (53.5cm) wide.
£500–600 *DMA*

A pine chest of drawers, with 2 short and 3 long drawers, on bracket feet, c1880, 20in (51cm) wide.
£650–800 *AL*

A pine chest with lift-up lid, on a drawer base, the front moulded, c1870, 38in (96.5cm) wide.
£500–600 *MIL*

A Dutch chest of 3 long drawers, c1880, 40in (101.5cm) wide.
£500–600 *AnD*

A Continental chest of drawers, with 4 long drawers, 40in (101.5cm) wide.
£500–600 *AnD*

A pine chest of drawers, with 2 short and 2 long drawers, pottery knobs, 19thC, 34in (86.5cm) wide.
£500–600 *LIB*

A pine chest, with 2 moulded long drawers, on bracket feet, 19thC, 42in (106.5cm) wide.
£500–600 *TPC*

A pine chest of drawers, with moulded drawer fronts, 37in (94cm) wide.
£500–600 *MIL*

A Georgian chest of drawers, with 2 short and 3 long drawers, 40in (101.5cm) wide.
£700–850 *AnD*

A pine mule chest, with 2 drawers, the front panelled, c1780, 45in (114.5cm) wide.
£600–750 *MIL*

A pine corner cupboard, with a glazed door and brass knob, c1900, 13in (33cm) wide.
£95–110 *FOX*

A miniature pine chest of drawers, with large wooden knobs, c1870, 13in (33cm) wide.
£200–250 *MIL*

A pine hanging cupboard, c1850, 25in (63.5cm) wide.
£185–230 *DMA*

A pair of pine hanging cabinets, with glazed doors, c1875, 14in (35.5cm) wide.
£150–200 *AnD*

A Dutch pine cabinet, with locking door, originally used as the base for a safe, c1890, 27in (68.5cm) high.
£250–300 *AnD*

A Victorian pine pot cupboard, c1840, 16in (40.5cm) wide.
£200–250 *DMA*

A pine pot cupbaord, with brass knob, c1880, 15in (38cm) wide.
£200–250 *AL*

A pine pot cupboard, with scroll decoration, on turned feet, 15in (38cm) wide.
£200–250 *AnD*

A pair of Continental pine bedside pot cupboards, c1890, 15in (38cm) wide.
£500–600 *AnD*

A pine box, 19thC, 30in (76cm) long.
£95–110 *LIB*

A pine mule chest, with brass handles, early 19thC, 36in (91.5cm) wide.
£450–550 *TPC*

A pine wall hanging cupboard, with an interior drawer, 19thC, 20in (51cm) wide.
£150–200 *FOX*

A pine box, late 19thC, 16in (40.5cm) wide.
£95–120 *FOX*

A pine chest of drawers, with a bonnet drawer at the bottom, c1860, 36in (91.5cm) wide.
£500–600 *AL*

A pine two-door cupboard, c1870, 42in (106.5cm) wide.
£400–500 *AL*

A pine chest of drawers, with 2 long drawers, one short drawer, and a pot shelf, c1880, 33in (84cm) wide.
£500–600 *AL*

A pine chest of drawers, with 2 short and 2 long drawers, c1880, 36in (91.5cm) wide.
£500–600 *AL*

A pine chest of drawers, with 3 long drawers, c1850, 37½in (95.5cm) wide.
£500–600 *AL*

A pine chest of drawers, with 2 short and 3 long drawers, c1830, 44½in (113cm)
£550–650 *AL*

A pine chest of drawers, with 4 long drawers and central handles, c1870, 49in (124.5cm) wide.
£400–500 *COP*

A pitch pine desk, with 3 drawers either side and bookshelves in the kneehole, on casters, c1890, 49½in (125.5cm) wide.
£700–850 *AL*

A pine chest of drawers, with 2 short and 2 long drawers, 39in (99cm) wide.
£500–600 *AL*

A Victorian pine chest of drawers, with 2 short and 2 long drawers, 33in (84cm) wide.
£450–550 *FOX*

A pine chest of drawers, with a marble top, tiled splashback, and 3 long drawers, c1890, 43in (109cm) wide.
£450–550 *AL*

A pine armoire, with 3 mirrored doors, and 2 long drawers beneath, c1880, 63in (160cm) wide.
£550–650 *COP*

A pine dresser, with 2 glazed doors above, 2 drawers and cupboard doors beneath, c1880, 50in (127cm) wide.
£550–650 *COP*

A pine breakfront bookcase, with astragal glazed doors above, one long and 2 short drawers above 3 cupboards, c1870, 72in (183cm) wide.
£2,500–3,000 *COP*

A pine armoire, with 2 doors, on bun feet, c1870, 46in (117cm) wide.
£500–600 *COP*

A Lincolnshire pine chiffonier, c1860, 72in (183cm) wide.
£1,000–1,200 *COP*

A pine dresser, with reeded and turned supports, 2 glazed doors above 2 short drawers and 2 cupboard doors below, c1875, 52in (132cm) wide.
£600–700 *COP*

A pine dressing table, with central mirror between 2 mirrored cupboards, 2 small drawers and 2 cupboards below, c1870, 56in (142cm) wide.
£500–600 *COP*

A pine linen press, c1865, 46in (117cm) wide.
£1,700–2,000 *COP*

A pine armoire, with 2 doors, c1870, 46in (117cm) wide.
£500–600 *COP*

A pine secrétaire, c1860,
42in (106.5cm) wide.
£1,700–2,000 *UP*

A pine pedestal pub table,
c1880, 30in (76cm) high.
£250–300 *AHL*

A pine dressing chest, the top with a mirror on turned supports over a drawer, a cupboard and 3 drawers, 19thC, 34in (86.5cm) wide.
£450–550 *TPC*

A pine gallery back washstand, with a shelf and drawer under, on turned legs, 19thC,
24in (61cm) wide.
£275–325 *TPC*

A Welsh high-backed turned spindle armchair, early 19thC.
£300–375 *TPC*

A pine picture frame, c1870,
35in (89cm) high.
£150–200 *AHL*

A Scandinavian pine dressing chest, c1900.
£350–400 *BEL*

A dairy table, c1850,
28in (71cm) wide.
£180–220 *SA*

A pine mule chest, with 2 drawers, early 19thC,
32in (81.5cm) wide.
£400–500 *TPC*

A pine armoire, with 2 doors, c1880, 55in (140cm) wide.
£500–600 *COP*

A pine chiffonier, c1865, 44in (112cm) wide.
£500–600 *COP*

A pine spice dresser, with 2 glazed doors, 6 small drawers, above 2 short drawers and 2 cupboard doors, c1875, 58in (147cm) wide.
£900–1,100 *COP*

A pine bookcase, with 2 glazed doors, c1880, 37in (94cm) wide.
£500–600 *COP*

An eastern European pine dresser base, c1850, 48in (122cm) wide.
£500–600 *COP*

A pine dresser, with 2 glazed doors, 2 short drawers, and 2 cupboard doors beneath, c1880, 42in (106.5cm) wide.
£650–750 *COP*

An Irish pine pantry cupboard, c1870, 54in (137cm) wide.
£750–900 *COP*

A pine armoire, with 2 doors, and 2 turned columns with urn finials, c1870, 47in (119cm) wide.
£650–800 *COP*

A pine food cupboard, with 4 doors, c1870, 49in (124.5cm) wide.
£1,400–1,700 *AL*

A pine chest of drawers, with 2 short and 2 long drawers, c1900, 34in (86cm) wide.
£450–550 *Ber*

A pine sideboard, with 2 drawers above 2 cupboard doors, c1870, 41in (104cm) wide.
£700–800 *AL*

A pine chest of drawers, with 2 short and 3 long drawers, and white pottery knobs, c1870, 40in (101.5cm) wide.
£500–600 *AL*

A Scottish pine chest of drawers, with 2 jewellery drawers and a concealed drawer, c1870, 52in (132cm) wide.
£800–950 *AL*

A pine chest of drawers, with 2 short and 3 long drawers, c1840, 43in (109cm) wide.
£500–600 *AL*

A pine cupboard, with panelled doors, one with a brass knob, c1870, 49½in (125cm) wide.
£550–650 *AL*

A pine chest of drawers, with 2 short and 2 long drawers, c1800, 31½in (80cm) wide.
£550–650 *AL*

A pine chest of drawers, with 2 short and 2 long drawers, c1880, 36in (91.5cm) wide.
£450–550 *AL*

A pine dresser base, with one long drawer above 2 cupboard doors, c1875, 40in (101.5cm) wide.
£400–500 *COP*

A pine chest of drawers, with 2 short and 2 long drawers, c1870, 40in (101.5cm) wide.
£450–550 *COP*

A pine sideboard, with one long drawer above 2 cupboard doors, with pine knobs, c1890, 39in (99cm) wide.
£400–500 *FAG*

A mid-Victorian pine kitchen side table, with 2 drawers and turned legs, c1870, 34in (86.5cm) wide.
£300–350 *POT*

A late Victorian table, on turned legs, 48in (122cm) wide.
£350–450 *POT*

A Victorian Irish pitch pine farmhouse table, with turned legs, 96in (244cm) long.
£1,100–1,300 *AF*

An early Victorian pine cricket table, c1840, 33in (84cm) diam.
£500–600 *POT*

A pine oval drop-leaf supper table, c1900, 45in (114.5cm) long.
£400–500 *OCP*

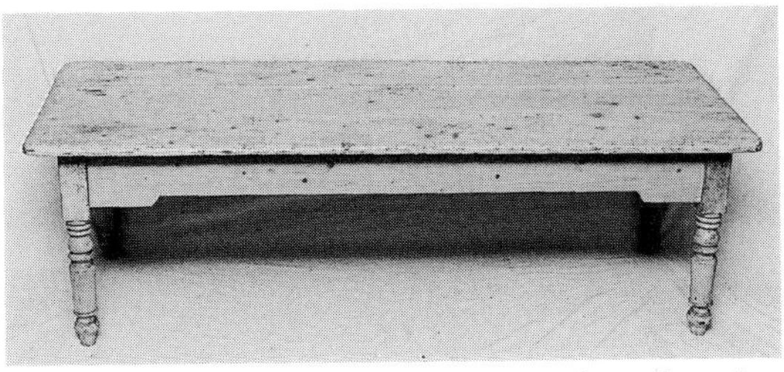

A pine coffee table, cut down to size, with single end drawer, on turned legs, c1870, 66in (167.5cm) wide.
£250–300 *SA*

A pine tripod table, c1880, 27in (68.5cm) high.
£350–450 *OCP*

A pine drop-leaf table, c1860, 48in (122cm) long.
£300–375 *OCP*

r. A pine side table, with gallery back and single drawer, c1850, 24in (61cm) wide.
£250–300 *DMe*

A pine side table,
33in (84cm) wide.
£250–300 *AL*

A pine cricket table,
c1850, 30in (76cm) high.
£450–550 *PIN*

An Irish pine double stretcher table,
c1850, 84in (213.5cm) wide.
£800–1,000 *PIN*

A pine and elm tilt-top
pedestal table, c1860,
46in (117cm) diam.
£750–900 *SSD*

A pine writing table, with
a hinged drop leaf, c1820,
36in (91.5cm) wide.
£350–450 *AL*

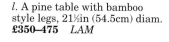

A pine cricket table, c1850,
27in (68.5cm) high.
£550–650 *AL*

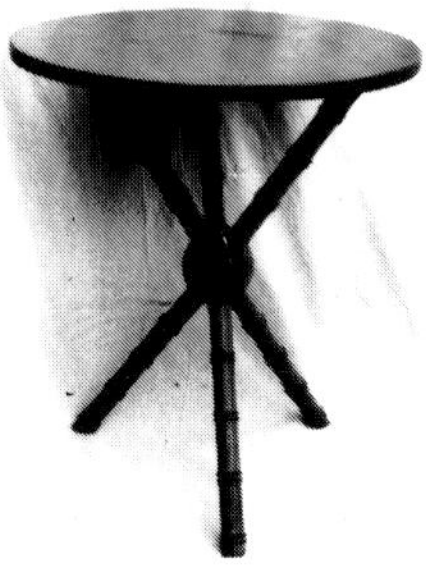

l. A pine table with bamboo
style legs, 21½in (54.5cm) diam.
£350–475 *LAM*

A pine cricket table, c1850,
29in (73.5cm) diam.
£500–600 *AL*

A pine lamp table,
22½in (57cm) high.
£150–200 *AL*

An adjustable bedside table,
c1850, 32in (81.5cm) high.
£250–300 *AL*

A small pine base, c1880,
24in (61cm) wide.
£200–250 *AL*

A pine dining table, with one
drawer, c1840, 34in (86.5cm) wide.
£500–600 *AL*

A pine table with slatted shelf,
c1850, 59in (150cm) wide.
£400–500 *AL*

. shaped pine side table, c1870,
1in (130cm) long.
350–400 *AL*

l. A two-drawer work table, c1850, 72in (183cm) wide.
£700–800 *AL*

. Devonshire pine table, with
ıaped top rail and tapered legs,
)8in (274.5cm) long.
1,000–1,200 *PF*

A pine table, with concealed drawer at one end, late 19thC, 38in (96.5cm) wide.
£150–200 *CHA*

A Georgian pine side table, on tapering legs, 23in (58.5cm) wide.
£400–500 *OA*

. Welsh pine drop-leaf
ıble, with one drawer
nd ogee scrolls each end,
0in (76cm) wide.
450–550 *PF*

A German shoemaker's pine bench, 47in (119.5cm) long.
£150–200 *CHA*

r. A pine dairy table, handles replaced, 19thC, 22in (56cm) wide.
£300–400 *AL*

. pine extending table, on dual
:roll carved supports joined by
on's mask stretchers and iron
:oss struts, possibly Spanish,
22½in (311cm) wide extended.
2,500–3,000 *CSK*

. Victorian pine tripod table,
3in (84cm) diam. **£750–900** *OA*

A pine side table, with one drawer and porcelain knobs, 36in (91.5cm) wide.
£350–400 *AL*

A Spanish pine table, with shaped side rails and one drawer, 24in (61cm) wide.
£250–300 *SM*

A pine and elm cricket table, c1840, 26in (66cm) high.
£350–450 *SSD*

An Irish pine table, c1860, 31in (78.5cm) wide.
£450–550 *UP*

A pine side table, 33in (84cm) wide.
£300–350 *AL*

A pine cricket table, 28in (71cm) diam.
£500–600 *PH*

A Georgian pine carving table, with 2 drawers and 6 legs, c1810.
£800–1,000 *PIN*

A Georgian pine cricket table, c1820, 29in (73.5cm) diam.
£550–650 *PIN*

A pine gateleg table, c1850, 34in (86.5cm) wide extended.
£500–600 *AL*

A pine gateleg table, with a drawer, c1850, 59in (150cm) wide extended.
£500–600 *AL*

A Victorian pine serving table, c1880, 40in (101.5cm) wide.
£375–475 *PIN*

A pine serving table, c1840, 63in (160cm) wide.
£700–850 *SSD*

A Victorian pine side table, c1880, 36in (91.5cm) wide.
£375–475 *PIN*

A pine side table, with turned legs and double stretchers, 65in (165cm) wide.
£650–800 *PH*

A pine farmhouse table, with stretcher, 66in (167.5cm) wide.
£450–550 *OCP*

A pine side table, with single drawer and turned legs, c1850, 31in (78.5cm) wide.
£225–275 *DMe*

A pine cricket table, c1880, 27in (68.5cm) high.
£225–275 *DFA*

A pine table, with a drawer in one end, cut down, 48in (122cm) wide.
£300–400 *SA*

An Irish rustic pine table, with 3 drawers, c1800, 30in (76cm) high.
£400–500 *DFA*

A pine table, c1870, 94in (238cm) diam extended.
£400–500 *DFA*

A pine drop-leaf table, c1850, 52in (132cm) wide.
£500–650 *DFA*

An Irish pine cricket table, c1860, 27in (68.5cm) high.
£400–500 *DFA*

A small pine table, early 18thC, 26in (66cm) wide.
£650–800 *AL*

A Victorian pine side table, with a frieze drawer, 27½in (70cm) wide.
£350–450 *OA*

A pine gateleg table, c1840, 47½in (120.5cm) wide.
£550–650 *AL*

A Victorian pine serving table, 44in (112cm) wide.
£400–500 *OA*

A baker's table, with a marble top, 19thC, 37in (94cm) long.
£500–600 *BR*

An early pegged straight leg pine table, c1830, 26½in (67.5cm) wide.
£300–400 *AL*

A Victorian one-flap table, with 2 frieze drawers, 48in (122cm) wide.
£500–600 *OA*

A mid-Victorian pine side table, 36in (91.5cm) wide.
£350–450 *OA*

A pine side table, 30½in (77.5cm) wide.
£300–350 *AL*

A Georgian pine side table, with original swan neck handles, 34in (86.5cm) wide.
£350–450 *OA*

A Georgian pine side table, 32in (81.5cm) wide.
£350–450 *OA*

A Victorian pine side table, 32in (81.5cm) wide.
£375–475 *OA*

A Victorian three-plank pine farmhouse kitchen table, c1870s, 96in (244cm) wide.
£700–850 *OA*

A pine farmhouse kitchen table, c1870, 84in (213.5cm) long.
£700–800 *OA*

l. A Victorian extending pine dining table, with a single leaf, 60in (152.5cm) long extended.
£800–1,000 *OA*

l. A sycamore and pine cricket table, mid-18thC, 30in (76cm) diam.
£500–650 *CHA*

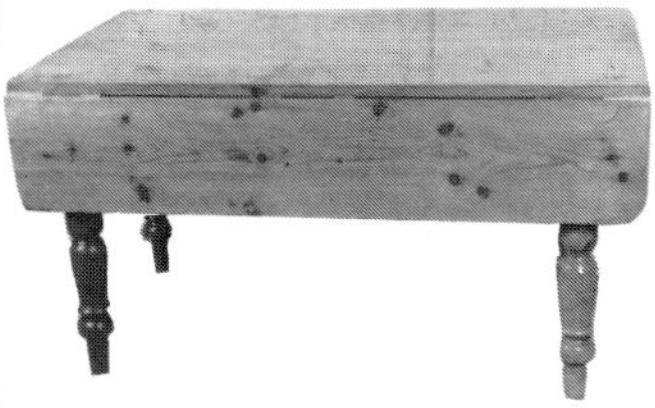

A pine drop-leaf table, with a drawer under, 59½in (151cm) long.
£400–500 *CHA*

A pine cricket table, c1840, 26in (66cm) diam.
£500–600 *AL*

l. A pine work bench, c1840, 46in (117cm) long.
£300–375 *AL*

l. A picnic table and 4 folding chairs, c1930.
£350–400 *MCA*

A French pine side table, with one drawer, on turned legs, c1890.
£200–275 *TPF*

A pine bench table, 19thC, 84in (213.5cm) long.
£175–225 *MS*

A Victorian pine desk, with a mahogany top and 3 frieze drawers, 80in (203cm) wide.
£550–700 *AL*

A pine work table, with an applewood top, 19thC, 78in (198cm) long. **£1,100–1,300** *AL*

An Irish pine country table, with a double rail, c1850, 25in (63.5cm) wide.
£600–750 *CC*

A pine table, c1860, 96in (244cm) long.
£1,200–1,500 *Sca*

A Regency pine side table, with original handles, 32in (81.5cm) wide.
£400–500 *AL*

An octagonal pine table, c1880, 47½in (120.5cm) diam.
£900–1,100 *AL*

A pine table, c1840, 35in (89cm) long.
£350–450 *Sca*

A Victorian pine table, c1880, 43in (109cm) wide.
£350–450 *Far*

A Regency pine side table, with 'bamboo' legs, original handles, c1820, 36in (91.5cm) wide.
£450–550 *AL*

A pine cricket table, c1810, 30in (76cm) diam.
£500–600 *AL*

A Scandinavian oval pine table, c1680–1720, 30in (76cm) high.
£650–750 *W*

A pine table, with 2 drawers, c1860, 40in (101.5cm) wide.
£400–500 *AL*

A pine side table, c1860, 35½in (90cm) wide.
£250–325 *AL*

A pine two-drawer single leaf table, 55in (139.5cm) wide.
£400–500 *AL*

A pine table, with turned legs, c1870, 28in (71cm) high.
£250–300 *AL*

A pine single flap table with drawer, original porcelain handles, c1850, 28in (71cm) high.
£350–450 *AL*

l. An Edwardian pine writing table, with 3 drawers, 48in (122cm) wide.
£650–750 *W*

A pine serving table, c1840.
£500–600 *CPA*

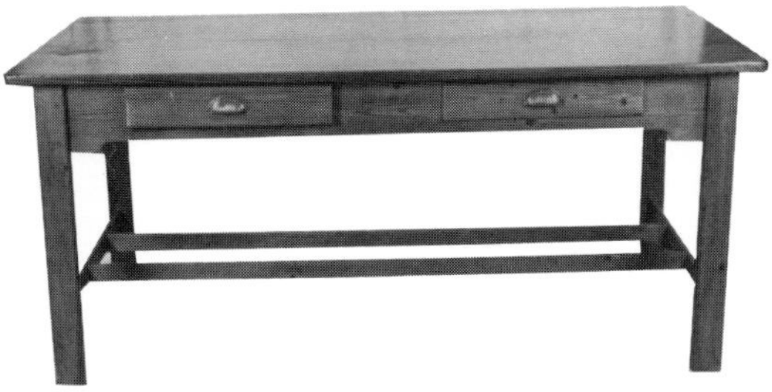

A pine farmhouse table, with a sycamore top, c1880.
£900–1,100 *CPA*

A pine serving table, from the North of England, with original handles, c1800, 74in (188cm) wide.
£1,000–1,200 *BH*

A pine table, reduced in height, c1800, 36in (91.5cm) wide.
£250–325 *AL*

An adjustable pine bed table, 23½in (59.5cm) wide.
£250–300 *AL*

A pine console table, 58in (147.5cm) wide.
£1,000–1,250 *PH*

A pine table, c1720, 36in (91.5cm) wide.
£500–600 *W*

A pine gateleg table, c1850, 29in (73.5cm) high.
£450–550 *AL*

A pine bench table, c1860, 26in (66cm) wide.
£150–200 *AL*

A pair of pine potboard bases, c1880, 46in (117cm) wide.
£1,600–1,900 *AL*

A pine drop-leaf table, with a drawer, c1860, 35in (89cm) wide open.
£400–475 *AL*

A pine writing table, with carved supports, c1860, 50in (127cm) wide.
£650–750 *BH*

A pine side table, c1880, 60in (152.5cm) wide.
£800–1,000 *UP*

l. A pine hunt table, American, used for cutting up game after hunting, 74in (188cm) wide.
£800–1,000 *PAC*

l. A pine gateleg table, with drawer under, 48in (122cm) wide.
£550–650 *AL*

A Victorian pine lyre-end library table, 36in (91.5cm) wide.
£550–650 *AH*

A pine table, c1850, 82in (208.5cm) long.
£650–750 *DFA*

A pine drop-leaf table, with drawers, c1880, 35in (89cm) wide.
£350–450 *AL*

A pine table, with turned legs, c1880, 47in (119.5cm) wide.
£400–500 *AL*

An Irish pine farmhouse table, c1880, 34in (86.5cm) long.
£350–450 *DFA*

A pine side table, with 2 drawers, c1870, 36in (91.5cm) diam.
£275–350 *AL*

A pine cricket table, on turned legs, c1860, 29½in (75cm) diam.
£500–600 *AL*

A pine side table, with one long drawer, on turned legs, c1870, 33in (84cm) wide.
£350–450 *AL*

A pine cricket table, c1860, 34½in (87.5cm) diam.
£500–600 *AL*

A low pine table, with two-way drawer, on turned legs, c1890, 27in (68.5cm) wide.
£275–350 *AL*

A pine press table, c1870, 18½in (47cm) wide.
£350–450 *AL*

l. A pine side table, with drawer, on turned legs, c1880, 38in (96.5cm) wide.
£275–350 *AL*

A pine cricket table, c1860, 30in (76cm) diam.
£500–600 *AL*

l. A pine cricket table, with bobbin turned legs, c1870, 27in (68.5cm) diam.
£275–350 *AL*

A pine table, with a single drop leaf, c1860, 35in (89cm) wide.
£350–450 *AL*

A pine drop-leaf table, c1860, 50in (127cm) wide extended.
£400–500 *AL*

A pine writing table, c1860, 42½in (108cm) wide.
£350–425 *AL*

A Danish pine side table, c1890, 31in (78.5cm) high.
£250–325 *RK*

An pine cricket table, c1840, 24in (61cm) diam.
£350–450 *PIN*

An Irish pine wine table, with an unusual carved Celtic design, 1820–40, 21in (53.5cm) diam.
£550–650 *PIN*

A pine writing table, c1860, 36in (91.5cm) wide.
£350–425 *AL*

A pine table, 52in (132cm) wide.
£300–400 *CHA*

A baker's pine table from North Wales, with lift-off lid revealing a dough trough, 56in (142cm) wide.
£500–600 *CHA*

A pine work table, c1860, 60in (152.5cm) long.
£350–450 *AL*

A pine table, c1860.
£300–400 *AL*

An Irish pine bobbin leg three-tier cake table, c1860, 27in (68.5cm) high.
£400–500 *BH*

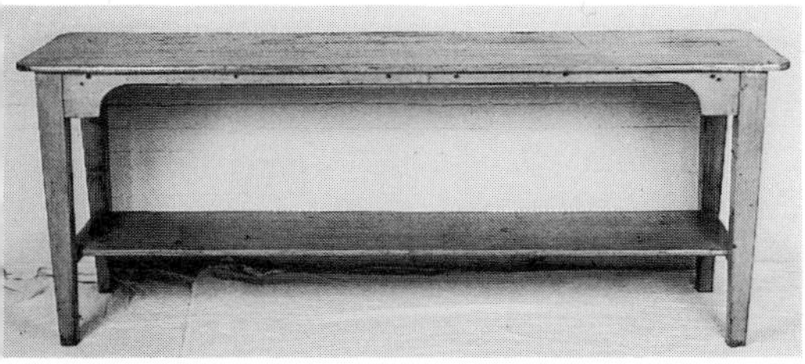

A pine serving table, with a shelf, c1870, 87in (221cm) long.
£750–900 *AL*

A pine side table, with drawer, c1870, 36in (91.5cm) wide.
£250–300 *AL*

A pine cricket table, with turned legs, burn mark to top, c1870, 20in (51cm) diam,
£400–475 *AL*

A pine stretcher table, with three-plank top, c1860, 81in (205.5cm) long.
£750–950 *HON*

An Irish pine drop-leaf table, on square legs, c1870, 42in (106.5cm) diam.
£200–250 *Byl*

A pine dairy table, with single drawer, c1850, 24in (61cm) wide.
£250–300 *SA*

A harbour commissioner's pine boardroom table, with 6 turned legs and 2 side drawers, c1850s, 53in (134.5cm) wide.
£1,800–2,200 *SA*

A pine coffee table, cut down to size, on square legs and stretchers, c1805, 60in (152.5cm) wide.
£300–400 *SA*

A pine coffee table, cut down to size, with turned legs, c1890, 48in (122cm) diam.
£300–400 *SA*

A pine cupboard, c1850, 72½in (183cm) wide.
£750–900 *AL*

A Co. Galway pine cupboard, c1840.
£2,000–2,400 *HON*

A Victorian housekeeper's pine cupboard, on a nine-drawer base, c1840, 78in (198cm) high.
£2,900–3,500 *PIN*

A German pine cupboard, with interior shelves.
£500–600 *CPA*

An Irish pine food cupboard, 18thC, 63in (160cm) wide.
£2,800–3,300 *Ad*

A Victorian pine pantry cupboard, 75in (190.5cm) high.
£4,000–4,700 *OA*

A Victorian pine press/cupboard, doors enclosing shelves, 48in (122cm) wide.
£1,700–2,100 *OA*

A pine huffer, c1840, 31½in (80cm) high.
£600–700 *AL*

A two-door pine cupboard, c1850, 83½in (212cm) high.
£1,200–1,500 *AL*

An Irish cupboard, with drawers, 72in (183cm) high.
£2,000–2,400 *RK*

A pine cupboard, c1840, 21in (53.5cm) high.
£400–500 *AL*

A pine unit, the centre cupboard with shelves, 19thC, 55½in (141cm) wide.
£500–600 *AL*

An Irish pine food cupboard, 58in (147.5cm) high.
£1,900–2,300 *RK*

A narrow pine cupboard, with 2 doors, c1840, 22½in (57cm) high.
£1,100–1,300 *AL*

A Gothic pine cupboard, 53½in (136cm) wide.
£1,700–2,000 *PH*

A Northern Irish panelled pine food cupboard, c1800, 58in (147.5cm) wide.
£1,800–2,200 *HG*

An Irish pine food cupboard, c1850, 54in (137cm) high.
£1,800–2,200 *PH*

A pine fielded panelled food cupboard, c1800, 56in (142cm) wide.
£2,200–2,700 *UP*

An Irish pine food cupboard, c1870, 46in (117cm) wide.
£1,700–2,100 *UP*

An Irish pine food cupboard, 58in (147.5cm) high.
£2,200–2,700 *PH*

A French pine display cupboard, c1890.
£550–650 *TPF*

A Welsh pine food cupboard, 18thC, 40in (101.5cm) wide.
£2,100–2,500 *PH*

l. An Irish rustic pine food cupboard, with oak and pine frame, early 18thC, 51in (129.5cm) high.
£1,700–2,000 *PIN*

A pair of Continental pine bedside cupboards, c1920.
£300–400 *TRU*

A pine food cupboard, 50in (127cm) wide.
£1,350–1,650 *Far*

A Victorian housemaid's pine cupboard, c1860, 44in (112cm) high.
£1,300–1,600 *PIN*

A pine cupboard, 84in (213.5cm) high.
£1,000–1,200 *SAn*

A small pine cupboard, c1870, 13in (33cm) wide.
£100–150 *AL*

A pine cupboard, with a shaped door, shelf inside, c1860, 50in (127cm) high.
£350–450 *AL*

An Irish pine food cupboard, with a knife drawer, c1820, 76½in (194.5cm) high.
£2,800–3,400 *W*

A pine cupboard, with 4 shelves and shaped mahogany base, c1800, 71in (180.5cm) high.
£1,150–1,400 *AL*

A pine wall cupboard, c1860, 29in (73.5cm) wide.
£300–400 *AL*

A twelve-door food cupboard, with original escutcheons, 19thC, 87in (221cm) wide.
£1,800–2,200 *AL*

A pine warming cupboard, c1830, 43in (109cm) wide.
£600–700 *AL*

A pine cupboard, c1850, 24in (61cm) high.
£250–300 *AL*

A pine cupboard, 20in (51cm) high.
£150–200 *LAM*

A pine huffer, c1840, 39in (99cm) wide.
£600–700 *AL*

A Georgian two-door pine cupboard, with raised and fielded panels, shelved interior, c1780, 58in (147.5cm) wide.
£2,000–2,400 *TPC*

A pine cupboard, with canted sides and pigeonhole fitted interior, 19thC, 48in (122cm) wide.
£1,000–1,200 *TPC*

An Irish pine four-door panelled cupboard, with dentil mouldings, c1850, 60in (152.5cm) wide.
£1,200–1,500 *HON*

A Victorian pine farmhouse cupboard, c1885, 30in (76cm) wide.
£150–200 *TPC*

r. A Victorian pine wall cupboard, c1860, 22½in (57cm) high.
£100–150 *OPH*

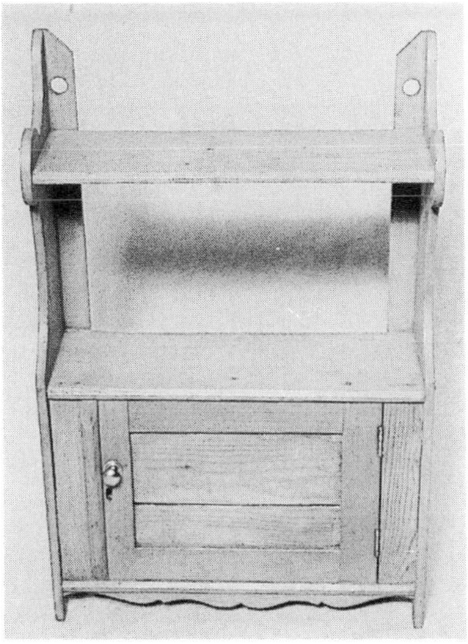

An Irish pine cupboard with breakfront top, panelled sides and 4 fielded panelled doors, c1820, 58in (147.5cm) wide.
£2,200–2,700 *HON*

A pine tack cupboard, late 19thC, 30in (76cm) wide.
£1,100–1,300 *CUL*

A pine wall cupboard, 19thC, 43in (109cm) high.
£250–350 *LIB*

A pine cupboard,
52in (132cm) high.
£1,400–1,700 *SAn*

A pine cupboard, with
shelves and a drawer
in base, c1800,
74in (188cm) high.
£1,100–1,300 *AL*

An Irish panelled pine
food cupboard, c1780,
50in (127cm) high.
£1,300–1,600 *UP*

A panelled pine cupboard,
c1840, 75½in (192cm) high.
£650–800 *AL*

A pine wall cupboard.
£100–150 *WEL*

A pine cupboard, with shelves
inside, 40in (101.5cm) high.
£200–250 *AL*

A pine wall cupboard,
15in (38cm) wide.
£150–200 *AL*

An Irish food cupboard,
with fitted interior, c1800,
51in (129.5cm) high.
£1,300–1,600 *UP*

An Irish pine food cupboard,
49in (124.5cm) wide.
£2,200–2,700 *PH*

A pine wall cupboard, c1860,
37in (94cm) wide.
£220–280 *AL*

A pine cupboard, with 4 doors,
and 2 drawers, c1850.
£1,800–2,200 *HON*

A Welsh pine hanging cupboard
18thC, 52in (132cm) high.
£2,200–2,700 *PH*

A Spanish pine food cupboard, with 2 doors, c1780, 40in (101.5cm) wide.
£1,700–2,000 *Ced*

r. A Regency pine wall cupboard, with 2 moulded panelled doors, enclosing a fitted shelf and drawer, 40in (101.5cm) wide.
£450–550 *TPC*

r. An Irish pine food cupboard, late 19thC, 60in (152.5cm) wide.
£2,100–2,500 *CUL*

l. An Irish pine food cupboard, c1780, 48in (122cm) wide.
£1,350–1,650 *CUL*

An Irish pine food cupboard, with 4 doors and 3 centre drawers, painted interior, late 19thC, 60in (152.5cm) wide.
£2,200–2,700 *HeR*

A pine food cupboard, c1850, 58in (147.5cm) wide.
£1,700–2,000 *UP*

A Georgian pine cupboard, with arch panelled doors, standing on bracket feet, 57in (145cm) wide.
£2,500–3,000 *Ad*

An Edwardian pine hanging bookcase, 36in (91.5cm) wide.
£200–250 *OA*

A Danish pine cupboard, with a fall front, 40in (101.5cm) wide.
£850–1,000 *RK*

A pitch pine cupboard, c1900, 71in (180.5cm) wide.
£750–950 *PCL*

A pine two-door cupboard, with adjustable shelves, c1880, 60in (152.5cm) wide.
£275–350 *AL*

A pine livery cupboard, with 3 short and 2 long drawers, 19thC.
£2,200–2,700 *ARK*

A pine wall cupboard, c1900, 71in (180.5cm) wide.
£150–200 *PCL*

A pine estate cupboard, c1820, 96in (244cm) wide.
£4,000–5,000 *SPA*

An Irish pine food cupboard, c1800.
£2,750–3,500 *UP*

An Irish pine fielded panelled food cupboard, c1800, 50in (127cm) high.
£2,250–2,750 *UP*

An Irish pine food cupboard, 18thC, 56in (142cm) wide.
£2,500–3,000 *Ad*

A Georgian pine panelled cupboard, with 2 doors, 48in (122cm) wide.
£450–550 *TPC*

r. A Victorian pine wall cupboard, with panelled door, c1880, 26½in (67.5cm) high.
£150–200 *COT*

An Irish pine butler's pantry cupboard, with panelled doors, c1850, 54in (137cm) wide.
£2,800–3,300 *UC*

A Welsh pine harness cupboard, c1790, 58in (147.5cm) wide.
£2,800–3,300 *UC*

A German pine cupboard with one single drawer, beech turned legs and carvings, mid-19thC, 74in (188cm) high.
£600–700 *HGN*

l. A pine hanging kitchen cupboard, original iron hinges, c1820, 36in (91.5cm) wide.
£300–400 *HGN*

A Victorian pine floor standing cupboard, replacement chicken wire panels, new handles, 35in (89cm) high.
£550–650 *HGN*

An Irish pine food cupboard, c1780, 57in (145cm) high.
£2,600–3,200 *UP*

An architectural pine cupboard, c1780, 50in (127cm) high.
£1,800–2,200 *UP*

An Irish panelled pine food cupboard, c1790, 53in (134.5cm) high.
£3,000–3,600 *UP*

A Scottish panelled pine cupboard, c1800, 73in (185.5cm) high.
£1,300–1,600 *HG*

A pine cupboard, 39½in (100.5cm) wide.
£200–250 *WHA*

An Irish pine food cupboard, 18thC, 78in (198cm) high.
£2,600–3,200 *Ad*

A pine food cupboard, 19thC, 50in (127cm) high.
£1,400–1,700 *RK*

A pine proving cupboard, c1840, 46in (117cm) high.
£600–700 *AL*

A pine proving cupboard, tin-lined, c1840, 44in (112cm) wide.
£600–700 *AL*

A Dutch pine kitchen cupboard, with decorative cornice, 19thC, 35in (89cm) wide.
£600–700 *CI*

An Irish pine food cupboard, with panelled doors and sides and fantail moulding to cupboard doors, c1850, 80in (203cm) high.
£3,700–4,500 *CC*

A pine two-door cupboard, c1860, 36½in (92.5cm) high.
£275–350 *AL*

A pine single door cupboard, with false press front, c1840, 33in (84cm) wide.
£800–1,000 *GD*

r. A German pine cupboard, with beech carvings and feet, original escutcheons and lock, replacement knob handles, c1870, 32in (81.5cm) high.
£550–650 *HGN*

r. A set of 3 pine stacking campaign cupboards, each with 2 doors and lifting handles, 19thC, 48in (122cm) wide.
£1,150–1,400 *TPC*

A Czechoslovakian pine food cupboard, with original ribbed china knobs, 19thC, 34in (86.5cm) wide.
£650–750 *ERA*

l. A pine cupboard, with shelves, 18thC, 57in (145cm) wide.
£1,200–1,450 *WV*

A Continental pine food cupboard, c1860, 40in (101.5cm) wide.
£550–650 *GD*

A small pine cupboard, with 2 drawers and 2 cupboard doors, early 19thC, 48in (122cm) wide.
£1,000–1,200 *GD*

A pine cupboard, with 2 drawers at the top, c1885, 38in (96.5cm) wide.
£275–350 *DFA*

A Georgian Irish pine food cupboard, with dentil cornice, raised and fielded panelled doors, bracket feet, c1770, 80in (203cm) wide.
£3,000–3,600 *AF*

A pine food cupboard, in 2 sections, the top with 2 doors, the base with 2 drawers and 2 doors, c1830, 49in (124.5cm) wide.
£1,400–1,700 *UC*

An Irish pine food cupboard, c1860, 82in (208.5cm) high.
£1,800–2,200 *AF*

A pine cupboard, c1880, 37in (94cm) wide.
£550–650 *DFA*

l. A pine press cupboard, with hinged top, 2 panelled doors enclosing shelving and 13 small drawers with brass ring handles, panelled sides and plinth base, 18thC, 43½in (110.5cm) wide.
£1,700–2,100 *AH*

A Continental pine hanging cupboard, late 19thC, 69in (175.5cm) high.
£650–800 *HGN*

A pine two-door food cupboard, with lift-up shoe press above, dated '1829', 83in (211cm) high.
£1,700–2,000 *OCP*

A pine cupboard, c1840, 45in (114.5cm) wide.
£250–300 *DFA*

A pine cupboard, c1870, 37½in (95.5cm) wide.
£250–300 *DFA*

A pine linen cupboard, in 2 parts, c1870, 42½in (108cm) wide.
£1,000–1,200 *HON*

An Irish pine cupboard, with 2 centre drawers and 4 panelled cupboard doors, c1860, 53in (134.5cm) wide.
£1,800–2,200 *HON*

A pine wall cupboard, c1880, 36in (91.5cm) wide.
£175–225 *AL*

A pine wall cupboard, with adjustable shelves, c1880, 36in (91.5cm) wide.
£350–450 *HON*

An Irish pine architectural cupboard, with 4 doors and sunburst decoration, c1840, 57½in (146cm) wide.
£2,500–3,000 *HON*

An Irish pine cupboard, with breakfront top, 2 panelled doors, with rope-twist columns to either side and panelled sides, c1820, 61in (155cm) wide.
£2,500–3,000 *HON*

A pine cupboard, with dentil moulded top and 2 panelled doors, c1850, 57in (145cm) wide.
£1,200–1,500 *HON*

A pine cupboard, with 2 doors, one side of interior with shelves, c1875, 48in (122cm) wide.
£600–700 *Byl*

A pine cupboard, with single four-panel door, c1875, 38in (96.5cm) wide.
£500–600 *Byl*

A pitch pine school cupboard, with 3 doors, the interior fitted with shelves, c1880, 54in (137cm) wide.
£500–600 *Byl*

A pine cupboard, with 2 panelled doors, c1870, 55in (139.5cm) wide.
£600–750 *Byl*

A pine cupboard, with 4 panelled doors and 2 centre drawers, c1880, 48in (122cm) wide.
£1,150–1,400 *Byl*

A pine food cupboard, with 4 doors and decorated surround, c1860, 64in (162.5cm) wide.
£1,000–1,250 *Byl*

An Irish pine food cupboard, with 2 glazed doors to top and 2 panelled doors to base, c1865, 49in (124.5cm) wide.
£1,150–1,400 *Byl*

A Georgian pine wall cupboard, with single glazed door, c1790.
£400–500 *SA*

A pine cupboard, with 2 panelled doors and 2 drawers to base, c1875, 50in (127cm) wide.
£750–950 *Byl*

A pine cupboard, with 4 panelled doors, c1860, 48in (122cm) wide.
£1,000–1,250 *SA*

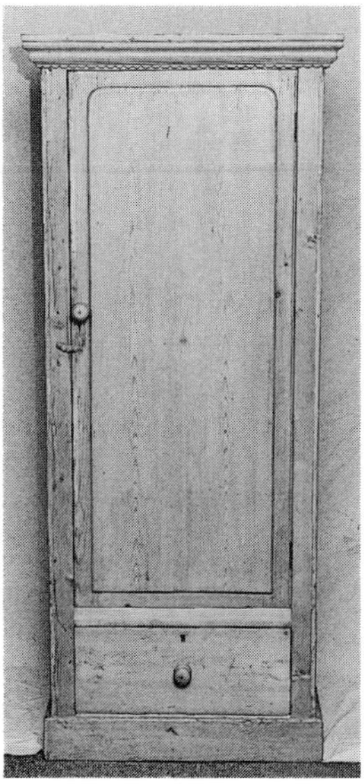

A pine cupboard, with single door and drawer beneath, late 19thC, 27in (68.5cm) wide.
£500–600 *SA*

A pine cupboard, with glazed top, c1860, 54in (137cm) wide.
£750–900 *TPC*

A Victorian pine china cupboard, with 2 astragal glazed doors above 2 blind panelled doors, 50in (127cm) wide.
£1,100–1,350 *TPC*

A Continental pine cupboard, with glazed doors to top, 42in (106.5cm) wide.
£650–800 *SA*

A Continental pine medicine cupboard, 19thC, 18in (45.5cm) high.
£100–150 *Cou*

A pine wall cabinet, with glazed doors, c1880, 23½in (59.5cm) high.
£175–225 *OPH*

r. A European pine wall cabinet, c1900, 18in (45.5cm) high.
£150–200 *OPH*

An Irish pine glazed cupboard, c1820, 77in (195.5cm) high.
£2,200–2,700 *Ad*

A pine two-door glazed cupboard, originally with metal mesh, c1825, 72½in (184cm) high.
£1,100–1,300 *AL*

A pine glazed cupboard with enclosed drawers, c1879, 15in (38cm) high.
£350–450 *AL*

An Irish pine pantry cupboard, late 19thC, 51in (129.5cm) wide.
£2,100–2,500 *Ad*

A pine glazed cupboard, with an arched top, 36in (91.5cm) wide.
£275–350 *CHA*

A pine glazed cupboard, 26in (66cm) wide.
£275–350 *PH*

A Georgian Irish pine cupboard, 48in (122cm) wide.
£2,100–2,500 *Ad*

l. A pine glazed cupboard, with adjustable shelves, c1860, 39½in (100.5cm) high.
£350–450 *AL*

An Irish pine glazed cupboard, c1780, 56in (142cm) wide.
£1,200–1,500 *UP*

An Irish pine corner cupboard, c1800, 52in (132cm) wide.
£2,500–3,000 *UP*

A pine food cupboard, c1880, 39in (99cm) wide.
£1,850–2,200 *W*

A pine glazed cupboard, unrestored, c1840.
£1,300–1,600 *CPA*

A German pine bedside cupboard, c1900.
£150–200 *CPA*

A pair of South German pine bedside cupboards, c1900.
£350–450 *TPF*

A German pine bedside cupboard.
£175–225 *CPA*

A pair of pine bedside cupboards, with one drawer and cupboard below, 20thC, 24in (61cm) wide.
£175–225 *PC*

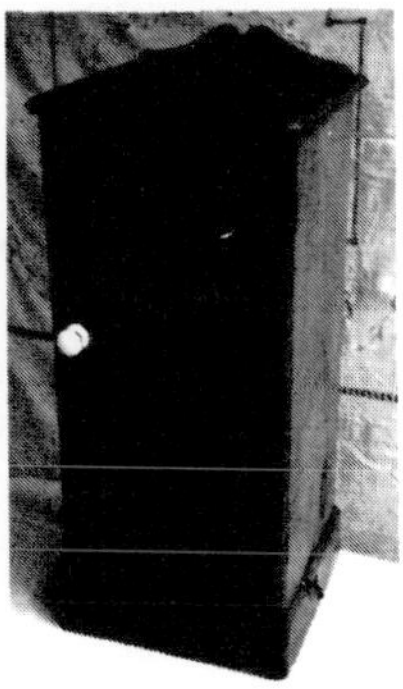

A pine bedside cupboard, 30in (76cm) high.
£250–300 *PAC*

A Danish pine bedside cupboard, c1870, 25in (63.5cm) wide.
£175–225 *RK*

l. A Victorian pine bedside cupboard, 16in (40.5cm) wide.
£220–275 *OA*

l. A Victorian pine bedside cupboard, c1880, 15in (38cm) wide.
£220–275 *OA*

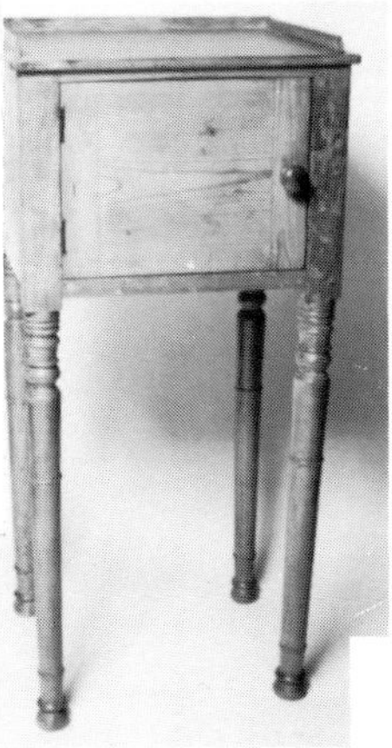

A pine bedside cupboard, 15in (38cm) wide.
£250–325 *AL*

A Regency tambour-fronted bedside cupboard, c1820, 18in (45.5cm) wide.
£300–350 *OL*

A pine pot cupboard, c1850, 15½in (39.5cm) wide.
£250–300 *W*

A deep two-door pine cupboard, c1840, 34in (86.5cm) wide.
£300–400 *AL*

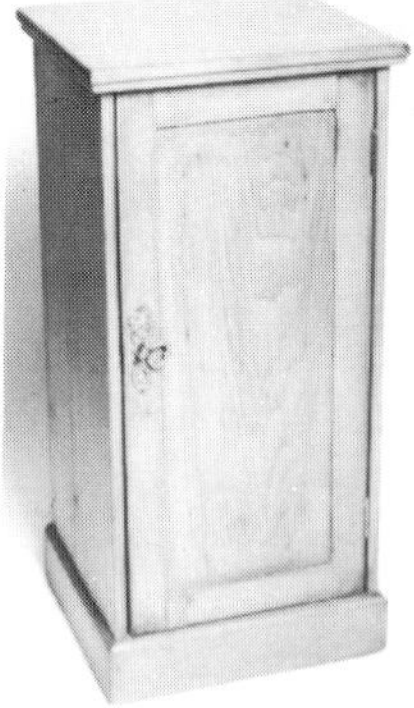

A pine pot cupboard, c1900, 30in (77.5cm) high.
£200–250 *W*

A pine drum-shaped pot cupboard, with marble top, c1840, 15½in (39.5cm) diam
£400–500 *LAM*

A Victorian pine cupboard on stand, 19in (48.5cm) wide.
£200–250 *AL*

A pine cupboard with drawer, c1840, 22in (56cm) wide.
£225–275 *AL*

A late Victorian pine pot cupboard, 15in (38cm) wide.
£225–275 *W*

A pine pot cupboard, with original porcelain handle, 14in (35.5cm) wide.
£250–300 *AL*

A pine cupboard, with adjustable shelves, original lock and key, c1840, 51in (129.5cm) high.
£125–175 *AL*

A pine pot cupboard, 19thC, 15in (38cm) wide.
£225–275 *AL*

A central European pine pot cupboard, c1920, 12in (30.5cm) wide.
£150–200 *SPA*

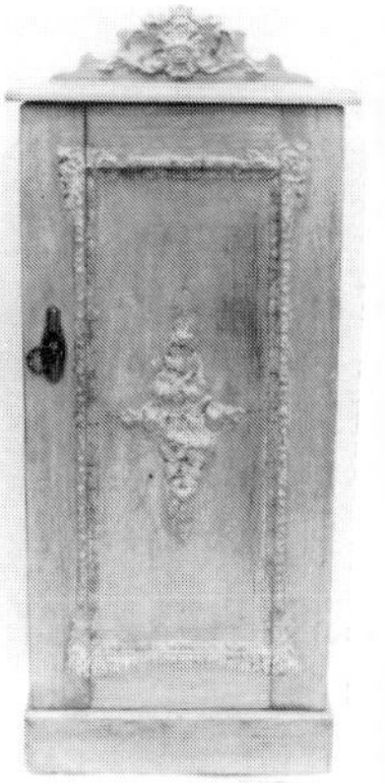

A pine pot cupboard, with gesso decoration, c1880, 15in (38cm) wide.
£225–275 *AL*

A Swedish pine pot cupboard, c1910, 24½in (62cm) wide.
£175–225 *BEL*

l. A Regency pine pot cupboard, with tapered legs, 32in (81.5cm) high.
£250–300 *AL*

r. A mid-European pot cupboard, 17in (43cm) wide.
£150–200 *RK*

A pine food cupboard, on bracket feet, c1820, 45in (114.5cm) wide.
£1,150–1,400 *POT*

r. A pine glazed food cupboard, with 2 drawers and pillar sides, c1880, 74in (188cm) wide.
£950–1,150 *OCP*

An Irish pine cupboard with 2 glazed doors above 2 small doors, c1880, 36in (91.5cm) wide.
£800–975 *SA*

r. A pine vitrine, original lock and key, late 19thC, 66in (167.5cm) high.
£650–800 *HGN*

l. A Dutch pine corner cupboard, c1865, 20in (51cm) wide.
£275–350 *AnD*

A pine cupboard, with 2 glazed doors to top and 2 panelled doors to base, c1875, 56in (142cm) wide.
£950–1,150 *SA*

A pine bowfronted corner cupboard, c1780, 34in (86.5cm) wide.
£1,700–2,000 *UP*

A pine bowfronted barrel back corner cupboard, with carved shelves and a slide, c1740.
£4,500–5,500 *LAM*

A mid-Georgian corner cupboard, with a breakfront moulded cornice above a recess with open shelves and semi-domed top, flanked by moulded uprights, 48in (122cm) wide.
£2,000–2,500 *CSK*

A George III Cumbrian pine corner cupboard, 76in (193cm) high.
£1,500–1,800 *UP*

A pine corner cupboard, with barrel back and shaped shelves, c1840, 79in (200.5cm) high.
£3,000–3,600 *Ad*

A pine two-piece corner cupboard, c1780, 44in (112cm) wide.
£2,400–2,900 *UP*

An astragal glazed, barrel-backed pine corner cupboard, c1840, 80in (203cm) high.
£2,500–3,000 *AL*

A pine corner cupboard, 18thC.
£1,500–1,800 *ARK*

A George III pine corner cupboard, on moulded apron and block feet, 41½in (105.5cm) wide.
£3,500–4,200 *P(L)*

l. A pine corner cupboard, 80in (203cm) high.
£1,350–1,650 *RK*

r. A late George III pine standing corner cupboard, the moulded cornice with a foliate carved frieze above a central lion's head and spandrels with paterae and trailing husks, a single arched astragal glazed door between reeded uprights, with a panelled door below between similar uprights, 32½in (82.5cm) wide.
£2,800–3,300 *CSK*

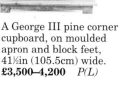

l. A Welsh pine corner cupboard, 71in (180.5cm) high.
£1,400–1,750 *RK*

A Georgian pine corner cabinet, the upper cupboards with shaped shelves, 50in (127cm) wide.
£2,000–2,400 *Ad*

A pine corner cupboard, c1860, 46in (117cm) wide.
£1,200–1,500 *WHA*

A late Georgian full length pine standing corner cabinet, 39in (99cm) wide.
£1,800–2,200 *OA*

A pine corner cupboard, 19thC.
£3,300–4,000 *PH*

A pine corner cupoboard, 43in (109cm) wide.
£1,600–2,000 *LAM*

r. An astragal glazed pine corner cupboard, 39in (99cm) wide.
£2,400–2,900 *PH*

l. A Scandinavian pine corner cupboard dated '1731', 72in (183cm) high.
£1,000–1,200 *W*

A Victorian Cornish pine corner cupboard, 33in (84cm) wide.
£1,150–1,400 *Ad*

A Georgian stripped pine corner cabinet, 86½in (219.5cm) high.
£2,500–3,000 *AG*

r. A pine glazed corner cupboard, c1860, on a new base, 84in (213.5cm) high.
£1,200–1,500 *AL*

A pine architectural corner cupboard, with barrel back and shaped interior display shelves, early 19thC, 90in (228.5cm) high.
£3,300–4,000 *Ced*

A Victorian pine wall corner cupboard, 36in (91.5cm) high.
£350–450 *WaH*

A Victorian pine hanging corner cupboard, 30in (76cm) wide.
£350–450 *ERA*

A pine corner cupboard, the panelled doors with original hinges, enclosing shaped shelved interior, 18thC, 40in (101.5cm) wide.
£1,400–1,700 *TPC*

A Georgian barrel-back corner cupboard, c1740, 51in (129.5cm) wide.
£2,500–3,000 *COT*

A pine corner cupboard, with glazed door, early 19thC, 31in (78.5cm) wide.
£500–600 *POT*

l. A pine hanging corner cupboard, with single glazed door, c1900, 29in (73.5cm) wide.
£300–375 *SA*

r. A pine corner cupboard, the top with 2 panelled doors, the base with 3 small drawers and 2 panelled doors, c1830, 36in (91.5cm) wide.
£2,100–2,500 *HeR*

A pine corner cupboard, with raised and fielded panelled doors, enclosing shaped shelves, bull's-eyes and column mouldings to sides, 18thC, 42in (106.5cm) high.
£1,600–1,950 *TPC*

A pine corner cupboard, with 2 glazed and 2 panelled doors, original blue painted interior, c1810, 46in (117cm) wide.
£2,500–3,000 *UC*

A pine corner cupboard, with glazed cupboard doors, on bracket feet, c1860.
£1,200–1,500 *POT*

A pine corner cupboard, with glazed top section, c1880, 51in (129.5cm) wide.
£1,200–1,500 *OCP*

A Georgian barrel-back pine recess cupboard, with domed hood and shaped shelves, 37in (94cm) wide.
£2,100–2,500 *ERA*

A pine glazed corner cupboard, the 2 upper doors with carved decoration and cut-outs, c1880, 54in (137cm) wide.
£1,400–1,700 *OCP*

l. A Georgian pine barrel-back corner cupboard, with arched interior and shaped shelves, 2 raised and fielded panel doors with original iron work, by T. Greer, N. Ireland, c1811, 74in (188cm) high.
£2,250–2,750 *AF*

r. A pine glazed corner cupboard, c1870, 40in (101.5cm) wide,
£1,100–1,300 *DFA*

A pine corner cupboard, with key, c1830, 41in (104cm) high.
£450–550 *AL*

A bowfronted pine corner cupboard, with original handles, 12½in (32cm) high.
£175–225 *AL*

A pine corner cupboard, c1870, 27in (68.5cm) wide.
£400–500 *RK*

A Georgian bowfront pine cupboard, 35in (89cm) high.
£400–500 *JAC*

A Scottish pine corner cupboard, 16in (40.5cm) wide.
£175–225 *BH*

A pine hanging corner cupboard, c1790, 37in (94cm) wide.
£550–650 *UP*

A Victorian pine corner cabinet, 25in (63.5cm) wide.
£400–500 *AL*

A Victorian pine corner cabinet, with a single locking door, 18in (45.5cm) wide.
£350–450 *AL*

A pine hanging corner cupboard, c1790, 37in (94cm) wide.
£450–550 *UP*

A pine corner cupboard, c1840, 27in (68.5cm) wide.
£350–425 *W*

A two-door pine hanging corner cupboard, c1850, 32in (81.5cm) high.
£450–550 *AL*

A pine hanging corner cupboard, c1840, 36in (91.5cm) high.
£300–400 *AL*

An Austrian pine corner cupboard, with 3 coloured glass panels in the single door, 31½in (80cm) high.
£350–450 *CHA*

A pine corner cupboard with semi-arched moulded panelled doors, 19thC, 31in (78.5cm) wide.
£650–800 *OK*

A pine hanging corner cupboard, 19thC, 28in (71cm) wide.
£500–600 *CHA*

A late Georgian pine corner cupboard, with a panelled and moulded door, 31in (78.5cm) wide.
£500–600 *OA*

An astragal glazed pine corner cupboard, c1800, 39in (99cm) wide.
£500–600 *UP*

A pine corner cupboard, c1800, 55½in (141cm) high.
£500–600 *AL*

l. A bowfront pine corner cupboard, 32in (81.5cm) high.
£550–700 *PH*

r. A pine corner cupboard, with handmade butterfly hinges, c1800, 21in (53.5cm) high.
£450–550 *AL*

l. A mid-Georgian pine hanging corner cabinet, the fielded panel door flanked by reeded and moulded sides, 28in (71cm) wide.
£500–650 *OA*

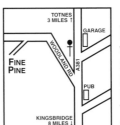

A late Victorian pine bedside cabinet, with shaped shelf beneath, on tapered legs, 16in (40.5cm) wide.
£200–250 *TPC*

A Continental pine pot cupboard, c1890, 29in (73.5cm) high.
£150–200 *ASP*

A pine bedside locker, c1880, 29in (73.5cm) high.
£150–200 *Byl*

A pine pot cupboard, with 2 doors, c1879, 30in (76cm) high.
£225–275 *AL*

A pine bedside locker, c1880, 31½in (80cm) high.
£150–200 *Byl*

A pine bedside locker, c1880, 30in (76cm) high.
£150–200 *Byl*

A pine pot cupboard, with single drawer, replacement handles, early 20thC, 16in (40.5cm) wide.
£150–200 *HNG*

A pine pot cupboard, c1879, 30in (76cm) high.
£175–225 *AL*

A pine pot cupboard, c1879, 30in (76cm) high.
£175–225 *AL*

An Eastern European pine chest of 3 drawers, with half-cut pillars, 1860s, 39in (99cm) wide.
£450–550 *NWE*

An Eastern European pine chest of drawers, 1880–1900, 23in (58.5cm) wide.
£300–400 *NWE*

An Eastern European chest of 3 drawers, 1880, 42½in (108cm) wide.
£400–475 *NWE*

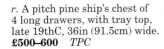

A pine chest of 2 short and 2 long drawers, 19thC, 36in (91.5cm) wide.
£500–600 *TPC*

r. A pitch pine ship's chest of 4 long drawers, with tray top, late 19thC, 36in (91.5cm) wide.
£500–600 *TPC*

A Shaker pine chest of drawers, the moulded cornice above 5 graduated moulded drawers, on bracket feet, Havard Community, Massachusetts, c1840, 60in (152.5cm) high.
£2,000–2,500 *S(NY)*

l. A pine chest of 2 short and 3 long drawers, with carved mouldings to fronts, on solid plinth base, 19thC, 48in (122cm) wide.
£550–650 *TPC*

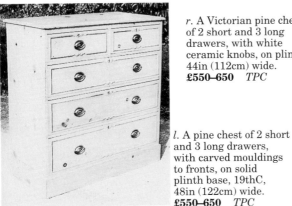

r. A Victorian pine chest, of 2 short and 3 long drawers, with white ceramic knobs, on plinth, 44in (112cm) wide.
£550–650 *TPC*

l. An early Victorian pine chest of drawers, c1840, 39in (99cm) wide.
£450–550 *COT*

r. A Georgian pine Winchester chest of 2 short and 3 long drawers, with original brass handles, on bracket feet, 54in (137cm) wide.
£800–1,000 *TPC*

A pine miniature chest of drawers, c1880, 14in (35.5cm) wide.
£250–300 *UP*

A pine bowfronted chest of drawers, c1860.
£850–1,000 *PIN*

A pine chest of drawers, c1860, 42in (106.5cm) wide.
£400–500 *SPA*

A pine chest of drawers, with original knobs and bracket feet, c1830, 34in (86.5cm) wide.
£550–650 *SPA*

A Federal pine bowfronted chest of drawers, painted and grained all over in brown and ochre to simulate mahogany, New England, c1810, 40in (101.5cm) wide.
£1,500–1,800 *S(NY)*

A pine chest of drawers, with new brass handles, c1890, 36in (91.5cm) wide.
£450–550 *SPA*

A small pine chest of drawers, 14in (35.5cm) wide.
£150–200 *AL*

A German pine chest of drawers, with turned columns original handles and fittings, c1850, 43in (109cm) wide.
£450–550 *Sca*

A box-shaped pine chest of drawers, with locking fall front, c1860, 34in (78.5cm) wide.
£600–750 *AL*

A pine chest of drawers, c1870, 36in (91.5cm) wide.
£400–500 *SPA*

A late Georgian pine chest, 34in (86.5cm) wide.
£500–600 *UP*

A Victorian pine chest of drawers.
£400–500 *PIN*

A pine chest of drawers, c1860, 34in (86.5cm) wide.
£400–500 *AL*

A Georgian pine chest of 3 long drawers, on bracket feet, 36in (91.5cm) wide.
£550–650 *TPC*

A pine chest of 2 short and 2 long drawers, c1920, 35½in (90cm) wide.
£275–350 *BEL*

A mid-Victorian pine chest of 5 drawers, 39in (99cm) wide.
£450–550 *ERA*

A pine chest of 4 drawers, flanked by columns, c1870, 37½in (95.5cm) wide.
£400–500 *BEL*

A pine chest of 3 drawers, c1920, 37½in (95.5cm) wide.
£300–400 *BEL*

r. A pine bowfront chest of drawers, c1860, 38½in (98cm) wide.
£500–600 *BEL*

A Scandinavian pine chest of 5 drawers, c1840, 39in (99cm) wide.
£500–600 *BEL*

A pine chest of 3 long drawers, c1900, 36in (91.5cm) wide.
£400–475 *FAG*

r. A Victorian pine chest of 5 drawers, 1875, 41in (104cm) wide.
£500–600 *OPH*

A pine five-drawer narrow chest, the top drawer containing 3 secret drawers, Lincolnshire, c1850, 41½in (105.5cm) high.
£800–1,000 *UC*

A Victorian pine chest of drawers, with original handles, 34in (86.5cm) wide.
£450–550 *OA*

A chemist's shop pine flight of drawers, with original knobs, 19thC.
£550–700 *AF*

A Victorian pine chest of drawers, with original handles, 34in (86.5cm) wide.
£450–550 *OA*

A Victorian pine chest of drawers, c1840, 45in (114.5cm) wide.
£500–600 *Sca*

A pine chest of drawers, unrestored, c1835.
£800–1,000 *CPA*

A Scottish pine chest of drawers, with bobbin turning at the sides, c1850, 49in (124.5cm) high.
£750–950 *AL*

A pine chest of drawers, with new handles, 19thC, 40in (101.5cm) wide.
£500–600 *AL*

A pine bowfronted chest, with graduated drawers, 18thC, 36in (91.5cm) wide.
£900–1,100 *RdeR*

A pine chest of drawers, 19thC, 27in (68.5cm) high.
£500–600 *AL*

A Georgian pine chest of drawers, with high bracket feet and original brass handles, 39in (99cm) high.
£800–1,000 *AF*

l. A pine three-piece bedroom suite, comprising: a chest of drawers, 45in (114.5cm) wide, a wardrobe, 49in (124.5cm) wide, and a dressing table, 50in (127cm) wide.
£3,200–3,800 *Sca*

A pine chest of drawers, with original handles, 36in (91.5cm) wide.
£400–500 *ASP*

A mid-Victorian pine chest of 4 drawers, with porcelain knob handles, 34in (86.5cm) wide.
£400–500 *ERA*

A pine chest of drawers, c1860, 41in (104cm) wide.
£400–500 *ASP*

r. A Victorian pine chest of 2 short and 3 long drawers, c1880, 37in (94cm) wide.
£500–600 *WaH*

l. A Victorian pine chest of 2 short and 2 long drawers, 33in (84cm) wide.
£400–500 *WaH*

A pine chest of 4 graduated drawers, on plinth base, 35in (89cm) wide.
£500–600 *CCP*

A Victorian pine chest of drawers, c1850, 38in (96.5cm) wide.
£500–600 *DMe*

A Continental pine chest, with 5 drawers, c1880, 37in (94cm) wide.
£400–475 *ASP*

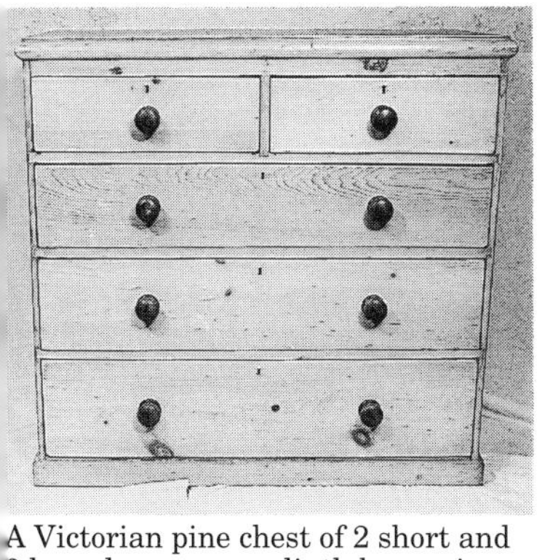

A Victorian pine chest of 2 short and 3 long drawers, on plinth base, pine knob handles, 41in (104cm) wide.
£500–600 *CCP*

A Scandinavian pine chest, with 4 drawers and one cupboard, c1900, 37in (94cm) wide.
£400–500 *BEL*

A Scottish pine chest of drawers, with one deep top drawer made to appear as 5 small drawers, 44in (112cm) wide.
£800–1,000 *PF*

A pine chest of drawers, with 3 drawers and mahogany handles, 19thC, 40in (101.5cm) wide.
£500–600 *PD*

A Scandinavian pitch pine chest of drawers, with split turned decorations to the side and original small brass handles, 19thC, 36in (91.5cm) wide.
£450–550 *CC*

A pair of Victorian pine chests of drawers, one on legs, 44in (112cm) wide.
£600–750 *AL*

A Georgian pine chest of drawers, 42in (106.5cm) wide.
£700–900 *AL*

A serpentine-fronted chest of drawers, with splashback and applied split turnings, late 19thC, 39in (99cm) wide.
£700–900 *PF*

A pine plan chest, c1880, 48in (122cm) wide.
£550–700 *RK*

A pine chest of drawers, c1890, 36in (91.5cm) wide.
£400–500 *RK*

A pine chest of drawers, c1840.
£450–550 *CPA*

A pine chest of drawers, c1820.
£600–750 *CPA*

A waxed pine miniature chest of drawers, 11in (28cm) wide.
£150–200 *TRU*

A pine chest of drawers, 1880, 36in (91.5cm) wide.
£400–475 *TRU*

A Continental pine chest, the 4 drawers with beech and rosewood mouldings, replaced handles, late 19thC, 43in (109cm) wide.
£450–550 *HNG*

A late Victorian pine chest, with 2 long drawers at top and bottom and 2 small in the middle, original glass handles, replacement feet, 46in (117cm) wide.
£400–500 *HNG*

An Eastern European pine chest, with 4 drawers, replacement handles and escutcheons, late 19thC, 39in (99cm) wide.
£400–500 *HNG*

r. A German pine chest of drawers, with 2 small and 3 long drawers, original brass handles, new feet, c1840, 31½in (80cm) wide.
£400–500 *HGN*

Use the Index!

Because certain items might fit easily into any number of categories, the quickest and surest method of locating any entry is by reference to the index at the back of the book. This index has been fully cross-referenced for absolute simplicity.

A pine chest of drawers, with splashback, 19thC, 28in (71cm) wide.
£450–550 *WV*

A North Country chest of drawers, with splashback and shelf, 19thC, 36in (91.5cm) wide.
£500–600 *WV*

r. A mid-Victorian pine chest of 4 drawers, with original porcelain knobs, and turned feet, 35in (89cm) wide.
£400–500 *ERA*

l. A mid-Victorian pine chest of 4 drawers, with original ebonized handles and feet, c1870, 36in (91.5cm) wide.
£400–500 *ERA*

A pine chest of drawers, with 2 short and 3 long drawers, c1870, 45in (114.5cm) wide.
£550–650 *SSD*

A pine chest of drawers, with replacement handles, c1850, 46in (117cm) wide.
£500–600 *AL*

A chest of drawers, with 2 short and 3 long drawers, c1860, 45in (114.5cm) wide.
£500–600 *SSD*

A Scottish pine chest of drawers, with original cockbeading and handles, c1830, 42½in (108cm) wide.
£750–900 *AL*

A Victorian pine chest of drawers, 36in (91.5cm) wide.
£400–500 *FP*

A pine chest of drawers, with 3 long drawers, c1890, 39in (99cm) wide.
£400–500 *SSD*

A pine chest of 2 short and 2 long drawers, c1890, 39in (99cm) wide.
£400–500 *SSD*

A pine chest of drawers, with bracket feet, c1820, 36in (91.5cm) wide.
£650–800 *AL*

A pine chest of drawers, with a splash back, 41½in (105.5cm) wide.
£550–650 *PH*

A pine chest of 2 short and 3 long drawers, c1860, 45in (114.5cm) wide.
£400–500 *SSD*

A Victorian pine chest of drawers, with a shaped back and scrolled ends, 31in (78.5cm) wide.
£500–600 *AH*

A Yorkshire pine chest-on-chest, with original ebonized handles, c1860, 40in (101.5cm) wide.
£1,500–1,800 *UC*

A Regency Suffolk pine and sycamore chest of drawers, with original feet and brass, c1810, 37in (94cm) wide.
£850–1,000 *UC*

r. A Victorian pine five-drawer chest, with original knobs, on turned feet, c1880, 42in (106.5cm) wide.
£500–600 *POT*

l. A late Victorian pine chest, with 2 short and 2 long drawers, 35in (89cm) wide.
£400–500 *HNG*

A pine chest of drawers, with gallery, c1845, 36in (91.5cm) wide.
£450–550 *DMe*

A Victorian pine chest of drawers, with original knobs and elm bun feet, c1860, 47in (119.5cm) wide.
£500–600 *POT*

A pine chest of drawers, with 2 small and 2 long drawers, on turned feet, c1880, 38in (96.5cm) wide.
£400–500 *SA*

A pine chest of drawers, with 2 short and 2 long drawers, c1880, 40in (101.5cm) wide.
£400–500 *OCP*

A pine breakfront side cabinet, c1875, 54in (137cm) wide.
£1,000–1,200 *DFA*

l. A pine chest of drawers, with 2 small above 2 long drawers, c1810, 32½in (82.5cm) wide.
£400–500 *AL*

r. A pine chest, with 2 short and 3 long drawers, c1860, 39½in (100.5cm) wide.
£500–600 *AL*

A pine chest of drawers, the 2 small and 2 long drawers with glass knob handles, 38in (96.5cm) wide.
£400–500 *AL*

A Welsh pine chest of 3 drawers, c1870, 36in (91.5cm) wide.
£450–550 *AL*

A pine chest of drawers, with shaped back above 2 small and 2 long drawers, c1880, 40in (101.5cm) wide.
£450–550 *SA*

A pine chest of drawers, on bun feet, c1840, 46in (117cm) wide.
£400–500 *DMe*

Make the most of Miller's

In *Miller's Pine & Country Buyer's Guide* we do NOT just reprint saleroom estimates. Our consultants work from realised prices and then calculate a price range for similar items, avoiding uncharacteristic 'one off' high or low results.

A Continental pine chest of 3 drawer with carved corbels, brass handles, c1870, 49½in (125.5cm) wide.
£400–500 *AF*

l. A pine blanket box, in the form of a chest of drawers, with lift-up top, c1885, 36in (91.5cm) wide.
£600–700 *BEL*

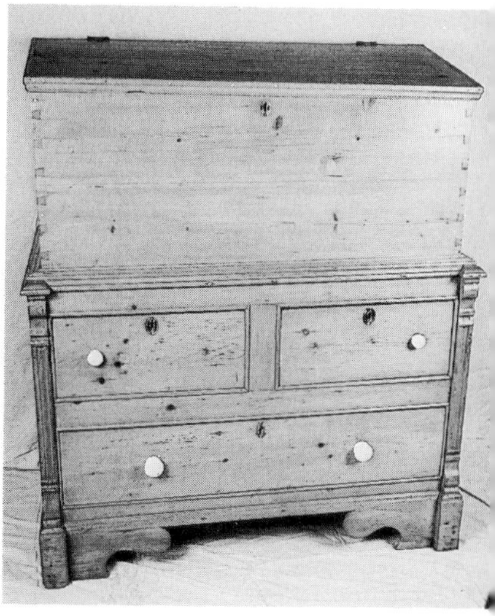

r. An Irish chest-on-chest, all original, c1800, 50in (127cm) wide.
£650–800 *COT*

A pine drop-leaf table, with a drawer at one end, on turned legs, c1880, 44½in (113cm) wide.
£350–400 *AL*

A pine drop-leaf table, with a drawer at each end, on turned legs, c1850, 42in (106.5cm) wide.
£325–400 *DMA*

A pine draw-leaf table, c1880, 37in (94cm) wide, extended.
£300–350 *AL*

A Victorian pine drop-leaf table, with one drawer, on turned legs, c1850, 47in (119cm) wide.
£350–400 *DMA*

A pine drop-leaf table, with a drawer, c1880, 36in (91.5cm) wide.
£350–400 *AL*

A pine washstand, with gallery back, c1880, 24in (61.5cm) wide.
£250–300 *AL*

A pine table, with turned legs, and shelf beneath, c1880, 30in (76.5cm) wide.
£225–275 *AL*

A pine table, with a drawer, c1870, 55in (139.5cm) wide.
£400–500 *AL*

A French pine dough bin, lid missing, c1870, 72in (182.5cm) wide.
£400–475 *AL*

A pine table, with one leaf, c1880, 40in (101.5cm) wide.
£250–300 *AL*

A pine side table, with 2 drawers, c1870, 45in (114cm) wide.
£420–480 *AL*

A pine serving table, with one small and 2 large drawers, c1850, 57in (144.5cm) wide.
£900–1,100 *AL*

A pine side table, with 2 drawers, and turned legs, 38in (96.5cm) wide.
£300–375 *LIB*

A pine tray-top washstand, c1870, 26in (66in) wide.
£325–375 *AL*

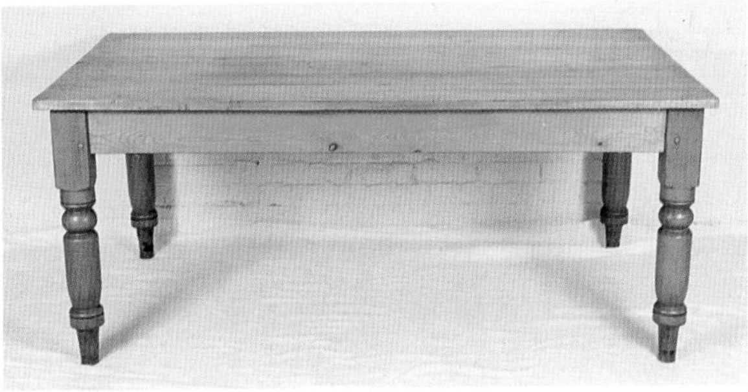

A pine table, with turned legs, c1880, 72in (182.5cm) wide.
£1,100–1,300 *AL*

A pine writing table, with new leather top, c1880, 36in (91.5cm) wide.
£550–650 *AL*

A pine side table, with one drawer, on turned legs, 28½in (72.5cm) wide.
£250–300 *AL*

A pine refectory table, with 3 drawers, on turned legs with stretchers, 19thC, 60in (152cm) long.
£800–950 *TPC*

A pine farmhouse table, with one long end drawer with a wooden knob, c1820, 66in (167.5cm) long.
£550–650 *DMA*

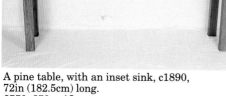

A pine table, with an inset sink, c1890, 72in (182.5cm) long.
£550–650 *AL*

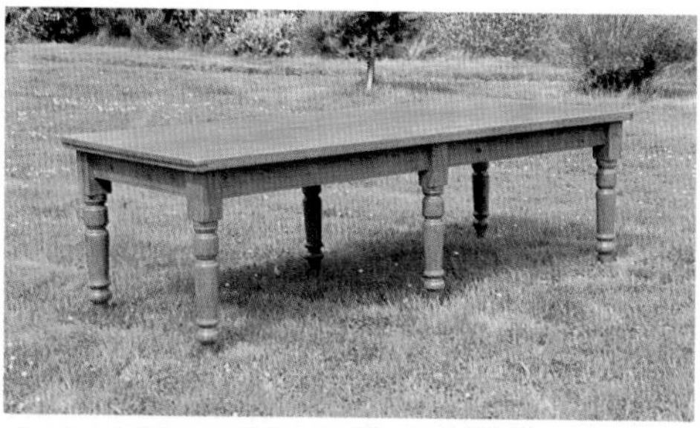

A pine table, on 6 turned legs, 19thC, 96in (244cm) long.
£1,100–1,350 *TPC*

A Victorian pine table, with drawers, on turned legs, c1840, 36in (91.5cm) long.
£500–550 *DMA*

A pine side table, c1870, 67in (170cm) long.
£400–500 *AL*

A pine farmhouse table, on turned legs, c1835, 84in (213.5cm) long.
£900–1,100 *DMA*

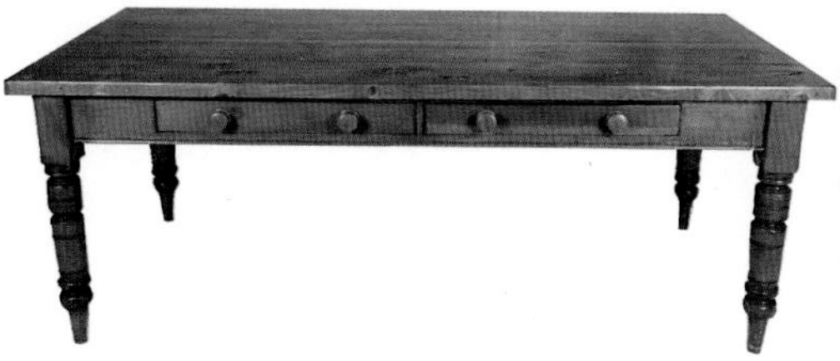

A pine farmhouse table, with 2 drawers, on turned legs, c1850, 85½in (217cm) long.
£1,000–1,250 *DMA*

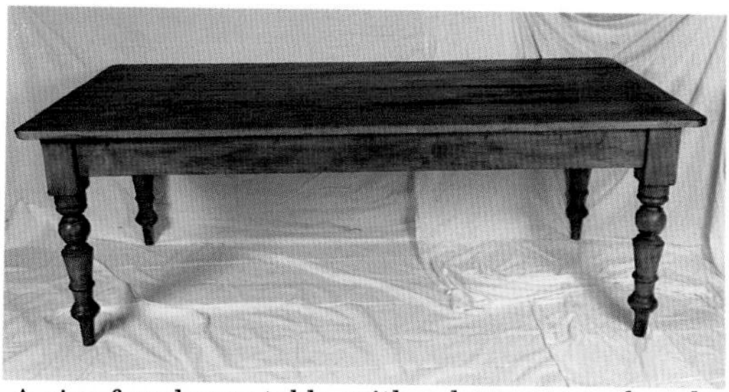

A pine farmhouse table, with a drawer at each end, on turned legs, c1830, 82in (208cm) long.
£900–1,100 *DMA*

A pine dressing table, with 2 small drawers below the mirror, c1885, 30in (76cm) wide.
£350–450 *COP*

A Victorian pine dressing table, c1865, 60in (152cm) wide.
£1,150–1,400 *AnD*

A pine dressing table, with spindle galleries, 19thC, 38in (96.5cm) wide.
£450–550 *TPC*

A pine dressing table, with 2 small and one long drawer, on turned legs, c1900, 39in (99cm) wide.
£370–450 *CCP*

A pine dressing chest, with 2 long drawers below 2 small drawers, c1880, 33in (83.5cm) wide.
£400–500 *DMA*

A pine dressing table, with oval mirror, c1880, 48in (122cm) wide.
£450–550 *COP*

A Victorian pine four-drawer dressing chest, on bun feet, handles replaced, 42in (106.5cm) wide.
£500–600 *CCP*

A pine dressing chest, with carved mirror supports, 19thC, 42in (106.5cm) wide.
£750–900 *TPC*

A pine dressing table, on casters, c1880, 48in (122cm) wide.
£1,150–1,400 *AL*

A pine compactum wardrobe, with gesso decoration, 19thC, 68in (172.5cm) wide.
£1,200–1,500 *TPC*

A pine 2 door 'knock down' wardrobe, c1875, 42in (106.5cm) wide.
£550–700 *AnD*

A pine collapsible wardrobe, with 3 drawers, c1880, 60in (152cm) wide.
£650–800 *AnD*

A pine wardrobe, with 2 doors and one long drawer, c1880, 43in (109cm) wide.
£500–600 *AnD*

A German pine cupboard, c1860, 34in (86cm) wide.
£500–600 *AnD*

A Victorian Gothic-style pine press cabinet, c1860, 53in (134.5cm) wide.
£1,150–1,400 *AnD*

A pine wardrobe, with 2 doors and 2 drawers, 41in (104cm) wide.
£650–800 *AnD*

A collapsible pine armoire, the 2 doors with raised and fielded panels, c1880, 53in (134.5cm) wide.
£650–800 *AnD*

An Eastern European pine wardrobe, with glazed panels and one drawer, early 20thC, 75in (190.5cm) wide.
£500–600 *AnD*

A beech and ash butcher's block, on original pine base, with trademark 'Herbert & Sons Ltd, West Smithfields, London', 24in (61cm) wide.
£650–800 *CCP*

A beech butcher's block, with a galleried knife back, on a pine base with a drawer, raised on casters, early 19thC, 42in (106.5cm) wide.
£1,150–1,400 *CCP*

A pine chopping block, c1880, 18in (46cm) wide.
£500–650 *MIL*

A beech and maple butcher's block, on beech legs, early 19thC, top 18in (46cm) thick.
£1,300–1,600 *CCP*

A sycamore coffee table, on a pine trestle base, early 19thC, 56in (142cm) wide.
£750–900 *CCP*

A Dutch pine washstand, with replaced decoration, 38in (96.5cm) wide.
£400–500 *AnD*

A German pine washstand, with brass knob and handle, c1890, 24in (61cm) wide.
£300–400 *AnD*

A Czechoslovakian pine washstand, with 2 small drawers above 2 cupboard doors, the splashback with a narrow shelf, c1865, 36in (91.5cm) wide.
£500–600 *AnD*

A Victorian pine washstand, with metal towel rails on each side, a drawer with 2 wooden knobs, on turned legs, c1845, 30in (76cm) long.
£275–350 *DMA*

A Victorian pine washstand, the drawer with a wooden knob, on turned legs, c1890, 24in (61cm) wide.
£250–300 *AnD*

A Victorian pine washstand, with 2 small drawers, on shaped end supports joined by a shaped stretcher, c1850, 39in (99cm) wide.
£400–500 *AnD*

A Victorian pine washstand, with 3 drawers and 2 cupboard doors, on turned feet, c1850, 44½in (113cm) wide.
£650–800 *DMA*

A Victorian pine washstand, with elaborately turned legs, 36in (91.5cm) wide.
£500–600 *AnD*

A pine corner washstand, with a shelf below, c1860, 28in (71cm) wide.
£550–650 *MIL*

A pine washstand, with a gallery top, turned legs, shaped undershelf, early 19thC, 42in (106.5cm) wide.
£450–550 *TPC*

A Victorian pine washstand, with a drawer under, on turned legs, 35in (89cm) wide.
£350–400 *WaH*

A Victorian pine washstand, with spindled gallery back, on turned legs, with a shaped undershelf, 36in (91.5cm) wide.
£400–500 *TPC*

A pine two-door washstand, with gallery top, and a marble worktop, c1870, 29½in (75cm) wide.
£300–400 *CCP*

A pine washstand, with a marble top, on turned legs, c1880, 30in (76cm) wide.
£250–300 *AnD*

A pine washstand, with slab ends, one drawer and a shaped stretcher, c1870, 34in (86cm) wide.
£450–550 *MIL*

A pine washstand, with a marble top, on straight legs, c1885, 36in (91.5cm) wide.
£250–300 *AnD*

A Victorian pine washstand, with a marble top, one drawer, on turned front legs joined by a shaped stretcher.
£500–600 *WaH*

A pine washstand, with 3 drawers, on turned legs c1870, 38in (96.5cm) wide.
£300–400 *MIL*

A pine washstand, with a shaped gallery top, a drawer below, on turned legs, c1880, 33in (84cm) wide.
£300–400 *WaH*

A pine washstand cupboard, with a lift-up top, c1890, 30½in (78cm) wide.
£275–350 *HeR*

A French Henry II pine buffet, 59in (150cm) wide.
£1,300–1,600 *AnD*

A pine two-door corner cupboard, c1865, 47in (119cm) wide.
£1,000–1,250 *AnD*

A pine panelled food cupboard, early 19thC, 48in (122cm) wide.
£1,700–2,000 *TPC*

A French Provincial pine buffet, c1840, 59in (150cm) wide.
£900–1,100 *AnD*

A pine linen press, with 8 short drawers, c1880, 58in (147cm) wide.
£1,600–1,900 *AnD*

A pine hanging corner cupboard, late 19thC, 47in (119cm) wide.
£550–650 *AnD*

A pine dresser, with glazed top cupboard doors, 2 drawers and 2 cupboards beneath, c1870, 41in (104cm) wide.
£750–900 *AnD*

A Dutch pine kitchen cupboard, with drawers, c1865, 37½in (95cm) wide.
£750–850 *AnD*

A pine dresser, with glazed top cupboard doors, 2 short drawers and 3 internal drawers, c1870, 43in (109cm) wide.
£750–850 *AnD*

A housemaid's pine press cupboard, with 4 cupboard doors, and 2 drawers, on bun feet, c1855, 51in (129.5cm) wide.
£1,700–2,000 *DMA*

A pine linen press, with 2 short and 2 long drawers, below 2 cupboard doors, 46in (116.5cm) wide.
£1,500–1,800 *DMA*

A Cumbrian pine linen press, with fitted interior slides, 18thC, 62in (157cm) wide.
£1,700–2,000 *BOA*

A pine linen press, with 2 short and 2 long drawers, below 2 cupboard doors, on bracket feet, c1840, 48½in (123cm) wide.
£1,700–2,000 *DMA*

A pine linen press, with carved corbels and interior slides, c1850.
£1,700–2,100 *BOA*

A pine linen press, with a fitted interior, on bracket feet, c1850.
£1,700–2,100 *BOA*

A Regency pine linen press, with fitted interior slides, on splayed feet, c1830, 48in (122cm) wide.
£1,700–2,000 *BOA*

A Yorkshire pine linen press, with fitted interior slides, c1850, 48in (122cm) wide.
£1,600–1,900 *BOA*

A Scottish pine linen press, with bonnet and glove drawers, c1840, 48in (122cm) wide.
£1,700–2,000 *BOA*

A George III pine standing corner cupboard, the moulded cornice above an astragal door, enclosing painted shaped shelves, 35½in (90cm) wide.
£1,600–1,900 *S(S)*

A pine corner cupboard, with one door, c1880, 34in (86cm) wide.
£400–500 *LIB*

A Victorian pine glazed corner cupboard, c1860, 37in (94cm) wide.
£1,150–1,400 *DMA*

A Victorian pine corner cabinet, with shaped shelves and barrel back, 1865, 42in (106.5cm) wide.
£1,700–2,000 *AnD*

An Irish pine corner cupboard, with astragal glazed doors, above 2 cupboard doors, c1810, 46in (116.5cm) wide.
£2,300–2,800 *TPC*

An Austrian painted pine food cupboard, with original paint finish, c1870, 36in (91.5cm) wide.
£750–950 *UC*

A pine corner cabinet, with a glazed door and 2 shelves, c1870, 17in (43cm) wide.
£350–450 *AnD*

A Dutch pine corner cupboard, on bun feet, c1880, 28in (71cm) wide.
£500–600 *AnD*

A pine bowfront corner cupboard, with a panelled door, c1850, 39½in (100cm) wide.
£1,000–1,200 *DMA*

A Danish pine wardrobe, c1880, 40in (101.5cm) wide.
£700–850 *UP*

An Irish pine food cupboard, with panelled doors, c1850, 78in (198cm) high.
£1,700–2,100 *RK*

A pine wardrobe, with turned pillars, c1880, 50in (127cm) wide.
£800–1,000 *UP*

A pine food safe, c1900, 25½in (65cm) high.
£170–200 *AHL*

An Irish food cupboard, with glazed doors, c1870, 50in (127cm) wide.
£2,000–2,500 *UP*

An Irish pine cupboard, c1820, 50in (127cm) wide.
£2,000–2,500 *RK*

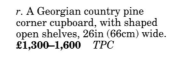

A pine linen press, c1860, 46in (116.5cm) wide.
£1,500–1,800 *SA*

A pine display cabinet, with 3 glazed doors above 3 drawers, c1840, 78in (198cm) wide.
£2,500–3,000 *UP*

r. A Georgian country pine corner cupboard, with shaped open shelves, 26in (66cm) wide.
£1,300–1,600 *TPC*

A French pine buffet, with 2 drawers, and 2 cupboard doors, c1850, 52in (132cm) wide.
£1,000–1,200 *UP*

An Irish pine cupboard, with 2 cupboard doors, and 6 drawers below, c1820, 54in (137cm) wide.
£2,100–2,500 *RK*

A pine press cupboard, with 3 panelled cupboard doors, above 2 short and 2 long drawers, c1840, 88in (223.5cm) high.
£1,800–2,200 *RK*

A pine single wardrobe, c1850, 40in (101.5cm) wide.
£750–900 *UP*

A Danish pine single wardrobe, c1870, 40in (101.5cm) wide.
£600–750 *RK*

A French pine buffet base, c1880, 44in (111.5cm) wide.
£650–800 *UP*

An Irish pine cupboard, with 4 panelled doors, c1850, 65in (165cm) wide.
£1,300–1,600 *RK*

A pine double wardrobe, with an elaborately carved cornice, c1890, 48in (122cm) wide.
£550–700 *UP*

An Irish pine corner cupboard, with astragal glazed doors above, decorated with shamrocks, c1850, 45in (114cm) wide.
£2,200–2,700 *RK*

. pine chest of 5 drawers,
1880, 42in (107cm) wide.
750–900 *UP*

An Irish pine bed, from County Clare, c1820, 66in (168cm) wide.
£1,900–2,300 *UP*

A pine harness cupboard, c1820, 60in (152cm) wide.
£2,200–2,600 *UP*

. pine linen press, c1790,
8in (122cm) wide.
2,100–2,500 *UP*

A housemaid's pine cupboard, c1890, 96in (244cm) high. **£2,500–3,000** *UP*

A pine bureau, c1780, 42in (107cm) wide.
£1,700–2,000 *UP*

A French pine glazed cupboard, c1870.
£800–950 *UP*

A French pine cupboard, c1870, 76in (193cm) high.
£900–1,100 *UP*

A pine corner cupboard, c1770.
£1,000–1,200 *RK*

. Scandanavian pine
hest of drawers, c1860,
8in (122cm) wide.
800–900 *RK*

. pine breakfront bookcase, c1820,
68in (427cm) wide.
3,800–4,500 *UP*

An Irish pine food cupboard, c1850, 58in (147cm) wide.
£1,800–2,200 *UP*

An Irish pine glazed cupboard, c1850, 82in (208cm) high.
£1,800–2,200 *UP*

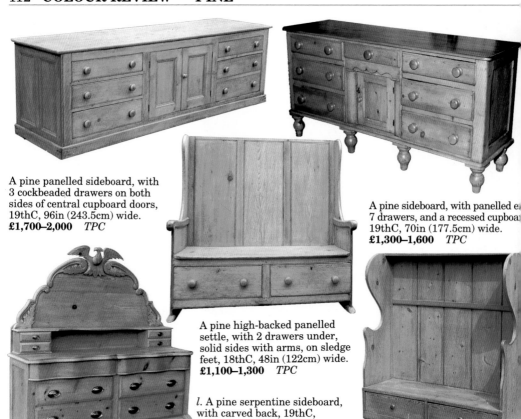

A pine panelled sideboard, with 3 cockbeaded drawers on both sides of central cupboard doors, 19thC, 96in (243.5cm) wide.
£1,700–2,000 *TPC*

A pine sideboard, with panelled e
7 drawers, and a recessed cupboa
19thC, 70in (177.5cm) wide.
£1,300–1,600 *TPC*

A pine high-backed panelled settle, with 2 drawers under, solid sides with arms, on sledge feet, 18thC, 48in (122cm) wide.
£1,100–1,300 *TPC*

l. A pine serpentine sideboard, with carved back, 19thC, 66in (167.5cm) wide.
£1,400–1,700 *TPC*

A Welsh pine high-backed settle, with 2 drawers under, early 18thC, 52in (132cm) wide.
£1,100–1,300 *TPC*

A pine chest of drawers, with 2 short and 4 long drawers, and original handles, c1860, 32in (81cm) wide.
£900–1,100 *SSD*

A pine chest of 2 short and 2 long drawers, with a gallery back, c1865, 42in (106.5cm) wide.
£750–900 *SSD*

A pine chest of 2 short and 2 long drawers, with a gallery back, c1865, 42in (106.5cm) wide.
£500–600 *SSD*

A pine chest of 3 long drawers, c1820, 37in (94cm) wide.
£550–600 *UP*

A Victorian pine chest of drawers, 30in (76cm) wide.
£500–600 *OA*

l. A Scandinavian bowfronted pine chest of drawers, 38in (96.5cm) wide.
£550–700 *BEL*

A Victorian pine chest of 2 short and 2 long drawers, 26in (66cm) wide.
£500–600 *AL*

A pine specimen chest, c1880, 40in (101.5cm) wide.
£650–750 *UP*

l. An Irish pine mule chest, with mock drawer fronts and original knobs, c1850, 42in (106.5cm) wide.
£500–600 *PIN*

A south German pine chest of 4 long drawers, c1880.
£450–550 *TPF*

A Scottish pine chest, c1850, 48in (120cm) wide.
£750–900 *RK*

A mid-European pine chest of drawers, 37in (94cm) wide.
£400–500 *RK*

A Victorian bowfront veneered chest of drawers, c1850, later painted with an east coast maritime theme, 42in (106.5cm) wide.
£500–600 *PIN*

A Victorian pine chest of drawers, with a shaped gallery back, 33in (84cm) wide.
£500–600 *AF*

A pine chest of drawers, c1870, 32in (81.5cm) high.
£400–500 *AL*

A pine bowfronted chest of drawers, 34in (86.5cm) wide.
£900–1,100 *PH*

A pine dressing chest, c1850, 42in (106.5cm) wide.
£600–750 *AL*

A pine chest, with lift-up lid and 2 opening drawers, c1830, 42in (106.5cm) wide.
£500–550 *AL*

A pine chest of drawers, with scroll decoration, c1850, 36in (91.5cm) wide.
£400–500 *AL*

A pine chest of drawers, with plywood drawer bottoms, c1900, 45in (114.5cm) high.
£800–950 *AL*

A pine chest of drawers, c1880, 33in (84cm) wide.
£400–500 *PAC*

A pine serpentine front chest of drawers, with an apron, original crystal knobs and mahogany feet, c1860.
£600–700 *CHA*

A Scandinavian or south German pine chest of drawers, 44in (112cm) wide.
£400–500 *CHA*

A pine chest of drawers, c1820, 42in (106.5cm) wide.
£500–600 *PH*

A pine combination chest of drawers c1860, 40in (101.5cm) wide.
£650–800 *AL*

A Regency pine chest of drawers, with original handles, c1835, 33in (84cm) wide.
£750–900 *AL*

A Victorian pine chest of drawers, with a splashback, c1840, 39in (99cm) wide.
£400–500 *W*

A pine chest of drawers, with original brass escutcheons, on turned feet, c1840, 37in (94cm) wide.
£450–550 *W*

A pine chest of drawers, c1860, 41in (104cm) wide.
£400–500 *W*

A pine flour barrel, made to resemble a chest of drawers, c1850, 26in (66cm) high.
£300–400 *AL*

A pine chest of drawers, c1880, 18in (45.5cm) wide.
£150–200 *AL*

A low pine chest of drawers, c1860, 41in (104cm) wide.
£400–500 *W*

l. A pine chest of drawers, 49½in (125.5cm) wide.
£550–650 *PH*

l. A pine chest of drawers, with original handles and escutcheons, c1840, 34½in (87.5cm) wide.
£450–550 *Sca*

A Regency pine two-door wardrobe, with applied hardwood mouldings, on shaped bracket feet, 54in (137cm) wide.
£1,000–1,200 *TPC*

A pine single wardrobe, with panelled door and one long drawer to base, 19thC, 30in (78.5cm) wide.
£500–600 *TPC*

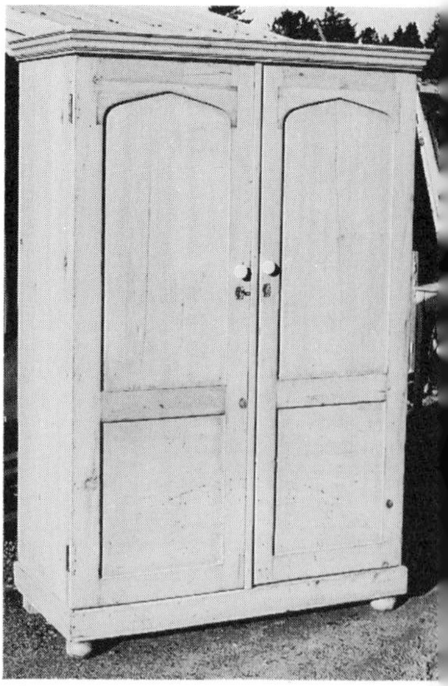

A pine two-door wardrobe, 19thC, 54in (137cm) wide.
£700–850 *TPC*

A pine panelled wardrobe, with mirrored door and long drawer to base, on bun feet, 19thC, 52in (132cm) wide.
£550–700 *TPC*

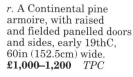

A mid-Victorian pine wardrobe, with 2 short and 2 long drawers to base, all original, c1860, 48in (122cm) wide.
£900–1,100 *COT*

A late Victorian pine wardrobe, with applied gesso urn decoration to 2 small upper doors, 50in (127cm) wide.
£1,000–1,250 *TPC*

r. A Continental pine armoire, with raised and fielded panelled doors and sides, early 19thC, 60in (152.5cm) wide.
£1,000–1,200 *TPC*

l. A Continental pine three-door wardrobe, c1890, 66in (167.5cm) wide.
£750–900 *AnD*

l. A Continental pine armoire, with columns flanking moulded and fielded panelled doors, 19thC, 42in (106.5cm) wide.
£700–850 *TPC*

r. A Dutch pine wardrobe, with 3 drawers to base, c1890, 66in (167.5cm) wide.
£700–850 *AnD*

A Dutch armoire, with 2 doors and one drawer to base, c1920, 42in (106.5cm) wide.
£550–700 *AnD*

A Continental pine wardrobe, with 2 doors, c1865, 40in (101.5cm) wide.
£650–800 *AnD*

A Spanish pine armoire, with double fielded panels to sides and doors, 18thC, 50in (127cm) wide.
£750–950 *TPC*

r. A Continental pine wardrobe, c1890, 34in (86.5cm) wide.
£400–500 *AnD*

l. A Dutch pine armoire, c1920, 42in (106.5cm) wide.
£650–800 *AnD*

A German pine wardrobe, c1900, 42in (106.5cm) wide.
£500–600 *AnD*

A pine wardrobe, c1890, 41½in (105.5cm) wide.
£400–500 *BEL*

A Continental pine armoire, with 2 doors and 2 drawers to base, late 19thC, 54in (137cm) wide.
£700–850 *TPC*

A Dutch pine armoire, c1810, 42in (106.5cm) wide.
£1,000–1,200 *AnD*

A pine single wardrobe, c1890, 41½in (105.5cm) wide.
£500–600 *BEL*

A pine wardrobe, with 2 panelled doors and a drawer to base, c1820, 51½in (131cm) wide.
£650–800 *BEL*

l. A Continental pine armoire, with 2 panelled doors flanked by turned columns, 19thC, 54in (137cm) wide.
£650–800 *TPC*

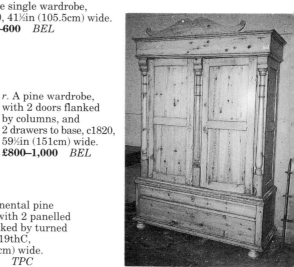

r. A pine wardrobe, with 2 doors flanked by columns, and 2 drawers to base, c1820, 59½in (151cm) wide.
£800–1,000 *BEL*

A pine wardrobe, with rounded corners, c1880, 36in (91.5cm) wide.
£600–750 *SPA*

A pine double wardrobe, 96in (244cm) wide.
£4,000–5,000 *SAn*

A French pine armoire, c1780, 50in (127cm) wide.
£1,800–2,200 *MCA*

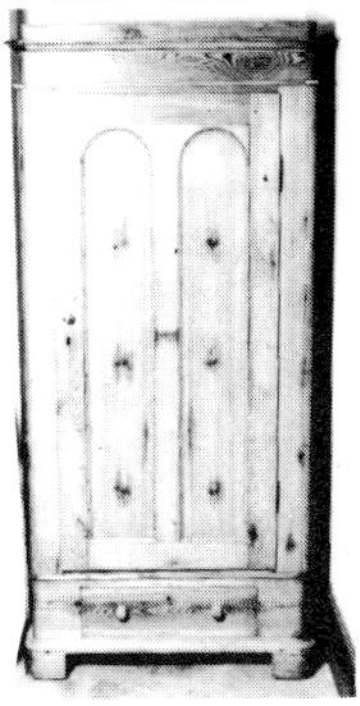

A pine wardrobe, 19thC, 35in (89cm) wide.
£500–600 *Ad*

A Scottish pine two-door wardrobe, with carved decoration, 45in (114.5cm) wide.
£900–1,100 *LAM*

r. An Edwardian pine wardrobe, with fielded panels flanking a central door, 48in (122cm) wide.
£500–600 *OA*

A pine wardrobe, with mirror door and brass fittings, c1890, 42in (106.5cm) wide.
£650–800 *SPA*

A two-door cupboard, with 9 drawers, c1860, 78in (198cm) high.
£1,200–1,500 *AL*

A Scandinavian pine wardrobe, with 2 drawers under, c1870, 55in (139.5cm) wide.
£800–950 *AHL*

l. A hazel pine combination wardrobe, with feature panels in East Indian satinwood, dated '1891', 72in (183cm) wide.
£1,700–2,000 *SSD*

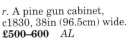

r. A pine gun cabinet, c1830, 38in (96.5cm) wide.
£500–600 *AL*

A pine wardrobe, with 2 drawers under, c1880, 48in (122cm) wide.
£600–750 *SSD*

A Danish pine wardrobe, with pagoda top, c1880, 38in (96.5cm) wide.
£600–700 *RK*

A pine wardrobe, 44in (112cm) wide.
£600–700 *PH*

A pine wardrobe, c1875, 84½in (214.5cm) high.
£500–600 *BEL*

A Danish pine wardrobe, with one door and one drawer, c1860, 37in (94cm) wide.
£500–600 *R*

A German pine wardrobe, with 2 panelled doors.
£600–750 *CPA*

l. A pitch pine and pine wardrobe, c1880, 46in (117cm) wide.
£500–600 *CPA*

A Continental pine wardrobe/armoire, 19thC, 78in (198cm) wide.
£650–750 *CHA*

l. A pine wardrobe, 41½in (105.5cm) wide.
£650–800 *PH*

A Danish pine wardrobe, c1860, 37in (94cm) wide.
£600–700 *BEL*

A hazel pine wardrobe, c1890, 54in (137cm) wide.
£650–750 *SSD*

A European pine armoire, c1910, 60in (152.5cm) wide.
£700–850 *AnD*

An Eastern European pine two-door wardrobe, with arched top and dummy drawers, 19thC, 55½in (141cm) wide.
£550–700 *NWE*

An Eastern European pine wardrobe, with a single door, one drawer and decorative moulding, c1880, 43½in (110.5cm) wide.
£500–600 *NWE*

A pine wardrobe, c1880, 43½in (110.5cm) wide.
£500–600 *NWE*

An Eastern European pine wardrobe, with arched top, 2 doors and one drawer, late 19thC, 40½in (103cm) wide.
£550–650 *NWE*

An Eastern European pine wardrobe, with carved arched top, c1880, 41in (104cm) wide.
£500–600 *NWE*

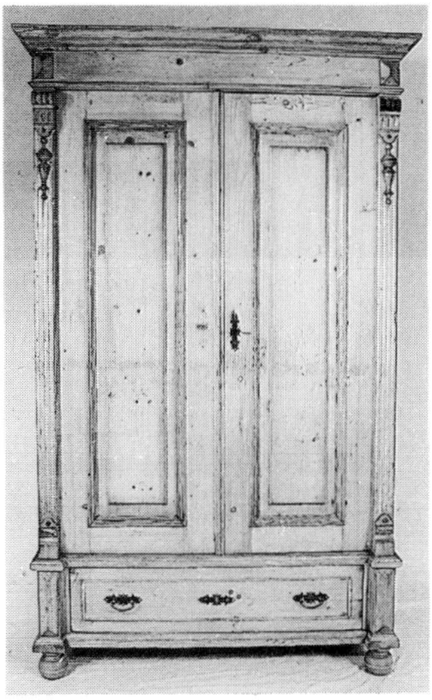

An Eastern European carved pine wardrobe, c1860, 41½in (105.5cm) wide.
£550–700 *NWE*

r. A pine wardrobe, with bowed doors, flanked by columns, c1820, 59½in (151cm) wide.
£700–850 *BEL*

An Edwardian pitch pine wardrobe, with deep drawer to base and porcelain handles, 32in (81.5cm) wide.
£500–600 *MM*

A Scandinavian seven-piece pine wardrobe, with panelled doors, one drawer in base, standing on bun feet, 19thC, 76in (193cm) high.
£750–950 *CC*

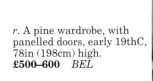

l. A German pine wardrobe, 37in (94cm) wide.
£400–500 *BEL*

A Scandinavian pine wardrobe with 2 fielded panelled doors, interior fitted with swivel pegs and a drop well in the base, 19thC, 79in (200.5cm) high.
£600–700 *CC*

A pine wardrobe, with shelves and hanging space in the upper part, c1850, 57in (145cm) high.
£1,000–1,200 *AL*

A pine wardrobe, with marked Wedgwood insets, carved top and garland decoration, 46in (117cm) high.
£700–800 *LAM*

A pine wardrobe and washstand, with 2 drawers and cupboard with panelled doors, 19thC, 77in (195.5cm) wide.
£1,100–1,300 *AL*

A pine wardrobe, with glazed insets, 48in (122cm) high.
£650–800 *LAM*

A gentleman's pine wardrobe, c1740, 165in (419cm) high.
£1,700–2,000 *UP*

r. A pine wardrobe, with panelled doors, early 19thC, 78in (198cm) high.
£500–600 *BEL*

A pitch pine wardrobe, early 20thC, 46in (117cm) wide.
£600–700 *HNG*

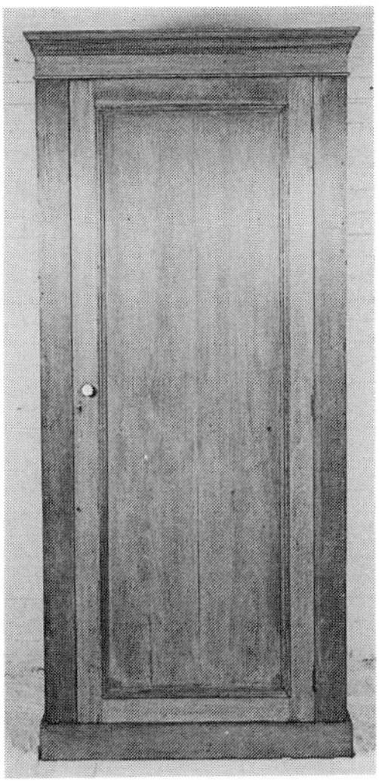

A pine single wardrobe, c1870, 35in (89cm) wide.
£500–600 *AL*

A German wardrobe, with single drawer and original fittings, some beech carvings, early 20thC, 45in (114.5cm) wide.
£600–700 *HNG*

A carved pine two-door press/television cupboard, with 2 upper drawers, 77in (195.5cm) high.
£800–950 *OCP*

A 'knock-down' armoire, with rounded fielded panels, rounded cornice, on bun feet, c1890, 61in (155cm) wide.
£800–950 *POT*

A Continental pine double wardrobe, c1880, 72in (183cm) high.
£600–700 *ASP*

A pine 'knock-down' armoire, with fielded panelled doors, late 19thC, 56in (142cm) wide.
£800–950 *POT*

A mid-Victorian pine wardrobe, with removable cornice, panelled doors and bun feet, c1870, 57in (145cm) wide.
£600–700 *POT*

A pine cupboard, with fielded panelled doors, originally with 6 drawers inside, mid-19thC, 48in (122cm) wide.
£650–800 *POT*

A pine wardrobe, with drawers under, 76in (193cm) high.
£500–600 *AL*

A pine wardrobe, c1860, 81in (205.5cm) high.
£500–600 *AL*

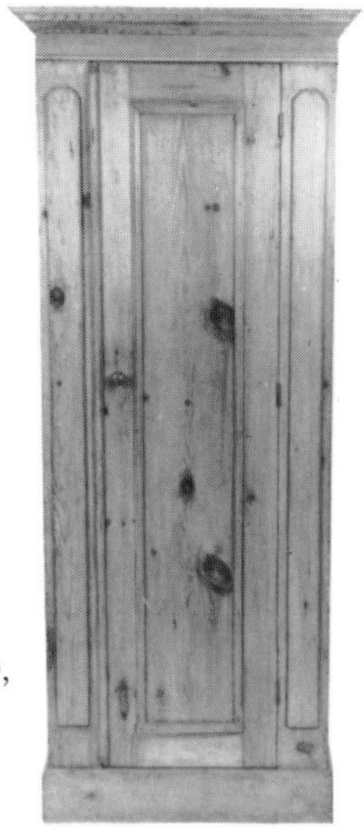

A pine wardrobe, 77in (195.5cm) high.
£500–600 *AL*

A pine wardrobe, with arched doors and shelves on one side, 54in (137cm) wide.
£900–1,100 *AF*

A Danish pine wardrobe 76in (193cm) wide.
£600–700 *RK*

A Hungarian pine wardrobe, c1885.
£500–600 *TPF*

A Danish pine single door wardrobe, 72in (183cm) wide.
£450–550 *RK*

A pine wardrobe, 67in (170cm) wide.
£750–900 *PH*

A Victorian pine wardrobe with reeded decoration, 54in (137cm) wide.
£400–500 *OA*

A Georgian pine bachelor's wardrobe/press.
£1,500–1,800 *DM*

A pine three-section wardrobe, c1880, 83in (211cm) high.
£1,200–1,500 *W*

A Danish two-door pine wardrobe, 69in (175.5cm) high.
£500–650 *BR*

A pine combination wardrobe, c1870, 79in (200.5cm) high.
£1,200–1,500 *AL*

A pine wardrobe, with ceramic knobs, c1890, 45in (114.5cm) high.
£550–700 *SPA*

A pine 'knock-down' armoire, with hanging space and storage drawers below, c1910, 63in (160cm) wide.
£700–800 *POT*

An Eastern European pine wardrobe, with arched top and single door, c1860, 37½in (95.5cm) wide.
£450–550 *NWE*

A Continental pine single door wardrobe, with single drawer, the legs with carved decoration, steel barrel hinges, original escutcheons, c1860, 72in (183cm) high.
£500–600 *AF*

A Victorian three-piece pine wardrobe, with bevelled mirror door and fielded panelled doors, 43in (109cm) wide.
£400–500 *POT*

A pine wardrobe, with 2 doors, c1880, 38½in (98cm) wide.
£500–600 *Byl*

An Edwardian pine single door mirror wardrobe, with a drawer in base, 75½in (192cm) high.
£400–500 *AF*

A pine wardrobe, with 2 doors and interior drawer, c1896, 45in (114.5cm) wide.
£500–600 *SA*

A European pine wardrobe, with decorated cornice, c1860, 82½in (209.5cm) high.
£650–800 *AF*

A pine wardrobe, with chamfered panelled doors and sides, c1895, 44in (112cm) wide.
£500–600 *SA*

A pine press cupboard, 50in (127cm) wide.
£1,400–1,700 *SAn*

A pine linen press, with slides, in 2 sections, c1860, 50in (127cm) wide.
£1,700–2,000 *AL*

A Danish pine panelled double armoire, with 2 drawers to base, c1870, 73½in (186.5cm) high.
£750–900 *UC*

A butler's pine cupboard, c1870, 106in (269cm) wide.
£3,000–3,500 *UP*

A Victorian pine linen press, with shelves, 40in (101.5cm) wide.
£1,300–1,700 *AL*

A housekeeper's breakfront pine cupboard, 19thC.
£3,300–4,000 *PH*

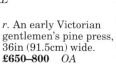

A Scottish pine linen press, with 2 interior drawers and a secret drawer, c1780, 72in (183cm) high.
£1,300–1,600 *BH*

r. An early Victorian gentlemen's pine press, 36in (91.5cm) wide.
£650–800 *OA*

A North Wales housekeeper's pine cupboard, 75in (190.5cm) wide.
£4,000–4,800 *PH*

A pine linen press, c1840, 47½in (120.5cm) wide.
£1,500–1,800 *AL*

A pine press cupboard, with panelled sides, 44in (112cm) wide.
£1,600–1,900 *PH*

A mid-Victorian pine linen press, with arched, moulded panelled doors, enclosing 5 linen slides, original white ceramic knobs, 48in (122cm) wide.
£1,700–2,000 *TPC*

A pine linen press on chest, early 19thC, 48in (122cm) wide.
£1,700–2,000 *TPC*

A housekeeper's pine cupboard, with 2 short and 2 long drawers in base, 44in (112cm) wide.
£1,500–1,800 *ASP*

A late Georgian pine linen press, on bracket feet, c1830, 50in (127cm) wide.
£1,500–1,800 *POT*

A Georgian pine linen press, with unusual drawer arrangement, on original bracket legs, c1830, 47in (119.5cm) wide.
£2,000–2,500 *POT*

An early Victorian pine linen press, with original knobs, c1850, 50½in (128.5cm) wide.
£1,500–1,800 *POT*

r. A pine livery cupboard, with sunburst design, in 2 pieces, c1835, 58in (147.5cm) wide.
£1,800–2,200 *DMe*

l. A housekeeper's pine cupboard, with unusual cornice, original turned feet, c1850, 62in (157.5cm) wide.
£2,500–3,000 *POT*

A pine linen press,
feet replaced, c1860,
78½in (199.5cm) high.
£1,500–1,800 *AL*

A Cumberland pine press,
c1850, 58in (147.5cm) wide.
£2,500–3,000 *UP*

A pine linen press,
35in (89cm) wide.
£1,500–1,800 *AL*

An Irish pine food press,
c1840, 72in (183cm) high.
£1,700–2,100 *BH*

A pine linen press,
by Heal & Co, London,
with porcelain knobs,
c1850, 43in (109cm) wide.
£1,700–2,000 *AL*

A Dutch carved
pine linen press,
93in (236cm) high.
£3,000–3,500 *RK*

A Victorian pine
linen press, c1800,
49in (124.5cm) wide.
£1,600–1,900 *PIN*

A Georgian linen press,
47½in (120.5cm) wide.
£1,700–2,000 *PH*

A pine linen press, 19thC,
49in (124.5cm) wide.
£1,600–1,900 *AL*

A Scottish pine linen
press, late 18thC,
77½in (197cm) high.
£1,700–2,000 *BH*

A pine press, c1840,
51in (129.5cm) wide.
£1,900–2,300 *UP*

l. A pine press/
cabinet, late 19thC,
58in (147.5cm) wide.
£1,700–2,000 *Ad*

r. An unusually small
housekeeper's cupboard,
fitted with a clock,
from Shropshire,
85in (216cm) wide.
£5,000–6,000 *HG*

A pine two-door wardrobe, with decorative linen drawer, c1900, 74in (188cm) high.
£750–900 *OCP*

An Irish pine linen cupboard, on bracket feet, restored, c1800, 52in (132cm) wide.
£1,200–1,500 *DFA*

An Irish pine linen cupboard, with panelled sides, County Donegal, restored, c1830, 49in (124.5cm) wide.
£1,700–2,100 *DFA*

A pine linen press, with shelved interior, c1800, 65in (165cm) wide.
£1,700–2,000 *DFA*

A housekeeper's pine cupboard, with original interior paint, c1860, 97in (246.5cm) wide.
£2,500–3,000 *OCP*

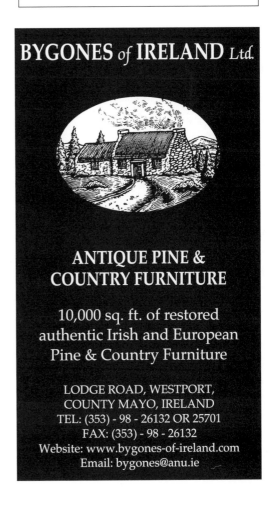

Use the Index!

Because certain items might fit easily into any number of categories, the quickest and surest method of locating any entry is by reference to the index at the back of the book. This index has been fully cross-referenced for absolute simplicity.

A glazed pine bookcase, with broken pediment, 50in (127cm) wide.
£2,500–3,000 *RK*

l. A stripped pine bookcase on cupboard, 84in (213.5cm) high.
£1,500–1,800 *Wor*

Above and left. A Victorian glaze secrétaire pine bookcase, with etched glass doors and fitted interior, c1820.
£3,500–4,000 *PIN*

A pine bookcase, 83in (211cm) wide.
£2,000–2,500 *PH*

An Irish pine bookcase, 18thC, 54in (137cm) wide.
£2,500–2,800 *AD*

An Austrian pine bookcase, the upper cupboard with original frosted glass doors, 19thC, 48in (122cm) wide.
£850–1,000 *AD*

l. A William IV pine bookcase, with false drawers, 50in (127cm) wide.
£1,000–1,200 *UP*

A pine secrétaire bookcase, c1820, 39½in (101cm) wide.
£3,000–3,500 *W*

A pine bookcase, 71in (181cm) wide.
£1,500–1,700 *LAM*

A Victorian pine bookcase, c1860, 44in (112cm) wide.
£1,000–1,200 *AL*

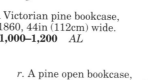

r. A pine open bookcase, early 19thC, 46in (117cm) high.
£800–950 *DN*

A pine bookcase, with adjustable shelves, original handles, c1860, 76½in (195cm) high.
£1,200–1,500 *AL*

A Victorian pine bookcase, the glazed doors with carved moulding, cushion moulded drawers, 48in (122cm) wide.
£2,000–2,300 *OA*

A pine bookcase, 46in (117cm) wide.
£1,500–1,800 *UP*

A late Georgian pine bookcase, 42in (106cm) wide.
£1,500–1,700 *UP*

r. A Continental pine bookcase, c1860, 43in (109cm) wide.
£1,000–1,100 *UP*

A William IV pine bookcase, 47in (120cm) wide.
£2,000–2,200 *UP*

A Victorian pine bookcase, 50in (127cm) wide.
£2,000–2,200 *OA*

r. A George III style pine breakfront bookcase, 74in (188cm) wide.
£4,000–5,000 *Bon*

A pine bookcase, with glazed top cupboards, c1880, 36in (91.5cm) wide.
£700–800 *SPA*

l. A Georgian bookcase, with astragal glazing, on bracket feet, 54in (137cm) wide.
£2,300–2,700 *Ad*

l. An Edwardian pine bookshelf, 36in (91.5cm) wide.
£250–300 *OA*

l. A pine bookcase in 2 parts, the 2 doors carved with shield-shaped panels, c1870, 44in (112cm) wide.
£800–900 *Byl*

A pine bookcase, with glazed door to top enclosing shelves, and cupboard base, c1900, 39in (99cm) wide.
£700–800 *BEL*

A pitch pine bookcase, on a plinth base, c1880, 48in (122cm) wide.
£800–900 *POT*

A pine country bureau bookcase, with astragal glazed door, over a desk and two-door cupboard, the fall revealing a fitted interior, 19thC, 38in (96.5cm) wide.
£1,100–1,250 *TPC*

A pine bookcase, with glazed door, arched top and single drawer, 1860s, 32½in (82.5cm) wide.
£800–900 *NWE*

An Eastern European pine bookcase, with glazed doors, originally a wood panelled wardrobe, c1810, 35½in (90cm) wide.
£450–500 *NWE*

l. A pine bookcase, with glazed door, and 2 drawers, restored, 1860s, 21½in (54.5cm) wide.
£650–750 *NWE*

A Victorian pine bookcase, with tray top and plinth base, 54in (137cm) wide.
£500–600 *TPC*

A George II pine bookcase cabinet, some damage, 118in (299.5cm) wide.
£32,000–35,000 *S(NY)*

A George II-style pine bookcase, the pierced broken scroll pediment with acanthus ornament and central urn above a pair of astragal glazed doors and a pair of panelled cupboard doors, on a plinth base, 50in (127cm) wide.
£3,500–4,500 *C*

A George III-style pine bookcase, with breakfront stiff-leaf, egg-and-dart and dentil moulded cornice, on a plinth base, some carving, 18thC, 90in (228.5cm) wide.
£6,000–7,000 *C*

r. A George III-style pine bookcase, on a stiff-leaf carved plinth base, some carving, 18thC, 78½in (199.5cm) wide.
£7,500–9,000 *C*

l. A pine wall-hanging bookcase, c1880, 24in (61cm) wide.
£350–400 *SPA*

A Victorian pine bookcase, c1860, 82in (208.5cm) high.
£1,500–1,800 *BH*

A pine bookcase, early 18thC, 90in (228.5cm) wide.
£4,000–4,500 *PCL*

A pine glazed top bookcase, 19thC, 43in (109cm) wide.
£1,500–1,800 *SV*

A pine glazed bookcase, 39in (99cm) wide.
£350–400 *AL*

A two-piece double arch door pine bookcase, c1820.
£1,500–1,800 *PIN*

An Edwardian pine bookcase, with original doors and brasswork, 95in (241.5cm) wide.
£3,500–4,000 *OA*

A pine bookcase, with frieze drawer, late 19thC, 45in (114.5cm) wide.
£1,500–1,800 *Ad*

An Irish pine glazed dresser/bookcase, c1840, 80in (203cm) high.
£1,100–1,300 *BH*

A Welsh pine glazed bookcase, with 2 bowfront drawers, 2 cupboards below with raised panel doors, on ball feet, c1840, 55in (139.5cm) wide.
£2,500–3,000 *Sca*

A Victorian Gothic-style pedestal bookcase, with adjustable shelves, 74in (188cm) wide.
£1,100–1,250 *OA*

A pine bookcase, c1780, 43in (109cm) wide.
£1,400–1,700 *UP*

A pine bookcase, the doors with coloured glass borders, c1880, 42in (106.5cm) wide.
£700–800 *SSD*

A pine breakfront bookcase, made from old timber, 90in (228.5cm) wide.
£2,500–3,000 *UP*

An Irish pine glazed cabinet, c1840, 51in (129.5cm) wide.
£1,500–1,800 *UP*

A German pine kitchen cabinet, with original ceramic spice drawers, c1900s, 71in (180.5cm) high.
£400–500 *WHA*

A Victorian collector's pine cabinet, with pigeonholes, 24in (61cm) wide.
£550–700 *Ad*

A Georgian pine filing cabinet, 54in (137cm) wide.
£1,700–2,000 *AL*

A pine display cabinet, c1780, 27½in (70cm) wide.
£300–350 *W*

A bedside cabinet, with gallery top, c1900, 31in (78.5cm) wide.
£300–350 *LAM*

A Regency pine display cabinet, 49in (124.5cm) wide.
£2,200–2,600 *W*

A European pine cabinet, c1860, 32in (81.5cm) wide.
£400–500 *UP*

A pine corner cabinet, with astragal glazed upper doors, 41in (104cm) wide.
£1,700–2,000 *PH*

An Irish astragal glazed pine cabinet, c1800, 49in (124.5cm) wide.
£2,000–2,400 *UP*

r. A Quicksey pine kitchen cabinet, with original fittings, glass storage jars and drawers, spice rack, flour bin, and memoranda panels inside top doors, enamel work surface, 48in (122cm) wide.
£1,300–1,500 *OC*

l. A mid-European draper's pine cabinet, 71in (180.5cm) wide.
£1,700–2,000 *MofC*

A Continental kitchen cabinet, with 3 shelves, replacement bottom frieze, early 20thC, 35in (89cm) high.
£250–300 *HGN*

r. A pine china cabinet, with specimen drawers and 2 glazed side doors, c1860, 45in (114.5cm) wide.
£600–700 *ASP*

A Victorian pine collector's cabinet, c1870, 37½in (95.5cm) wide.
£600–700 *MofC*

A Continental pine bedside cabinet, with one door, 1890, 18in (45.5cm) high.
£200–250 *ASP*

A pine sewing cabinet, 15in (38cm) wide.
£145–175 *ASP*

r. A pine wall-hanging pipe rack cabinet, 17½in (44.5cm) high.
£85–100 *ASP*

A pitch pine wall cabinet, c1880, 20in (51cm) high.
£125–150 *ASP*

l. A Victorian entomologist's ten-drawer pine cabinet, with original stain on inside, 29in (73.5cm) wide.
£800–950 *CCP*

A Georgian pine mule chest, with bracket feet, c1780, 44in (112cm) wide.
£450–500 *COT*

A Georgian pine mule chest, restored, c1800.
£450–500 *COT*

A Baltic region pine coffer, c1800, 51½in (131cm) wide.
£550–650 *HeR*

A panelled pine coffer on shaped bracket feet, 18thC, 48in (122cm) wide.
£450–500 *TPC*

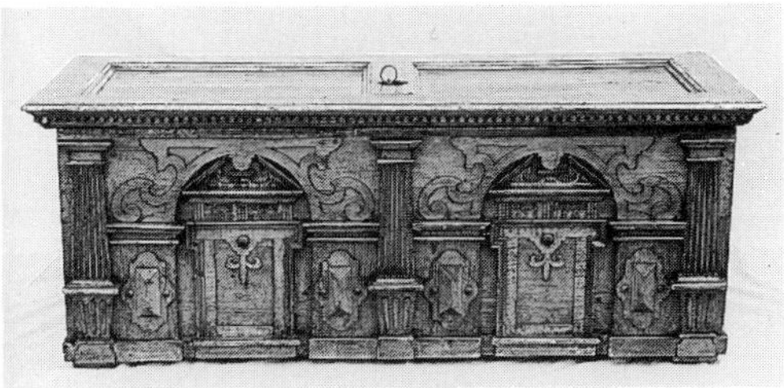

A German pine marriage chest, with carved front, dated '1614', 68in (172.5cm) wide.
£1,650–2,200 *CCP*

A pine mule chest, with long base drawer, with key, on bracket feet, 19thC, 33in (84cm) wide.
£450–500 *CCP*

A pine mule chest, with 2 drawers, fitted internal candle box and original lock and key, 37in (94cm) wide.
£500–550 *CCP*

A Victorian pine carpenter's tool box, 38in (96.5cm) wide.
£250–275 *WaH*

l. A Victorian pine trunk, 36in (91.5cm) wide.
£200–250 *CCP*

A Welsh pine mule chest, c1820, 35in (89cm) wide.
£500–600 *HG*

A pine box on stand, 19thC, 27½in (70cm) wide.
£250–275 *AL*

A pine box, 22in (56cm) wide.
£200–250 *AL*

r. An Austrian pine chest, dated '1861'.
£400–500 *TPF*

l. A pine mule chest, with 2 drawers c1860.
£450–500 *PIN*

r. A pine mule chest, c1840, 42½in (108cm) wide.
£450–500 *AL*

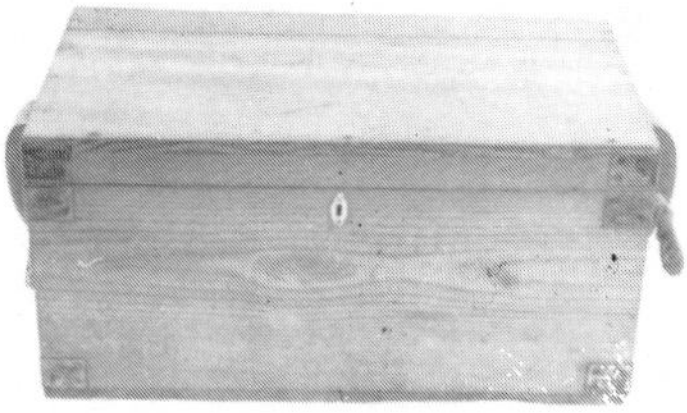

l. A pine sea chest, with fitted tray, c1880, 27in (69cm) wide.
£250–300 *AL*

A pine box, c1860, 35in (89cm) wide.
£250–300 *AL*

A pine offertory box, c1900, 29½in (75cm) wide.
£150–175 *UC*

A pine box, c1880, 24in (61cm) wide.
£160–200 *SPA*

A mid-Victorian pine chest, with side carrying handles, fitted interior, 43½in (110.5cm) wide.
£300–350 *OA*

A mid-Victorian pine trunk, with side handles, 33in (84cm) wide.
£300–350 *OA*

A pine box, c1900, 36in (91.5cm) wide.
£125–175 *SPA*

A pine box, with iron hinges, 26½in (67.5cm) wide.
£160–175 *AL*

A Continental pine dome-topped box, 43in (109cm) wide.
£200–225 *CPA*

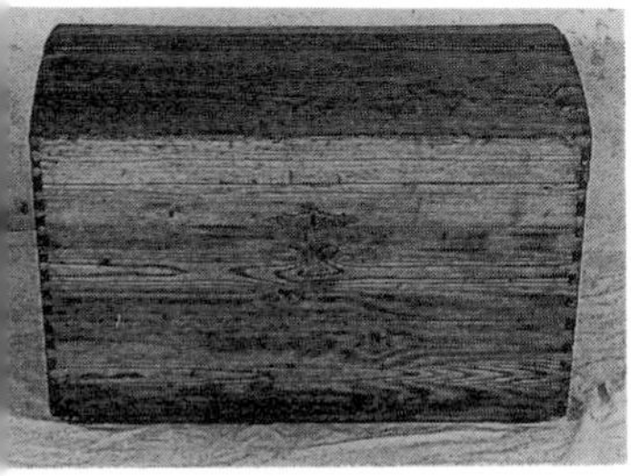

A pine dome-topped box, restored,
.860, 31in (78.5cm) wide.
'180–220 *NWE*

A Continental pine box, with domed top and original iron furnishings, dated '1868', 39in (99cm) wide.
£180–220 *ASP*

A Continental pine blanket box, with original
urnishings, c1900, 35in (89cm) wide.
:150–300 *HNG*

A pine carpenter's chest, with fitted interior, c1860, 31in (78.5cm) wide.
£300–350 *ASP*

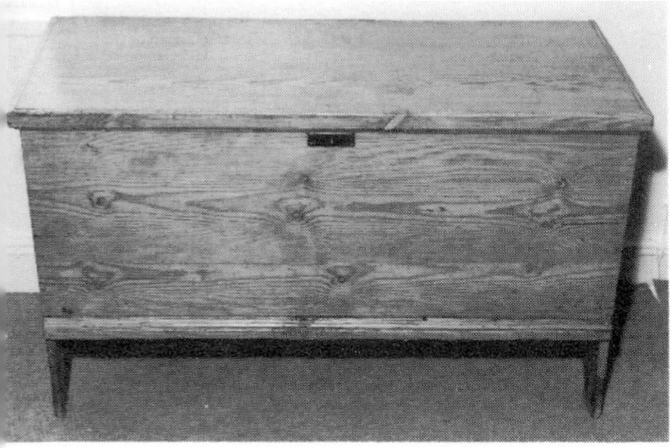

A pitch pine and elm coffer, with original candle
ɔox and fittings, mid-19thC, 43in (109cm) wide.
£325–375 *HNG*

A Continental pine box, with domed top, c1870, 41in (104cm) wide.
£230–270 *HNG*

An Austrian pine dome-topped coffer, 18thC, 48in (122cm) wide.
£450–500 *GD*

A German pine blanket box, with original iron fittings and original lock and key, 47in (119.5cm) wide.
£350–400 *HGN*

An English pine linen chest, with candle box, 1850, 36½in (92.5cm) wide.
£225–250 *ASP*

A pine deed box, c1900, 21in (53cm) long.
£125–150 *ASP*

A Victorian blanket box, c1880, 34½in (87cm) wide.
£220–270 *POT*

l. A pine grain/flour bin, c1890, 48in (122cm) wide.
£200–250 *OCP*

A European carved pine mule chest, the single drawer with original handles, c1840, 45in (114.5cm) wide.
£450–500 *AF*

A pine mule chest, with fitted interior, drawers and candle box, all original, 45in (114.5cm) wide.
£450–500 *ASP*

A Continental pine trunk, with domed top and metal bands, c1880, 32in (81.5cm) wide.
£170–200 *ASP*

A pine rug chest/mule chest, with candle box, c1835, 41½in (105.5cm) wide.
£250–300 *DMe*

A pine grain/flour bin, c1840, 31in (78.5cm) wide.
£250–300 *DMe*

A European pine dome-topped linen chest, with iron hinges, c1860, 34in (86.5cm) wide.
£170–200 *DMe*

r. A pine box, with domed top, c1880, 27½in (70cm) wide.
£170–200 *DFA*

A pine box, with nameplate, c1850, 26in (66cm) wide.
£170–200 *DFA*

A pine box, c1870, 42in (106.5cm) wide.
£170–200 *DFA*

A pine iron-bound box, c1870, 30in (76cm) wide.
£150–175 *AL*

A small pine blanket box, with original handles, c1850, 31in (78.5cm) wide.
£150–175 *SA*

An Austrian pine linen box, with handles, c1880, 44in (112cm) wide.
£125–150 *Byl*

A pine sea chest, with rope handles, c1860, 38½in (96.5cm) wide.
£325–375 *AL*

l. An Irish pine metal-bound document box, c1880, 28in (71cm) wide.
£125–150 *Byl*

A pine blanket box, c1850, 36in (91.5cm) wide.
£150–175 *SA*

A pine box, with handles, c1880, 47in (119.5cm) wide.
£300–350 *AL*

A pine box, c1880, 47in (119.5cm) wide.
£200–250 *AL*

Two sailors' pine diddy boxes, c1890, 12in (30.5cm) wide.
£50–60 each *AL*

A pine box, with one drawer and a candle box, c1860, 40in (101.5cm) wide.
£300–350 *AL*

A pine fishing rod box, c1890, 45in (114.5cm) wide.
£85–100 *AL*

A small pine box, with a tray, c1880, 15in (38cm) wide.
£85–100 *AL*

A pine box, c1890, 32in (81.5cm) wide.
£85–100 *AL*

An iron-bound pine box, c1890, 26in (66cm)wide.
£150–175 *AL*

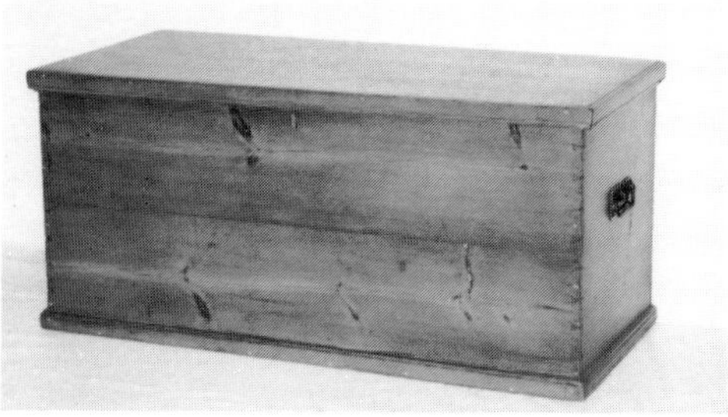

l. A pine box, with a candle box, c1870, 42in (106.5cm) wide.
£250–275 *AL*

A pine blanket chest, with dovetail joints, c1875.
£200–250 *PIN*

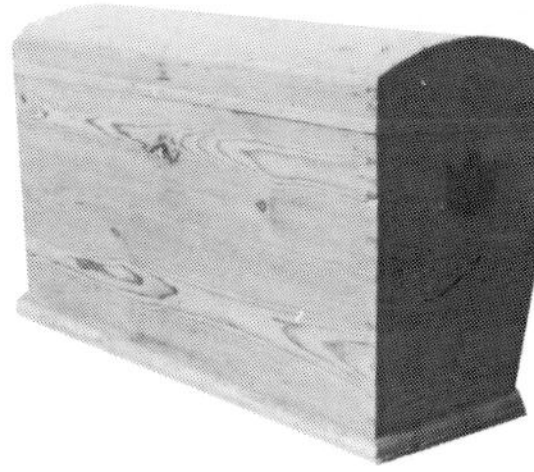

A Danish pine dome-topped box, c1860, 43in (109cm) wide.
£200–250 *RK*

A pine chest, with a divided top, original locks, 48in (122cm) wide.
£800–950 *AL*

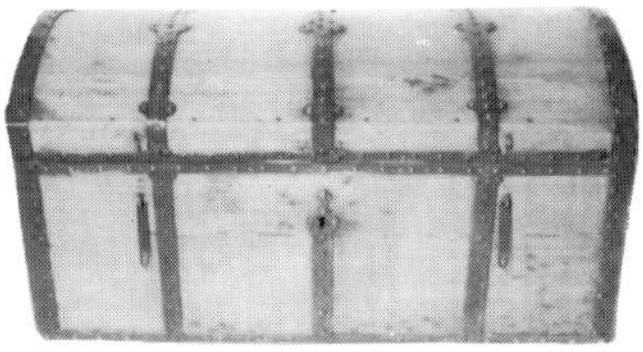

A Scandinavian pine dome-topped coffer, all original iron, c1800.
£200–250 *W*

A pine chest, some damage, to mouldings, c1750, 46in (117cm) wide.
£450–500 *AL*

A small pine box, c1890, 29in (73.5cm) wide.
£125–150 *PAC*

A pine chest, with original ironwork, c1850, 24in (61cm) wide.
£100–120 *W*

A pine box, 20in (51cm) wide.
£75–90 *AL*

A child's pine dome-topped box, with original ironwork, c1860, 18½in (47cm) long.
£125–150 *MPA*

A pitch pine box, 44in (112cm) wide.
£200–225 *LAM*

A pine mule chest with wooden hinges to lid, c1790, 39in (99cm) wide.
£400–450 *W*

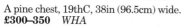

A pine chest, 19thC, 38in (96.5cm) wide.
£300–350 *WHA*

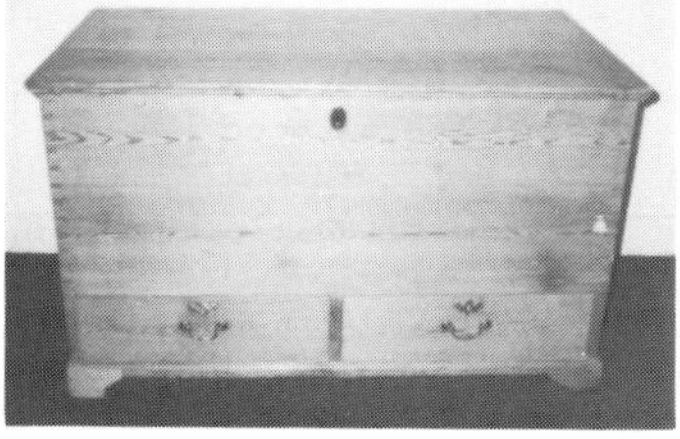

A pine mule chest, with rising top and 2 drawers under, 19thC, 28in (71cm) wide.
£500–600 *PM*

A pine chest, with dovetail joints and original brass handles, c1880, 44in (112cm) wide.
£250–300 *Sca*

A pine box, with a trim round the base, 29in (73.5cm) wide.
£200–225 *AL*

A pine box, with a candle box, c1860, 41in (106.5cm) long.
£300–360 *AL*

\ pine box, c1880, 42in (106.5cm) wide.
:170–200 *SPA*

r. A pine mule chest, with a drawer, c1840, 42½in (108cm) wide.
£450–550 *AL*

l. A pine panelled coffer, 51½in (131cm) wide.
£375–450 *PAC*

A pine coffer, c1800, 66in (167.5cm) wide.
£170–200 *SSD*

A pine box, 36in (91.5cm) wide.
£170–200 *PAC*

. pine box, c1850, 20in (51cm) wide.
250–300 *AL*

A pine coffer, c1800, 66in (167.5cm) wide.
£375–450 *SSD*

. pine coffer, carved 'In this chest re the books and maps belonging ɔ the Commission of Severs for he Eastern part of the County f Kent, 1715', with original scutcheons, feet replaced, 8in (198cm) long.
1,000–1,200 *LAM*

A small pine box, 15in (38cm) wide.
£125–150 *LAM*

A pine trunk, with side carrying handles, 19thC, 25in (63.5cm) wide.
£325–375 *OA*

. pine fitted box, c1880, 9in (99cm) wide.
325–375 *AL*

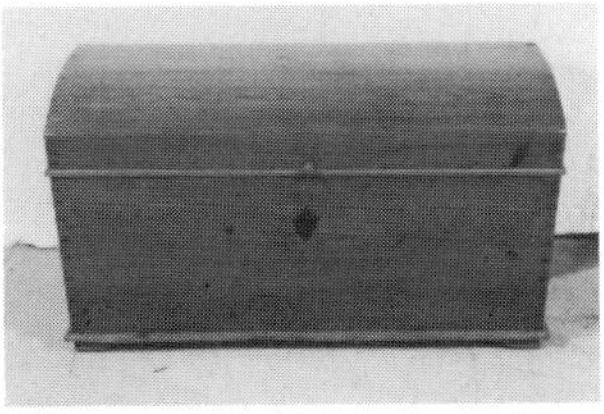

A German pine dome-topped box.
£200–225 *CPA*

l. A pine tool chest, with two trays, c1860, 36in (91.5cm) wide.
£250–300 *AL*

A pine dome-topped box, with iron straps, c1840, 41in (104cm) wide.
£180–220 *AL*

r. A pine tool chest, with 2 trays, c1860, 36in (91.5cm) wide.
£275–325 *AL*

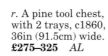

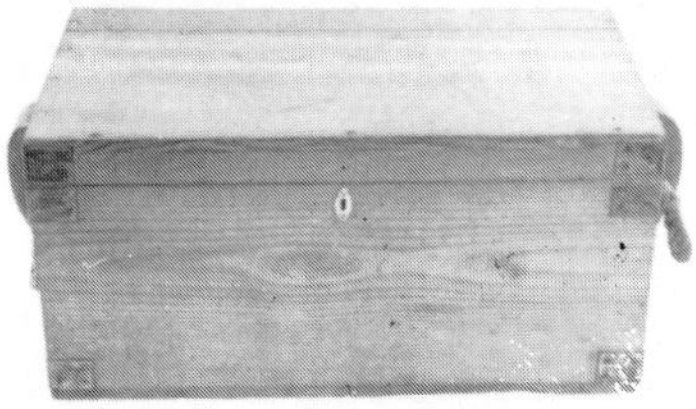

l. A pine sea chest, with a fitted tray c1880, 27in (68.5cm) wide.
£275–325 *AL*

A pine fitted tool box, c1850, 33in (84cm) wide.
£350–400 *AL*

A pine mule chest, with a hinged top and 4 drawers beneath, 19thC, 36in (91.5cm) wide.
£600–700 *CC*

r. A pitch pine coffer, with interior candle box, 19thC, 36in (91.5cm) wide.
£250–300 *SSP*

A pine chest, with well-concealed secret drawers, c1860, 35in (89cm) wide.
£300–350 *Far*

l. A Victorian pin workbox, with a sectioned tray, 20in (51cm) wide
£100–120 *CI*

r. A pine deed box, with original iron handles and spearhead hinges, pegged sides to lid, date on exterior added later, 3 earlier dates inside, 18thC.
£170–200 *PF*

A pine box, with padlock and key, 21in (53.5cm) wide.
£150–180 *AL*

A pine box, with original fittings, c1820, 45in (114.5cm) wide.
£350–400 *AL*

A German pine dome-topped box.
£200–250 *CPA*

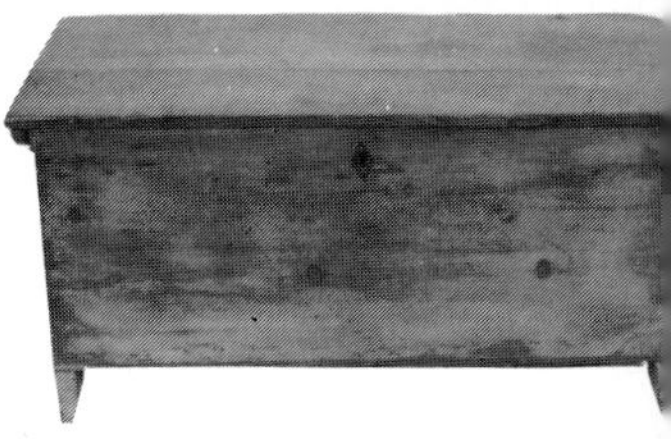

A Spanish pine coffer, original ironwork, c1840, 43in (109cm) wi
£325–375 *UC*

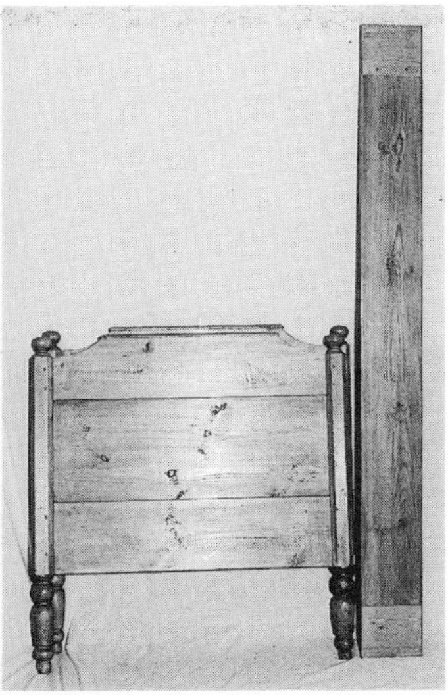

A pine single bed, with knob finials, c1890, 39in (99cm) wide.
£250–300 *ASP*

A Continental pine single bed, with decorative headboard, carved corbels and turned legs, c1860, 76in (193cm) long.
£500–600 *AF*

A pine sleigh bed, c1870, 74in (188cm) wide.
£550–650 *AnD*

Did you know?
***Miller's Antiques Price Guide* builds up year by year to form the most comprehensive antiques photo-reference library available.**

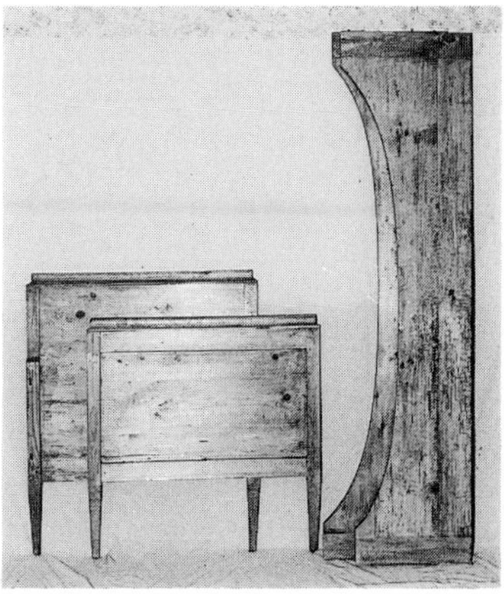

r. A Continental pine 'roll-over' bed, c1890.
£350–400 *ASP*

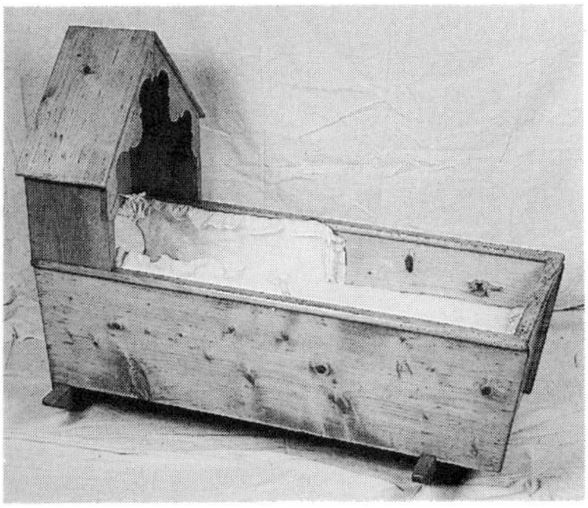

A Victorian pine crib, c1860, 40in (101.5cm) long.
£400–450 *COT*

A child's pine extending bed, c1910, 51in (129.5cm) long before extending.
£350–400 *BEL*

A pine bed, c1890,
36in (91.5cm) wide.
£350–400 *AL*

A carved pine and cane bed head and foot, 66in (167.5cm) wide.
£600–700 *LAM*

An Irish two-door pine bed cupboard, with panelled sides, c1840, 48in (122cm) wide.
£850–1,000 *LC*

A Scandinavian pine extending bed in 3 sections, c1800, opening to 72in (182.5cm) long.
£350–400 *W*

A pine Victorian bed, with oak posts and legs, and close-boarded base, c1850, 78in (198cm) long.
£650–750 *CC*

A Irish pine bed/ cupboard, c1840, 72in (182.5cm) long.
£1,200–1,400 *LC*

A German pine bed, c1890, 75½in (191cm) long.
£300–350 *Sca*

A pine single bed head and foot, from an Austrian sleigh bed, 75in (190cm) long.
£350–400 *CHA*

A pine bed, (head only shown), with original sides and slats, 54in (137cm) wide.
£550–650 *AL*

r. A pine sleigh bed, c1880.
£300–350 *TPF*

l. A pine bedstead, with high 'ship's' sides, 19thC, 72in (180cm) long.
£300–350 *AF*

A Texan yellow pine daybed, with outward flared ends, each with horizontal slats, on square tapering chanfered legs, retains traces of original blue paint, mid-19thC, 77½in (197cm) long.
£400–500 *CNY*

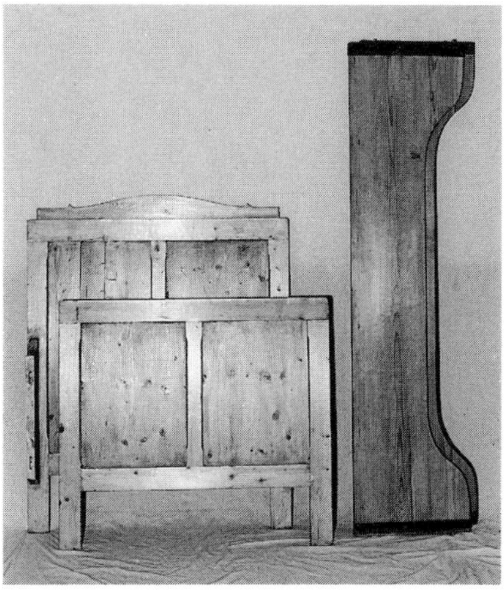

A Continental pine bed, c1890.
£300–350 *ASP*

An Irish settle bed, c1870, 72in (183cm) wide.
£550–650 *AF*

An Eastern European pine sleigh bed, early 20thC, 76in (193cm) long.
£300–350 *HNG*

l. A German sleigh bed, c1890, 78in (198cm) long.
£250–300 *AnD*

A Welsh pine bed, c1870, 64in (162.5cm) wide.
£450–500 *AL*

A Continental pine bed, with panelled head and foot, c1890.
£250–300 *ASP*

A Dutch pine sideboard, c1870, 48in (122cm) wide.
£700–850 *FAG*

A pine buffet, c1900, 45½in (115.5cm) wide.
£400–500 *BEL*

A carved pine sideboard, with 3 drawers and 2 doors, c1890, 54in (137cm) wide.
£600–700 *OCP*

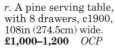

r. A pine serving table, with 8 drawers, c1900, 108in (274.5cm) wide.
£1,000–1,200 *OCP*

A French pine serving table, with 2 drawers, c1850, 49in (124.5cm) wide.
£550–650 *GD*

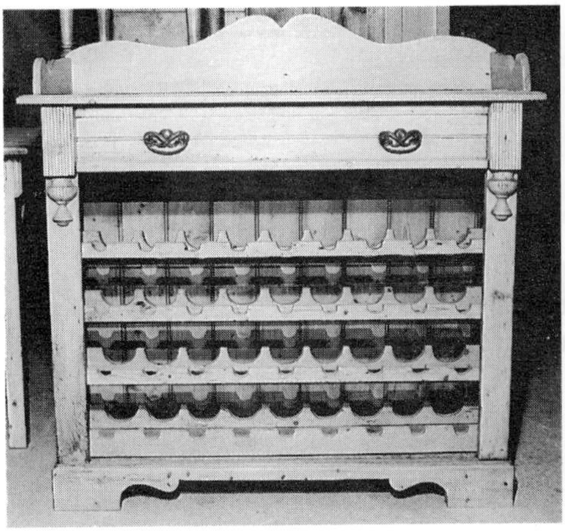
A pine wine rack, converted from a buffet, c1880, 45in (114.5cm) wide.
£350–400 *OCP*

A Danish carved pine sideboard, with mirrored back, c1870, 50in (127cm) wide.
£1,000–1,150 *UC*

r. A pine side server, c1880, 37in (94cm) wide.
£500–600 *OCP*

A Victorian pine chiffonier, 64in (162.5cm) wide.
£1,400–1,600 *Ad*

A Regency pine chiffonier, c1820, 46in (117cm) wide.
£1,100–1,300 *AL*

A Welsh pine chiffonier, c1830, 68in (172.5cm) wide.
£1,200–1,400 *Sca*

A pine chiffonier, 33½in (85cm) wide.
£600–700 *PH*

A pine chiffonier, c1860, 42in (106.7cm) wide.
£800–950 *AL*

An Austrian pine chiffonier, 19thC, 36in (91.5cm) wide.
£750–900 *Ad*

l. A pine chiffonier, with brass escutcheons, c1850, 34½in (87.5cm) wide.
£800–950 *AL*

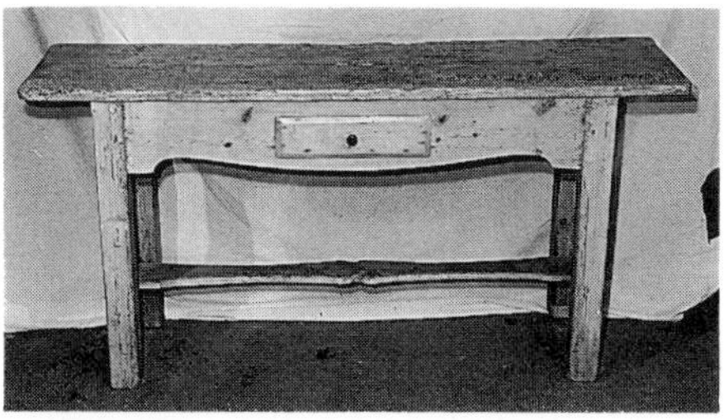

l. A pine side table, with single drawer, and stretcher, c1840, 60½in (153.5cm) wide.
£400–450 *DFA*

An Irish pine buffer, from Co. Laois, c1845, 36in (91.5cm) wide.
£350–400 *DMe*

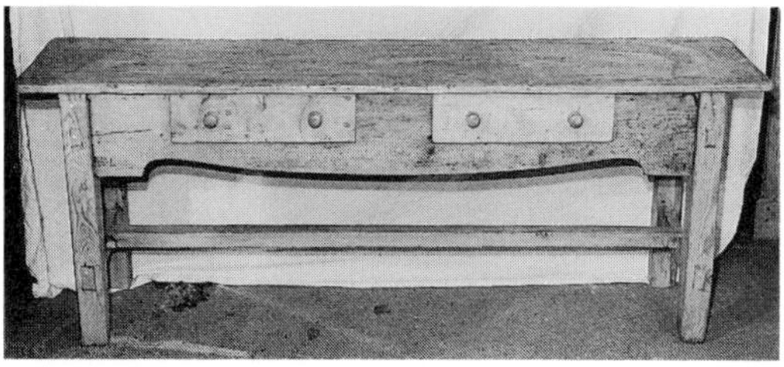

A pine side table, with stretcher, c1870, 28½in (72.5cm) high.
£500–600 *DFA*

A pine serving table, the drawers with glass knobs, c1870, 69in (175.5cm) wide.
£750–900 *AL*

A pine side cabinet, c1870, 45in (114.5cm) wide.
£350–400 *DFA*

A pine sideboard, with a single frieze drawer, c1865, 45½in (115.5cm) wide.
£375–450 *DFA*

A pine breakfront sideboard, with 3 central drawers flanked by 2 cupboard doors, c1870, 71in (180.5cm) wide.
£1,000–1,100 *DFA*

A pine side/serving table, c1870, 42½in (108cm) wide.
£350–400 *AL*

A pine sideboard, with bull's-eye decoration on doors, c1870, 48in (122cm) wide.
£750–850 *AL*

A pine sideboard, c1880, 50in (127cm) wide.
£450–500 *DFA*

A North Country pine sideboard, c1880, 58in (147.5cm) wide.
£1,000–1,100 *Sca*

A mid-Victorian sideboard, with gallery back, c1860, 78in (198cm) wide.
£1,000–1,200 *PIN*

A carved pine sideboard, with original handles, 35in (89cm) wide.
£800–950 *AL*

A pine sideboard, with arched panelled doors, c1860, 54in 137cm) wide.
£1,100–1,300 *UP*

A Victorian sideboard, with 6 small drawers above, 3 large drawers each side of a central cupboard and central drawer, c1860, 74in (188cm) wide.
£1,500–1,800 *PH*

A pine sideboard, 47in (119.5cm) wide.
£800–950 *SAn*

l. A pine sideboard, with Gothic panelled doors, 70in (178cm) wide.
£2,100–2,500 *PH*

l. A pine sideboard, with beaded and panelled doors and carved side pillars, 19thC, 49in (124.5cm) wide.
£700–800 *MS*

A Regency pine sideboard, 54in (137cm) wide.
£1,000–1,200 *UP*

l. A pine sideboard, 72in (183cm) wide.
£800–950 *SAn*

A pine sideboard, with gallery back, 2 drawers and 2 panelled doors, c1870, 48in (122cm) wide.
£450–500 *Byl*

A pine sideboard, with shaped back, 2 drawers, 2 panelled doors and pillars to sides, c1875, 39in (99cm) wide.
£500–600 *Byl*

A Victorian pine sideboard, carved in relief with ribbon and bow decoration, 50in (127cm) wide.
£500–600 *SA*

'Antique' Pine

Made today out of antique or reclaimed wood, 'antique' pine furniture is often made in contemporary styles, and both accurate and inaccurate copies of original pieces.

A pine server, with gallery back and 2 cupboard doors, c1900, 45in (114.5cm) wide.
£450–500 *SA*

A pine sideboard, with shaped back, 2 drawers, 2 panelled doors and pillars to sides, c1875, 39in (99cm) wide.
£450–500 *Byl*

A pine sideboard, with gallery back, one drawer, and 2 panelled doors, 42in (106.5cm) wide.
£450–500 *SA*

An Edwardian sideboard, with one drawer and 2 carved doors, c1910, 41in (104cm) wide.
£400–450 *SA*

A pitch pine chiffonier, c1885, 49in (124.5cm) wide.
£600–700 *ASP*

l. A pine chiffonier, with raised shelf on turned column supports, early 19thC, 48in (122cm) wide.
£800–950 *TPC*

A Victorian pine chiffonier, 48in (122cm) wide.
£850–1,000 *WV*

A pine bureau bookcase, with glazed doors to top, fitted interior and 3 drawers, early 19thC, 38in (96.5cm) wide.
£2,000–2,250 *TPC*

A pine filing chest, with 2 fitted drawers, c1910, 29in (73.5cm) high.
£500–600 *BEL*

A pine desk, with 4 drawers, c1890, 22½in (57cm) wide.
£300–350 *BEL*

A pine clerk's chest, with slope top above 7 graduated drawers, 19thC, 30in (76cm) wide.
£800–900 *TPC*

A pine school desk, with lift-up top, c1910, 20in (51cm) wide.
£150–175 *DMe*

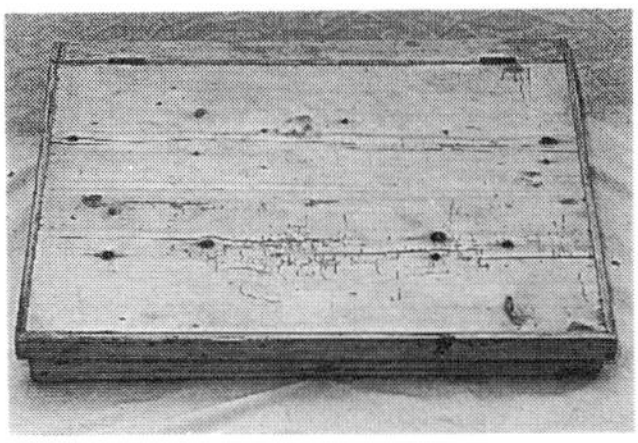

A Welsh pine clerk's desk, c1880, 20in (51cm) wide.
£200–250 *ASP*

l. A Victorian pine writing slope, c1860, 22in (56cm) wide.
£55–65 *SA*

A pine pedestal desk, c1900, 55in (140cm) wide.
£650–750 *BEL*

A pine kneehole desk, with 18 drawers, c1830, 46½in (118cm) wide.
£1,400–1,600 *GD*

A pine secrétaire, c1890, 37in (94cm) wide.
£1,500–1,800 *W*

A pine desk.
£125–150 *AL*

A German Biedermeier-style pine secrétaire, late 19thC, 37in (94cm) wide.
£1,000–1,200 *CPA*

A pine writing desk, 74in (188cm) wide.
£900–1,100 *RK*

A clerk's pine desk, with a slide, pegged construction, c1860, 43½in 110.5cm) high.
£250–300 *AL*

A pine desk, with later leathered slope, c1860, 53in (134.5cm) wide.
£1,000–1,200 *AL*

A glazed pine bureau bookcase, with 6 interior drawers and 2 drawers below, 19thC, 42in (106.5cm) wide.
£3,500–4,000 *CC*

A pine desk, fitted with pigeonholes, 22½in (57cm) wide.
£170–200 *AL*

A pine desk, with new leather and handles, 19thC, 49in (124.5cm) wide.
£1,000–1,200 *AL*

r. A kneehole desk, 47in (119.5cm) wide.
£1,000–1,250 *RK*

A Queen Anne pine bureau, with fitted interior, 35in (89cm) wide.
£2,000–2,500 *GC*

A pine secrétaire, 40in (101.5cm) wide.
£1,200–1,400 *W*

A clerk's pine desk, with cupboards at the back, 2 shelves and a china ink well with brass cover, c1850, 47in (119.5cm) high.
£450–500 *AL*

A Danish pine secrétaire, 1880, 38in (96.5cm) wide.
£1,300–1,500 *UP*

A pine pedestal desk, 61in (155cm) wide.
£1,000–1,200 *PH*

A pine desk/cupboard mid-19thC, 34in (86.5cm) wide.
£450–500 *WHA*

A pine desk, with cupboards under, 44½in (113cm) wide.
£1,000–1,100 *AL*

A pine writing table, with 3 drawers, c1820, 31½in (80cm) high.
£650–750 *AL*

A Georgian lady's pine work box, fitted with a sliding shelf, 30½in (77.5cm) wide.
£600–700 *LAM*

A carved pine writing desk, with cabriole legs, c1880, 72in (183cm) wide.
£2,000–2,200 *PH*

A Victorian pine desk, 47in (119.5cm) wide.
£1,100–1,300 *AL*

A pine pedestal desk, with a central drawer, and 4 drawers each side, 36in (91.5cm) wide.
£1,200–1,400 *PC*

A Scandinavian pine desk, with an oak top, c1910, 51in (129.5cm) wide.
£650–750 *BEL*

A pine pedestal, desk, c1880, 57in (145cm) wide.
£1,000–1,100 *RK*

A pine partners' desk, 51in (129.5cm) wide.
£1,400–1,600 *AL*

A Regency simulated bamboo pine desk, with new leather top, c1820, 45in (114.5cm) wide.
£1,300–1,500 *AL*

A pine fitted desk, with new sledge feet, c1870, 48in (122cm) high.
£1,150–1,350 *AL*

A pine desk, with black china knob handles, new leather top, c1860, 47in (119.5cm) wide.
£2,500–3,000 *AL*

A pine desk, c1870, 59in (150cm) wide.
£700–800 *AL*

A pine desk, 26in (66cm) wide.
£1,000–1,100 *PH*

A pine bureau, c1840, 43in (109.2cm) wide. **£1,300–1,500** *UP*

A pine kneehole desk, with gallery back and original knobs, c1880, 50in (127cm) wide.
£900–1,100 *SSD*

A pine estate desk, with turned legs, the interior with pigeonholes, early 19thC, later gallery, 24in (61cm) wide.
£800–950 *OA*

A pine pedestal desk, with new leather top and handles, c1860, 54in (137cm) wide.
£1,750–2,000 *AL*

l. A Victorian pine partners' desk, c1880, 60in (152.5cm) wide.
£2,500–3,000 *DDS*

A Victorian pine pedestal desk, 48in (122cm) wide.
£1,200–1,400 *PM*

A Victorian pine school desk, with a slot for a slate, c1880, 29in (73.5cm) high.
£170–200 *COT*

A pine cupboard, with a writing slope, c1860, 23½in (59.5cm) wide.
£250–300 *DME*

An Irish shopkeeper's pine desk, c1880, 24in (61cm) wide.
£110–125 *Byl*

A Continental pine two-seater school desk, with original inkwell, c1900, 46in (117cm) wide.
£170–200 *ASP*

A pine lady's writing table, with a single drawer c1900, 36in (91.5cm) wide.
£250–300 *OCP*

A clerk's pine desk, with lift-up lid, c1900, 44in (112cm) wide.
£450–500 *OCP*

A French pine desk, with split fall and kneehole, 3 drawers one side and a cupboard the other, panelled back, c1880, 47in (119cm) wide.
£800–950 *GD*

An Irish pitch pine desk, with 2 doors enclosing bookshelves, c1900, 41in (104cm) wide.
£550–650 *Byl*

A pine kneehole desk, with 7 drawers, c1860, 50in (127cm) wide.
£850–1,000 *DFA*

A pine kneehole desk, with waxed finish, c1890, 55in (139.5cm) wide.
£1,000–1,100 *DFA*

A Victorian pine desk, with a hinged top, the doors enclosing 2 sets of sliding trays, 48in (122cm) wide.
£600–700 *AL*

A Georgian pine estate desk on stand, the interior with 3 drawers, 24in (61cm) wide.
£750–900 *OA*

A Georgian pine estate desk, 26in (66cm) wide.
£750–900 *OA*

A pine desk, c1850, 29in (73.5cm) wide.
£400–500 *AL*

A pine bureau, with fitted interior, c1830, 41in (104cm) wide.
£1,500–1,800 *W*

A pine breakfront kneehole desk, c1860, 47in (119.5cm) wide.
£1,100–1,300 *AL*

A pitch pine desk, c1860, 42in (106.5cm) wide.
£1,000–1,250 *SSD*

A late Georgian slope-top estate desk, with a bank of drawers, 1800–30.
£750–900 *PIN*

A Victorian pine desk, leather top renewed, 49in (124.5cm) wide.
£500–600 *Far*

A Georgian pine double teller's desk, with spindle gallery, c1780.
£700–800 *PIN*

A pine flat-topped desk, c1850, 19in (48.5cm) wide.
£100–120 *AL*

A Georgian pine bureau, the top drawer acts as a support for the fall front, oak interior, c1800.
£1,700–2,000 *PIN*

A Victorian pitch pine school-teacher's desk, with rising lid and cupboard below.
£250–300 *PM*

A pine bowfronted kneehole writing table, with a leather top, on turned legs with brass casters, 19thC, 42in (106.5cm) wide.
£750–900 *TPC*

A pine pedestal desk, with 9 drawers, leather top renewed, c1840, 54in (137cm) wide.
£1,000–1,200 *DMA*

A Victorian pine partner's desk, with 32 drawers, 1875, 102in (259cm) wide.
£1,600–1,900 *AnD*

A Danish pine kneehole desk, with 5 drawers, on turned legs, c1870, 44in (112cm) wide.
£1,000–1,100 *UC*

A late Victorian clerk's pine desk, with a tooled leather writing slope, 52in (132cm) wide.
£750–900 *WAT*

A Victorian pine writing table, with 5 drawers, and original brass handles, on turned legs, c1845, 54in (137cm) wide.
£1,000–1,100 *DMA*

A pine partners' desk, one side with 3 pedestal drawers and one cupboard, the other side with 2 cupboards and a centre drawer, c1860, 60in (152.5cm) wide.
£1,000–1,100 *HOA*

An architect's pine flight of drawers, c1875, 42in (106.5cm) wide.
£400–450 *AnD*

A mid-Victorian pine pedestal partners' desk, 54in (137cm) wide,
£1,400–1,600 *TPC*

An Eastern European pine kneehole desk, with 7 drawers, on turned feet, the date '1867' carved under the left pedestal, 49in (124.5cm) wide.
£900–1,000 *HeR*

A Victorian pitch pine desk, with a cupboard and one drawer to the right side, a central drawer, and 4 drawers to the left side, the drawers with scallop-shaped handles, c1860, 49in (124.5cm) wide.
£700–800 *COT*

A Victorian pine pedestal desk, with 3 drawers above 2 cupboard doors each concealed as 3 false drawers, 48in (122cm) wide.
£900–1,000 *CCP*

An eastern European pine kneehole desk, with a leather top, 3 drawers, and 2 cupboard doors, c1900, 53in (134.5cm) wide.
£750–850 *HeR*

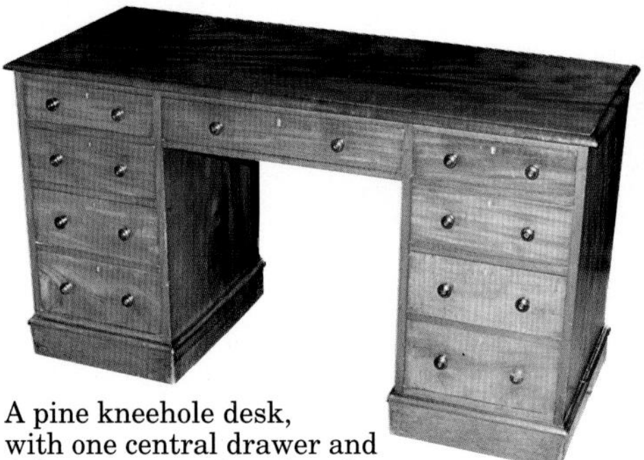

A pine kneehole desk, with one central drawer and 4 drawers to each pedestal, 54in (137cm) wide.
£1,400–1,600 *TPC*

A Victorian pine kneehole desk, with a shaped frieze below a central drawer, and 4 drawers to each pedestal, 47in (119.5cm) wide.
£900–1,000 *HeR*

A Victorian pine davenport, leather top replaced, c1880, 26½in (67.5cm) wide.
£650–750 *OPH*

A pine panelled coffer, c1820, 46in (117cm) long.
500–600 *DMA*

A German seaman's pine chest, c1890, 45in (114.5cm) long.
£250–275 *AnD*

An Austrian pine chest, originally painted with naïve decoration, c1860, 40in (101.5cm) long.
£250–300 *AnD*

A pine mule chest, with 2 drawers, c1780, 45in (114.5cm) long.
£550–650 *MIL*

A Bavarian pine chest, c1860, 72in (183cm) long.
£450–500 *AnD*

This chest was used to store heavily embroidered ceremonial religious garments. It was made to collapse, to enable it to get through chapel doors.

A pine mule chest, with original bale handles, 45in (114.5cm) long.
£500–600 *DMA*

A German pine box, c1870, 48in (122cm) long.
£250–300 *AnD*

A Continental seaman's pine chest, c1880, 36in (91.5cm) long.
£250–275 *AnD*

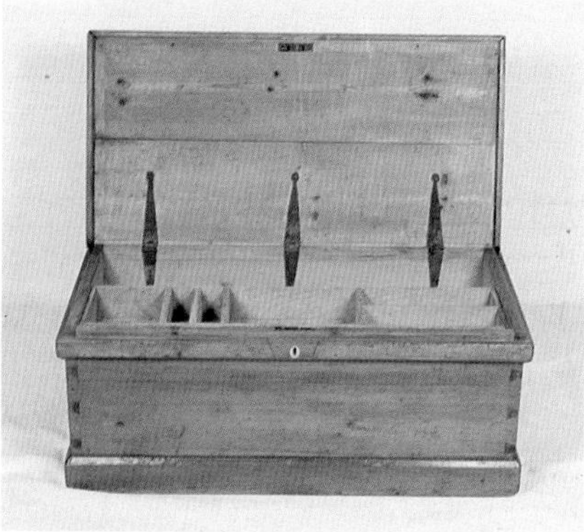

A pine box, fitted with a tray, c1870, 37in (94cm) wide.
£250–300 *AL*

A pine blanket box, with original finish, c1870, 38in (96.5cm) wide.
£250–300 *MIL*

A pine box, with a domed top, c1870, 42in (106.5cm) long.
£250–275 *AnD*

A pine blanket box, with a domed top, fitted with a candle box, c1890, 36in (91.5cm) wide.
£250–275 *MIL*

A pine box, with a domed top, fitted with a candle box, c1880, 33in (84cm) wide.
£250–275 *AnD*

A pine box, c1880, 45in (114.5cm) wide.
£250–300 *AnD*

A carpenter's pine tool chest, c1870, 35in (89cm) wide.
£350–400 *AnD*

A pine box, c1870, 27in (68.5cm) wide.
£300–350 *AnD*

A pine curved settle, c1820, 55in (139.5cm) wide.
£700–800 *MIL*

An elm and pine curved settle, with a panelled back, and 3 drawers, 64in (162.5cm) wide.
£1,000–1,250 *DMA*

A pine barrel-back settle, c1850, 84in (213.5cm) high.
£1,100–1,300 *COP*

A pine settle, with open arms and turned spindle back, c1860, 72in (183cm) wide.
£450–500 *COP*

A pine settle, with solid back and slatted arms, c1860, 72in (183cm) wide.
£450–500 *COP*

A Czechoslovakian pine buffet dresser, c1880, 38in (96.5cm) wide.
£750–850 *AnD*

A pine dresser, with glazed cupboard doors, above 2 drawers and cupboards, 40in (101.5cm) wide.
£600–700 *MIL*

A Welsh pine dresser, with 6 drawers, c1820, 64in (162.5cm) wide.
£3,500–4,000 *UC*

A Continental pine dresser, c1900, 60in (152.5cm) wide.
£750–850 *AnD*

A Czechoslovakian dresser, the top with glazed doors, c1860, 60in (152.5cm) wide.
£750–850 *AnD*

A Cornish pine dresser, with 3 glazed doors, 3 drawers with 3 cupboards beneath, and applied split turnings, 59in (150cm) wide.
£1,300–1,600 *MIL*

An Irish pine and elm farmhouse dresser, with fretted frieze, c1850, 59in (150cm) wide.
£2,300–2,700 *UC*

A Dutch pine dresser, with 3 glazed doors, 60in (152.5cm) wide.
£750–900 *AnD*

A West Country pine dresser, with turned moulding to doors, 46in (117cm) wide.
£1,000–1,150 *MIL*

A Victorian dresser base, with central 'dog kennel', and original brass handles, 113in (287cm) wide.
£1,100–1,300 *CCP*

An Eastern European pine dresser base, with carved panel motifs, c1880, 41½in (105.5cm) wide.
£450–500 *NWE*

A Continental pine kitchen cupboard, with carved panel motifs, c1910, 44in (112cm) wide.
£450–500 *WAT*

A Victorian pine dresser base, with 3 serpentine drawers, above 4 cockbeaded drawers, with original glass handles, and solid mahogany worktop, 78in (198cm) wide.
£1,100–1,300 *CCP*

An Eastern European dresser base, with a serpentine front, 2 panelled doors below 2 drawers, c1860, 40in (101.5cm) wide.
£450–500 *NWE*

An Eastern European pine cupboard, with one small drawer above 2 panelled doors, c1830, 58½in (148.5cm) wide.
£800–900 *HeR*

A Victorian pine dresser base, with 4 drawers and later marble galleried top, 50in (127cm) wide.
£550–650 *CCP*

A pine dresser base, with 3 drawers above open shelving, and one side cupboard, mid-19thC, 70in (178cm) wide.
£900–1,000 *CCP*

An Irish pine and elm farmhouse dresser, with a fretted frieze, c1850, 59in (150cm) wide.
£2,500–2,700 *UC*

A Sussex pine dresser, with an open rack, c1830, 59in (150cm) wide.
£2,300–2,500 *UC*

A Suffolk pine cottage dresser, with an open rack, c1830, 56in (142cm) wide.
£1,700–2,000 *UC*

A pine Welsh dresser, with 2 narrow glazed cupboards, above 3 frieze drawers and 2 lower cupboards, c1860, 63in (160cm) wide.
£1,700–2,000 *BOA*

A pine dresser, with open shelves above 2 drawers and 2 cupboards, 58in (147.5cm) wide.
£1,400–1,650 *AL*

A Georgian pine Welsh dresser, with 6 drawers, c1820, 64in (162.5cm) wide.
£3,500–4,000 *UC*

l. A mid-Victorian pine dresser, in original condition, 61in (155cm) wide.
£1,500–1,700 *CCP*

A North Country pine dresser, restored, c1780, 98in (249cm) wide.
£2,000–2,500 *BOA*

A pine Welsh dresser, c1820,
58in (147.5cm) wide.
£3,500–4,000 *RK*

An Irish pine dresser, c1840,
78in (198cm) high.
£1,700–2,000 *RK*

A Scottish pine dresser, c1860,
55in (139.5cm) high.
£1,200–1,400 *RK*

l. An Irish pine dresser,
c1880, 52in (132cm) wide.
£1,500–1,800 *UP*

An Irish pine fiddle-front dresser,
c1820, 50in (127cm) wide.
£2,000–2,500 *UP*

An Irish pine dresser,
c1850, 49in (124.5cm) wide.
£1,500–1,750 *RK*

An Irish pine dresser,
c1860, 80in (203cm) high.
£1,800–2,100 *RK*

A Scottish pine dresser, c1860,
52in (132cm) wide.
£1,100–1,300 *RK*

An Irish pine dresser, c1880,
80in (205.7cm) wide.
£1,500–1,750 *RK*

An Irish pine dresser, c1860,
60in (152.5cm) wide.
£2,000–2,500 *UP*

An Irish pine settle, c1880,
75in (190.5cm) wide.
£600–700 *UP*

˛ pine bowfront chest of drawers,
ˈith a shaped frieze, 2 short and 3 long
rawers, on squat ball feet, 19thC.
900–1,100 *TPC*

A Danish pine bureau bookcase, c1860, 84in (213.5cm) high.
£2,000–2,500 *RK*

A pine bureau bookcase, c1790, 42in (106.5cm) wide.
£2,500–3,000 *UP*

ˎ pine chest of drawers, with 2 short and
ː long gesso decorated drawers, 19thC,
ˌ0in (101.5cm) wide.
ː900–1,000 *TPC*

A Scandinavian chest of drawers, c1880, 52in (132cm) wide.
£700–800 *RK*

n Irish pine glazed
ookcase, c1830,
ˌ4in (213.5cm) wide.
2,000–2,200 *RK*

A pine chest of 5 drawers, 41in (104cm) wide.
£550–650 *AL*

A painted pine chest, with a serpentine-fronted top and 8 drawers, early 19thC, 30in (76cm) wide.
£1,600–1,900 *DN*

A pine sideboard, c1850, 96in (244cm) wide.
£1,200–1,400 *SAn*

A pitch pine single wardrobe, c1870, 48in (122cm) wide.
£500–600 *PC*

l. A pine cupboard base, c1800, with a later breakfront display plate rack, 60in (152.5cm) wide.
£1,500–1,700 *PC*

A pine delft plate rack, c1840, 60in (152.5cm) wide.
£700–800 *AL*

r. A hazel pine wardrobe, c1890, 39in (99cm) wide.
£450–550 *PC*

A pine dresser base, with a gallery back, c1860, 66in (167.5cm) wide.
£1,200–1,400 *PC*

A pine and elm dresser base, c1850, with a later plate rack, 72in (183cm) wide.
£2,250–2,700 *PC*

A Yorkshire serpentine front pine dresser base, with original spice drawers, c1860, later plate rack, 54in (137cm) wide.
£1,500–1,800 *PC*

A pitch pine dresser base, c1900, with a later plate rack 42in (106.5cm) wide.
£1,200–1,400 *PC*

. pine stool, c1880,
6in (40.5cm) wide.
75–90 *AL*

A pine stool, c1890, 16in (40.5cm) wide.
£65–75 *MIL*

An Austrian pine chair, with shaped back, c1890,
£125–150 *AnD*

. pine folding chair,
y Thornet, c1930.
65–75 *Ber*

A pine stool, c1890,
15in (38cm) wide.
£65–75 *AL*

A pine milking stool, c1890,
11in (28cm) high.
£50–60 *MIL*

A pine stool, with a saddle seat, c1890, 26in (66cm) high.
£125–150 *AL*

A pine chair, with carved bar across the back.
£70–80 *LIB*

A pine milking stool, c1880,
14in (35.5cm) high.
£60–70 *MIL*

A tall stool, c1900,
29in (73.5cm) high.
£125–150 *AL*

A German pine wardrobe, with 2 doors flanking a central oval mirror, above 2 long drawers, c1900, 60in (152.5cm) wide.
£750–850 *AnD*

A Flemish pine armoire, c1870, 48in (122cm) wide.
£500–550 *AnD*

A Continental pine wardrobe, 19thC, 44in (112cm) wide.
£500–600 *LIB*

A pine 'break-down' wardrobe, 19thC, 66in (167.5cm) wide.
£600–700 *LIB*

A Continental pine wardrobe, with decorated cornice and door panels, 46½in (118cm) wide.
£750–900 *WAT*

A Dutch pine armoire, with 2 doors above 2 drawers, c1840, 60in (152.5cm) wide.
£750–900 *AnD*

A Danish pine armoire, with 2 doors above 2 drawers, c1850, 55in (139.5cm) wide.
£1,000–1,100 *UC*

A Continental pine wardrobe, with arched top, 19thC, 44in (112cm) wide.
£450–500 *LIB*

A pine armoire, with 2 doors above one long drawer, c1880, 48in (122cm) wide.
£500–600 *AnD*

A pine fire surround, 19thC, 48in (122cm) wide.
£300–350 *AnD*

A pine door, with frame, 19thC, 36in (91.5cm) wide.
£300–350 *WEL*

A pair of pine church doors, 19thC 62in (157.5cm) wide.
£800–900 *WEL*

A pair of pine chapel doors, of heavy braced construction, with decorative hand forged strap hinges, 18thC, 52in (132cm) wide.
£800–900 *TPC*

A cast-iron fireplace, with Art Nouveau tiled surround, c1900, 40in (101.5cm) wide.
£450–500 *WaH*

A Victorian pine bedroom fireplace, with fluted decoration, c1860.
£250–300 *OPH*

A Canadian Adam-style fire surround, with carved pilasters and paterae, early 19thC, 59in (150cm) high.
£2,500–3,000 *RIT*

A carved pine fire surround, with a leaf and flower-decorated frieze flanked by urn-toppe fluted and reeded column sides, the opening surrounded with egg-and-dart moulding, 18thC, 62in (157cm) wide.
£1,700–2,000 *TPC*

pitch pine dressing
est, c1870,
:in (106.5cm) wide.
'50–900 *SSD*

A hazel pine dressing chest, c1890, 42in (106.5cm) wide.
£500–600 *SSD*

A hazel pine dressing chest, c1890, 36in (92cm) wide.
£500–600 *SSD*

A pine dressing table, c1870, 39in (99cm) wide.
£500–600 *SSD*

pine dressing table,
ith original paint,
3in (92cm) wide.
500–600 *AL*

A pine dressing table, with new handles, 36in (92cm) wide.
£500–600 *AL*

A pine dressing table, c1890, 42in (106.5cm) wide.
£450–500 *W*

An Edwardian pine dressing chest, 34in (86cm) wide.
£500–600 *OA*

Pine

Pine is a soft, pale wood used in England and the United States as a secondary timber for the carcass of a piece, drawer linings, backboards etc. It was also used in the production of inexpensive furniture during the 19thC, when it was often painted.

\n Edwardian pine
lressing table,
;6in (92cm) wide.
:450–500 *OA*

A pine dressing table, with new handles, 36in (92cm) wide.
£450–500 *AL*

A pine dressing chest, with mahogany handles, 19thC, 39in (99cm) wide.
£500–600 *CC*

l. A pine dressing table, c1870, 39in (99cm) wide.
£550–650 *W*

l. A Swedish pine dressing chest, with unusual carving, 32in (81cm) wide.
£400–450 *BEL*

A pine dressing table, with an elm top, 34in (87cm) wide.
£450–550 *AL*

A pitch pine dressing chest, with carved mirror supports and shaped brackets below, 19thC, 36in (91.5cm) wide.
£500–600 *PF*

A pine washstand/ dressing table, c1860 30in (76cm) wide.
£550–650 *AL*

A pine dressing chest, with original handles and fittings, c1840, 44in (110cm) wide.
£550–650 *Sca*

A pine dressing table, with original handles, c1860, 38in (96.5cm) wide.
£550–650 *AL*

A Victorian pine dressing table, with a bevelled mirror, 36in (91.5cm) wide.
£450–500 *AH*

A pitch pine dressing table, c1880, 39in (99cm) wide.
£450–550 *SSD*

A pine dressing chest, with bevelled glass, porcelain knob handles, late 19thC, 42in (106.5cm) wide.
£500–600 *AL*

A pine dressing table, c1870, 30in (76cm) wide.
£400–450 *W*

A Victorian dressing chest, c1880, 42in (106.5cm) wide.
£500–600 *Sca*

late Victorian pine dressing
est, c1890, 43in (109cm) wide.
50–650 *COT*

A Victorian Gothic-style pitch pine dressing table, c1860, 44in (111.5cm) wide.
£450–500 *COT*

A late Victorian pitch pine dressing chest, 42in (106.5cm) wide.
£500–600 *WaH*

pine dressing chest, c1910,
7½in (20cm) wide.
450–500 *BEL*

A pine dressing chest, with 2 small cupboards above 3 long drawers, c1920, 57½in (145cm) wide.
£450–500 *BEL*

l. A mid-Victorian pine breakfront kneehole dressing table, with arched top mirror on carved supports, 52in (132cm) wide.
£1,000–1,100 *TPC*

r. A pine and elm dressing table, c1940, 43½in (110cm) wide.
£450–500 *BEL*

A dressing chest, with galleried mirror, c1880, 41in (104cm) wide.
£450–550 *ASP*

A late Victorian pine dressing chest, with gesso decoration, 2 short and 2 long drawers, on solid plinth base, 40in (101.5cm) wide.
£450–550 *TPC*

A pine and satin walnut dressing chest, original brass handles and bevelled glass mirror in excellent condition, early 20thC, 37in (94cm) wide.
£450–550 *HNG*

A late Victorian pine dressing chest, with gesso decoration, 42in (106.5cm) wide.
£600–700 *TPC*

A Victorian pine dressing table, 41in (104cm) wide.
£400–450 *GD*

r. A pine dressing chest, with 4 drawers in base, c1880, 38in (96.5cm) wide.
£500–600 *ASP*

A primitive washstand/dressing table, c1800, 41½in (105cm) wide.
£450–500 *COT*

r. A late Victorian pine dressing table, with gesso decoration, on tapered legs, 40in (101.5cm) wide.
£550–650 *TPC*

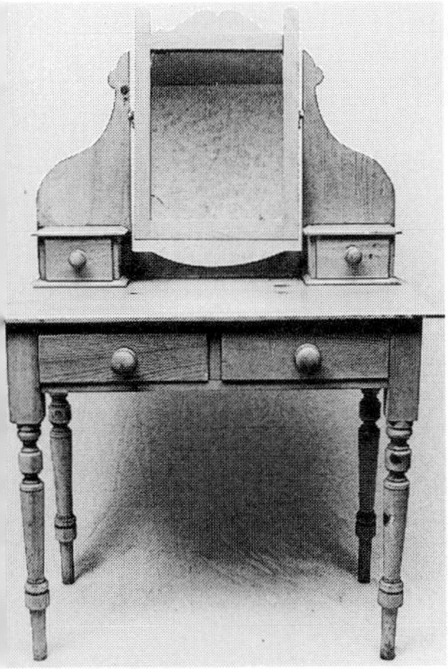

l. A pine dressing table, c1880, 36in (91.5cm) wide.
£350–400 *ASP*

A pine dressing table, with mirror and 2 drawers, c1940, 33in (84cm) wide.
£450–500 *OCP*

A pine dressing table, with a mirror, on turned legs, c1875, 41in (104cm) wide.
£350–400 *Byl*

l. A pine dressing table, by Maples, c1880, 36in (91.5cm) wide.
£450–500 *AL*

Old Pine

Old pine has often been restored, modified or customized, either because the piece has deteriorated beyond reasonable repair, or it is not suitable in its original state for modern use or taste.

. pine longcase clock, ith 30-hour movement, rched dial, painted face, 2in (208cm) high.
1,300–1,500 *MIL*

l. A pine longcase clock, with 30-hour movement, c1810, 78in (198cm) high.
£1,200–1,400 *HOA*

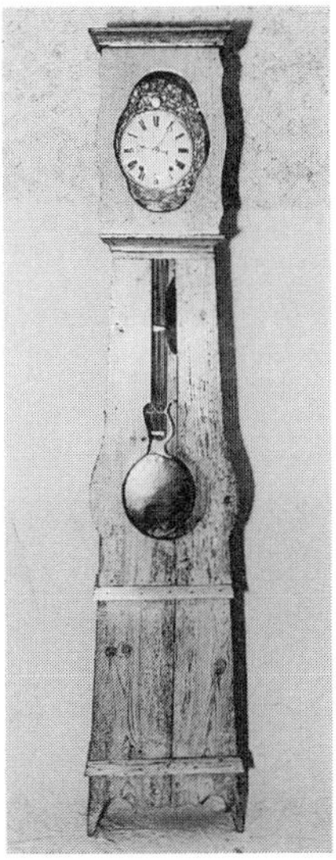

A French pine longcase clock, 92in (233.5cm) high.
£1,200–1,400 *ASP*

An Irish pine longcase clock, c1840.
£1,700–2,000 *HON*

A Victorian pine washstand,
36in (91.5cm) wide.
£350–400 *OA*

A Victorian pine washstand,
with a towel rail on either side,
41in (104cm) wide.
£350–400 *OA*

A Victorian pine washstand
39in (99cm) wide.
£450–500 *OA*

A pine washstand, c1880,
36in (91.5cm) wide.
£350–400 *OA*

A pine washstand, with a marble
top, the splashback with Art
Deco tiles, 36in (91.5cm) wide.
£325–375 *OA*

A Victorian pine washstand
with marble superstructure,
28in (71cm) wide.
£325–375 *Ad*

A pine washstand, c1860,
43½in (110cm) wide.
£500–600 *AL*

A Victorian pine washstand,
with a marble top and a pink tiled
splashback, 36in (91.5cm) wide.
£350–400 *OA*

A Victorian pine washstand,
24in (61cm) wide.
£250–300 *OA*

l. A Lincolnshire pine
washstand, original
paint, 35in (89cm) wide.
£500–600 *CPA*

r. A mid-Victorian
pine washstand,
36in (91.5cm) wide.
£325–375 *OA*

A late Victorian pine washstand, with marble top,
36in (91.5cm) wide.
£350–400 *OA*

A late Victorian pine
washstand, with a marble
top and tiled splashback.
£450–500 *OA*

A pine double washstand,
40½in (102cm) wide.
£350–400 *AL*

ı Georgian pine washstand,
4in (36cm) wide.
300–350 *W*

A pine washstand, with a drawer,
c1860, 23in (59cm) wide.
£300–350 *W*

A pine marble-topped
washstand, 36in (91.5cm) wide.
£350–400 *WHA*

ı Victorian pine washstand,
;7in (94cm) wide.
'350–400 *AH*

A pine washstand, c1850,
35in (89cm) wide.
£300–350 *W*

A Swedish pine washstand/side
cabinet, c1890, 32½in (82cm) wide.
£400–450 *Far*

\ pine washstand, c1900,
ʒ1in (84cm) wide.
ː250–275 *Ad*

A pine washstand, c1880,
28in (71cm) wide.
£200–250 *WEL*

A Regency pine washstand,
22in (55.5cm) wide.
£300–350 *W*

A pine washstand, with one door and one
drawer, c1880, 40in (102cm) high.
£500–600 *AL*

A pine washstand, with a marble
top, c1880, 42in (107cm) wide.
£350–400 *AL*

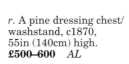

r. A pine dressing chest/
washstand, c1870,
55in (140cm) high.
£500–600 *AL*

A pine washstand, with a high splashback, a drawer under the potboard, c1860.
£250–300 *PIN*

A pine washstand, c1760, 13in (33cm) wide.
£350–400 *UP*

A pine bowfront washstand, c1780, 35in (89cm) high.
£600–700 *UP*

A pine washstand, c1850, 24in (61cm) wide.
£250–300 *AL*

A pine cupboard/washstand, with a marble top, c1910, 42½in (107cm) high.
£200–250 *BEL*

A pine washstand and shelf, c1860, 35in (89cm) high.
£200–250 *AL*

A pine washstand, c1870, 21in (52.5cm) wide.
£200–250 *AL*

A single pine washstand, c1860, 24in (61cm) wide.
£250–300 *SSD*

A pine washstand, 30in (76cm) wide.
£300–350 *AL*

A pine washstand, with a marble top, c1860, 30in (76cm) wide.
£350–400 *AL*

A hazel pine washstand, with a marble top, c1890, 42in (106cm) wide.
£350–400 *SSD*

A pine washstand, c1890, 31in (79cm) wide.
£250–300 *W*

An Arts and Crafts style grained pine washstand, c1880, 36in (91.5cm) wide.
£350–400 *COT*

A pine washstand, with square tapered legs, early 20thC, 36in (91.5cm) wide.
£250–300 *HNG*

A marble topped washstand, with cupboard and drawers, 19thC.
£350–400 *WV*

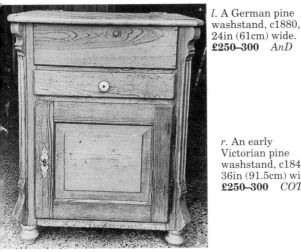

l. A German pine washstand, c1880, 24in (61cm) wide.
£250–300 *AnD*

r. An early Victorian pine washstand, c1840, 36in (91.5cm) wide.
£250–300 *COT*

A pine washstand with gallery back, Essex, c1880, 37in (94cm) wide.
£200–250 *ASP*

A pine tiled back washstand, c1880, 35½in (90cm) wide.
£250–300 *ASP*

A Victorian pine washstand, 24in (61cm) wide.
£250–300 *ERA*

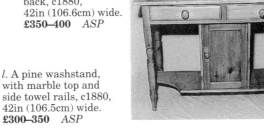

r. A pine marble-topped washstand, with tiled splash-back, c1880, 42in (106.6cm) wide.
£350–400 *ASP*

l. A pine washstand, with marble top and side towel rails, c1880, 42in (106.5cm) wide.
£300–350 *ASP*

A pine marble-topped washstand, with original green and white tiles, c1890, 36in (91.5cm) wide.
£250–300 *POT*

A pine washstand, with gallery back, single drawer, shaped undertier and turned legs, c1855, 36in (91.5cm) wide.
£225–250 *DMe*

A pine washstand, c1870, 33in (84cm) wide.
£225–250 *ASP*

A pine washstand with tiled back, original, c1880, 34in (86cm) wide.
£250–300 *ASP*

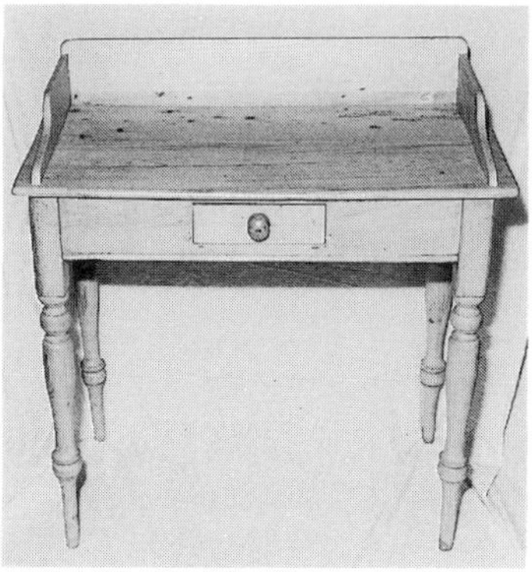

A pine washstand, with gallery back, small single drawer and turned legs, c1845, 31½in (80cm) wide.
£225–250 *DMe*

A pine washstand, c1880, 23in (59cm) wide.
£175–200 *DFA*

An Irish pine single washstand, c1870, 23½in (60cm) wide.
£175–200 *Byl*

A pine washstand, with single drawer and potboard, c1850, 42in (106.5cm) wide.
£225–250 *SA*

A pine washstand, c1880, 34in (86cm) wide.
£225–250 *AL*

r. A pine washstand, 19thC, 32in (81cm) wide.
£225–250 *ERA*

Use the Index!

Because certain items might fit easily into any number of categories, the quickest and surest method of locating any entry is by reference to the index at the back of the book. This index has been fully cross-referenced for absolute simplicity.

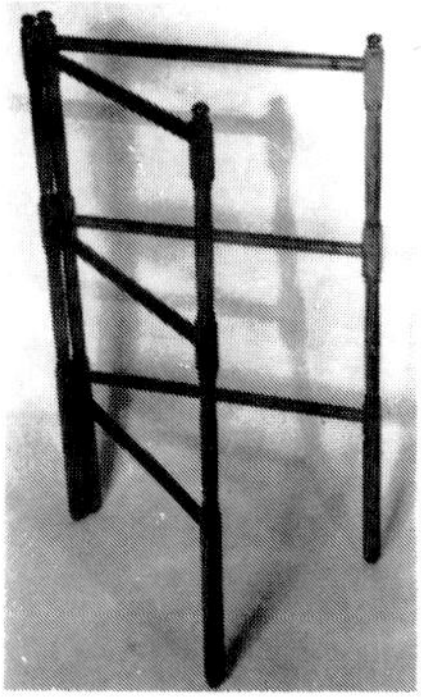
A pine towel rail,
35in (87.5cm) high.
£70–85 *AL*

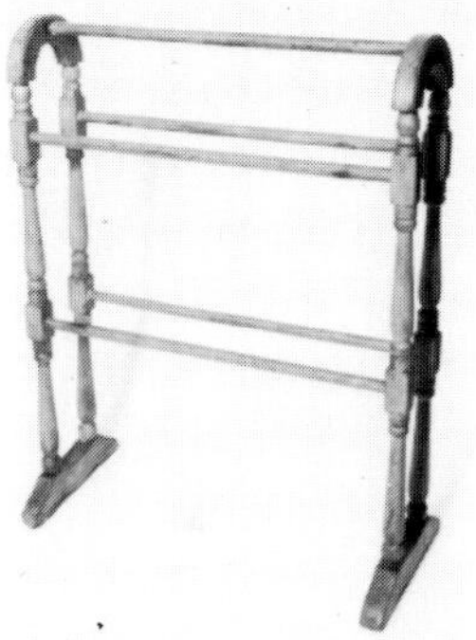
A pine towel rail, c1880,
36in (91.5cm) wide.
£90–100 *W*

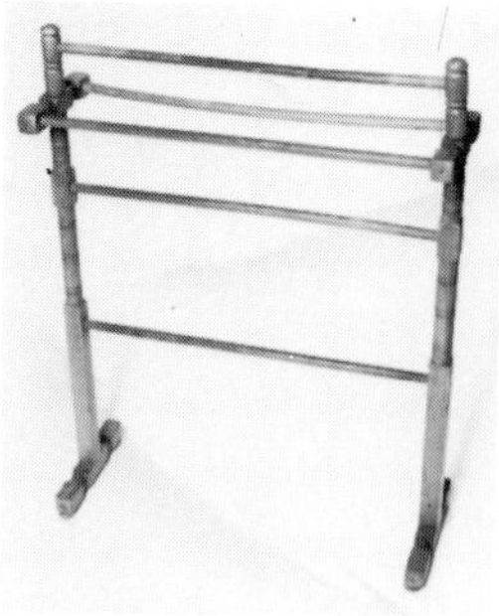
A pine towel rail, c1900.
£60–70 *W*

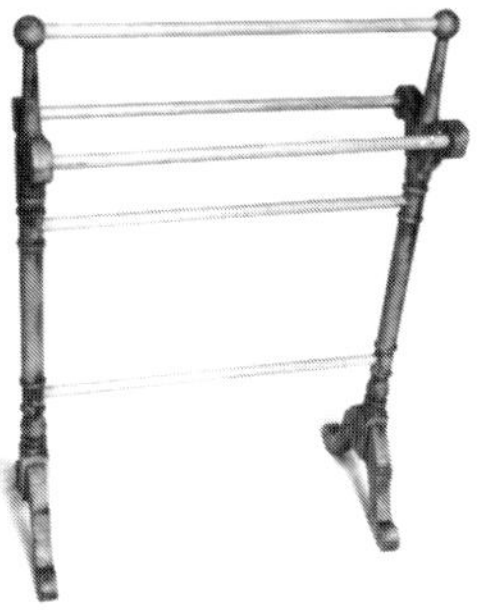
A pine towel rail,
25in (63.5cm) wide.
£90–100 *LAM*

A pine towel rail,
26½in (67cm) wide.
£110–130 *AL*

A pine towel rail,
29½in (75cm) high.
£110–130 *AL*

A pine towel rail, 19thC,
26in (65cm) wide.
£110–130 *PCL*

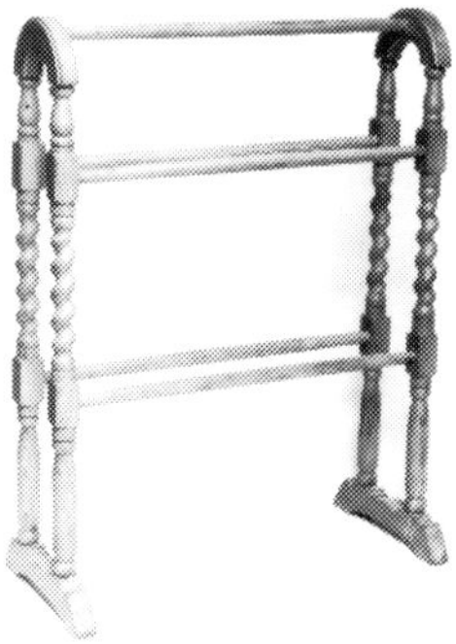
A hoop towel rail, with
barley-twist ends, 19thC.
£130–150 *PF*

A pine towel rail, 28in (71cm) wide.
£90–100 *TRU*

A pine towel rail,
with barley twist ends,
c1870, 30in (76cm) high.
£130–150 *SPA*

A pine towel rail, 34in (87cm) high.
£90–100 *AL*

A pine towel rail, all original,
c1880, 30in (76cm) high.
£110–130 *SPA*

A pine nest of drawers, c1860, 54in (137cm) wide.
£1,100–1,250 *UP*

A pine flight of 18 grocery drawers, 50in (127cm) wide.
£1,100–1,250 *BEL*

A pine nest of drawers, c1820, 43in (109cm) high.
£850–1,000 *UP*

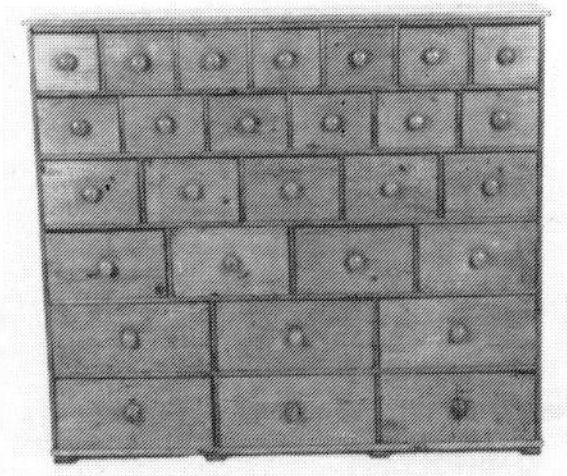

l. A pine flight of drawers, c1850, 56½in (143cm) wide.
£850–1,000 *AL*

A pine nest of drawers, 18in (45.5cm) wide.
£500–600 *PH*

A pine flight of 6 drawers, c1860, 16in (40.5cm) high.
£250–400 *BEL*

A pine flight of drawers, with original handles, c1840, 51in (129.5cm) wide.
£1,000–1,200 *AL*

A pine flight of 38 drawers, 54in (137cm) high.
£850–1,000 *AL*

A pine flight of drawers, c1850, 56½in (143cm) wide.
£850–1,000 *AL*

A pine flight of drawers, with original handles, c1850, 32in (81cm) wide.
£300–350 *AL*

A clockmaker's pine chest of 36 drawers, with brass knob handles, early 19thC, 26in (66cm) wide.
£450–500 *TPC*

A pine flight of drawers, late 19thC, 108in (274cm) wide.
£1,100–1,250 *CUL*

A pine set of 9 drawers, c1870, 34in (86cm) wide.
£250–300 *AL*

A pine Wellington chest, with original handles, c1880, 22in (56cm) wide.
£1,100–1,250 *ASP*

A Victorian pine bank of 4 drawers, 10in (25.5cm) wide.
£150–180 *OPH*

A Victorian pine specimen chest, with original brass handles, 46in (116.5cm) high.
£500–600 *ERA*

A pine military-style flight of 10 drawers, with original handles, 19thC, 54in (137cm) wide.
£450–500 *ERA*

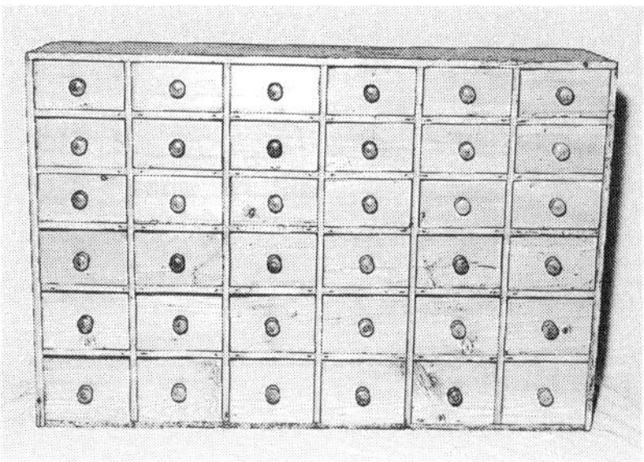

A chestnut flight of drawers, c1870, 38in (96.5cm) wide.
£500–600 *ASP*

. pine nest of drawers,
9in (48cm) wide.
450–550 *PH*

A bank of drawers, c1930,
24in (61cm) wide.
£450–550 *SPA*

A pine shop counter, c1880,
109in (277cm) wide.
£1,400–1,600 *UP*

l. A collector's pine cabinet,
29in (74cm) wide.
£550–650 *PH*

A pine flight of drawers, with original brass handles, c1806,
37in (94cm) wide.
£350–400 *AL*

l. A pine bank of drawers, c1880,
89in (226cm) wide.
£1,200–1,400 *RK*

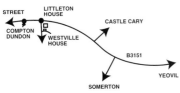

A pine tray-top commode, c1840, 19in (48cm) wide.
£500–600 *W*

A pine commode, c1850, 25in (63.5cm) wide.
£400–450 *AL*

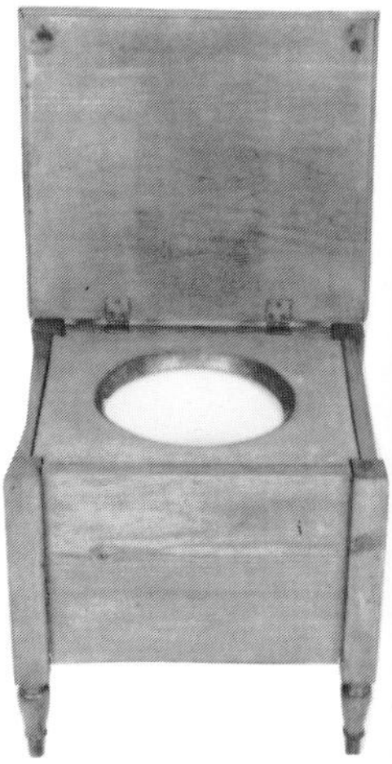

A pine commode, with pottery liner, c1860, 19in (48cm) wide.
£200–225 *AL*

A pine commode, 25in (64cm) wide.
£300–350 *WHA*

r. A pine step commode, new leather, c1850, 20in (51cm) square.
£300–350 *AL*

A pine commode, with liner, 18½in (47cm) high.
£200–225 *AL*

A Scandinavian pine commode table, c1890, 18in (46cm) wide.
£300–350 *W*

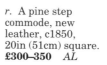

A pine commode, with black china knob handles, c1860, 26in (66cm) wide.
£350–400 *AL*

A pine commode, 19thC, 17in (42.5cm) wide.
£200–225 *AL*

A Scandinavian commode, with lift-up top, original fittings, c1890, 20in (50.5cm) wide.
£300–350 *W*

A pine step commode, c1860, 18in (46cm) wide.
£300–325 *AL*

A pine commode, with initials 'TD' on lid and dated '1890'.
£130–160 *CHA*

A Victorian pine bed cupboard, with a dummy chest of drawers front, 47in (119cm) wide.
£400–500 *AL*

A pine commode chair, c1850.
£170–200 *AL*

A Scandinavian pine commode, 19½in (49cm) wide.
£150–180 *W*

A mid-Victorian pine commode, 17in (43cm) square.
£170–200 *FP*

A pine step commode, 26in (66cm) high.
£450–500 *W*

A pine panel-backed settle, c1790, 76in (193cm) wide.
£800–950 *UP*

A Dutch pine settle, c1880, 40in (100cm) wide.
£650–750 *Sca*

An Austrian pine bench, 34in (86cm) long.
£700–850 *MCA*

A carved pine rustic bench, the back and arms in the form of naturalistic branches, carved with leaves and with a bear seated in the branches, the plank seat supported by carved standing bears, probably Swiss, c1860, 50½in (128cm) wide.
£2,500–3,000 *S*

r. A pine church pew, c1850, 64in (160cm) wide.
£300–350 *Sca*

A pine seat, 69in (175cm) long.
£170–200 *AL*

A pair of Georgian pine benches, c1800, 91in (231cm) long.
£600–700 *PIN*

A pine bed settle, c1740, 72in (183cm) wide.
£1,300–1,600 *UP*

A pine bench, 68in (172.5cm) long.
£170–200 *AL*

A pine bench, with clover leaf and other motifs carved into the back rail, c1900.
£700–800 *LRG*

A pine bench, with pegged back c1840, 72in (182.5cm) long.
£450–500 *AL*

A Dutch carved pine bench, in the baroque taste, on trestle end supports, 18thC, 74in (188cm) wide.
£2,000–2,500 *P*

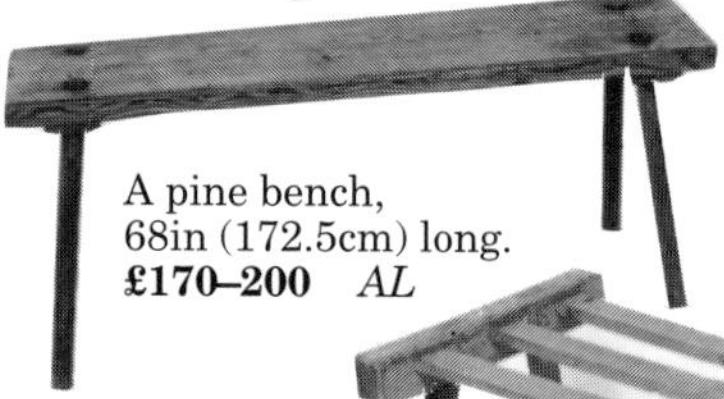

A pine bench, 68in (172.5cm) long.
£170–200 *AL*

r. A Cumbrian pine sheep shearing bench, individually made for each shearer, c1860, 44in (111.5cm) long.
£250–275 *AL*

pine panelled settle, with lift-up
eat, 19thC, 48in (122cm) wide.
450–500 *HeR*

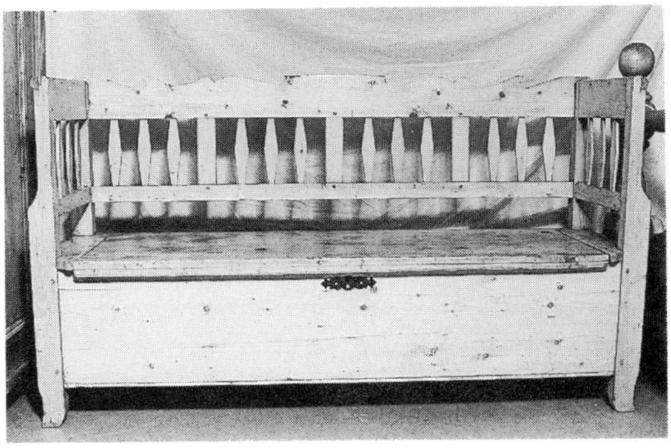

A Hungarian pine box settle, c1840, 65in (165cm) wide.
£500–600 *HeR*

A pine church pew, early 20thC, 85in (216cm) long.
£250–300 *HGN*

A pine panelled box settle, 19thC,
54in (137cm) wide.
£550–650 *TPC*

A pine barrel-back bench, c1880,
118in (300cm) wide.
£350–400 *AL*

A pine bench, c1870, 47½in (120cm) long.
£100–120 *ASP*

An Irish pine bed settle, with panelled
back, 72in (182.5cm) wide.
£700–800 *TPC*

l. A pine bench, 78in (198cm) long.
£100–120 *ASP*

A Georgian barrel-back pine settle, with a cupboard, c1830, 81in (205.5cm) wide.
£1,200–1,400 *BH*

A carved pine bench, 72in (182.5cm) wide.
£800–950 *SAn*

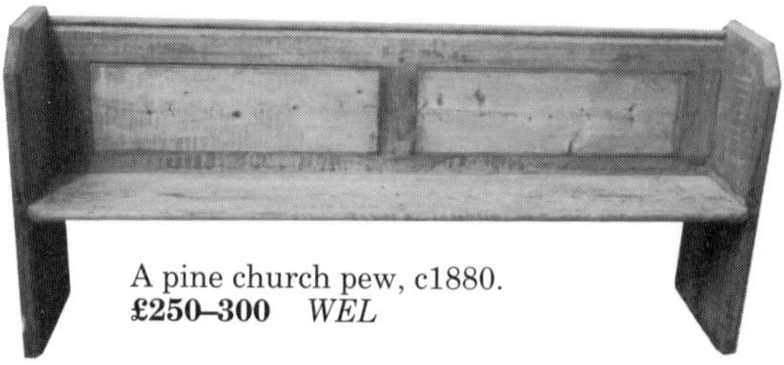

A pine church pew, c1880.
£250–300 *WEL*

l. A Georgian barrel-back pine settle, 69in (172.5cm) wide.
£1,500–1,800 *JMW*

An Irish high backed pine settle, c1820, 74in (188cm) wide.
£1,000–1,100 *UP*

A pine settle, c1850, 39in (99cm) wide.
£1,000–1,100 *AL*

An early Victorian pine box settle, 50in (127cm) wide.
£1,400–1,600 *W*

A pine bed-settle, in original condition, c1800.
£600–700 *CPA*

A barrel-back pine settle, c1840, 72in (182.5cm) wide.
£750–900 *AL*

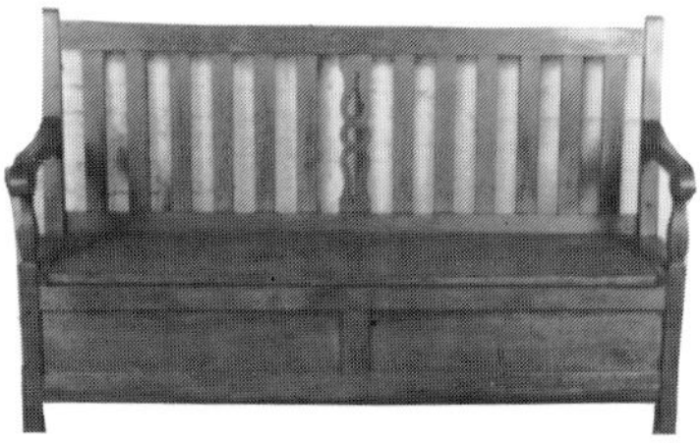

A Welsh pine box settle, c1840, 66in (167.5cm) wide.
£750–900 *BH*

A pine settle, c1840, 67in (170cm) high.
£1,500–1,800 *W*

An Irish pine settle, 72in (182.5cm) wide.
£750–850 *UP*

A concave wing-back pine settle, with a broad plank back, early 19thC, 66in (167.5cm) wide.
£950–1,100 *S(S)*

A pine bench, c1880, 50in (127cm) long.
£170–200 *ASP*

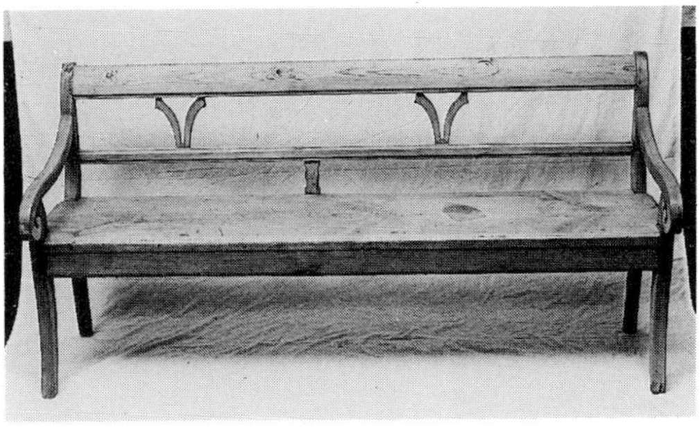

A Continental pine bench, c1870, 73in (185cm) long.
£400–475 *ASP*

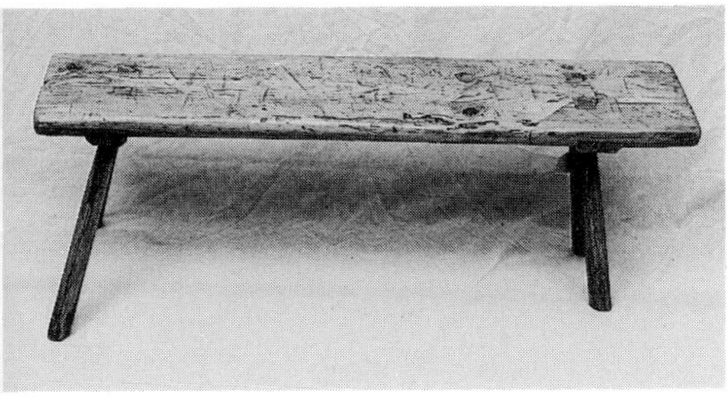

A pine country bench, 1870, 37½in (95cm) long.
£170–200 *ASP*

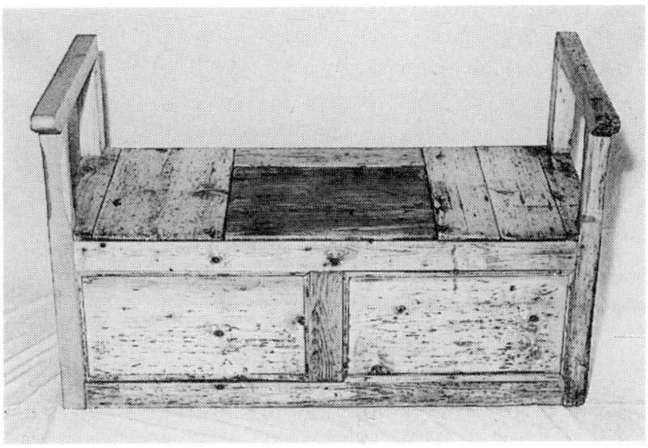

A late Georgian pine monk's bench, with panelled base, c1830.
£700–800 *POT*

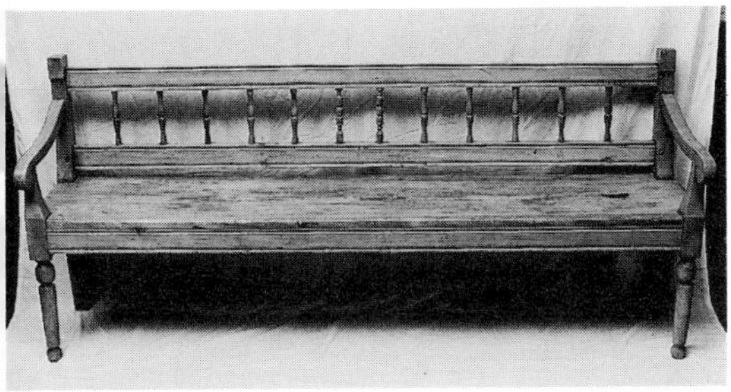

An Austrian pine bench, 1890, 78in (198cm) long.
£450–500 *ASP*

An early Victorian pine settle, with high panelled back, on sledge feet, c1840, 55½in (140cm) long.
£1,000–1,250 *POT*

A pine bench, c1870, 97in (246cm) long.
£250–300 *AL*

A pine settle/table, with worn top, c1860, 63in (160cm) long.
£950–1,100 *OCP*

An early Victorian pine monk's bench, with shaped back, 51in (129cm) wide.
£950–1,100 *POT*

A pine bench, c1870, 36in (91.5cm) wide.
£100–120 *AL*

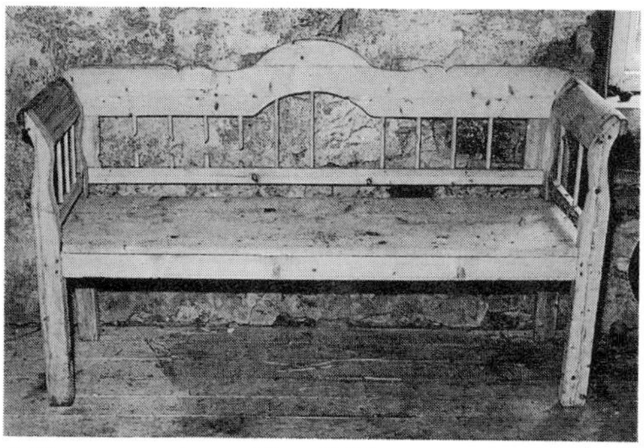

A European pine settle, c1870, 66in (167.5cm) wide.
£450–500 *AF*

A European pine and oak settle, c1840, 61½in (156cm) wide.
£450–500 *AF*

An Irish pine settle bed, c1875, 75in (190.5cm) long.
£450–500 *Byl*

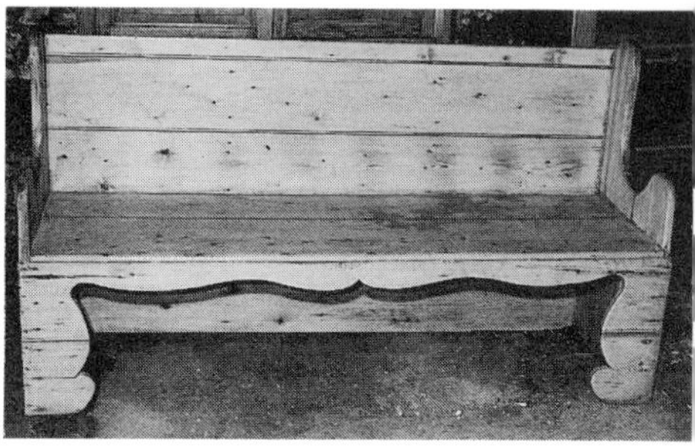

A pine settle, c1860, 72in (182.5cm) long.
£350–400 *OCP*

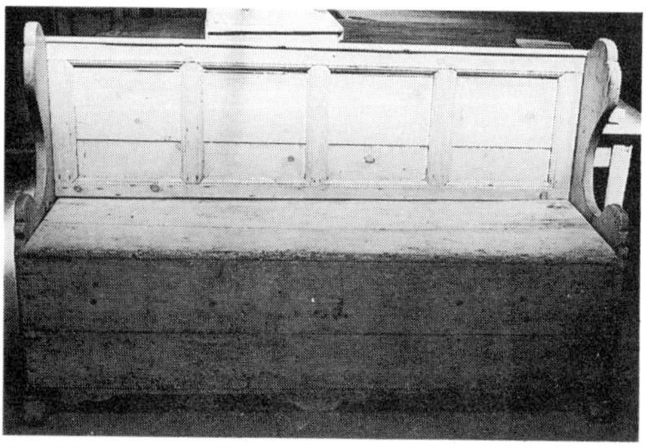

An Irish pine settle, with drop-down front, c1840, 72in (182.5cm) long.
£600–700 *DFA*

A carved pine bench, c1870, 73in (185cm) wide.
£350–400 *DFA*

A pine settle, c1870, 66in (167cm) long.
£850–1,000 *AL*

A carved pine high-back settle, c1780, 74in (188cm) long.
£1,700–2,000 *SA*

An Irish pine settle, with panelled back, 1850, 69in (175cm) long.
£850–1,000 *HON*

A round stick-back chair.
£60–70 *AL*

A balloon-back chair, with cane seat.
£60–70 *AL*

A pair of simulated bamboo chairs, c1840.
£200–250 *W*

A Regency cane-seated chair, 33in (84cm) high.
£250–300 *W*

A scroll back kitchen chair.
£70–80 *AL*

A set of 3 pine chairs, c1850.
£200–250 *W*

A stick-back chair.
£70–80 *AL*

A rocking chair, with cane seat and back, c1860, 34in (85cm) high.
£300–350 *AL*

A set of 4 pine chairs, pegged, 34½in (87cm) high.
£70–85 each *AL*

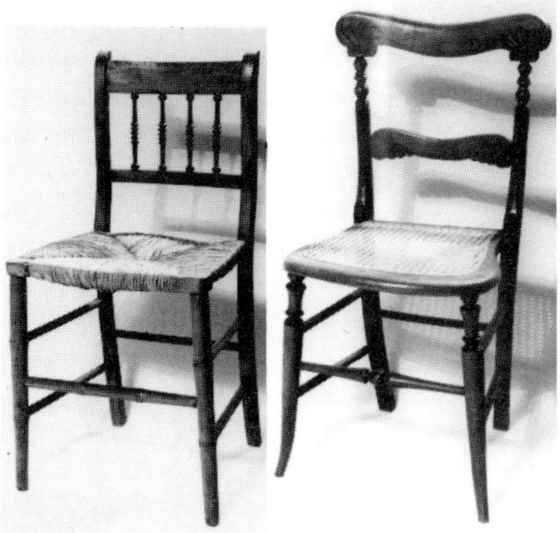
A rush-seated chair, and a cane-seated chair, c1860.
£60–70 each *AL*

An American pine and bleached mahogany rocking chair, on original casters, c1900, 42in (105cm) high.
£350–400 *LAM*

l. A pine chair, c1840.
£150–180 *AL*

A set of 4 beech chairs.
£250–300 *AL*

A beech chair, new cane seat, 31½in (80cm) high.
£85–100 *AL*

A reclining garden chair, c1880, 57in (144.5cm) wide.
£85–100 *PEN*

A pine captain's chair.
£275–325 *ASP*

A set of 4 pine slat-back kitchen chairs, 1870s.
£350–400 *ASP*

A Continental pine chair.
£170–200 *AF*

A set of 4 Victorian pine bar-backed kitchen chairs, c1860.
£350–400 *ASP*

A Continental pine rocking chair, with 8 legs, late 19thC.
£600–700 *ASP*

A primitive pine chair, with drawer under seat, c1880.
£350–400 *OCP*

A Continental kitchen chair, with shaped back and pine seat, c1860.
£70–80 *AF*

An Irish 'cock fighting' chair, 18thC.
£300–350 *AF*

A pub stool, with elm seat and beech legs, c1870, 19½in (49cm) high.
£70–80 *OPH*

A pub stool, with elm seat and beech legs, c1870, 19in (48cm) high.
£70–80 *OPH*

A country pine stool, c1860, 23in (59cm) high.
£70–85 *OPH*

l. A pine stool, original, c1860, 20½in (52cm) high.
£65–75 *FAG*

A pine stool, c1880, 26in (66cm) wide.
£70–80 *AL*

A pine milking stool, with 4 legs, c1870, 18in (46cm) wide.
£70–80 *OPH*

A pine stool, c1870, 18½in (47cm) wide.
£60–70 *OPH*

A round pine stool, c1880,
17½in (44cm) high.
£70–80 *CPA*

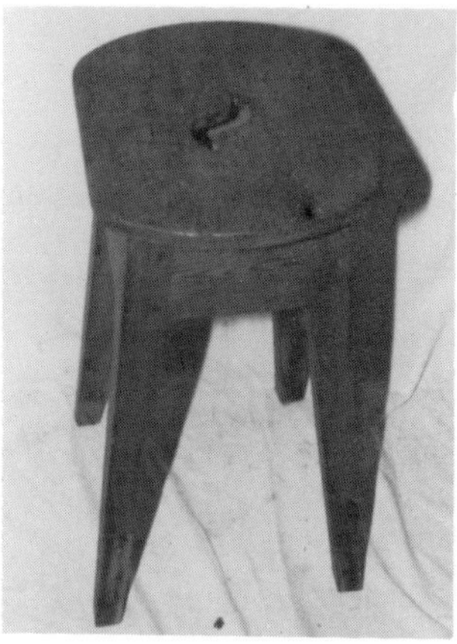

A pine stool.
£60–70 *WEL*

A pair of pine stools,
18in (45.5cm) high.
£100–110 *AL*

A set of pine steps, early 20thC,
28in (71cm) high.
£70–80 *AL*

A pine stool.
£50–60 *SPA*

A set of pine steps,
with metal fittings, c1900,
55in (140cm) high.
£75–90 *SPA*

A pine sloping desk stool,
29½in (73cm) high.
£85–100 *AL*

A pine stool,
14in (35.5cm) wide.
£60–70 *AL*

A pine stool, c1860, 12in (32cm) high.
£65–75 *AL*

A pine stool, 27in (67.5cm) high.
£100–120 *AL*

A Victorian pine stool,
48in (122cm) wide.
£130–150 *OA*

A pine stool, on turned legs,
28in (71cm) high.
£100–120 *AL*

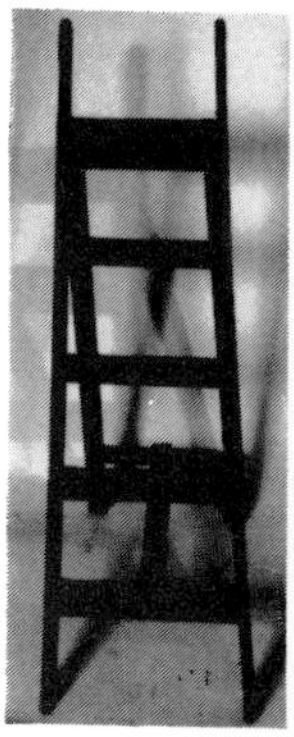

r. A set of pine
steps, 49in
(122.5cm) high.
£85–100 *AL*

A pine stool, c1880,
19in (48cm) high.
£70–80 *FAG*

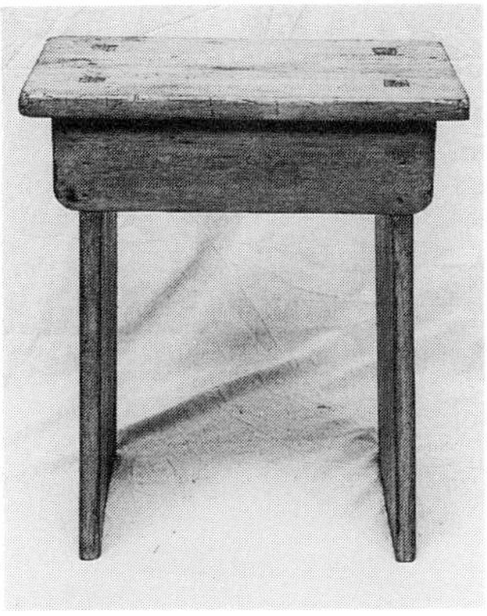

A pine country stool, c1880,
18in (46cm) wide.
£50–60 *ASP*

A pine bar stool, c1890,
21in (53cm) high.
£65–75 *ASP*

A pine bar stool, c1880,
18in (46cm) high.
£70–80 *ASP*

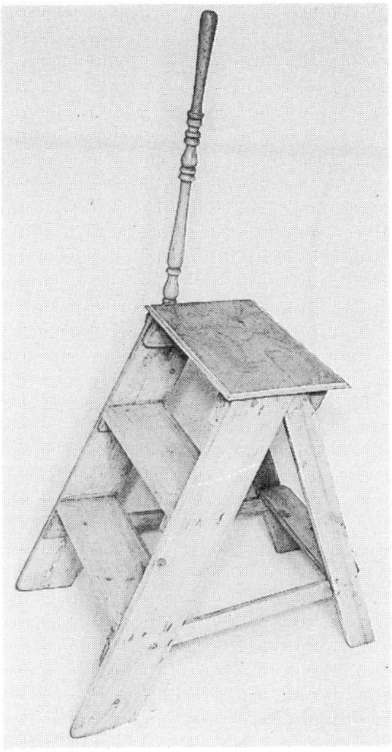

A set of pine library steps, c1880,
28in (71cm) high.
£400–450 *FAG*

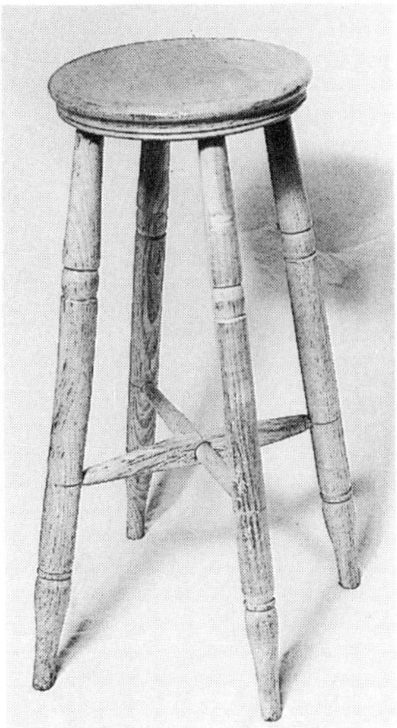

A Victorian bar stool, c1870,
29in (74cm) high.
£100–125 *OPH*

A pair of pine open-sided library
steps, c1900, 69in (175cm) high.
£100–125 *ASP*

A pine step ladder, c1890,
59in (149.5cm) high.
£100–125 *ASP*

A pine step ladder, c1900,
48in (122cm) high.
£85–100 *ASP*

A pine stool,
10in (25.5cm) diam.
£50–60 *AL*

A pine stool, 24in (61cm) wide.
£50–60 *AL*

A pine stool, c1880,
13in (33cm) wide.
£70–80 *AL*

A set of pine library
steps, restored, 18thC,
71in (180cm) high.
£850–1,000 *W*

A pine stool, 19thC,
12in (30.5cm) high.
£60–70 *AL*

A pine stool, 18in (45cm) wide.
£45–55 *AL*

A pair of pine stools, 19thC,
18in (46cm) high.
£100–120 *AL*

A rustic pine stool, c1840,
27in (69cm) wide.
£70–80 *AL*

A pine stool, c1880, 7in (17.5cm) high.
£60–70 *AL*

A stool, or small table, c1860,
15in (38cm) diam.
£50–60 *AL*

A pine shoe-cleaning
stool, 15in (38cm) hig
£80–95 *AL*

A pine stool, with hand-
hold in top, c1860,
24in (61cm) high.
£70–80 *AL*

A pine stool, 21in (53cm) high
£70–80 *AL*

A set of pine shelves, 21in (53cm) wide.
£90–110 *AL*

A French decorated pine shelf, Alsace region, c1880, 19in (48cm) wide.
£175–225 *MCA*

A pine pot rack, 37in (94cm) high.
£120–140 *AL*

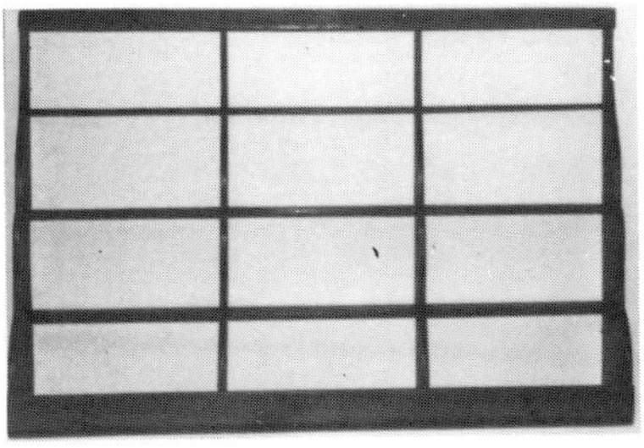

A set of pine hanging shelves, 38in (96.5cm) wide.
£175–250 *AL*

A set of pine hanging shelves, 17½in (44.5cm) wide.
£120–140 *AL*

A set of pine hanging shelves, c1860, 22in (56cm) wide.
£100–120 *AL*

A set of pine shelves, with bobbin-turned supports, c1850, 50in (127cm) high.
£350–400 *AL*

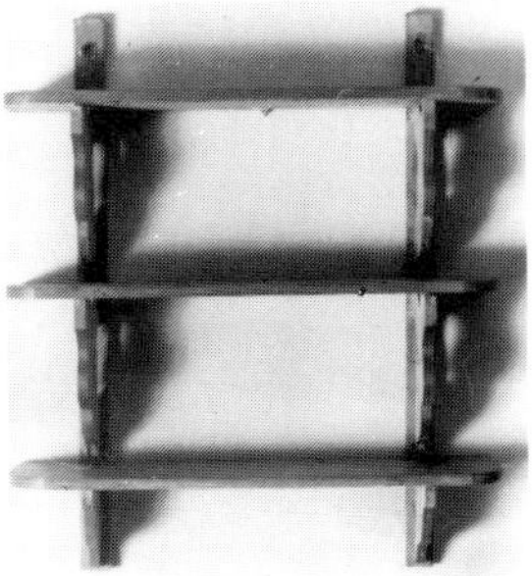

A set of pine hanging shelves, 23in (57.5cm) wide.
£125–150 *AL*

A set of pine shelves, c1860, 34in (87cm) wide.
£100–120 *AL*

A set of pine hanging shelves, 39in (97.5cm) wide.
£200–250 *PCL*

A set of pine bookshelves, c1860, 27in (68.5cm) wide.
£130–160 *AL*

A set of pine shelves, on a plinth base, 19thC, 27in (68.5cm) wide.
£175–225 *AL*

A pine corner unit, c1860, 31in (78.5cm) wide.
£250–300 *AL*

A tall pine shelf unit, c1860, 41in (104cm) wide.
£170–200 *AL*

A pair of George II-style carved pine open wall shelves, by Callow of Mount Street, with egg-and-tongue borders, each arched pediment centred by a female mask with adjustable shelves, c1930, possibly incorporating 18thC components, 38in (96.5cm) wide.
£2,500–3,000 *S(S)*

A set of pine shelves, c1860, 33in (84cm) wide.
£250–300 *AL*

A pine hanging wall shelf, c1860, 27½in (70cm) wide.
£170–200 *AL*

A pine rack, unpolished, early 19thC, 60in (152.5cm) wide.
£400–450 *CC*

A set of pine shelves, 36in (91.5cm) wide.
£125–150 *AL*

An early Victorian pine hanging delft rack, 43in (109cm) wide.
£550–650 *OA*

A set of Liberty pine shelves, c1890, 31in (78.5cm) high.
£100–120 *AL*

A pine hanging rack, 30in (76cm) wide.
£170–200 *OPH*

A set of pine shelves, c1870, 30in (76cm) wide.
£200–250 *AL*

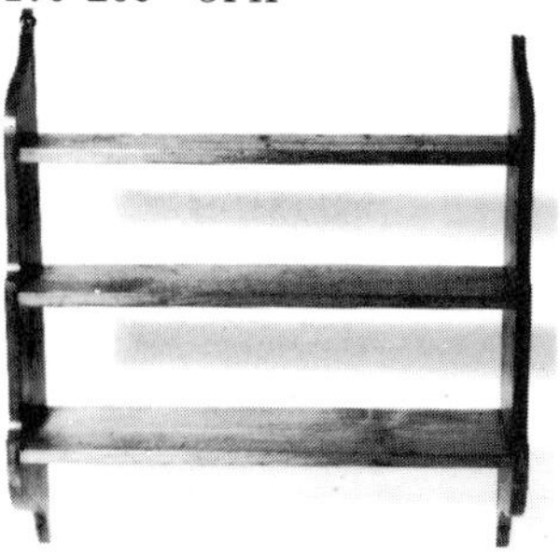

A Victorian pine hanging bookshelf, 30in (76cm) wide.
£85–100 *OA*

r. A set of pine bookshelves, 48in (122cm) high.
£200–250 *LAM*

set of German pitch pine hanging
ıelves, with fielded panels, late 19thC,
łin (62cm) high.
ł00–120 *HGN*

A pine shelf unit, with 'cotton reel' supports, 24in (61cm) wide.
£95–110 *FOX*

n Eastern European pine
hatnot, 48in (122cm) wide.
250–300 *AnD*

A pine wall shelf unit, c1890, 24in (61cm) wide.
£95–110 *AL*

A pine wall shelf unit, c1880, 36in (91.5cm) high.
£170–200 *AL*

. Victorian pine delft rack,
estored back and cornice, c1890,
0in (152cm) wide.
325–375 *POT*

A set of pine shelves, c1890, 29in (74cm) wide.
£95–110 *AL*

A pine dresser top, c1880, 44in (111.5cm) wide.
£170–200 *SA*

l. A pine wall shelf unit, 30in (76cm) wide.
£80–95 *FOX*

r. A pine wall shelf unit, c1880, 27in (69cm) wide.
£120–140 *AL*

A Victorian pine mirror frame, 38in (96.5cm) high.
£130–150 *Far*

A pine overmantel mirror, c1860, 44in (111.5cm) wide.
£140–160 *AL*

A pine-framed mirror, c1830, 34in (86cm) wide.
£200–250 *Far*

Two pine framed mirrors, 14 and 16in (36 and 41cm) square.
£65–75 *CPA*

A pine frame, 16in (41cm) wide.
£140–160 *AL*

A pine and elm dressing table mirror, c1860, 24 x 22in (60 x 55cm).
£200–250 *SSD*

A carved pine picture frame, 30 x 36in (76 x 92cm).
£250–300 *LAM*

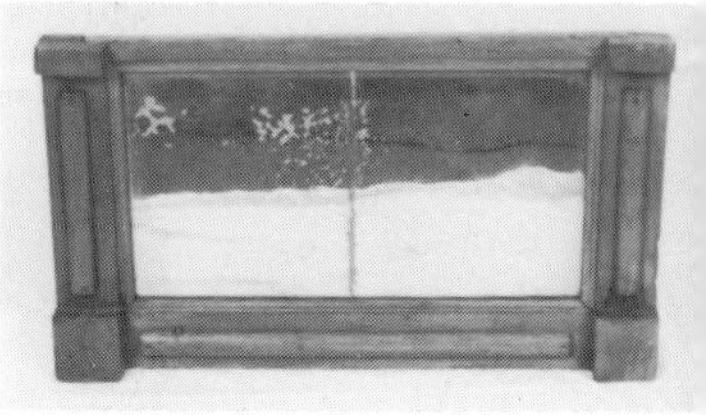

A pine overmantel mirror, 27in (69cm) wide.
£100–125 *AL*

A pine frame, c1860, 30 x 26½in (76 x 67cm).
£150–180 *SSD*

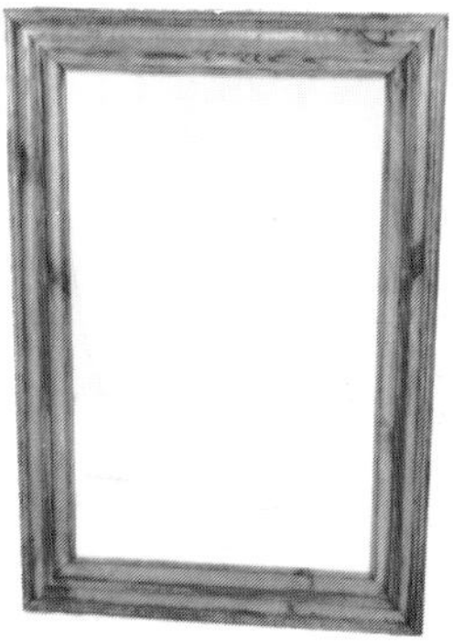

A pine mirror, 30in (77cm) wide.
£200–220 *AL*

A Victorian pine overmantel mirror, 40in (101.5cm) wide.
£200–250 *Far*

l. A pine cheval mirror, 19thC, 31in (77.5cm) wide.
£700–800 *PCL*

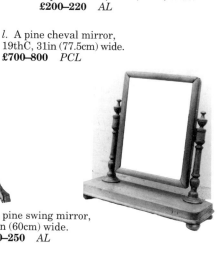

r. A pine swing mirror, 23½in (60cm) wide.
£200–250 *AL*

A pine dressing mirror, c1850, 23½in (60cm) wide.
£200–250 *AL*

A panelled pine fireplace, c1860.
£250–300 *AL*

A pair of French carved pine fireplace surrounds, 19thC, 79in (200cm) wide.
£6,500–7,500 *PH*

A pine door, with brass letter box, handles and finger plate, 26in (65cm) wide.
£200–250 *PCL*

A pine fireplace surround, 52in (132cm) high.
£250–300 *LAM*

A carved pine doorway, 59in (150cm) wide.
£3,000–3,500 *PH*

A pine fireplace, 38in (95cm) wide.
£250–300 *AL*

A Victorian pine fire surround, 40in (101.5cm) wide.
£250–300 *AL*

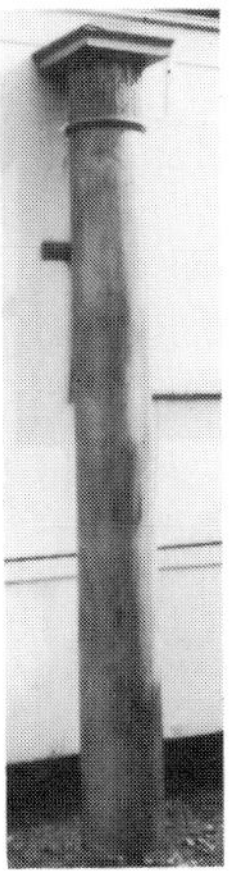

A pair of carved pine pillars, 95in (241cm) high.
£1,250–1,500 *GRF*

A reeded pine fire surround, 51in (129.5cm) wide.
£300–350 *LAM*

l. A Colonial white painted pine room section, comprising a fireplace surround and 2 cupboard doors with surrounds, each section with moulded corners above a fluted frieze with raised panels below, 96in (243.5cm) high.
£8,000–9,000 *S(NY)*

A pine and gesso fire surround, 18thC, 66in (167.5cm) wide.
£2,000–2,500 *AF*

l. An Irish pine internal door, with carved Gothic panels, c1800, 78in (198cm) high.
£450–500 *AF*

A pine architectural frame, c1880, 25in (64cm) wide.
£250–300 *HON*

A draper's display unit, with glazed doors and original handles and escutcheons, 75½in (191cm) wide.
£900–1,100 *LAM*

A set of West Country stocks, mid-19thC.
£700–800 *RP*

A hall stand, c1890, 71in (180cm) high.
£300–350 *AL*

A pine luggage rack, c1880, 25in (64cm) wide.
£100–120 *AL*

A pine plant stand, with tin liner, c1900, 46in (116cm) wide.
£170–200 *AL*

A brass gong, on a pine stand, c1860, 48in (122cm) high.
£300–350 *AL*

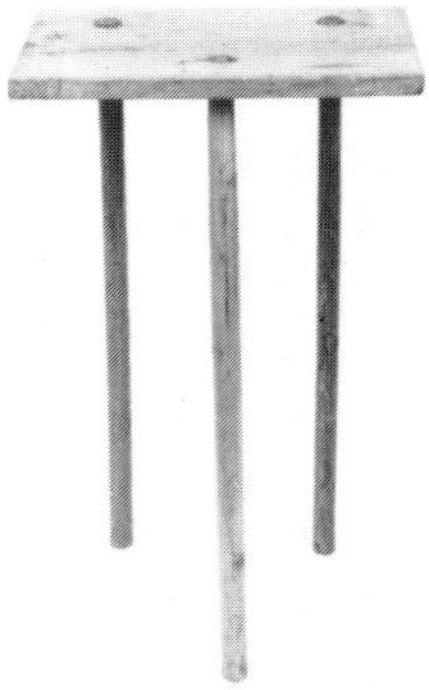

A primitive plant stand, c1840, 25in (64cm) high.
£75–90 *AL*

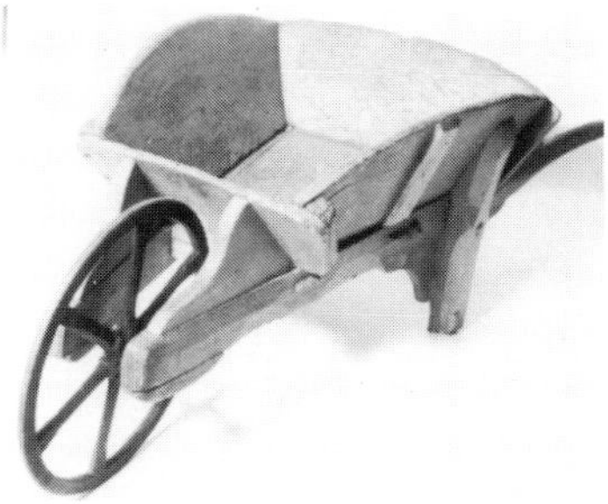

An elm wheelbarrow, with a wrought-iron wheel, c1860, 60in (152cm) long.
£300–350 *AL*

A pine stick stand, 41in (104cm) wide.
£350–400 *PH*

A Victorian pine screen, 70in (177.5cm) high.
£200–225 *AL*

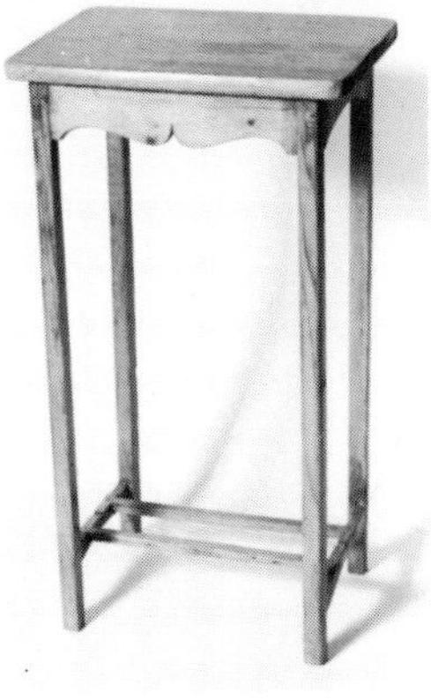

A small pine plant stand, 12in (30.5cm) wide.
£100–120 *AL*

A pine, fruitwood and tôle food cage, 18thC, 34in (86.5cm) wide.
£600–700 *MCA*

A pine game safe, with copper roof, for hanging 16 brace of game birds, 37in (94cm) high.
£500–600 *AL*

A pine easel, 43in (109cm) high.
£85–100 *AL*

A wheelbarrow, c1860, 26in (66cm) wide.
£250–300 *UP*

A large rocking horse, 87in (220cm) long.
£2,000–2,250 *PH*

l. An Irish pearwood rustic turf or peat box, Connemara, c1840, 36in (92cm) wide.
£700–800 *UC*

A pine shop counter, with a panelled back, 76in (193cm) wide.
£1,000–1,200 *RK*

A Victorian pine shop counter, c1870.
£1,000–1,250 *WEL*

A carved bear, with a flower holder, 22in (56cm) high.
£750–900 *PH*

A pine plant stand, c1910 60in (152cm) high.
£110–130 *SPA*

An iron-bound oak washtub on legs, Lincolnshire, c1890, 21in (53cm) diam.
£300–350 *UC*

A pair of painted carved fairground horses.
£2,000–2,200 *CSK*

A pine spinning wheel and spindle, late 19thC. **£200–250** *W*

A Victorian two-fold screen, restored, c1870.
£300–350 *PIN*

A pair of mid-Victorian mahogany hanging shelves, with shaped top rails, the shelves divided by turned baluster columns, 39in (99cm) wide.
£800–950 *C(S)*

A pine tub, 27in (69cm) diam.
£170–200 *AL*

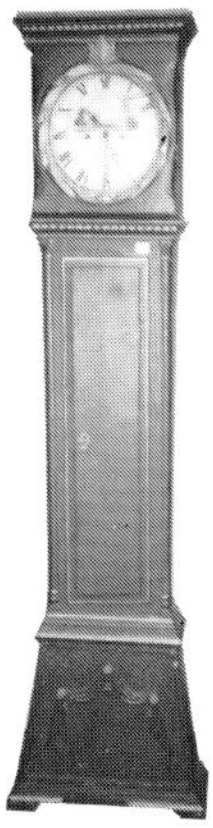

r. A Danish pine 8-day grandfather clock, with painted dial, c1862, 76in (192cm) high.
£1,200–1,400 *BEL*

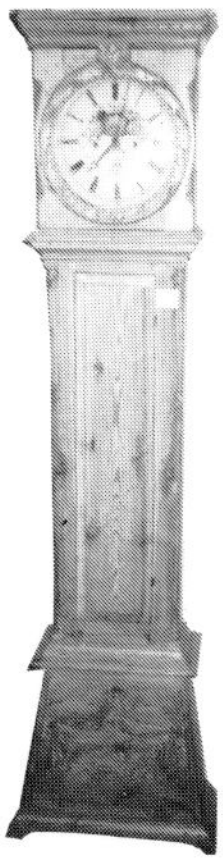

A pine frame, 23½in (60cm) wide.
£100–110 *LAM*

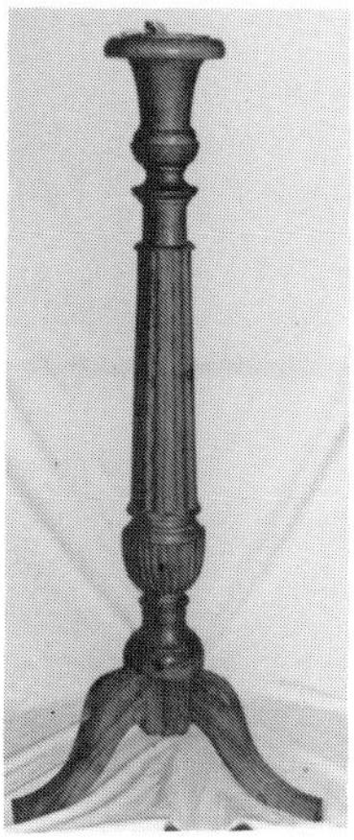

A pine torchère, 60in (152cm) high.
£450–500 *PH*

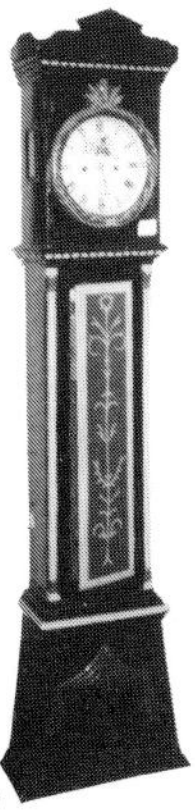

r. A Danish pine 8-day grandfather clock, with later paint, c1860, 73in (186cm) high.
£1,200–1,400 *BEL*

r. A Scandinavian pine sledge, 14in (36cm) long.
£90–110 *W*

A pine croquet box, 35½in (90cm) wide.
£120–140 *PAC*

Eleven German carved pine fairground gallopers, 19thC, smallest 36in (91.5cm) long.
£8,000–9,500 *CDC*

A pine writing box, 14½in (37cm) wide.
£150–180 *PH*

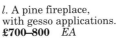

An easel, on a trestle base with casters, 92in (232.5cm) high.
£900–1,000 *CNY*

l. A pine fireplace, with gesso applications.
£700–800 *EA*

A pine box, on a later stand, c1880, 22in (56cm) high.
£150–170 *AL*

A pine hymn board.
£90–100 *WEL*

A set of pine pigeonholes, 37in (92.5cm) wide.
£130–150 *AL*

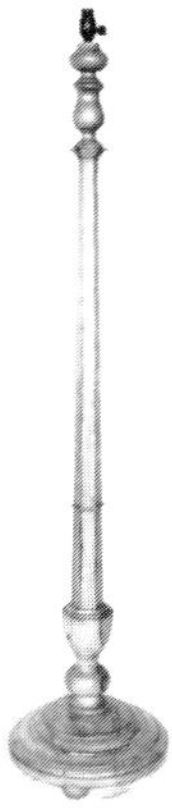

A pine standard lamp, 64½in (163cm) high.
£140–160 *LAM*

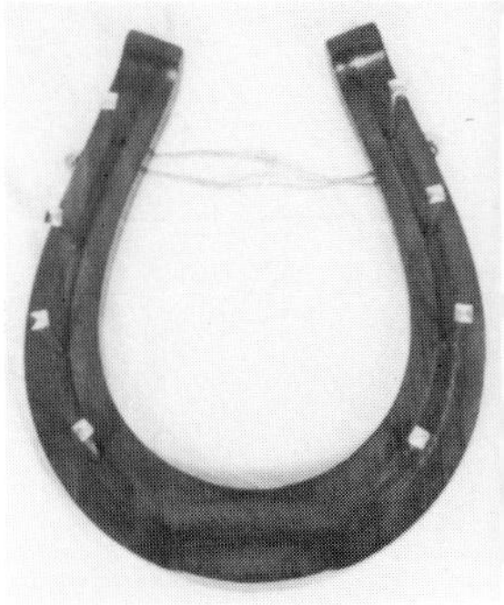

A set of pegs, on a horseshoe-shaped frame, c1920, 17½in (44cm) high.
£130–150 *AL*

A small pine stand, 19thC, 18in (45cm) high.
£100–120 *AL*

A carved and panelled pine mule chest, c1680, 48in (101.5cm) wide.
£1,300–1,500 *PH*

A pine umbrella stand, 23in (57.5cm) wide.
£130–150 *AL*

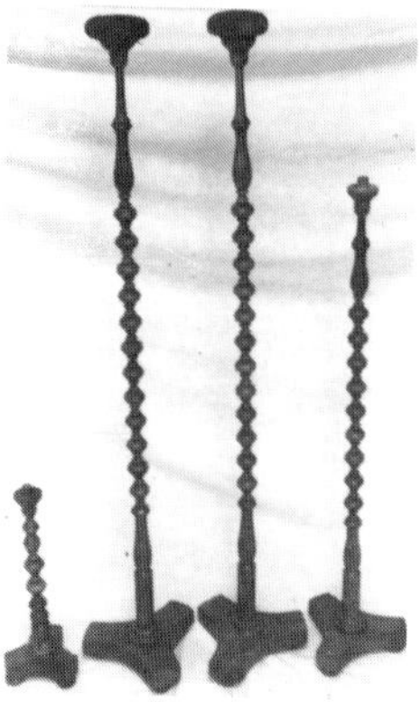

A set of pine hat stands, 2 with original pads, largest 38in (96.5cm) high.
£45–50 *PAC*

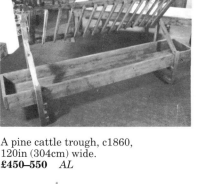

A pine cattle trough, c1860, 120in (304cm) wide.
£450–550 *AL*

An Edwardian pine coal box, with an iron carrying handle and brass side handles, 17in (43cm) wide.
£120–140 *OA*

A pine plant stand, c1850, 30in (76cm) high.
£80–95 *AL*

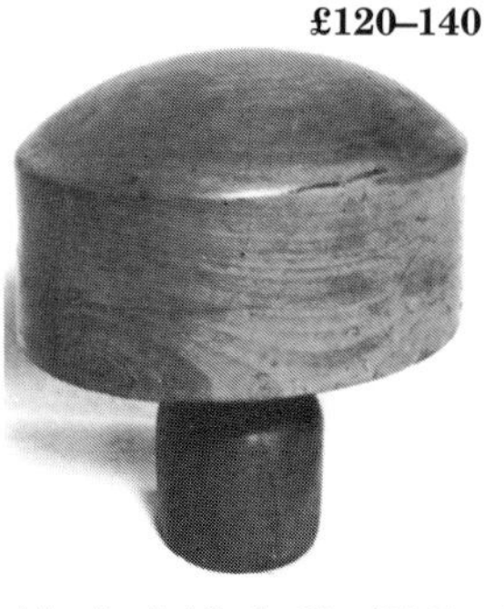

A hatter's block, 8in (20.5cm) high.
£40–50 *LAM*

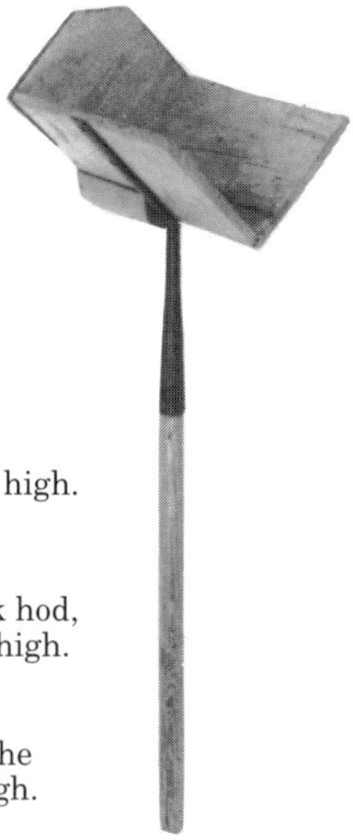

r. A pine brick hod, 48in (122cm) high.
£65–75 *AL*

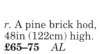

l. A pine hall stand, carved in the form of a bear, 85in (216cm) high.
£2,500–3,000 *Wor*

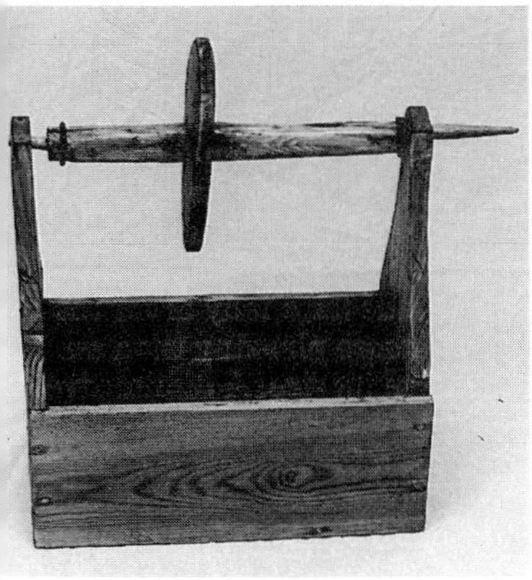

A pine Continental crofter's spinning box, 17in (43cm) wide.
£65–75 *ASP*

A treen pot, inscribed 'A.O. The Priory St. Ives, 1854', and 'Pear Tree'.
£100–120 *WaH*

A Welsh pine miniature chest of drawers, c1870, 14in (36cm) wide.
£130–150 *ASP*

A station master's pine luggage trolley, c1880, 48in (122cm) high.
£85–100 *ASP*

A pine coal scuttle, with metal mounts, 17in (43cm) wide.
£65–75 *OCP*

A pine tool box, with drawers, 18in (45.5cm) wide.
£75–90 *ASP*

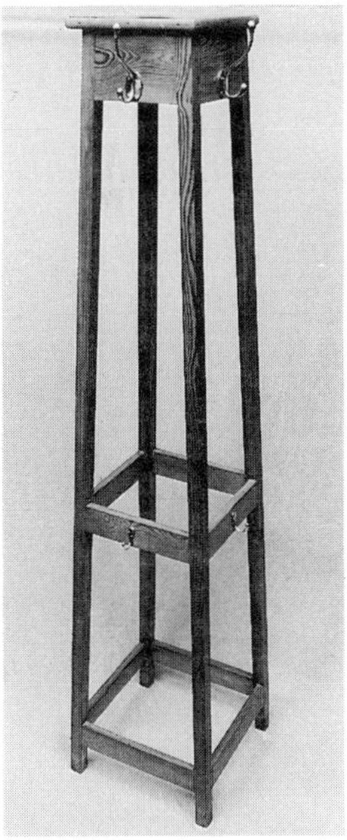

A pine hat and coat stand, c1900, 74in (188cm) high.
£130–150 *ASP*

r. A pine tool box, 1900, 18in (46cm) long.
£65–75 *ASP*

A carved pine eagle, c1900, 37½in (95cm) high.
£450–500 *ASP*

r. A varnished pine wheelbarrow, c1900, 28in (71cm) long.
£85–100 *ASP*

OAK & COUNTRY FURNITURE

Furniture historians recognize 'The Age of Oak' as being the years 1500 to 1660, coming before the ages of 'Walnut', 'Mahogany' and 'Satinwood'. One could easily be misled into thinking no furniture was made in oak after 1660 or, indeed, that any other timber could possibly have been used before that date. 'Oak furniture' seems to be a generic term applied to country-made pieces, as opposed to their sophisticated, city counterparts. Although much country furniture was made from oak, the generalisation encompasses a host of native timbers and country pieces are often found in chestnut, elm, ash, yew, walnut, pine, sycamore and the fruitwoods.

In the 18th century, these indigenous timbers were often stained with a dark dye, oiled and polished to simulate oak and thereby conform with popular fashion, and it is only in subsequent years that this finish has worn away, allowing us glimpses of the enchanting timbers hidden below. One could easily be forgiven for dismissing an early 18th-century side table as oak, when upon closer examination it was found to be walnut, fruitwood or even yew.

The type of timber, the condition of the piece, the proportion and patina, are important factors to collectors of this furniture, and as such can result in huge price differences. In general, all the country timbers are prized and have good colour and grain configuration, but rarer timbers such as yew, plum and cherry are infinitely more desirable. English cherry is rare, and as a rule was only used for smaller pieces (often constructed from narrow planks) or for turning or decorative work. It cannot be compared with French Provincial fruitwood furniture, which is of a softer, sunnier, more golden hue and fairly widely available.

Restoration work is tolerated in oak furniture, and often no attempt is made to conceal it. It is quite natural to find a 17th-century chair with an 18th-century replaced rail, or indeed a 19th-century seat – in 300 years of use it is only to be expected, but the restoration will be reflected in the price, especially when compared to a perfect example in museum condition. Restoration work that is unsympathetic or has attempted to enhance the object is not looked upon favourably. Late 17th-century panelled oak coffers were often 'carved-up' in the 19th century, and the panels emblazoned with flowers, dates and intricate patterns. This type of carving is totally different to the simple style of an early craftsman, and may explain why two carved oak coffers could have such different values.

The late 19th/early 20th century saw a revival in fashion of early, dark, carved oak, and many 1930s beamed properties are furnished with these early reproductions. Machine made and heavily varnished, they are worlds apart from their forefathers, but they nevertheless have their own following.

Style and proportion are important factors to consider, but rather hard to quantify. In general, 'small is beautiful'. A tiny oak bureau, probably made for a lady or for the smallest cottage, is more pleasing than an example almost twice its size. A diminutive North Wales dresser with perfectly proportioned panels, a full canopy rack and a host of tiny spice drawers with original patina is a superior piece to a large housekeeper's dresser recently removed from a farmhouse kitchen, stripped of its layers of gloss paint and refinished!

Outstanding craftsmanship is often apparent, but in general country pieces were not signed or stamped. Some early oak court cupboards, chests or chairs have been carved with the owner's initials, and possibly a date if the piece was a marriage or dowry item.

Extensive research has been undertaken into the history of English chairs and many Windsor chair varieties and certain ladderbacks bear the maker's stamp or date. However, early stick chairs, rustic tables and occasional pieces which seem to have been carved from a solid tree-trunk are often difficult to date or define. A dug-out, high-backed chair, carved from a massive section of elm begs the questions – when was the chair made? Moreover, how old is the elm tree from which it is carved? Rustic, simple items do have a unique charm, particularly if they have achieved a glorious colour and deep patina from daily use and polishing. Colour and patina are the foremost criteria for country furniture. Both go hand in hand, are impossible to fake and will be reflected in the asking price.

Ideally, one looks for a good colour, not just overall but with a variety of tones, the palest areas where wear would have been greatest and darker sections where neither hands nor sunlight has reached. The wood will be soft and silky to the touch and the piece should glow with a three-dimensional depth.

Oak furniture was never produced in great quantities in the 17th and 18th centuries, and was not fashionable for mass production after the Industrial Revolution. It is very good value and in general far less expensive than the later, mahogany equivalent. Oak furniture seems to be particularly fashionable in Britain at the moment, and also with Continental customers since changes in customs regulations have broken down trading barriers.

Prices have risen steeply over the last few years, particularly for untouched original pieces with genuine colour, surface and patina. Interest in the field is increasing, especially among the younger first-time furniture buyers and, as there is a finite supply, prices can only go one way and that is up! **Derek Green**

\n oak dresser, with 3 frieze
lrawers above 2 panelled
:upboards, c1780,
;8in (147cm) wide.
:3,000–3,500 *SKC*

An oak Welsh dresser,
18thC, 60in (152cm) wide.
£4,500–5,000 *DDM*

A Georgian oak Welsh
dresser, 64in (162.5cm) wide.
£3,500–4,000 *BMM*

A joined oak high dresser,
65in (165cm) wide.
£3,000–3,500 *L*

An oak Welsh dresser,
in original condition,
early 18thC, 51in (129.5cm) wide.
£4,000–4,500 *WIL*

An oak dresser, the lower
part with 3 frieze drawers,
mid-18thC, 63in (160cm) wide.
£4,000–4,500 *SC*

A George II oak and elm dresser,
c1740, 80in (203cm) wide.
£8,000–9,500 *SS*

An oak Welsh dresser, early
18thC, 54in (137cm) wide.
£4,000–4,500 *H*

An oak Welsh dresser, with
good colour and patination,
c1740, 63in (160cm) wide.
£5,000–6,000 *H*

r. A Georgian oak cottage
dresser, with good patina,
57in (144.5cm) wide.
£3,500–4,000 *L*

An oak dresser base, the inverted breakfront top above a central drawer and cupboard between reeded half columns, flanked by 3 drawers to either side, with outer channelled columns, on multiple bracket feet, one corner block missing, early 18thC, 72in (182.5cm) wide.
£8,000–9,500 *C*

An oak dresser, with moulded top above drawers, on barley-twist legs.
£2,500–3,000 *DN*

A George III elm dresser, with moulded top, three frieze drawers and shaped apron, on shell carved cabriole legs with pad feet, 66in (168cm) wide.
£3,000–3,500 *DN*

An oak low dresser, with 7 moulded panelled drawers around a fielded panelled door, 18thC, 68in (172cm) wide.
£3,000–3,500 *DN*

An oak dresser, the moulded fruitwood top above 3 frieze drawers and a pair of cupboard doors with geometric mitred mouldings, on turned stile feet, restored, c1700, 58½in (148cm) wide.
£6,000–7,000 *S(S)*

A George III fruitwood dresser, the back with a plain gallery above 3 drawers, on plain turned tapered legs, restored, c1800, 64in (163cm) wide.
£2,000–2,500 *Bon*

l. A George III oak enclosed dresser base, with moulded edged top, central drawer with ogee panelled door below, flanked on either side by 3 drawers with brass drop handles, panelled sides, moulded base and bracket feet, 73in (185cm) wide.
£6,000–7,000 *AH*

A George III oak dresser, the moulded cornice above an open shelf back, on bracket feet, possibly reduced in width, c1790, 46in (117cm) wide.
£3,000–3,500 *S(S)*

An oak dresser, with shaped apron carved with fan motifs and on square legs, early 19thC, 51in (129.5cm) wide.
£4,500–5,500 *S*

An oak dresser, inlaid with satinwood and boxwood, on turned tapering legs, parts 18thC, 74½in (189cm) wide.
£3,000–3,500 *CSK*

An oak Welsh dresser, on block feet, 18thC, 61in (154.5cm) wide.
£4,500–5,500 *CSK*

An oak dresser, with baluster turned uprights and bun feet, joined by an undertier, 94in (239cm) wide.
£2,000–2,500 *CSK*

An oak Welsh dresser carved with the letters 'A.M.O.W.B.', early 18thC, 64½in (163cm) wide.
£4,500–5,500 *Bon*

An oak dresser, mid-18thC, 58in (147cm) wide.
£2,500–3,000 *SBe*

An oak dresser base, on straight feet, having 3 fielded panelled doors and 3 drawers over, 18thC, 71in (180cm) wide.
£4,500–5,500 *JD*

A pair of oak dresser bases, probably adapted from a single dresser base, each with rectangular top above 2 frieze drawers and waved apron, on baluster turned uprights and block feet, part 18thC, 46in (117cm) wide.
£3,000–3,500 *CSK*

An oak dresser and rack, with moulded dentil cornice and waved frieze, 18thC and later, 70in (178cm) wide. **£3,000–3,500** *CSK*

l. An oak and pine dresser, with chamfered square legs joined by a platform stretcher, restored, late 18thC, 55in (139cm) wide.
£4,500–5,500 *S(S)*

An oak dresser, the upper section with a moulded cornice and 3 shelves flanked by inlaid uprights, the base with ebony stringing to the 3 frieze drawers and central simulated drawers, the 2 doors with crossbanded panels, on shaped stile feet, early 19thC, 63in (160cm) wide.
£4,500–5,500 *Bea*

An ash canopy cupboard dresser, with fielded panels to the doors and drawers, c1690.
£15,000–18,000 *Ced*

An oak dresser, with 3 shelves to the top, and 3 drawers to base, on 4 baluster supports and pot-board, 18thC, 68in (172.5cm) wide.
£5,500–6,500 *RBB*

A stained dresser, with 3 shelves, 7 drawers and 2 cupboards, mid-Wales, c1780.
£3,500–4,000 *COM*

An oak dresser, the upper section with planked plate rack, 3 small frieze drawers, block legs and potboard to base, 18thC, 57½in (146cm) wide.
£4,500–5,500 *WL*

A George III oak dresser, the top with moulded cornice above 3 shelves, 3 frieze drawers above a shaped apron with two further small drawers to base, on turned legs with a platform base, 54in (137cm) wide.
£4,500–5,500 *DN*

A Welsh oak dresser, the boarded backed top with 3 shelves and hooks, the base with 3 frieze drawers, on 4 turned front supports to a potboard, and bracket feet, 18thC, 67in (170cm) wide.
£4,500–5,500 *B*

An Irish dresser, with carved three-shelf top, 3 drawers and 2 cupboards to base, c1800.
£4,500–5,500 *B*

A Georgian fruitwood dresser, with open plate rack, above a base with 3 long drawers, on cabriole legs, alterations, 18thC, 62in (157cm) wide.
£2,500–3,000 *MMG*

n oak dresser base, the 3 drawers cockbeaded and ık lined, shaped apron, cabriole front legs, brackets issing, square section back of legs, old restoration, ırly 18thC, 73in (185cm) long.
3,500–4,000 *WIL*

An oak dresser, the rack with lambrequin frieze above 3 central shelves flanked by arcaded doors to cupboards on either side, on a base with 4 frieze drawers, above two central cupboards, each with 2 arcaded fielded panels flanked on either side by 2 further drawers, and canted reeded corners, 18thC, 96in (243.5cm) wide.
£12,000–14,500 *B*

A George III Montgomeryshire oak dresser base, with 3 cockbeaded frieze drawers above cockbeaded and shaped aprons, baluster turned legs, framed pot board, 75in (190.5cm) wide.
£8,000–9,500 *P(S)*

A George II oak dresser, with open shelf back above a pair of frieze drawers and an ogee arched apron, the turned and square supports joined by a platform stretcher, reduced in size from a larger dresser, back probably associated, altered, 51½in (130cm) wide.
£2,800–3,500 *S(S)*

n oak Anglesey dresser, with pine ack, three-shelf rack, breakfront ase, with 4 central drawers and uarter columns, one drawer and ıpboard to each side, 19thC, 7in (170cm) wide.
3,500–4,000 *WIL*

A Charles II style oak dresser, with moulded cornice above open shelves and a pair of geometrically panelled frieze drawers, on turned and square legs, 54½in (138cm) wide.
£12,000–14,500 *S(S)*

n oak dresser base, the moulded top above frieze drawers, with columnar turned and ąuare supports, mid-18thC, 75½in (192cm) wide.
4,000–4,500 *S(S)*

An oak dresser, the shallow raised back with small drawers, the base with drawers surrounding a cupboard, now on casters, damaged, late 18thC, 71in (180cm) wide.
£5,000–6,000 *S(S)*

Welsh Furniture

It may be a surprise to some that a small country such as Wales could have such an impact on the furniture market. But it is a strong indication of the quality and variety of furniture produced there, that such an astonishingly large proportion of collectable country furniture originated in Wales.

Produced from the early 16th century, evolving styles showed considerable innovation in response to local needs and owed little to urban fashion. Certain cupboards and chests, such as the 'coffor bach', the 'cwpwrdd tridarn' and 'cwpwrdd deuddarn', are so distinctive that they are known universally by their Welsh names.

An oak 'coffor bach', with inlaid decoration in holly and bog oak in a design typical of West Wales, 1750–80.

However, it is the dresser that has achieved the greatest fame. So diverse that no two are identical, the Welsh dresser admirably combines both practical and decorative features, and the overall market for the more unusual examples has never been healthier.

With a reputation for being solidly constructed, with a fine polished finish, Welsh furniture was made to be functional, designed for a specific purpose, and often for a specific location. Local carpenters preferred to use native timbers – the most sought-after type of Welsh furniture today is made from figured red-black oak, which grew on exposed mountain-sides. Although other woods such as ash, elm and fruitwood were used, a mixture of woods is often found in the same piece. This is an indication of the suitability of certain timbers for the particular parts, the availability of usable boards, or cost considerations.

During the 19th century 'oak' dressers, for example, may commonly have comprised shelves and even potboards made from pine. The craftsmen, who were not full-time furniture makers, would also have produced everyday items, from spinning wheels to gates, using a range of techniques. This resulted in unexpected and interesting methods of construction, reflected in the frequent absence of dovetails from drawers, especially in the finely panelled cupboards from North Wales.

The demand for useful pieces had always been strong, but of course the requirements of the modern home do not match those of the 18th century farmhouse. Certain items such as long tables and sets of chairs, were always scarce – cupboards deep enough to hold a hi-fi are decidedly rare! Furniture was traditionally an important acquisition, intended to be handed down to future generations. The sheer quantity of large presses, dressers and chests found in Wales has led to much 'recycling', so be wary when buying – you may well be offered pieces that have been substantially altered to make them more suited to 20th century life.

Although basically utilitarian, Welsh dressers typically contain decorative embellishments including shaped panels, fretted friezes and carved or inlaid dates and initials. The presence of such elements adds considerably to the desirability of an item, and is reflected in the higher price. Remember, too, the fact that pieces were made to be used will have resulted in everyday wear and tear, minor damage and variation in colour – all factors forming an important part of the furniture's appeal.

Recently, there has been emphasis on the identification of the precise regional origins of pieces, and the singularity of certain features suggests that local styles should be discernible. For instance, flowing designs of floral inlay were confined to a few areas in South Wales, and the famed 'cwpwrdd tridarn' was only found in Snowdonia. But plainer forms, such as stick chairs and stools, were produced over a wide area, thus making specific identification difficult.

An oak 'cwpwrdd tridarn', carved and inlaid with marriage initials and '1731', Conwy Valley, Caernarfonshire.

The last few years have witnessed a significant increase in interest from the home market for more unusual items, or those with a reliable provenance. Trade from North America and the Continent, who have both in the past imported vast numbers of Welsh dressers, cupboards and chests, still remains active.

There is a continually growing demand for the best original pieces that are now becoming scarcer and increasingly valuable.

Richard Bebb

n oak and inlaid dresser, the pen shelf back with pilasters, ne base with frieze drawers, pair of panel doors with fan nedallions flanking a central rawer and 2 dummy drawers, tile feet with shaped brackets, Jorth Wales, early 19thC, 3in (160cm) wide.
5,000–6,000 *S(S)*

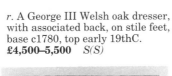

r. A George III Welsh oak dresser, with associated back, on stile feet, base c1780, top early 19thC.
£4,500–5,500 *S(S)*

A George III elmwood Welsh dresser, late 18thC, 52½in (133cm) wide.
£3,500–4,000 *SKB*

r. An oak dresser, the associated open shelf back above 4 shallow drawers, 5 frieze drawers above turned supports with fan-shaped angle brackets, on a platform base and square feet, South Wales, early 19thC, 60½in (153cm) wide.
£6,000–7,000 *S(S)*

An oak dresser, the associated open shelf ack with a pair of cupboards, the base vith 4 frieze drawers, an open recess and pair of panelled doors, on shaped bracket eet, restored, North Wales, early 19thC, 2½in (234cm) wide.
2,500–3,000 *S(S)*

A Georgian elmwood and fruitwood Welsh dresser, the base with 3 drawers, on cabriole legs, rack replaced, restored, 62in (157cm) wide.
£1,000–1,200 *MMG*

An oak Welsh dresser, the 2 cupboards and 2 drawers below a panelled plate rack, c1720, 50in (127cm) wide.
£5,000–6,000 *KHD*

An oak dresser, in original condition, replaced brasses, North Wales, 50in (127cm) wide.
£8,000–9,500 *H*

An oak Welsh dresser, the bas with 3 frieze drawers, above 3 short drawers flanked by a pair of cupboards, c1750, 62½in (159cm) wide.
£4,000–4,500 *S(S)*

An George III oak dresser, c1770, 64in (162.5cm) wide.
£5,000–6,000 *S*

An oak Welsh dresser, with raised ogee arched panels, on ogee bracket feet, mid-18thC, 72in (182.5cm) wide.
£8,000–9,500 *Bea*

A late Georgian oak Welsh dresser, with 6 drawers and 2 cupboard doors, later turned ebony handles, 69in (174.5cm) wide.
£3,500–4,000 *C*

An oak Welsh dresser, with 3 frieze drawers and 2 cupboard doors below, mid-18thC.
£17,000–20,000 *PHA*

An oak Welsh dresser, with spice drawers, all crossbanded in burr oak, mid-18thC, 74in (188cm) wide.
£7,000–8,500 *PJ*

An oak Welsh dresser, with fielded panelled cupboard doors, in original condition, 69in (175cm) wide.
£6,000–7,000 *H*

l. An oak Welsh dresser, 18thC, 64in (162.5cm) wide.
£4,000–4,500 *LRG*

. matched set of 6 Charles II carved oak 'orkshire chairs, now with figured seat ushions and loose covers, c1680.
8,000–9,500 *S(S)*

A Charles I oak coffer, with moulded top above a fluted frieze, the panelled front carved with stylized flowerheads and initials 'AW' flanked by foliate strapwork and stile supports, Somerset, c1640, 42in (106cm) wide.
£2,000–2,500 *S(S)*

A Windsor chair, one arm repaired, mid-19thC.
£2,500–3,000 *C*

\n oak bench, with a padded seat covered in close-nailed)rown leather, on turned legs and square channelled ;tretchers, mainly 17thC, 60in (152.5cm) wide.
:3,500–4,000 *C*

An ebonized oak and fruitwood chest in 2 sections, inlaid with ivory and mother-of-pearl, dated '1652'.
£6,000–7,000 *C*

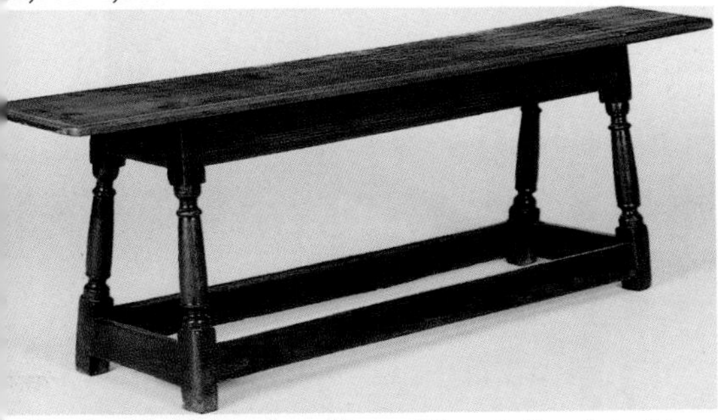

\ Charles II oak bench, with a solid seat, the plain frieze vith channels, on 4 baluster legs joined by stretchers, ›ne stretcher replaced, 67in (170cm) wide.
:3,000–3,500 *C*

A William and Mary line-inlaid burr-yew chest, with later veneer and bun feet.
£7,000–8,000 *C*

. Welsh primitive chair, ry-scraped down to its riginal paint finish.
1,500–1,800 *SWN*

A Queen Anne oak bureau bookcase, with associated top, on later bun feet, c1710, 79in (200.5cm) high.
£3,500–4,000 *S(S)*

r. An oak bureau, on bracket feet, early 19thC, 36in (91.5cm) wide.
£2,000–2,500 *GAK*

A beech and elm slat-back chair, c1880.
£50–60 *AL*

A Continental oak strong box, with 3 locks and keys, c1730, 22in (55.5cm) wide.
£1,000–1,200 *KEY*

A miniature oak chest of drawers, 19thC, 8in (20.5cm) wide.
£180–200 *Ber*

r. An oak spice cabinet, with 11 interior drawers, 16in (40.5cm) wide.
£500–600 *JH*

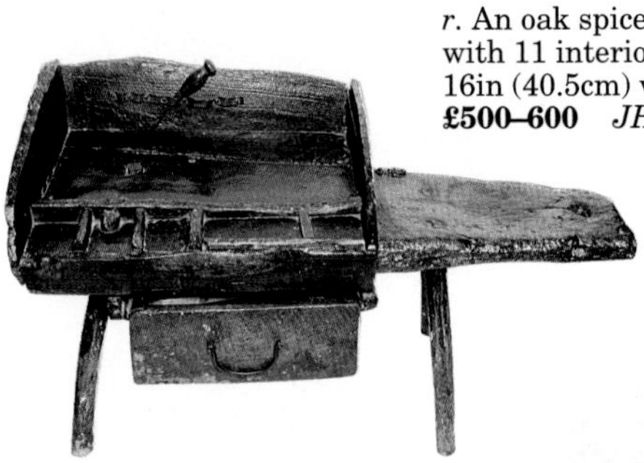

A Welsh cobbler's oak bench, in original condition, early 19thC, 38in (96.5cm) wide.
£850–1,000 *RYA*

A child's school desk, 26in (66cm) high.
£25–30 *Ber*

A shepherd's ash dug-out chair, with a cupboard beneath the seat, early 18thC, 24½in (62cm) wide.
£8,500–10,000 *RYA*

An early Victorian child's nursery table with original paint.
£475–500 *SWN*

An oak side table, c1690, 26in (66cm) high.
£3,000–3,500 *KEY*

An American bentwood chair, with carving on the seat and back, c1910.
£180–200 *Ber*

A scroll-back Windsor chair, c1880.
£70–80 *AL*

A table, the sycamore top with cleats, over a painted elm base with 3 drawers, c1800.
£1,200–1,400 *SWN*

An oak refectory table, 17thC, 57in (144.5cm) long.
£3,000–3,500 *SPa*

A farmhouse Windsor carver, with original green paint, 18thC.
£500–600 *SWN*

A pair of yew-wood high-back Windsor chairs, 19thC.
£2,500–3,000 *SPa*

A Windsor chair, with hickory arms, original paint, possibly American, 18thC.
£950–1,100 *SPa*

A beech and elm child's chair, c1920.
£35–45 *AL*

An elm night commode, with carving, late 17thC.
£750–900 *SWN*

A Welsh Windsor chair.
£250–300 *PC*

A pine tavern table, heavily carved through use, late 18thC, 60in (152cm) wide.
£2,500–3,000 *SWN*

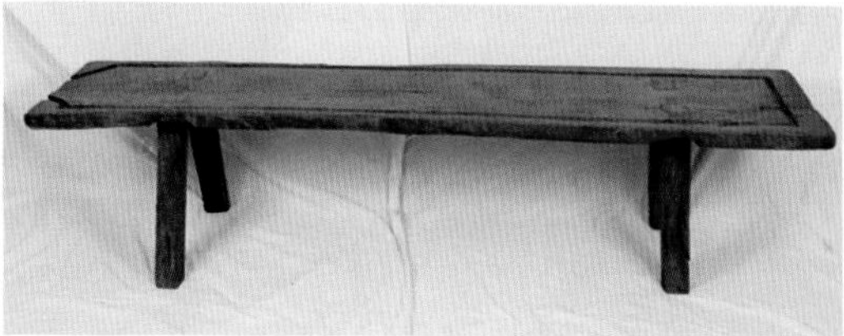

A chestnut washboard, with oak legs, 19thC, 69in (175cm) long.
£400–450 *SPa*

A primitive Windsor comb-backed armchair, with traces of original paint, c1780.
£2,500–3,000 *RYA*

A child's fruitwood chair, 19thC.
£250–300 *SWN*

A stick back chair, c1880.
£60–70 *AL*

A country stool, c1900, 10½in (26.5cm) high.
£40–50 *Ber*

A set of wedge/wheel-back Windsor chairs, comprising: 3 side chairs and one carver, c1890.
£400–450 *AL*

An oak panelled-back carver chair, with a primitive crest, early 17thC.
£1,500–1,800 *SWN*

A comb-back Windsor chair, with original paint, c1870.
£1,000–1,200 *PC*

Eight ash and elm Windsor chairs, with draught patterned splats, 18thC.
£2,800–3,200 *SPa*

l. A child's stick chair, with panelled seat, late 18thC.
£1,500–1,800
c. A comb back beech and ash stick chair, c1800.
£1,200–1,500
r. A Welsh oak child's backstool/stick chair, c1700.
£2,000–2,500 *CAL*

A Celtic elm box chair, early 19thC.
£1,000–1,200 *FHA*

A set of 4 Dutch ladder back chairs, with rush seats, c1880, 43in (109cm) high.
£1,000–1,200 *AnD*

An ash reclining ladderback chair, with wrought iron ratchet mechanism, c1800.
£1,800–2,000 *CAL*

A pair of ladderback chairs, with rush seats, early 20thC.
£120–150 *AnD*

A Continental lignum vitae turned ladderback chair, early 19thC.
£1,900–2,200 *CAL*

A rustic stick chair of angular design and construction, showing traces of original paint.
£2,000–2,500 *CAL*

l. A yew-wood comb-back Windsor chair, with cabriole legs, c1740.
£5,000–6,000 *CAL*

A yew-wood turner's chair, with an oak panelled seat, early 17thC.
£8,500–10,000 *CAL*

A pair of stick-back chairs, the back with 2 iron rods, c1880.
£100–120 *AL*

A school chair, c1920.
£30–35 *Ber*

A bar-back Windsor chair, c1880.
£50–55 *AL*

A spindle-back Windsor chair, c1880.
£60–70 *AL*

A beech and elm chair, c1920.
£35–40 *FAG*

A smoker's bow chair, c1900.
£160–200 *FAG*

A penny seat chair, c1900.
£45–55 *AL*

A folding chapel chair, c1900.
£40–50 *AL*

A set of 4 French chairs, with rush seats, c1930.
£350–400 *Ber*

A French chair, with rush seat and original paintwork, early 19thC.
£40–50 *FOX*

A pine step ladder, early 20thC, 58in (147cm) high.
£70–80 *FOX*

An Irish painted stool, with rush seat, 13in (33cm) high.
£70–80 *Ber*

A chopping bench, c1850, 54in (137cm) wide.
£150–180 *MIL*

An oak joined stool, the plain top above a shaped frieze on ring-turned tapering legs tied by block stretchers, mid-17thC, 19½in (49.5cm) wide.
£5,000–6,000 *Bon*

An oak country stool, early 19thC, 17in (43cm) high.
£100–120 *SHA*

An oak joined stool, the associated top above a moulded frieze on turned column supports tied by block stretchers, mid-17thC and later, 18in (46cm) wide.
£200–250 *Bon*

A kitchen stool, c1900, 22in (56cm) high.
£85–100 *MIL*

A pair of oak joined stools, the bevelled plank seats above moulded friezes on ring-turned column supports and peg feet, 18in (46cm) wide.
£4,000–4,500 *Bon*

An oak stool, c1850, 22in (55.5cm) wide.
£130–150 *MIL*

George III Provincial oak nd pollard oak linen press, ith a moulded cornice above panelled doors, plain interior ith a well, 40in (101.5cm) wide.
2,500–3,000 *C*

A North Wales oak clothes press, with arched panelled doors above fielded drawers, on a later plinth base, late 18thC, 79in (201cm) wide.
£3,500–4,000 *S(S)*

A yew wood cupboard or press, early 18thC, 72in (183cm) wide.
£4,500–5,500 *CAL*

An oak press cupboard, with moulded cornice above 2 panelled doors, the base with panelled front and 2 drawers below, on stile feet, 51in (129.5cm) wide.
£1,500–1,800 *C*

A French oak buffet 'deux corps', with 4 doors, c1840, 57in (145cm) wide.
£2,000–2,500 *UC*

An oak clothes press, with a pair of fielded panelled doors above drawers, on bracket feet, cornice damaged, late 18thC, 61in (155cm) wide.
£2,750–3,250 *S(S)*

A Welsh sycamore two-part cupboard, 54in (137cm) high.
£4,500–5,000 *CAL*

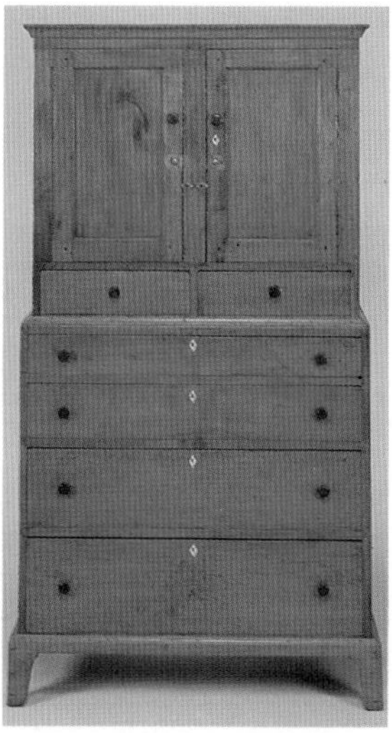

A Shaker bone-inlaid butternut cabinet, over 4 drawers, from Harvard Community, Mass, 36in (91.5cm) wide.
£25,000–30,000 *S(NY)*

An oak press cupboard, the moulded cornice above 2 fielded panelled doors, above 4 panels and 5 drawers, 61in (155cm) wide.
£3,500–4,500 *S(S)*

A Spanish walnut bread table, c1600, 37in (94cm) wide.
£1,800–2,200 *FHA*

An oak gateleg occasional table, with elliptical leaves, on bobbin turned column, with square section stretcher support, c1670, 26in (66cm) wide.
£3,800–4,200 *Bon*

A burr-oak joined folding table, the tilt-top on slender baluster supports with a single gateleg action, c1680, 31in (78.5cm) diam.
£4,500–5,000 *Bon*

An oak refectory table, the later three-plank top with end cleats, the frieze carved with a leaf scroll border, with 6 baluster turned square legs joined by stretchers, mid-17thC, 89in (226cm) wide.
£5,000–6,000 *S(S)*

An oak refectory table, with a cleated three-plank top, the frieze carved with a foliate border, on baluster turned and square legs, mid-17thC, 80in (203cm) long.
£3,500–4,200 *S(S)*

A sycamore and ash cricket table, the turned legs joined by a platform stretcher, early 18thC.
£3,500–4,000 *S*

An oak gateleg table, with a later pine frieze drawer, the baluster turned legs joined by conforming stretchers, mid-18thC, 76in ((193cm) wide.
£5,500–6,000 *S(S)*

An oak refectory table, the reduced top above a channel moulded frieze carved with lunettes, on block feet, mid-17thC, 87in (220cm) long.
£2,200–2,800 *S(S)*

. Welsh oak bureau cabinet, with stepped nterior, mid-18thC, 37in (34cm) wide.
'9,500–11,000 *CoA*

A Welsh oak and fruitwood food cupboard, 18thC, 31½in (80cm) wide.
£5,000–6,000 *CoA*

A Welsh oak 'cwpwrdd tridarn', 17thC, 54in (37cm) wide.
£8,500–10,000 *CoA*

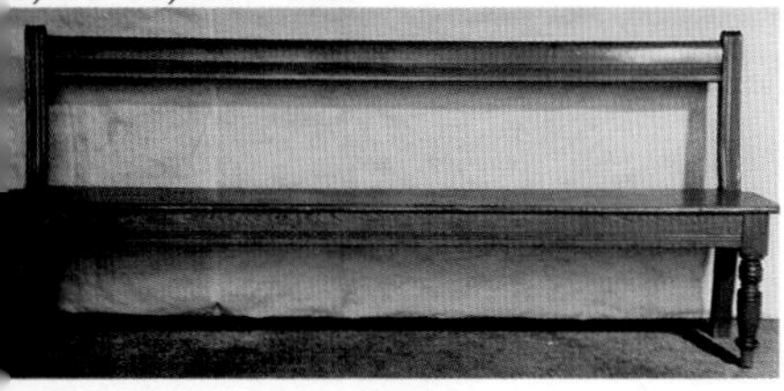

. pair of Victorian benches, 2in (182.5cm) wide.
200–250 *AnD*

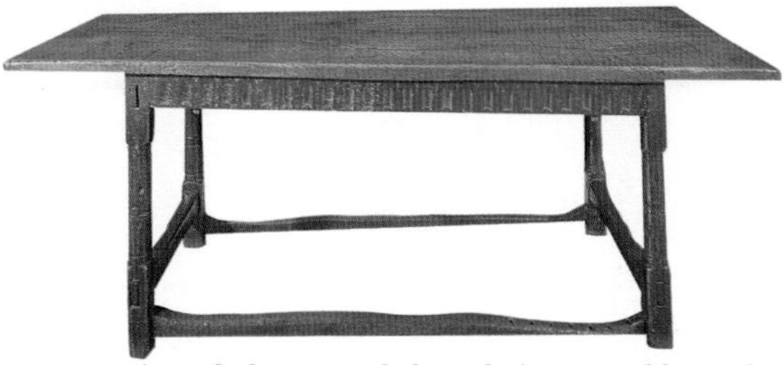

An oak dining and shove ha'penny table, with incised diagonal lines and arcaded frieze, on ring turned legs joined by stretchers on block feet, early 18thC, 81½in (207cm) long.
£8,500–10,000 *C*

\ Welsh oak chest of 3 long drawers, 1790, 18in (46cm) wide.
:1,200–1,500 *KEY*

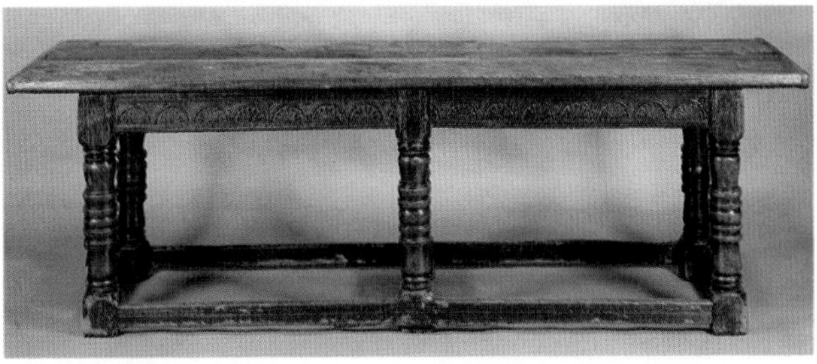

An oak refectory table, with carved frieze, initials 'WD', early 17thC, 103½in (263cm) wide. **£8,500–10,000** *Bon*

.n oak chest of drawers, with 2 hort and 3 long drawers, on bracket eet, c1820, 47in (119cm) wide.
:800–900 *UC*

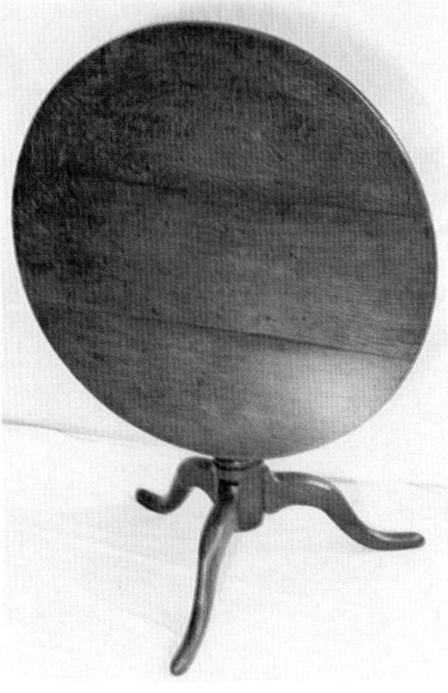

An oak tilt-top table, c1760, 34in (86cm) diam.
£450–500 *MIL*

An oak chest of 2 short and 4 long drawers, 42in (106.5cm) wide.
£2,200–2,800 *S(S)*

A Welsh cottage dresser, with potboard, original hooks, late 18thC, 56in (142cm) wide.
£3,500–4,000 *SWN*

An oak dresser, the rack with a moulded cornice above 2 shelves, the base with 3 frieze drawers and 4 false central drawers, on bracket feet, mid-18thC, 56½in (143cm) wide.
£3,800–4,200 *Bon*

An oak Welsh dresser, on stile feet, late 18thC, 69in (175cm) wide.
£6,500–8,000 *S(S)*

An oak Welsh dresser, the raised back with projecting cornice above notched beading, the base with 3 frieze drawers, on stile feet, mid-18thC, 58in (147cm) wide.
£12,000–15,000 *S(S)*

An oak Welsh dresser, with potboard and 3 shelves above 3 drawers, c1770, 56in (142cm) wide.
£4,500–5,500 *KEY*

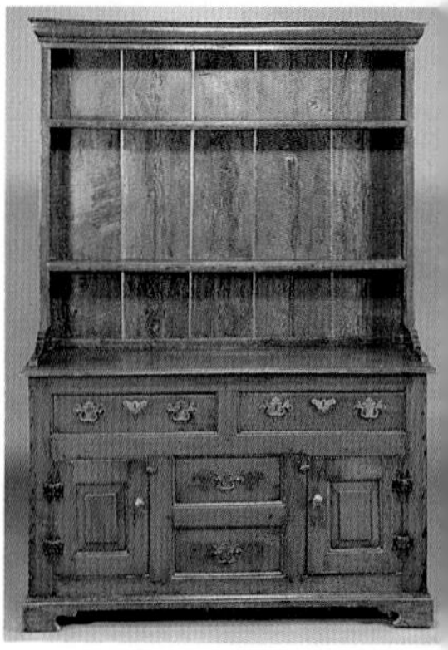

An oak dresser, the rack with ogee moulded cornice, the base with 2 frieze drawers, 2 false central drawers, and 2 cupboard doors, on bracket feet, mid-18thC, 55in (139.5cm) wide.
£4,800–5,500 *Bon*

A George II oak dresser, with 3 plate rails, on chamfered legs with a platform base, 58in (147cm) wide.
£4,800–5,500 *DN*

A George III oak Welsh dresser, with a shaped apron, on baluster legs, with a platform base and stump feet, 67½in (171.5cm) wide.
£10,000–12,000 *DN*

An oak Welsh dresser, the associated shelf back above 5 mahogany drawers and 2 cupboard doors, on later bracket feet, 79½in (202cm) wide.
£3,500–4,000 *S(S)*

George III oak Welsh dresser, e shelf back above 5 frieze awers and a pierced apron, turned column supports, ith a platform undertier on ock feet, restored, late 18thC, in (165cm) wide.
,000–5,000 *Bon*

An oak Welsh 'cwpwrdd tridarn', the canopy with columns, the central section with turned pendants and recessed cupboards, 2 frieze drawers and 2 panelled doors below, Harrods label, restored, early 18thC, 52in (132cm) wide.
£5,000–6,000 *S(S)*

A West Country oak dresser, the associated open shelf back above 3 frieze drawers, on reduced turned legs, early 19thC, 69in (175cm) wide.
£2,500–3,000 *S(S)*

North West region oak dresser, the oulded cornice above an open shelf ack, the base with 3 crossbanded ieze drawers and a valanced apron, cabriole legs with pad feet, late 8thC, 78in (198cm) wide.
7,500–9,000 *S(S)*

An oak and pitch pine dresser/bookcase, with glazed doors above 6 drawers and 2 cupboard doors, 19thC, 72in (183cm) wide.
£5,000–6,000 *CCP*

A North Country oak dresser, the open back rack with 3 open shelves, the base with 2 tiers of 3 graduated drawers and a central drawer over 2 panelled doors, on 3 front bracket supports, 18thC, 82in (208cm) wide.
£4,500–5,500 *LAY*

n oak Welsh dresser, on profile aluster and square supports joined y a platform base, late 18thC, 7in (170cm) wide.
4,000–4,800 *S(S)*

An oak Welsh dresser, with a pair of frieze drawers, on square supports, late 18thC, 57in (145cm) wide.
£4,500–5,000 *S(S)*

An oak dresser, with dentil cornice and shaped frieze above 3 open shelves, the base with 3 drawers, on cabriole legs, c1770, 72in (183cm) wide.
£4,500–5,000 *S(S)*

An oak dresser/mule chest, with 6 false and 3 real drawers, late 18thC, 61in (155cm) wide.
£2,500–3,000 *S(S)*

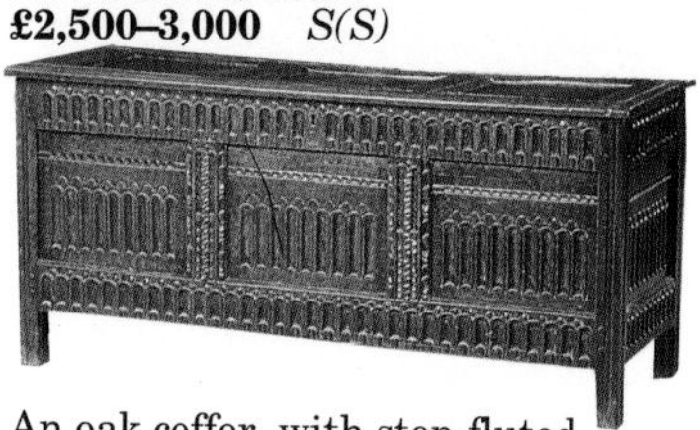

An oak coffer, with stop-fluted panelled front and sides, mid-17thC, 57in(145cm) wide.
£2,200–2,800 *S(S)*

An Essex County, Massachusetts, Pilgrim Century oak blanket chest, with geometric carving, c1660, 45in (114cm) wide.
£60,000–70,000 *S(NY)*

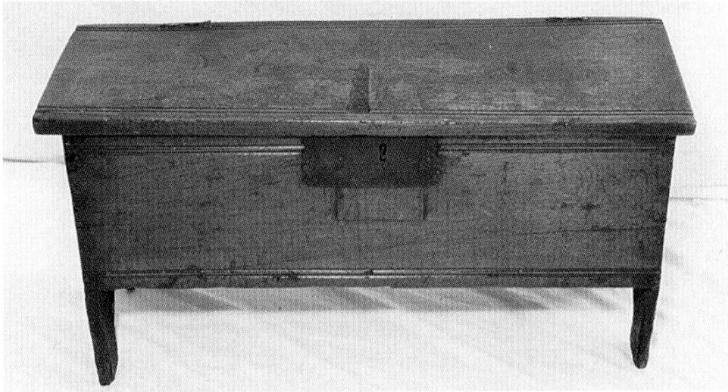

An oak plank coffer, c1870, 37in (94cm) wide.
£700–800 *MIL*

An oak mule chest, with 2 small drawers, 18thC, 25in (63.5cm) wide.
£350–450 *WaH*

An oak mule chest, with 4 arched panels, 2 drawers, the interior fitted with a candle box, 2 drawers, 18thC, 57in (145cm) wide.
£1,200–1,500 *CCP*

An oak and mahogany crossbanded mule chest, the front with 4 panels and 3 drawers, late 18thC, 59in (150cm) wid
£1,200–1,500 *S(S)*

An oak coffer, of 6 planks, original hinges and lock, mid-17thC, 56in (142cm) wide.
£1,000–1,250 *SWN*

An oak plank coffer, with original carving and ironwork, c1650, 44in (112cm) wide.
£1,200–1,500 *KEY*

n elm bacon settle, with riginal interior wrought iron ieat hooks, 30in (76cm) wide. **5,000–6,000** *CAL*

A primitive elm settle, of bowed plank construction, carved with various initials, late 17thC, 98in (249cm) wide. **£3,000–3,500** *Bon*

An oak high-backed winged armchair or settle, with a drawer to the base, c1780. **£4,000–5,000** *CAL*

An arched back miniature elm settle, with lift-up seat, constructed in the manner of a six-plank coffer, c1740, 36in (91.5cm) wide. **£2,500–3,000** *CAL*

A walnut dresser base, 48in (122cm) wide.
£12,000–15,000 *CAL*

An oak dresser base, with 3 frieze drawers, 2 central drawers flanked by panelled cupboard doors on block feet, restored, mid-18thC, 72in (182cm) wide. **£2,800–3,200** *Bon*

A Canadian Waterloo County Mennonite cherrywood sideboard, c1880, 50in (127cm) wide.
£1,000–1,200 *RIT*

An oak serving table, with 3 drawers, late 17thC 72in (183cm) wide.
£8,000–10,000 *CAL*

A French carved and decorated cherrywood low buffet, with original ironwork, c1790, 50in (127cm) wide.
£3,500–4,000 *CAL*

A cherrywood dresser base, with 2 panelled doors beneath 3 drawers, c1690, 72in (183cm) wide.
£10,000–12,000 *CAL*

A Georgian oak Welsh dresser base, with 3 frieze drawers interspersed with fluted panels above an apron fitted with 3 ogee arches, on ring turned baluster supports joined by a platform stretcher, on bracket feet, restored, mid-18thC, 76in (193cm) wide.
£18,000–22,000 *S(NY)*

A French Provincial cherrywood low buffet, with scratch-carving to the drawers, and original wrought iron, c1780, 50in (127cm) wide.
£3,200–3,800 *CAL*

A Welsh oak cricket table, 18thC.
£500–600 *OSc*

An oak tavern table, c1830.
£1,400–1,800 *CCA*

A George III oak and elm cricket table, with a shelf, c1800.
£1,000–1,200 *PHA*

An oak gateleg table, fitted with a drawer, 17thC.
£1,800–2,200 *NCr*

An oak gateleg dining table, c1900, 53in (135cm) wide.
£1,500–2,000 *SC*

An oak gateleg table, late 17thC, 64in (163cm) extended.
£3,500–4,500 *SC*

A Welsh oak and elm farmhouse table, with 2 drawers, c1820.
£1,000–1,200 *OSc*

A George III country oak farmhouse table, one leaf missing, 94in (239cm) long.
£1,800–2,200 *L*

A Tudor refectory table, mid-16thC, 125½in (317.5cm) long.
£6,500–8,000 *SBA*

A William and Mary oak double action gateleg table, with frieze drawer and twelve square baluster turned supports with conforming stretchers, 74in (188cm) extended.
£12,000–15,000 *S(S)*

A French walnut folding wine tasting table, c1850, 42in (106.5cm) diam.
£1,100–1,300 *UC*

l. A cherrywood table, with turned legs, c1880, 45in (114cm) wide.
£700–800
MofC

An oak gateleg table, the oval moulded top above two frieze drawers, on block and turned legs with shaped aprons, joined by stretchers, the flaps re-tipped, 18thC, 59in (149cm) wide.
£1,800–2,200 *P*

A Charles II oak gateleg table, the top with eliptical leaves above a drawer, on baluster turned columns, joined by ball turned stretchers, c1670, 59in (149.5cm) wide.
£1,200–1,500 *Bon*

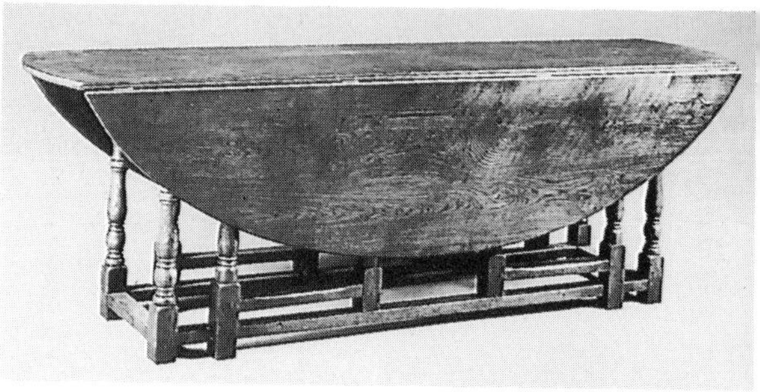

An oak gateleg table, on turned baluster supports joined by stretchers, on block feet, 20thC, 96in (244cm) extended.
£800–1,000 *CSK*

A Charles II oak gateleg table, the drop-leaf top raised above a shallow frieze drawer with moulded front, on spiral-twist legs, stretchers and gates on either side, late 17thC, 48in (122cm) wide.
£2,500–3,000 *B*

A New England maplewood 'butterfly' table, the base with old colour, restored top and drawers, 38in (96.5cm) wide.
£1,000–1,200 *SK(B)*

n oak gateleg circular table, arly 18thC, 52in (132cm) diam.
1,400–1,800 *DA*

An oak gateleg dining table, late 17thC, 73in (185cm) extended.
£8,500–10,000 *B*

gateleg table, with a earwood top, mid-17thC, 9in (74cm) wide.
2,500–3,000 *SKC*

An oak gateleg table, late 17thC, 45in (114cm) extended.
£1,200–1,500 *SKC*

An oak gateleg table, with twin-flap top and one panelled drawer, on later bun feet, restorations to top, some replacements to legs, top extended, part late 17thC, 60in (153cm) wide.
£1,500–1,800 *C*

An 18thC-style oak gateleg dining able, with single frieze drawer, supported on ring turned legs with plain stretchers, 40in (101.5cm) wide.
£800–1,000 *DDM*

An oak oval gateleg dining table, with plain top, frieze drawer, turned supports and plain stretchers, 60in (152cm) extended.
£1,500–2,000 *DDM*

A William and Mary oak gateleg table, with a drawer, on square and bobbin turned legs, late 17thC, 56in (142cm) extended.
£3,500–4,000 *S(S)*

A Charles II oak gateleg table, with spiral twist end supports, restored, late 17thC, 30½in (78cm) extended.
£1,800–2,200 *S(S)*

A George III oak side table, the moulded top above one long and 2 short drawers, with a shaped apron, on chamfered square legs, damaged, late 18thC, 33½in (85cm) wide.
£800–1,000 *S(S)*

A Shaker cherrywood trestle-base work table, the top with rounded corners above a two-drawer frieze, the supports joined by a turned stretcher, on slightly arched shoe feet, Kentucky, 1850–70, 24½in (62cm) wide.
£3,500–4,000 *S(NY)*

r. An oak credence table, the circular top falling over a single gate to a base of 4 cannon barrel turned legs beneath an incised frieze with a potboard beneath, early 17thC, 37in (94cm) wide.
£3,500–4,000 *B*

l. An oak side table, with a moulded top above one long and 3 short drawers, with a shaped apron, on tapered square legs, South Wales, late 18thC, 31in (79cm) wide.
£1,500–2,000 *S(S)*

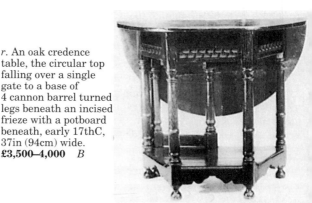

An oak side table, the moulded top above a frieze drawer, on block and turned legs, joined by stretchers, turned feet, early 18thC, 29in (74cm) wide.
£1,000–1,200 *P*

l. A Continental oak refectory table, the top above 2 frieze drawers, on rounded square tapering legs joined by box stretchers, associated, 18th/19thC, with 2 later stretchers, 87½in (222cm) wide.
£6,500–8,000 *C*

A Spanish walnut rustic table, 18thC.
£1,000–1,500 *Ced*

A late Victorian oak press table with 2 drawers, turned ebony handles, with splayed front legs, 35in (89cm) extended.
£175–225 *AP*

A dairy table, in original finish, c1870, 20in (51cm) wide.
£220–250 *MIL*

An oak and ash tavern table, the three-plank top above X-shaped end supports, early 19thC, 61½in (156cm) wide.
£2,750–3,250 *S(S)*

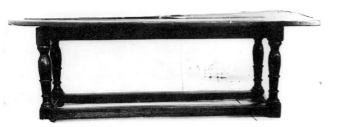

A Charles II oak refectory table, with three-planked top, on a separate base of 4 baluster-turned legs united by one carved and one plain frieze, inscribed '1667', with a heavy all-round stretcher at the base, good colour and original patination, 99in (251.5cm) wide.
£8,500–10,000 *B*

A Jacobean oak refectory table, the plank top on bulbous gadrooned pedestals and X-form plinths, 147in (373.5cm) wide.
£28,000–35,000 *C(NY)*

A pine and ash long tavern table, with shove-halfpenny markings, c1800.
£2,300–2,800 *COM*

r. An oak tavern table, the top supported by X-form base, with faceted supports, 19thC, 56in (142cm) wide.
£8,000–9,000 *S(NY)*

An oak side table, the projecting top above columnar-turned and square legs joined by peripheral stretchers, c1700, possibly associated, 48½in (123cm) wide.
£1,200–1,400 *S(S)*

An oak side table, the top above a plain frieze, on baluster turned legs, joined by stretchers, late 17thC, 35in (89cm) wide.
£650–800 *SK(B)*

A New England William and Mary tavern table, on turned legs joined by a stretcher, painted black, restored, 22in (56cm) wide.
£650–800 *SK(B)*

A pine and elm tavern table, with X-frame, c1830.
£1,500–1,800 *COM*

Colour and patina

Simple rustic items have a unique charm, particularly if they have achieved a glorious colour and deep patina from daily use and polishing. Colour and patina are the foremost criteria for country furniture. Both go hand-in-hand, are impossible to fake, and will be reflected in the asking price. Ideally, one looks for a good colour – not just an overall blanket of colour, but a variety of tones from almost blond to black. The palest areas are where wear would have been greatest, and darker sections that were out of reach of hands or sunlight. The wood will be soft and silky to the touch, and the piece should glow with a three-dimensional depth.

An oak gateleg table, the top above an end frieze pine-lined drawer, baluster ogee turned block legs and stretchers, on turned feet, late 17thC, 42in (106.5cm) wide.
£1,200–1,500 *WW*

r. A New England pine and poplar harvest table, the top supported on 4 angled legs with stretchers, 78in (198cm) wide.
£4,000–5,000 *MMG*

A French cherrywood table, on brass casters, c1830, 42in (106.5cm) diam.
£800–1,000 *GD*

An oak refectory table, on 6 inverted baluster legs united by stretchers at floor level, early 17thC with a new solid oak top, 157½in (402cm) long.
£2,000–2,500 *WL*

A Charles II oak credence table, with folding demi-lune top above a central panelled frieze drawer, on turned baluster column supports tied by block stretchers, c1640, 49in (124.5cm) wide.
£6,500–8,000 *Bon*

A Charles I-style oak monk's table, with boarded hinged top, boarded seat and drawer, the square and turned legs joined by peripheral stretchers, made-up, 42½in (108cm) wide.
£900–1,000 *S(S)*

A pine and walnut wine table, with carved dolphin base, c1870, 23in (58.5cm) diam.
£300–400 *AF*

A Charles II oak side table, with moulded rectangular top, on bobbin-turned and square legs joined by peripheral stretchers, late 17thC, 33in (84cm) wide.
£1,200–1,500 *S(S)*

A Queen Anne oak side table, with moulded top above a frieze drawer, the slender turned and square legs joined by peripheral stretchers, early 18thC, 30in (76cm) wide.
£900–1,000 *S(S)*

An oak and fruitwood draw-leaf dining table, French or Flemish, the cleated top above turned and square legs joined by shaped stretchers, on later turned feet, mid-18thC, 106in (269cm) long.
£5,000–6,000 *AF*

l. An oak table, c1920s, 16½in (42cm) diam.
£120–150 *JHW*

A chestnut table, with quartered top, late 19th/early 20thC, 60in (152.5cm) diam.
£600–700 *CUL*

An Irish yew-wood wake table, with oval drop leaf, 18thC, 29in (73.5cm) high.
£4,000–5,000 *AF*

A French Provincial Normandy pearwood table, with oak frame, single centre drawer, tapered legs, 80in (203cm) long.
£1,200–1,500 *AF*

French Provincial Furniture

The past few years have seen a huge increase in the importation of French Provincial antique country furniture to England. As 'French country' becomes a recognized look, it is important to consider certain factors before buying French furniture.

Invariably, the French 'restore' their tables, a process that involves noticeable and unacceptable practices, including removing the top to close up shrinkage gaps by trimming down one side of the cleats (the smaller plank at each end binding the main plank at right angles), leaving one side with a new worked surface. Many work tables were altered to make them more valuable as dining tables, by removing drawers and shaping rails to leave low corner brackets, and cut up to a shallow rail leaving knee space.

Age and style are important: one type of table from northern France, dated 1680–1780, is very similar in style to a late 17th/early 18th-century English table – with large square section chamfered legs and a generous thick top – usually in chestnut or elm. Many have been sold as English, and go well with English furniture. Very plain tables with square section legs joined by H-stretchers from about 1760 to 1880, follow a popular style in England and France, marrying well with English vernacular chair types. By the mid-19th century, French tables had heavily turned legs, often in well-figured walnut, and are used in England as kitchen dining tables. These are commanding between £1,200 and £2,000.

A late 18th-century English ten-seater farmhouse dining table, that has a thick two-plank cleated top with a good overhang at each end, in well patinated oak, elm, ash or sycamore, would command in excess of £10,000. The French equivalent in oak, elm, ash, chestnut or cherrywood, mostly from northern France and much prized in England, would cost about £6,000.

Quality French (and English) dining tables have doubled in value over the past few years and the price differential is narrowing. As fine French tables are becoming rarer in Britain, the French are more reluctant to part with them.

French country chairs are not popular in Britain, although recently there has been a vogue for painted rush-seated ladder backs from Provence. Original sets are very desirable reaching prices of £4,000–6,000 for a three-seater banquette. But be warned – reproductions exist complete with distressed paint surface. We tend to match French farmhouse tables with our traditional English country ladder-back, spindle-back or Windsor-type chair.

The desirability and value of an exceptional dresser, court cupboard or chest of drawers means they exact a high price, but it is still possible to buy fine French provincial pieces for relatively competitive prices. Commodes or chests of drawers are the highlight of French provincial furniture. Offered frequently at £10,000 or more they are often considered too flamboyant for English taste, usually outshining heavily geometrically moulded English chests and plain, flat-fronted ones.

Armoires (wardrobes) with 'Napoleon hat' type cornices are very popular – usually inlaid, decorative and elegant, as opposed to the rare, rather ungainly, early English country form. A plain armoire would fetch between £2,500–3,500, and fine examples now command up to £7,000 or even £10,000. A huge advantage of the French armoire is that the doors are removable and the carcass may be knocked apart for easy transportation.

Whatever one chooses to buy it is, above all, important to look for a genuine patina over the scars of generations. It is this that gives any piece of country furniture its vital magic.

When looking at 'restored' tables, look for a new worked surface on the cleats, showing shrinkage gaps have been closed up. Shadow marks on the underside of the table top planks indicate that recentring on the frame has taken place, and look for 'length shrinkage' – a sure sign of trouble as one has been reduced to create a bigger overhang. Note any signs of a mechanical circular saw as these do not predate 1840. On altered work tables, fresh underside rail edges or even staining to conceal them are of note.

Wear to both English and French tables can be easily identified: wear to stretchers, finger marks, grimy patina around underside edges of tops, shrinkage of timber, wear to feet. Colour, surface and patina are most important – washed off and repolished tables lose value and evidence of age. **Robert Young**

‹ 17thC-style oak cupboard, ‚ith split bobbin and turned nouldings, the triple panel front ncluding a pair of arched panel loors, the square and turned legs oined by peripheral stretchers, ·5½in (115.5cm) wide.
'950–1,200 *S(S)*

An oak cupboard in 2 parts, possibly East Anglian, with a frieze drawer and 3 panelled doors above a shaped apron, alterations, late 17thC, 41½in (106cm) wide.
£2,500–3,000 *S(S)*

A George III oak wall cupboard, with shelves enclosed by a panelled door, 26½in (67.5cm) wide.
£650–800 *DN*

An oak cupboard, with shelves ·nclosed by one panelled door ‚with iron hinges, 17thC, 21½in (54.5cm) wide.
£450–550 *DN*

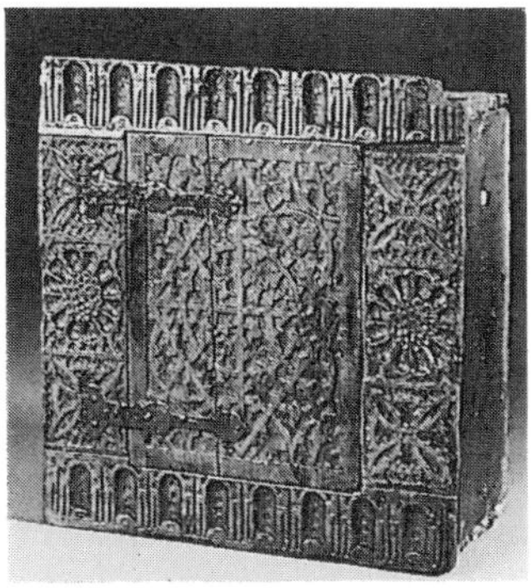

An oak cupboard, with punch decoration of lunettes, stylized paterae and dentil geometric motifs, enclosed by a panelled door, traces of green paint, 17thC, 20½in (52cm) wide.
£4,000–5,000 *C*

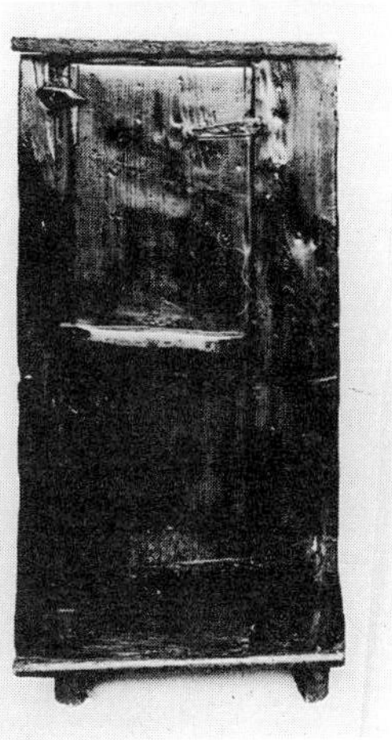

A Spanish dug-out cupboard, with single door and iron strap hinges, c1750.
£3,800–4,200 *B*

A small oak food cupboard, with potboard base, c1870, the handles and hinges later replacements.
£4,000–5,000 *Ced*

A George III oak food cupboard, inlaid with mahogany geometric motifs, the moulded cornice above a pair of doors with perforated panels enclosing shelves, the base with 2 short and 2 long drawers, lacking feet, late 18th/early 19thC, 43½in (110.5cm) wide.
£2,200–2,600 *S(S)*

An oak press cupboard, the pair of panelled doors above a panelled frieze, on stile feet, restored, c1670, 49½in (125.5cm) wide.
£2,500–3,000 *Bon*

A Queen Anne oak press cupboard-on-chest, the panelled doors enclosing hanging space, 4 panels below, on stile feet, restored, early 18thC, 46½in (118cm) wide.
£1,200–1,500 *S(S)*

An oak court cupboard, with fielded panelled doors, 17thC, 53in (134.5cm) wide.
£2,200–2,600 *RBB*

A Welsh oak cupboard, in 2 parts, fitted with cupboard doors and drawers, with engaged columns, on bracket feet, inscribed 'A.I. 1798', late 18thC, 60in (152.5cm) wide.
£7,500–9,000 *S(NY)*

A Federal cherrywood cupboard, with projecting cornice over glass doors enclosing shelves, above 3 panelled drawers and a pair of cupboard doors, on bracket feet, 19thC, 63in (160cm) wide.
£2,500–3,000 *LHA*

An oak hanging corner cupboard, enclosing 3 shelves, the shaped moulded panel door with central inlaid rosette, 27in (68.5cm) wide.
£650–800 *DA*

A Pennsylvanian walnut cupboard, with glazed doors to top, 3 drawers and cupboards to base, restored, 70in (178cm) wide
£4,500–5,000 *SK(B)*

A George III oak hanging corner cupboard, the moulded cornice above a fielded panelled door enclosing shaped shelves, the canted sides with stop-fluted pilasters, late 18thC, 36in (91.5cm) wide.
£1,100–1,300 *S(S)*

A George III oak hanging corner cupboard, the moulded cornice above a pair of mahogany crossbanded and floral inlaid panelled doors with one true and 2 false drawers beneath, late 18thC, 35in (89cm) wide.
£800–1,000 *Bon*

An oak corner cupboard, the moulded cornice above a crossbanded door with central inlaid paterae, on a moulded plinth base, 18thC, 32in (81.5cm) wide.
£650–800 *P*

A walnut carved and glazed buffet, probably mid-Atlantic States, with 3 painted shaped shelves, glazed door and a single shelf behind the recessed door flanked by fluted columns, old darkened surface, restored, 1790–1820, 48in (122cm) wide.
£3,500–4,000 *SK(B)*

A Federal cherrywood four-door corner cabinet, late 18thC, 55in (139.5cm) wide.
£2,000–2,500 *LHA*

A New England cherrywood corner cupboard, old refinish, minor imperfections, c1810, 42in (106.5cm) wide.
£2,700–3,200 *SK(B)*

r. A poplar wood glazed corner cupboard, probably Pennsylvania, refinished, minor repairs, c1810, 43in (109cm) wide.
£3,500–4,000 *SK(B)*

A George III oak standing corner cupboard, the moulded cornice above 2 fielded panelled doors, flanked by canted corners, mid-18thC, 40in (101.5cm) wide.
£2,300–2,800 *Bon*

A Federal inlaid cherrywood corner cupboard, the shaped pediment with 3 carved urn finials above a pair of glazed doors enclosing shelves, 2 drawers and a pair of raised panelled doors enclosing a shelf, on plinth base, 49in (124.5cm) wide.
£5,000–6,000 *CCS*

l. An elm standing corner cupboard, with dentil cornice and a pair of arched doors, 19thC.
£3,750–4,500 *DN*

Locate the source

The source of each illustration in *Miller's Pine & Country Buyer's Guide* can easily be found by checking the code letters at the end of each caption with the Key to Illustrations located at the front of the book.

An oak chest, with 2 short and 2 long drawers, on bracket feet, some original brass handles and escutcheons, early 18thC, 36in (91.5cm) wide.
£1,200–1,500 *WIL*

Followers of fashion

The fashion in furniture hardware – handles, locks, hinges and escutcheons – changed regularly, and owners can be seen to have updated their furniture, leaving behind the evidence of time. Look closely at a chest of drawers. You may well see evidence of the original drop handles, replaced by later plates, sometimes by two or even three progressively larger sets and lastly, perhaps, a Victorian glass or china knob. Dealers will often rehandle a piece, putting back whatever is most appropriate, but the scars are hard to disguise and original hardware is obviously at a premium.

A simulated maple chest of drawers, c1860, 36in (91.5cm) wide.
£500–600 *PEN*

An oak chest of drawers, with linen press, c1800.
£1,500–2,000 *Ced*

An oak chest of drawers, late 18thC, 44in (112cm) wide.
£700–850 *WV*

An oak chest of drawers, with mitred mouldings and later pierced bracket feet, late 17thC, 42½in (108cm) wide.
£1,200–1,500 *S(S)*

A William and Mary oak chest of drawers, restored, late 17thC, 35½in (90cm) wide.
£2,000–2,400 *SK(B)*

A George III oak chest of drawers, with 4 long graduated drawers, on bracket feet, c1770, 34in (86.5cm) wide.
£850–1,000 *Bon*

l. A James II oak chest, the moulded top above 2 short and 3 long geometrically moulded drawers, on later shaped bracket feet, 36in (91.5cm) wide.
£1,300–1,700 *P*

r. A maple chest of 4 drawers, New England, original brass handles, refinished, restored, c1790, 33in (84cm) wide.
£1,500–1,800 *SK(B)*

A Jacobean oak tester bed, with cup-and-cover turned end posts below a nine-panel tester with moulded cornice, legs rebuilt, tester possibly of a later date, 54in (137cm) wide.
£5,000–6,000 *P(M)*

A pair of French fruitwood bedsteads, each with arched panelled headboard and footboard, panelled uprights and joined by side rails with shaped spandrels, mid-19thC, 80in (203cm) wide.
£800–1,000 *CSK*

r. An oak cradle, with a domed canopy, tapering sides and lunette-shaped rockers, 18thC, 35½in (90cm) wide.
£300–400 *P*

An oak tester bed, the panelled canopy with cavetto moulded cornice and headboard, the footboard with turned posts and moulded panels, on solid end supports, parts 17thC, 58in (147.5cm) wide.
£3,500–4,000 *Bon*

An oak tester bed, the headboard with a pair of floral marquetry panels, above carved arcades with recessed foliate fruiting tendrils, and the box spring, Yorkshire, parts 17thC, 69in (175.5cm) wide.
£8,500–10,000 *CSK*

A French chestnut enclosed double bed, early 19thC.
£2,500–3,000 *Ced*

An oak tester bed, the panelled headboard carved with a figure, on square block feet, 17thC and later, made up, 58in (147.5cm) wide.
£3,500–4,500 *S(S)*

r. An oak tester bedstead, known as 'The Lovely Hall Bed', with 24 pierced carved panels, the end posts carved with 'R' and 'I', early 16thC, 158in (401.5cm) wide.
£30,000–40,000 *S(S)*

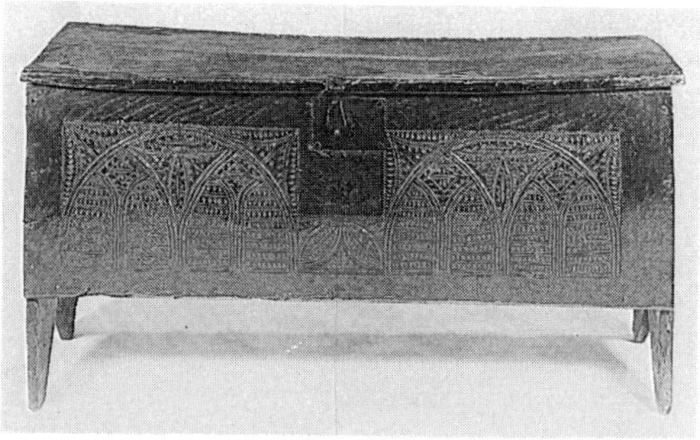

An oak chest, the moulded plank top enclosing a lidded candle box above a lunette and chip-carved painted front, with arcaded end supports, restored, mid-17thC, 48½in (123cm) wide.
£1,800–2,200 *Bon*

A Charles II joined oak chest, the panelled top above a frieze applied with ovoid bosses and 3 leaf and sunburst carved panels flanked by split balusters, Yorkshire, c1660, 49in (124.5cm) wide.
£1,500–1,800 *Bon*

A Jacobean oak chest, the moulded hinged top above a panelled and carved case, plank legs, late 17thC, 55½in (141cm) wide.
£1,200–1,500 *SK(B)*

An oak coffer, the rising plank top above a front with a gouge-decorated frieze and 2 arcaded panels with carved decorations and stylized pilasters, early 17thC, 40in (101.5cm) wide.
£1,800–2,200 *B*

An oak coffer, the panelled hinged top enclosing a plain interior with a till, the linen-fold panelled front above block feet, restorations, part 16thC, 49¼in (125cm) wide.
£2,500–3,000 *C*

An oak joined chest, with panelled hinged top and a frieze of stop-flutes, 17thC, 40½in (103cm) wide.
£750–900 *DN*

An oak mule chest, the moulded top previously hinged at the back, above a fall-front of 4 fielded arched panels, 3 drawers and ogee arched aprons, on scrolling plank feet, alterations, mid-18thC, 55½in (141cm) wide.
£800–1,200 *P*

An oak coffer, the hinged lid with 4 moulded panels above an arcaded frieze and conforming panelled front, on plank feet, 17thC, 51¼in (130cm) wide.
£500–600 *P*

An oak six-plank chest, with scratch-carved decoration, c1700, 24in (61.5cm) wide.
£900–1,100 *OSc*

A Commonwealth oak coffer, the moulded hinged top above a twin panel front, on stile feet, c1650, 37½in (95cm) wide.
£1,300–1,700 *S(S)*

An oak coffer, 18thC, 60in (125.5cm) wide.
£1,000–1,200 *C*

A small oak six-plank chest, mid-17thC, 31½in (80cm) wide.
£900–1,100 *S*

An oak coffer, 17thC, 41in (104cm) wide.
£1,000–1,200 *OB*

An oak 3 panelled coffer, with carved top rail and ebony and holly chevron inlay, raised on high stiles, 17thC, 42in (106.5cm) wide.
£900–1,100 *TM*

An oak coffer, with plain hinged top and front, 18thC, 35in (89cm) wide.
£550–700 *DDM*

An oak chest, with moulded hinged lid, 3 moulded panels to the front and 2 drawers in the base, on bracket feet, c1740, 51in (129.5cm) wide.
£900–1,100 *M*

An elm blanket chest, 18thC, 42in (106.5cm) wide.
£120–150 *JMW*

A carved elm coffer, 18thC, 38in (96cm) wide.
£900–1,100 *PCA*

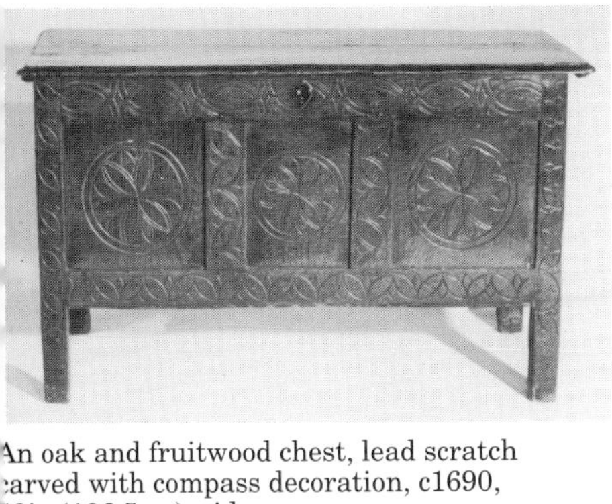

An oak and fruitwood chest, lead scratch carved with compass decoration, c1690, 42in (106.5cm) wide.
£1,500–1,800 *OSc*

An oak chest, with scratch carved decoration, c1670, 36in (91.5cm) wide.
£1,200–1,400 *OSc*

An oak coffer, with panelled top and sides, 18thC.
£550–700 *DaD*

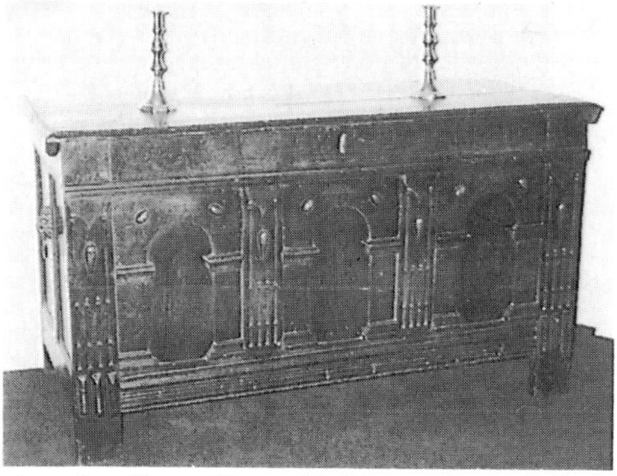

An oak coffer, with moulded top and panelled front with arcaded fluted decoration, 17thC, 39in (99cm) wide.
£900–1,100 *AP*

An oak chest, with two-plank top, 4 shaped, raised and fielded panels to front and 2 drawers to base, on ogee bracket feet, restored, late 18thC, 55in (140cm) wide.
£700–800 *WIL*

A mule chest, 18thC, 48in (122cm) wide.
£650–750 *WV*

An oak triple panel coffer, with iron latch, late 17thC, 50in (127cm) wide.
£650–800 *AP*

An oak coffer, with carved front, 57in (144.5cm) wide.
£550–700 *GD*

An oak coffer with 3 panels, late 17thC, 47in (119cm) wide.
£900–1,100 *AP*

An oak chest, the top with 3 panels, original hinges, the front panels carved with roundels and arcading to top rail, slight restoration to lid, 17thC, 42in (107cm) wide.
£1,200–1,500 *WIL*

An oak and mahogany crossbanded blanket chest, the panelled top above 4 dummy and 3 real drawers flanked by reeded pilasters, on ogee bracket feet, Cheshire, late 18thC, 55½in (141cm) wide.
£1,500–1,800 *S(S)*

A Charles II oak chest, the moulded hinged top above a triple panel front carved with stylized arches within S-scroll borders, on stile feet, late 17thC, 55½in (140cm) wide.
£750–900 *S(S)*

A North Country carved oak chest, the moulded hinged top above a lunette frieze and a triple panel front with stylized foliate motifs within inlaid geometric borders, on stile feet, mid-17thC, 58in (147cm) wide.
£900–1,100 *S(S)*

An oak plank ecclesiastical chest with iron strap hinges and hasps, the rising lid enclosing a fitted interior with an ecclesiastical safe compartment with further rising lid, on sledge feet, formerly with 3 internal locks, 16thC, 53in (134.5cm) wide.
£2,500–3,000 *B*

r. A William and Mary carved oak boarded chest, with hinged cover, the carved front bearing the initials 'WS' and dated '1696', 40½in (103cm) wide.
£2,500–3,000 *S(S)*

A small oak coffer, with three-panel rising lid above a front of 3 panels with stylized foliate decoration and spandrels beneath, 17thC, 44in (111.5cm) wide.
£600–700 *B*

An oak five-panelled coffer, 17thC, 37in (94cm) wide.
£850–1,000 *MIT*

An oak coffer, the plank top above a frieze of scrolls and a three-panel front with moulded decoration, late 17thC, 62in (157cm) wide.
£850–1,000 *B*

An oak coffer, 18thC, 30in (77cm) wide.
£500–600 *DaD*

An oak coffer, the rising plank top above a carved front and lunette carved frieze, 3 panels with applied lozenge decoration within carved arcades, 17thC, 53in (134.5cm) wide.
£650–800 *B*

r. A Charles I small oak boarded coffer, with punch-work roundels and banding within gouge carved boarders, mid-17thC, 24in (61cm) wide.
£1,400–1,800 *S(S)*

A Westmorland oak coffer, the rising top above a three-panelled front with gouged decoration, above applied arcades and pilasters, 17thC, 51in (129.5cm) wide.
£900–1,100 *B*

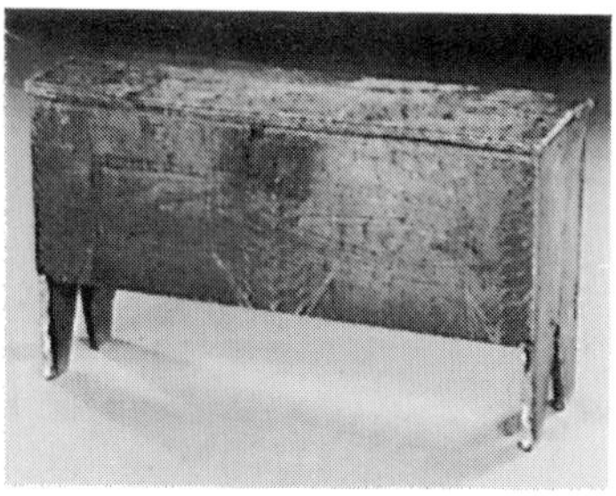

A Queen Anne oak boarded coffer, the hinged top above an incised front panel with an iron lockplate, flanked by the date '1709', on trestle shaped supports, early 18thC, 35½in (91cm) wide.
£700–850 *S(S)*

A Yorkshire oak double coffer, the panelled top above a frieze with incised decoration surrounding the initials 'P.S. 1702', early 18thC, 72in (182cm) wide.
£900–1,100 *B*

Chests and coffers

Oak was mainly used for chests in northern Europe, while walnut was used further south. A simple chest consists of six planks nailed or dovetailed together, with the vertical 'slab' ends shaped at the bottom to form feet. Another kind of boarded chest was the hutch (from the French *huche* meaning chest) – the horizontal planks of the front and back are housed at either end in wide vertical members (stiles), which extend downwards as the feet.

Chests of framed and panelled construction were developed during the 15thC, and by the 16thC were produced in considerable quantities. They were used widely for storage in the home, and were often fitted with a small compartment, or 'till', which might be lockable for valuables.

A late Victorian oak blanket box, with original hinges, c1820, 44in (111.5cm) wide.
£200–240 *POT*

A military camphor wood box, brass hinges, 38in (96.5cm) wide.
£350–400 *AF*

An elm plank coffer, with arcadian carving, original lockplate, 17thC, 54in (137cm) wide.
£550–650 *AF*

A George III oak bureau, with fall front and fitted interior, the base with 4 graduated drawers, brass bail handles, on bracket feet, 37in (94cm) wide.
£1,800–2,200 *WIL*

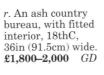

r. An ash country bureau, with fitted interior, 18thC, 36in (91.5cm) wide.
£1,800–2,000 *GD*

r. A George III oak bureau, the cleated fall enclosing fitted interior above 4 graduated drawers, on later ogee bracket feet, late 18thC, 36in (92cm) wide.
£1,500–2,000 *S(S)*

An oak bureau, the interior with pigeonholes, 5 drawers, 3 secret drawers and a sliding well, the lower section with 2 short drawers and 2 long drawers, on bracket feet, early 18thC, 37in (94cm) wide.
£1,300–1,800 *P*

A George III oak and mahogany crossbanded bureau, late 18thC, 39in (99cm) wide.
£1,800–2,200 *S(S)*

Locate the source

The source of each illustration in *Miller's Pine & Country Furniture Buyer's Guide* can easily be found by checking the code letters at the end of each caption with the Key to Illustrations located at the front of the book.

A George II oak bureau, the fall front enclosing a fitted interior above 2 short and 2 long drawers, on bracket feet, 33½in (85cm) wide.
£3,500–4,000 *DN*

A George III oak bureau, with fall front enclosing a fitted interior, above 4 long drawers, on bracket feet, 38in (96.5cm) wide.
£1,500–1,800 *DN*

A George III oak bureau, with fitted interior, above 4 long drawers with brass handles, on bracket feet, 40in (101.5cm) wide.
£1,500–1,800 *DN*

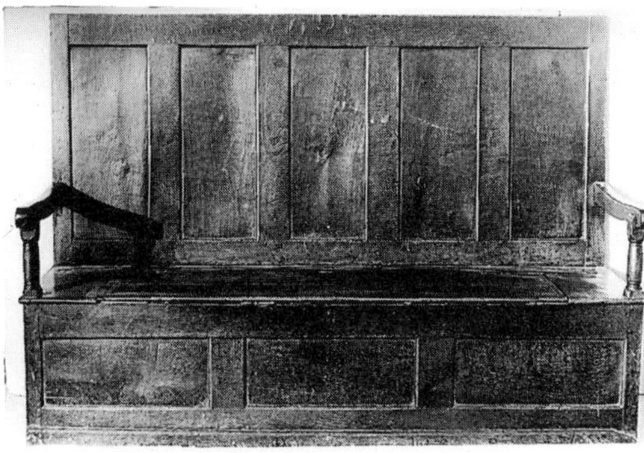

An oak high-back settle, the five-panel back above a box base with lift-up seat and panels beneath, turned supports to side arms, original colour and patination, 18thC, 67in (170cm) wide.
£2,200–2,800 *B*

A George II style oak settle, with moulded crested rail above five arched fielding panels to the back, shaped arm supports, square fluted legs with a gold dralon squab cushion, basically 18thC, 80in (203cm) long.
£650–800 *HCC*

An oak settle, the back with 3 panels, the base with open arms and single central drawer, 45in (115cm) long.
£900–1,100 *LAY*

An oak settle, the back with 5 stylized foliate carved panels, solid seat and chamfered legs, restored, Lancashire/Cheshire, late 17thC, 71in (180cm) long.
£1,500–2,000 *S(S)*

A George III oak settle, the back with 4 shaped panels.
£500–600 *DaD*

An oak settle, with four-panelled back and cushioned seat, Lancashire, 18thC.
£650–800 *W*

An oak box settle, the back with 4 raised and fielded panels, hinged seat, front of base with 5 square fielded panels, open arms, base replaced, 17thC, 51in (130cm) long.
£3,000–3,500 *WIL*

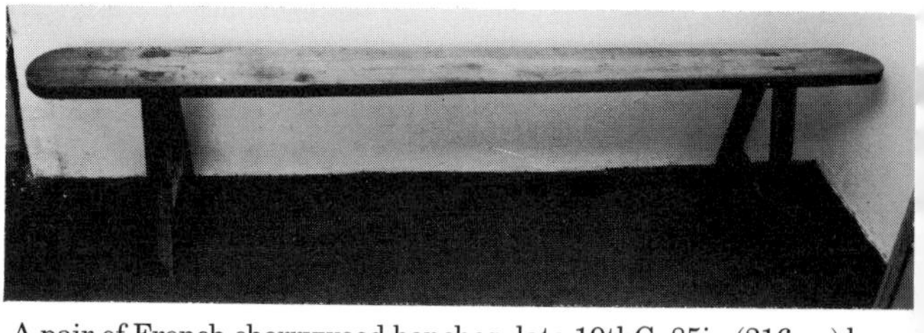

A pair of French cherrywood benches, late 19thC, 85in (216cm) long.
£300–350 *HGN*

An oak high wing-back concave settle, the seat with 2 drawers, 18thC, 50in (127cm) wide.
£1,800–2,200 *DDM*

An elm and oak hall bench, the back inscribed '1736', on reduced stump supports, mid-18thC, 60in (152cm) long.
£2,500–3,000 *SBA*

An elm bacon settle, c1800, 77in (195.5cm) high.
£3,500–4,000 *W*

A Welsh oak settle, the top rail carved and dated '1687', the base fully enclosed with a small removable lid inserted in the seat, the top 17thC, the base made up later, 46in (117cm) wide.
£800–1,200 *SC*

An elm bacon settle, the back with a single cupboard below 4 short drawers, solid seat, with a cupboard below, c1720, 56in (142cm) wide.
£3,750–4,500 *SKC*

An oak four-panel settle, 17thC, 72in (182.5cm) wide.
£2,500–3,000 *AGr*

An oak settle, dated '1740', 44in (111.5cm) wide.
£2,700–3,000 *JAC*

l. An oak and chestnut settle, 18thC, 58in (147cm) wide.
£1,300–1,700 *PCA*

A Charles II oak joined stool, with moulded top above a fretwork apron, on baluster turned and square legs joined by stretchers, late 17thC, 17½in (44cm) wide.
£2,500–3,000 *S(S)*

A Queen Anne oak close stool, with 3 dummy drawers, on later turned feet, early 18thC, 19in (48cm) wide.
£1,800–2,200 *S(S)*

An oak joined stool, c1850, 14in (36cm) wide.
£250–300 *MofC*

A Charles II oak joined stool, c1650, later carved, 17in (43cm) wide.
£2,000–2,500 *WaH*

r. An oak joined stool, with moulded top above a frieze carved with the initials 'HB', on bobbin turned legs tied by block stretchers, restorations, top possibly associated, mid-17thC, 18½in (47cm) wide.
£800–900 *Bon*

An elm rustic stool, early 19thC, 18in (45.5cm) high.
£45–60 *WCA*

An oak fireside or dairy stool, c1800.
£120–180 *Ced*

A child's oak joined stool on baluster turned legs, c1680, late 17th/early 18thC, 12in (30.5cm) square.
£1,200–1,500 *RYA*

l. A pine milking stool, c1870, 12in (30.5cm) wide.
£45–60 *ASP*

r. An oak joined stool, the moulded top above turned and square legs joined by stretchers, early 18thC, 15in (38cm) wide.
£2,200–2,700 *S(S)*

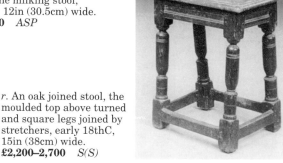

A country stool, 19thC, 25in (63.5cm) high.
£90–120 *JAC*

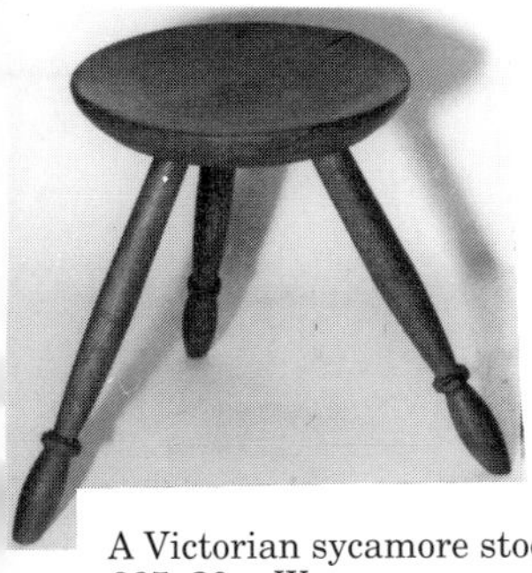

A Victorian sycamore stool.
£65–80 *W*

A saddle seat stool, c1860, 32in (81.5cm) high.
£65–80 *AL*

A milking stool, 1880, 12in (30.5cm) high.
£35–50 *AL*

A late Georgian elm and ash stool, 18in (45.5cm) wide.
£100–120 *OA*

An elm stool, c1880, 21in (53.5cm) high.
£65–80 *W*

A French cherrywood armoire, Normandy, c1820, 52in (132cm) wide.
£2,500–3,000 *PEN*

A French Provincial oak cupboard, with shell-carved crest over a double panelled door, on stile feet, 30in (76cm) wide.
£1,700–2,000 *MMG*

An oak armoire, 18thC.
£1,600–1,800 *CUL*

l. A French oak armoire, 17thC.
£450–550 *AnD*

r. A French chestnut armoire, Quimper, Brittany, c1790, 52in (132cm) wide.
£2,200–2,800 *GD*

A French or Spanish carved oak armoire, the flared cornice above a pair of rounded carved panelled doors with foliate borders enclosing hanging space, 4 carved apron panels, on stile feet, restored, early 18thC, 56½in (143cm) wide.
£2,200–2,800 *S(S)*

A chestnut armoire, 19thC, 48in (122cm) wide.
£2,000–2,500 *CUL*

An oak hanging press, with Gothic fielded panels, on bracket feet, c1760, 51in (129.5cm) wide.
£3,000–3,600 *POT*

A panel-back lambing armchair, with shaped toprail, fielded panel back, outset wings with flat arms and enclosed sides, the sprung seat with panelled base, c1740.
£3,800–4,500 *S*

A rare elm dug-out chair, 18thC, 26in (66cm) wide.
£8,500–10,000 *RYA*

An early Georgian elm lambing chair, with original paint.
£7,000–8,000 *SWN*

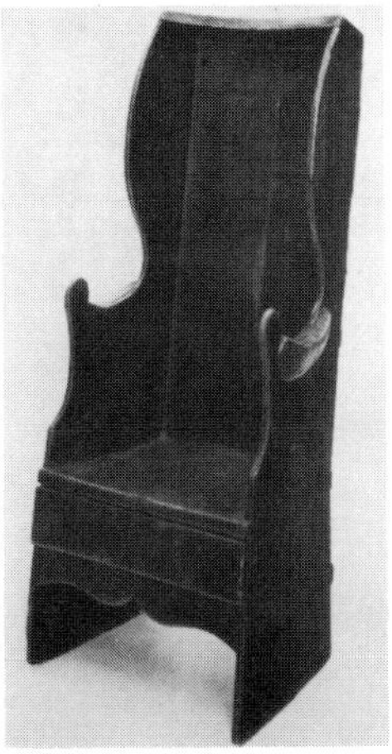

A lambing chair, of primitive form, partly in elm, the panel seat with drawer beneath, 55in (140cm) high.
£2,800–3,500 *L*

r. A George I oak lambing chair, with a rope seat, c1725.
£2,500–3,000 *PHA*

A William IV oak and alder rocking lambing chair, c1830.
£2,200–2,600 *PHA*

A yew-wood Windsor chair, 18thC.
£1,200–1,500 *MMB*

A pair of yew-wood Windsor elbow chairs, with bow backs and pierced splats, dished elm seats and crinoline stretchers joining the turned supports, early 19thC.
£4,000–4,500 *L*

A set of yew and elm high-ba elbow Windsor chairs, with pierced splats, mid-19thC.
£16,000–20,000 *N*

A walnut Windsor armchair, with arched cresting rail and outscrolled arms with spindle supports, damaged arm, mid-18thC.
£3,500–4,000 *Bea*

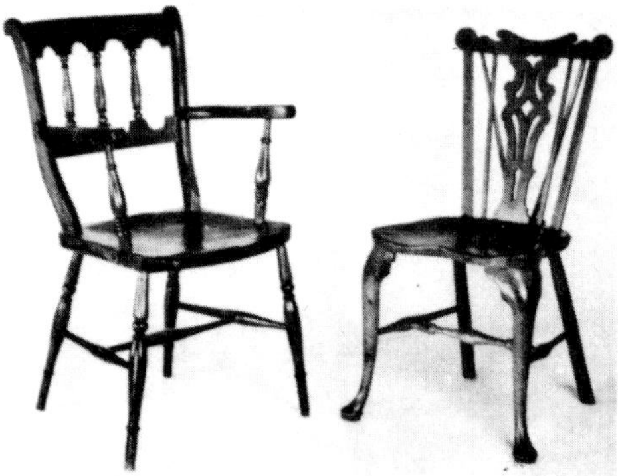

A beech and elm Mendlesham chair, with curved arms above a solid seat on turned legs and stretchers, and a Georgian beech and elm Windsor chair, 19thC.
l. **£480–600**
r. **£800–1,000** *CSK*

A yew and elm Windsor armchai with pierced vase-shaped splat, early 19thC, 35in (87.5cm) high.
£1,000–1,200 *TEN*

l. A set of 6 ash and elm Windsor chairs, including 2 armchairs, the arched backs with pierced baluster vertical splat flanked by stick splats, late 18thC.
£4,500–5,500 *Bon*

r. A set of 8 Robert Pryor design yew Windsor armchairs, c1800.
£12,000–15,000 *H*

A harlequin set of 8 yew-wood Windsor armchairs, with decorative splats, early 19thC.
£12,000–15,000 *H*

A set of 6 yew-wood Windsor style chairs, with crinoline stretchers.
£10,000–12,000 *BA*

A yew-wood Windsor chair, c1800.
£1,500–1,800 *MAT*

An elm Windsor armchair, c1825.
£450–550 *LL*

A Windsor armchair, with part yew-wood back, c1800, 35in (89cm) high.
£700–900 *S*

A beech and elm Windsor chair, c1840.
£550–650 *LL*

An elm Windsor chair, c1850.
£400–500 *LL*

An elm and ash Windsor chair, with crinoline stretcher, c1850.
£500–600 *DEB*

A yew-wood Windsor chair, c1800.
£1,200–1,500 *MAT*

A set of 6 country elm and ash Windsor chair, c1900.
£550–650 *DEB*

An elm and ash Windsor chair, c1850.
£480–600 *DEB*

A matched set of 8 low-back yew-wood Windsor armchairs, with standard splats, c1820.
£9,000–11,000 *H*

Two Victorian yew and elm Windsor armchairs, each with an arched pierced splat and spindled rail back, above outscrolled arms on bobbin-turned supports and a solid saddle seat.
£1,600–2,000 *CSK*

An elm and ash Windsor elbow chair, with pierced wheel splat, turned supports with an H-stretcher.
£400–500 *CDC*

An ash and elm comb-back Windsor chair, with a yoke-shaped crest rail, bowed arm rail with shaped front supports and turned legs, mid-18thC.
£1,200–1,500 *DWB*

Six yew, elm and beechwood Windsor armchairs, the bowed rail and pierced splat backs above saddle seats on ring-turned tapering legs, joined with crinoline cross stretchers.
£7,500–9,000 *CSK*

l. Four yew-wood Windsor elbow chairs, slightly different but each with bow backs and pierced central splats, elm seats and crinoline stretchers joining the turned supports.
£4,000–5,000 *L*

A yew-wood Windsor rocking chair, with an elm seat, c1790.
£1,200–1,500 *CDE*

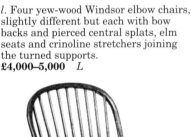

A Windsor yew and elm armchair, the arched back with pierced splat and baluster supports, moulded seat, on cut-down baluster legs, later rockers.
£800–1,200 *C*

A Windsor open armchair, with yew-wood hoop-back rails and arms, elm seat, on turned supports with crinoline hoop stretcher.
£900–1,200 *CDC*

A pair of yew-wood Windsor armchairs, 18thC.
£1,600–2,000 *B*

. A set of 6 Windsor armchairs, tamped 'F. Walker Rockley', arly 19thC.
:7,000–8,500 *CSK*

'rederick Walker was born at 'hornhill, near Leeds, in 1798. n 1823 he was a member of the ;amston Methodist Society, and y 1828 he was a member of Villiam Wheatland's class at tockley. He became class leader imself in 1831, and remained so or at least 30 years. By 1851, he nd his son, Henry, were the only emaining chair makers in the arish, and were specifically alled Windsor chair makers.

l. A harlequin set of 7 George IV elm and yew-wood Windsor armchairs, 2 stamped 'Wheatland Rockley'.
£8,000–10,000 *CSK*

William Wheatland is first recorded as a chair maker living and working at Beardsalls Row, East Retford, Notts, in 1822. In 1821 he was the Wesleyan leader in the small parish of Gamston which lies close to the hamlet of Rockley. By 1828 he is recorded as chair maker and Wesleyan class leader in Rockley. By 1841 William Wheatland is no longer recorded as living in the parish.

An elm Windsor armchair, mid-19thC.
£400–500 *OMH*

A small elm rail-back Windsor-type armchair, c1850.
£240–300 *OMH*

l. A low back yew-wood Windsor armchair, with an elm seat, late 18thC.
£750–900
r. A low-back Windsor armchair in elm and yew, early 19thC.
£1,200–1,500 *MAX*

r. A set of 8 yew-wood low back armchairs, late 18thC.
£12,000–16,000 *H*

A North Country elm broad-arm Windsor chair, c1860.
£800–1,200 *OMH*

A set of 5 yew-wood Windsor elbow chairs, with elm seats, early 19thC.
£4,500–5,000 *GD*

r. A matched set of 8 ash and elm Windsor armchairs, with stick backs and solid seats.
£3,500–4,500 *SS*

A harlequin set of 12 yew-wood broad arm Windsor chairs.
£12,000–15,000 *MGM*

l. An ash and elm high-back Windsor chair, c1830.
£480–600 *KEY*

A large yew and elm Windsor armchair, on ring-turned legs, c1830.
£3,500–4,000 *C*

A set of 6 small Windsor chairs with elm saddle-shape seats and front cabriole legs with pad feet, late 18thC.
£6,400–8,000 *L*

An ash and elm Windsor chair, early 19thC.
£400–500 *OSc*

An ash and elm Windsor chair, with crinoline stretcher, 19thC, 19in (49.5cm) wide.
£640–800 *PCA*

A fruitwood and elm Windsor chair, 19thC, 15in (38cm) wide.
£250–300 *PCA*

A broad arm yew-wood Windsor chair, 19thC.
£900–1,000 *TM*

Two yew-wood Windsor chairs, one with replaced crest rail, 19thC.
£1,200–1,500 *DWB*

A set of 8 elm ladder-back dining chairs, early 19thC.
£4,500–5,500 *PWC*

l. A pair of elm Windsor wheel-back farmhouse elbow chairs, with H-stretchers.
£800–1,200 *JD*

An ash, elm and fruitwood Windsor high-back chair, with 'Christmas tree' decorated splat, c1860.
£550–650 *OSc*

A scroll-back Windsor chair.
£80–100 *AL*

A George III ash Windsor armchair, with a fruitwood cresting rail and sycamore seat, on turned legs.
£1,800–2,200 *S(S)*

A mid-Georgian elm Windsor armchair, with waved top rail, railed back with pierced splat, cabriole legs and pad feet.
£3,200–3,800 *C*

Early Windsor armchairs of this style probably originated in the Thames Valley.

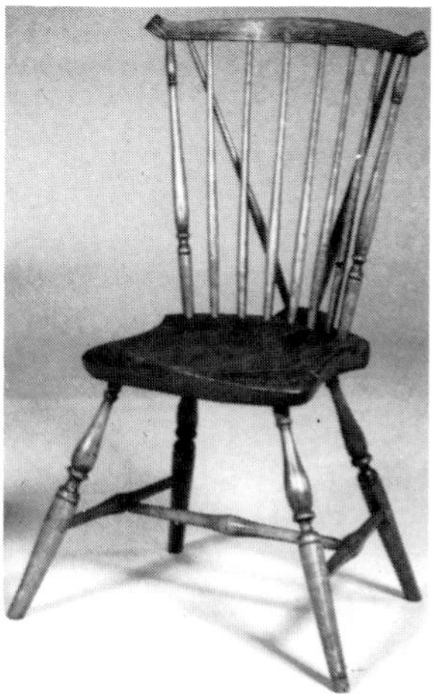

A pair of brace back Windsor side chairs, on baluster and ring turned legs joined by swelled stretchers, New England, late 18th/early 19thC.
£3,000–4,000 *CNY*

A simple rail back elm Windsor armchair, c1800.
£500–600 *OMH*

An elm, beech and yew-wood Windsor armchair, 18thC.
£800–1,000 *WHL*

Two comb-back Windsor elbow chairs, in ash and elm and some yew-wood, minor variations, 18thC.
£4,500–5,500 *L*

A sack-back Windsor armchair, on baluster and ring turned legs joined by turned stretchers, New England, 19thC.
£1,200–1,600 *CNY*

An ash Windsor armchair, early 19thC.
£750–900 *CSK*

A Windsor chair, with shaped seat and single bow back, c1780.
£1,000–1,200 *OSc*

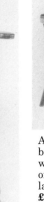

A pair of yew and elm Windsor low-back armchairs, the horseshoe arms with scroll terminals, the solid seats on turned legs joined by stretchers, late 18th/early 19thC.
£3,000–3,500 *Bea*

A set of 6 Windsor chairs, and 2 armchairs, c1840.
£2,500–3,000 *OSc*

Six ash and elm Windsor armchairs, with spindle filled hoop backs, horseshoe arms, solid seats and turned legs joined by stretchers.
£3,000–3,500 *Bea*

A yew-wood Windsor chair, with crinoline stretcher and pierced splat, c1850.
£800–1,000 *OSc*

A set of 7 beech, fruitwood and elm Windsor scroll back chairs, one with arms, each with triple baluster spindles beneath an arcaded top rail, dished panel seat and turned underframe, repaired, stamped 'RW' on rear edge of seat, 19thC.
£2,000–2,500 *L*

This style of chair was made by many of the High Wycombe chair manufacturers.

A West Country Windsor armchair, c1800.
£800–1,000 *KEY*

A yew-wood Windsor chair, c1900
£1,200–1,400 *AS*

Windsor Chairs

- unknown before 1720s
- basically Georgian tavern and coffee-house chairs
- earliest examples have comb backs, plain turned splayed legs, no stretchers
- cabriole legs suggest a date between 1740–70
- hoop back introduced c1740
- wheel splat introduced c1790
- Gothic Windsors, recognized by the carving of their spats and their pointed-arch backs, made 1760–1800
- some better quality Windsors stained black or japanned black or green; these are more valuable in original condition – do not strip them
- most desirable wood is yew, followed by elm
- some mahogany Windsors were made for the gentry, and are always of good quality
- curved stretchers, carved and well proportioned backs add to value

A fruitwood ladder-back elbow rocking chair, with rush seat on turned supports, 19thC.
£400–500 *GD*

A matched set of 6 Billinge Wigan ladder-back chairs, plus 2 armchairs, c1800.
£4,500–5,200 *H*

A set of George III elm ladder-back chairs, with pad feet, c1790.
£2,500–3,200 *SS*

A set of 7 oak ladder-back dining chairs, late 19thC.
£1,200–1,500 *PCh*

Eight ladder back dining chairs, with rush and string seats, including 2 carvers, late 18thC.
£4,500–6,000 *A*

l. A set of 6 George III oak and elm ladder-back chairs, c1800.
£1,500–2,000 *S(S)*

A set of 4 Macclesfield chairs.
£2,200–2,800 *Bro*

A set of 6 Wigan ash and elm ladder-back chairs, c1780.
£2,200–2,800 *P*

A set of 8 Macclesfield ladder-back chairs, with distinctive top rails.
£4,500–5,500 *H*

An ash and elm ladder-back elbow chair, 18thC.
£1,000–1,200 *CW*

A set of 6 elm and ash country ladder-back chairs, with American influence.
£2,500–3,000 *DEB*

An elm and ash country ladder-back chair, c1760.
£180–250 *DEB*

A set of 8 George III ash, elm and fruitwood ladder-back chairs, including a pair of armchairs.
£4,500–6,000 *Bon*

An 18thC ladder-back chair.
£200–250 *TJ*

A maple slat-back armchair, with ball and ring turned finials and flat arms, above a rush seat, on cylinder-and-ball turned legs joined by a double turned stretcher, New York or Connecticut, late 18thC.
£2,800–3,500 *CNY*

An 18thC-style ladder-back carver chair, with rush seat, on turned legs and stretcher.
£250–300 *DDM*

A George III oak ladder-back armchair, c1800.
£600–750 *SS*

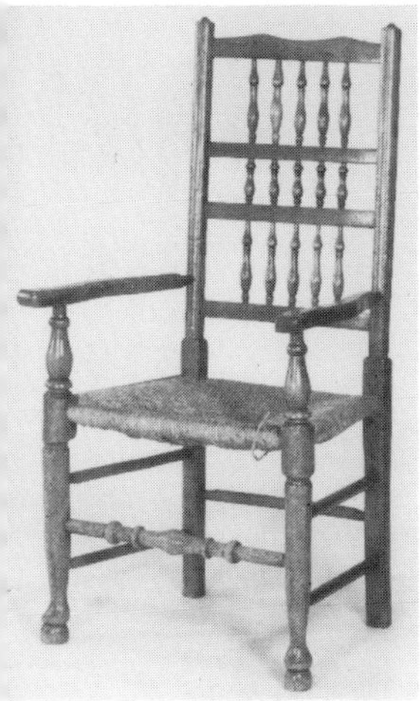

A set of 8 oak and ash spindle-back chairs, including a pair of armchairs, with rush and woven seats, on turned legs joined by stretchers, on pad and ball feet, spindle splats partially lacking, seats differ, early 19thC.
£2,500–3,000 *S(S)*

A harlequin set of 12 elm chairs, including 2 armchairs, with rush seats.
£4,500–5,000 *CSK*

A set of 6 ash spindle back chairs, each with a shell-carved top rail and rush seat, on turned legs joined by stretchers, pad feet, stamped 'C. Leicester', probably Cheshire, mid-19thC.
£2,500–3,200 *S(S)*

Charles Leicester is recorded as a chair maker with premises at 120–121 Chestergate, Macclesfield, Cheshire. He shared these premises with his son Charles, until they both moved to Derby Street c1855.

A matched set of 8 ash and birch spindle back chairs, including a pair of elbow chairs, with rush seats and turned tapering legs joined by stretchers, on pad and bun feet, seats re-rushed, Lancashire/Cheshire, c1900.
£3,000–3,500 *S(S)*

An ash spindle-back armchair, with a pierced splat back, and shaped seat, on turned supports with a hoop-form stretcher.
£800–1,200 *OL*

A matched set of 8 spindle-back dining chairs, on pad and ball feet, c1900.
£2,800–3,800 *S*

A mixed set of 5 Lancashire spindle back dining chairs, including one elbow chair, 19thC.
£1,200–1,600 *PC*

A matched set of 8 North Country fruitwood and ash spindle-back dining chairs, including one elbow chair, with rush seats, turned legs and stretchers, early 19thC.
£2,800–3,200 *P(S)*

An elm armchair, reduced in height, with rockers added.
£250–300 *CDE*

An elm smoker's bow chair, c1900.
£350–400 *Ph*

A Victorian elm and yew-wood smoker's bow chair.
£750–900 *JMW*

A desk chair, c1900.
£350–425 *Ph*

A set of 5 Irish beechwood penny seat and stick-back chairs, c1890.
£800–1,000 *UC*

A primitive oak and ash chair, 18thC.
£1,500–2,000 *RYA*

A set of 4 country stick-back chairs.
£480–600 *MGM*

A set of 3 Hereford-style kitchen chairs, late 19thC.
£250–300 *TRU*

A set of 6 elm kitchen chairs, early 20thC.
£450–550 *JMW*

An Irish ash and elm famine chair, Co. Kerry, 1840, 21in (54cm) high.
£450–550 *UC*

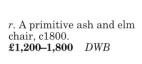

r. A primitive ash and elm chair, c1800.
£1,200–1,800 *DWB*

An elm bobbin-back farmhouse armchair, c1840.
£180–220 *OMH*

An elm slat-back cottage armchair, c1880, 26in (65cm) wide.
£90–110 *OMH*

A 'Busby's Stoop' rocking chair, c1880.
£200–250 *PIN*

A pair of Thonet beech dining chairs, c1910.
£80–100 *OMH*

A set of 6 wheelback chairs, with cabriole legs and crinoline stretchers, c1950.
£250–300 *PIN*

A pair of Georgian yew-wood and elm chairs.
£2,800–3,200 *HWO*

A wheelback chair.
£75–90 *AL*

A George III oak wing-back armchair, the panel back above a webbed seat and an enclosed base with a lateral frieze drawer, on stile feet, Lancashire/Yorkshire Dales, late 18thC.
£4,000–5,000 *S(S)*

An Irish fool's chair, 19in (48cm) wide.
£250–300 *PH*

A folding chair.
£110–140 *AL*

A matched set of 8 Lancashire spindle-back chairs, with Chippendale ears, late 18thC
£4,000–5,000 *H*

A Welsh primitive oak and ash comb-back armchair, with semi-circular seat and triple splayed legs.
£1,500–1,800 *S(S)*

A yew-wood comb back elbow chair, on cabriole legs with crinoline stretcher, 18thC.
£1,400–1,800 *JD*

An ash and elm comb-back chair, 41in (104cm) high.
£1,200–1,500 *LA*

l. An ash and elm comb back Windsor chair, 18thC.
£500–600 *TM*

An ash and elm comb-back corner chair, with a rush seat, 18thC.
£1,000–1,200 *OS*

A yew and elm low comb-back armchair, on turned legs with a bowed stretcher, late 18thC.
£1,000–1,200 *Bon*

A Suffolk Mendlesham chair in cherrywood with an elm seat and boxwood stringing, c1820.
£1,200–1,500 *OS*

Two elm and fruitwood Mendlesham open armchairs, each with a spindle back inlaid with boxwood, one with vase-shaped splat, solid seats on turned tapering legs joined by turned H-shaped stretchers, early 19thC.
£2,500–3,000 *C*

A pair of Mendlesham chairs, the backs line-inlaid, with turned spindle and ball decoration, the solid elm seats on turned legs.
£1,800–2,200 *NSF*

An elm Mendlesham chair.
£650–750 *GT*

A kitchen chair.
£75–90 *AL*

A yew-wood smoker's chair.
£850–1,000 *MAT*

A Victorian elm child's chair, from the village school at Preston, Kent, 24in (62cm) high.
£40–50 *PC*

A Tiverton chair, beech with elm seat, with contemporary tin repairs.
£300–350 *AL*

A pair of pine hall chairs, c1850.
£350–400 *AL*

An elm and beech kitchen chair.
£55–60 *WHA*

A kitchen chair.
£50–60 *AL*

A beechwood armchair, with a rush seat, 36in (92cm) high.
£200–250 *AL*

l. A set of 8 Victorian elm chairs, including 2 armchairs, on club legs joined with cross stretchers, and a set of 4 similar side chairs.
£3,800–4,200 *CSK*

r. A Scottish ash and walnut armchair, with burrwood veneered panel, repaired, front stretcher missing, veneer later, c1680.
£800–1,000 *S*

An ash and beech elbow chair, 19thC, 22in (56cm) wide.
£400–500 *PCA*

A set of 8 Wigan ladder-back chairs, in original condition, late 18thC.
£3,800–4,500 *H*

A rocking chair, c1880, 24in (61cm) wide.
£500–600 *W*

An Irish famine chair, c1840.
£350–400 *GPA*

A set of 4 smoker's chairs, c1860, 26in (66cm) wide.
£1,200–1,500 *W*

An armchair, with a new rush seat, c1870.
£250–280 *AL*

A pair of oak bobbin-turned elbow chairs, with vertical splats and finials, the solid seats on a similar turned underframe.
£1,800–2,200 *P*

A beech corner chair, with a rush seat, 27in (69cm) wide.
£200–250 *AL*

An elm and beech kitchen chair.
£80–100 *WHA*

A pine and wicker Orkney chair, 19thC.
£370–420 *ARK*

An Arts & Crafts hall chair, 24in (61cm) wide.
£500–600 *W*

An elm country chair, c1760.
£350–400 *PCL*

A Welsh primitive chair, with an oak seat and sycamore spindles, c1800.
£1,000–1,200 *OSc*

r. A set of 6 elm farmhouse dining chairs, c1820.
£500–600 *OMH*

r. A Yorkshire elm, ash and oak spindle back rocking chair, 42in (105cm) high.
£350–450 *SSD*

A set of 6 matched elm Windsor open arm elbow chairs, the saddle shaped seats on turned legs with stretchers.
£5,500–7,000 *GC*

A pair of elm side chairs, with spindle backs and panel seats, on turned supports with stretchers.
£650–800 *LRG*

A pair of yew Windsor domino back chairs, 18thC.
£1,500–1,800 *PCA*

A yew and elm Windsor armchair, with spindle filled hoop backs and horseshoe arms, solid seats and on baluster turned legs, joined by stretchers, stamped 'Hubbard', early 19thC.
£1,200–1,500 *Bea*

An elm chair, with a new rush seat, c1820.
£300–400 *AL*

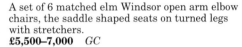

A pair of yew and beechwood Windsor chairs, c1800. **£1,500–2,000** *S*

r. An ash and elm Windsor rocking chair, c1830.
£750–900 *KEY*

An open arm Windsor chair.
£1,000–1,200 *AS*

A French fruitwood corner seat, with storage under seat, converted from a commode, 1880s, 22in (56cm) wide.
£350–450 *GD*

An oak panel-back armchair, the scroll cresting rail above a lozenge carved splat, the solid seat with columnar turned legs joined by peripheral stretchers, Yorkshire, feet restored, mid-17thC.
£2,800–3,500 *S(S)*

A Victorian Gothic-style chair.
£500–600 *WAH*

An English dug-out armchair, mid-18thC.
£6,500–7,500 *Ced*

An oak rocking chair, possibly Lancashire/Yorkshire, the foliate-carved cresting with the date '1748' flanked by later wings, the upholstered drop-in seat above a panelled base, on rocking supports, split back, late 18thC.
£1,500–1,800 *S(S)*

An oak lambing chair, with upholstered winged back, scrolled arms, webbed seat, panelled base with side drawer and pierced brass handle, 18thC.
£600–800 *AH*

A Welsh primitive commode chair, c1780.
£800–1,200 *COM*

A French child's chair, with rush seat, c1900, 21in (53cm) high.
£120–150 *WaH*

A primitive comb-back Windsor armchair, with lobster-pot cresting above a thick ash seat, c1770.
£2,500–3,000 *RYA*

A Victorian smoker's bow chair, with beech back and elm seat, c1890.
£150–180 *OPH*

An Irish súgán chair, replaced back rail, late 19thC.
£80–120 *FOX*

'Súgán' means twisted lengths of straw.

A Victorian pair of matched smoker's bow chairs.
£400–500 *POT*

An Irish ash and elm stick chair, original paint, early 19thC.
£350–400 *AF*

A beech desk chair, c1890.
£50–60 *AL*

An ash smoker's bow chair, c1870.
£180–200 *HON*

An Irish mixed wood famine chair, c1840.
£280–350 *Byl*

A Bavarian oak chair, with exotic wood inlays of birds and deer, on tapered legs.
£320–400 *AF*

An Irish beech carver chair, with string seat, c1880.
£140–180 *Byl*

An Irish pine child's dresser, c1870, 16½in (42cm) wide.
£100–125 *Byl*

A mixed wood child's chair, c1880.
£60–75 *HON*

A pine single door child's wardrobe, made from ceiling boards, c1900, 36in (91.5cm) wide.
£285–325 *OCP*

A Continental pine rocking cradle, c1890, 37in (94cm) long.
£150–175 *ASP*

A European pine cradle, c1870, 38in (96.5cm) wide.
£120–130 *AF*

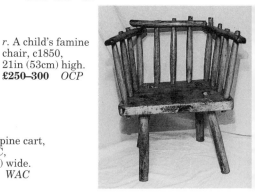

l. A child's pine cart, early 20thC, 18in (46cm) wide.
£130–180 *WAC*

r. A child's famine chair, c1850, 21in (53cm) high.
£250–300 *OCP*

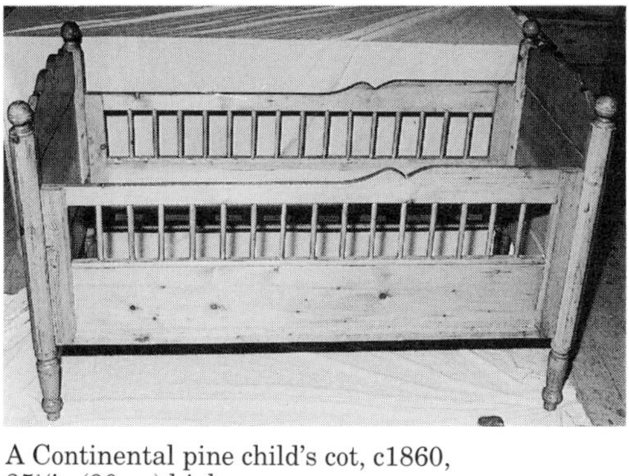

A Continental pine child's cot, c1860, 35½in (90cm) high.
£230–280 *AF*

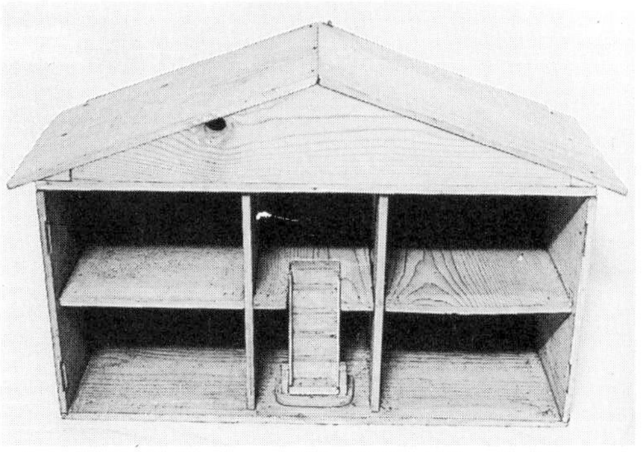

A pine doll's house, c1930, 26½in (67cm) wide.
£60–70 *OPH*

A child's Windsor chair, with original green paint, c1800.
£280–350 *KEY*

A Welsh comb back child's Windsor armchair, 18thC.
£1,200–1,400 *RYA*

A yew and elm Windsor elbow chair, with crinoline stretcher.
£700–900 *BHW*

An elm and ash child's school chair, c1880.
£250–300 *DEB*

A Welsh elm child's chair, with a shaped top rail over a spindle back, raised on splay supports, mid-18thC, 14in (36cm) high.
£800–1,000 *P(M)*

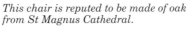

A Victorian Orkney oak framed child's chair, the enclosed curved back in bound rush, with open flat scroll arms and woven sea-grass seat.
£650–800 *GA(W)*

This chair is reputed to be made of oak from St Magnus Cathedral.

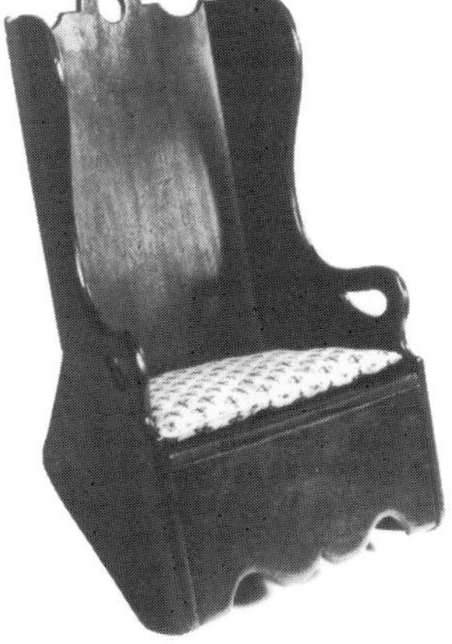

A child's mahogany rocking chair, c1770, 23½in (60cm) high.
£1,400–1,800 *PC*

A child's oak chair, c1800, 29½in (75cm) high.
£400–450 *PC*

A George III mahogany child's chair, and a stand.
£550–700 *PC*

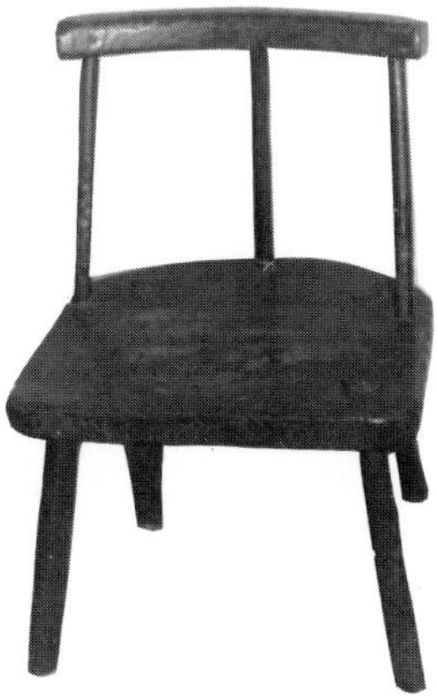

A primitive child's chair, with original red paint, 19thC, 18in (45.5cm) high.
£250–300 *PCA*

A child's Windsor chair, c1875.
£200–250 *PIN*

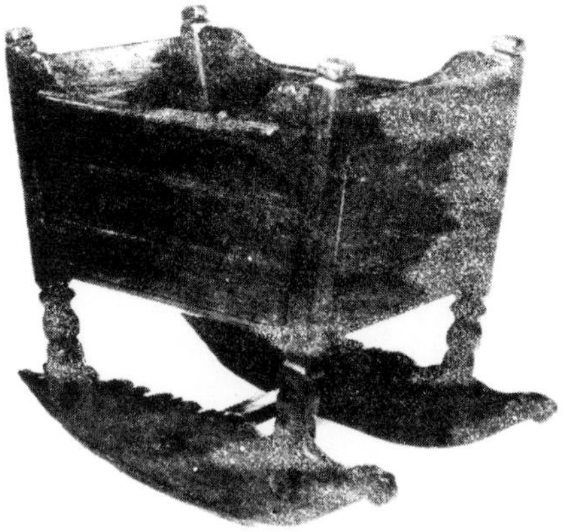

An oak cradle, Dutch or German, 17thC, 38½in (98cm) wide.
£1,500–2,000 *C*

A child's yew-wood and elm Windsor armchair, with an arched stick back and turned splayed legs joined by crinoline stretchers, early 19thC.
£1,200–1,500 *S(S)*

l. A child's walnut armchair with humped cresting rail, solid vase form splat, shaped arms and elm seat on outsplayed turned legs with baluster turned stretchers, damaged, 18thC.
£500–650 *NSF*

r. A child's school chair, c1920, 24in (52cm) high.
£40–50 *AL*

A spice rack, possibly a child's dresser, with blac porcelain knobs, 28in (71cm) high.
£240–300 *AL*

A Victorian baby walker, 18in (46cm) high.
£160–200 *PH*

A Welsh sycamore turned stool, 11in (29cm) high.
£150–200 *IW*

A primitive Welsh chair, c1780.
£1,250–1,750 *CC*

A child's trolley, late 19thC, 20in (51cm) wide.
£350–400 *PH*

A child's chair, 30½in (78cm) high.
£40–50 *AL*

. pine cot, with porcelain handles,
1in (104cm) long.
140–175 *CHA*

n early pine rocking
radle, c1830,
9in (99cm) long.
250–300 *AL*

pine doll's cradle,
1850, 18½in (47cm) long.
125–150 *AL*

pine cot/cradle, c1850,
4in (86cm) long.
300–350 *AL*

A beech high chair, which converts to a play pen, c1920.
£170–200 *AL*

A pitch pine child's washstand, c1880, 21½in (55cm) wide.
£250–300 *MCA*

A Welsh oak child's rocking armchair, 18thC, 22in (56cm) high.
£350–400 *SC*

A child's elm chair, mid-18thC, 12in (30.5cm) wide.
£650–750 *RYA*

A pine high chair which converts to a play table, with porcelain beads, 38in (96.5cm) high.
£140–180 *LAM*

Children's Furniture

The children's furniture illustrated in this guide no longer complies with EC safety regulations, and must not be used for its original purpose.

r. A pine high chair, c1850, 40in (101.5cm) high.
£160–200 *AL*

l. A child's beech high chair, with new cane seat.
£65–80 *AL*

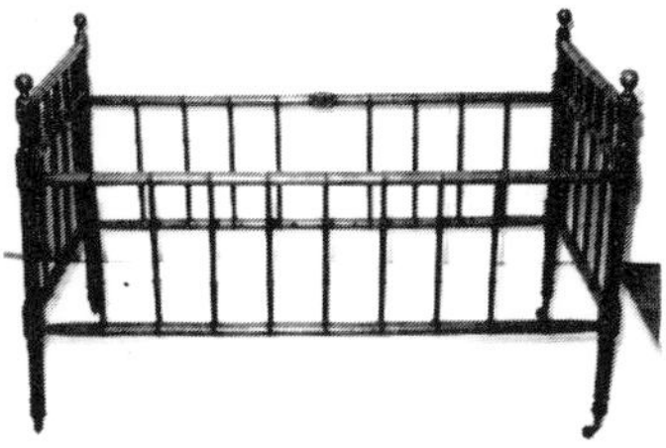

A simulated bamboo pine cot, 28in (71cm) wide.
£250–300 *PH*

A pine child's chair, c1920, 19in (49cm) high.
£45–50 *AL*

EARLY PAINTED FURNITURE

A late 17th century oak chest of drawers with original bun feet made £24,200 at auction. Without one addition to it, the price would have been nearer £1,500. Why? Because it was decorated with paint! This may seem surprising but the chest, not decorated until the early 19th century, is one of the many items of early painted furniture that is now attracting a great deal of interest. Although the species itself is not well documented, recent research is turning up many interesting facts about both materials and methods used for this particular type of decoration.

British domestic and ecclesiastical furniture has been decorated with paint and coloured pigment since medieval times and following the flamboyant Gothic period, the painting style of furniture and domestic wooden objects changed. It fell into three categories: monochrome, polychrome (geometric or floral) and simulation.

Monochrome, the most common form of decoration, was simply a coat or two of single-coloured paint usually applied as protection against weather and general household wear and tear. Used on uncarved softwood, its decorative merits lie within the colour chosen, and the effect that years of wear and tear, patina and fading has had on its surface. An early Irish 19th century monochrome painted pine dresser can make £3,000 on the merit of its attractive colour combination, and retained paint surface on the backboards and shelves. This is not an uncommon feature on dressers, corner cupboards and delft racks and one which may add considerably to their value.

Polychrome decoration is most prized on painted furniture as it demands more artistic ability and epitomizes the soul of 'folk art'. A simple child's moneybox, late 18th century, made and painted to imitate a Georgian house is worth around £800. British 17th and early 18th century free-hand painting is extremely rare and highly prized on furniture, but a certain amount of 'leopard spotted', 'striped' or 'chequerboard' decorated early furniture does come on the market, initialled and occasionally dated. The rarity of these pieces always ensures a healthy price, as was the case with the aforementioned bun-footed chest of drawers.

The simulated finish covers items made from ordinary oak or pine, which is then painted to imitate a finer or more exotic timber (often walnut or imaginary burrwood). A mid-17th century English oak joint stool, a rare example of imitation walnut, could fetch £2,500. This scumble-type decoration – achieved by drawing a comb, hard brush or feather through a wet dark glaze laid over a lighter coloured ground – became popular in the 18th century and common in the 19th century.

As fashions and tastes changed, much of the early painted furniture was redecorated to cover the cracks, chips and decoration of years gone by, and later added paint serves to protect the original from further damage. To remove these later layers, it is imperative that skilful and careful restoration of the furniture takes place as harm is easily done. Non-original layers of paint added later should be carefully scraped off with a scalpel or chisel to avoid damage to the original. Known as dry scraping, this slow but worthwhile process leaves a powdery, slightly rough finish, returning the item close to its original condition, complete with blemishes and chips. Only in very exceptional circumstances should chemical paint removers, solvents or hot air guns be used as they seriously damage the original surface.

Dry scraped furniture is the most desirable and easily identifiable. To avoid pitfalls such as claims that later paint has been 'washed off', which usually means that much or all of the 'old' paint has been 'washed on', follow a few guidelines. When examining an 'antique' or 'original' paint surface, look out for any 'original' paint found in worm holes, or worm tracking, on or towards the bottom of feet, covering repairs or patches, replaced hinges, and be wary of a paint surface without a ground. Bear in mind that brush strokes shouldn't be visible after 100 years and that a bubbled surface is easily achieved with a blowlamp! A black or coloured wax finish also indicates there may be something to hide.

Evidence of age is proudly displayed in original or dry scraped pieces – faded sun-bleached colours (especially blues, salmon pinks and turquoise greens), paintwork through to wood, built-up patina around handles, and bleached-out areas around polished handles, are all to be cherished. Look too for natural blistering, stains, water damage, and wear around feet.

Many pieces of country furniture were already 50 to 100 years old when painted, so naturally the question of originality occurs, even though a good piece of such furniture is now worth more than its equivalent in polished wood. It seems that the painted furniture market has now established its own rules in this respect. If the paint has not been touched up or otherwise enhanced, or if the paint is antique but not necessarily contemporary with the item, it may be considered acceptable. But bear in mind that 17th century furniture with original paint is very rare.

The furniture is simply a vehicle for the paint, which was not applied to deceive or copy, but merely to decorate and brighten up the home. This is British folk art, produced by ordinary unskilled people, but to be considered valuable and desirable, it must have character, colour, originality of design – basically the 'look'. This 'look' can lift a piece of painted furniture from the ordinary and everyday, to a much prized and valuable level.

Robert Young

A carved and painted pine schrank, with deep carved double-moulded cornice above a panelled case with shelved interior and 2 drawers in base, Pennsylvania, c1770, 69in (175cm) wide.
$25,000–30,000 *S(NY)*

A Hungarian painted pine coffer, c1850, 43in (109cm) wide.
£650–750 *UC*

A Hungarian painted pine dower chest, with original finish, c1850, 46in (116.5cm) wide.
£650–750 *UC*

A painted pine base, with 3 drawers and one door, c1880, 38in (96.5cm) wide.
£650–700 *AL*

An Irish painted pine open rack farmhouse dresser, with original finish, c1850, 55in (139.5cm) wide.
£2,200–2,800 *UC*

A Bohemian painted pine armoire, with canted corners, original finish, c1820, 48in (122cm) wide.
£2,200–2,500 *UC*

An Irish painted pine two-part hutch dresser, with original finish, c1860, 50in (127cm) wide.
£2,000–2,200 *UC*

An Irish painted pine fiddle-front farmhouse dresser, original paint worn, c1850, 51in (129.5cm) wide.
£2,500–2,800 *UC*

A painted pine chest of drawers, original finish, fitted with glass knobs, c1870, 41in (104cm) wide.
£500–600 *AL*

A Romanian painted pine bed, with original finish, c1880, 39in (99cm) wide.
£500–600 *UC*

A painted pine coffer, with original painted finish, on bracket feet, 18thC, 42in (106.5cm) wide.
£300–400 *SWN*

A painted pine chest of drawers, with upstand, 2 short and 2 long drawers, c1840, 42in (106.5cm) wide.
£550–600 *AL*

A Danish painted pine iron-bound seaman's chest, c1850, lined with newspaper dated '1893', 53in (134.5cm) wide.
£750–900 *UC*

A painted pine dresser, with 3 drawers, southern England, c1750, 42in (106.5cm) wide.
£3,500–4,000 *SWN*

A European painted pine cupboard, with elaborate floral design, 1806, 50in (127cm) wide.
£1,000–1,200 *AnD*

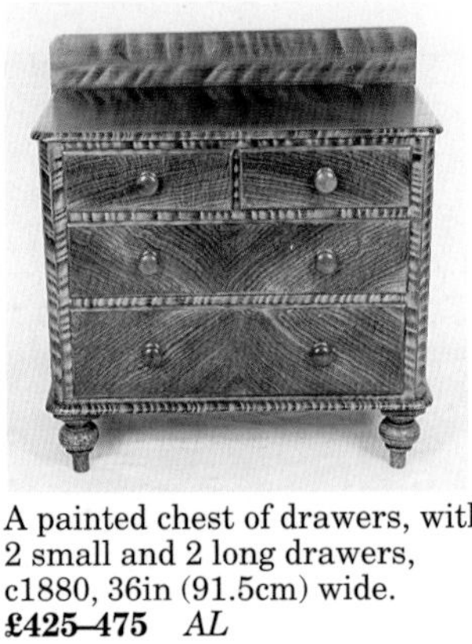

A painted chest of drawers, with 2 small and 2 long drawers, c1880, 36in (91.5cm) wide.
£425–475 *AL*

A painted pine stool, c1920, 13in (33cm) high.
£40–50 *Ber*

A painted pine chest, southern Germany, c1860, 48in (122cm) wide.
£450–500 *AnD*

A Russian pine dresser, with original paint, c1840, 30in (76cm) wide.
£500–600 *AnD*

A painted pine marriage chest, decorated with a tulip design, 18thC, 49in (124.5cm) wide.
£600–700 *SWN*

A painted pine toy cupboard, with turned baluster columns, early 18thC, 31in (78.5cm) wide.
£500–600 *SPa*

A Victorian painted pine washstand, 30in (76cm) wide.
£140–180 *FOX*

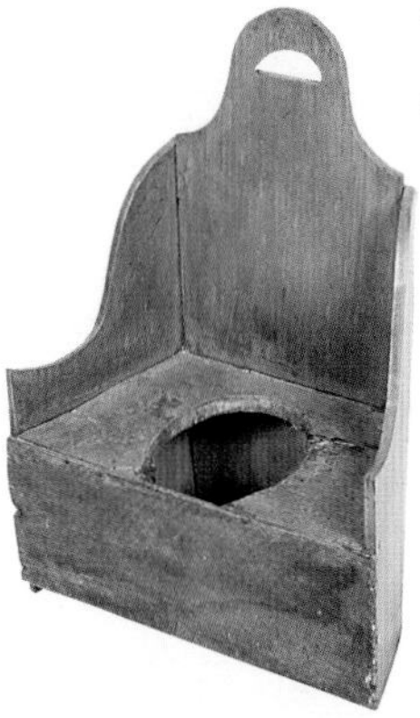

A child's painted latrine, c1880, 25in (63.5cm) high.
£150–180 *Ber*

A painted pine corner cupboard, with dentile cornice, the door with 4 panels, mid-18thC, 29in (74cm) wide.
£650–750 *SWN*

r. A painted pine corner cupboard, with original finish, 19thC, 25in (63.5cm) wide.
£425–475 *FOX*

A painted pine food cupboard, mid-18thC, 33in (83.5cm) wide.
£700–800 *SWN*

A painted pine stool, with lifting lid, 19thC, 16in (41cm) wide.
£120–150 *SWN*

A pine candle stand, with a stool base, the top painted, c1760, 16in (41cm) wide.
£900–1,100 *RYA*

A hanging meat safe, with original paint and iron hooks, c1840, 52in (137cm) high.
£350–450 *COT*

A five-drawer hanging spice cabinet, with original paint, c1880, 18in (45.5cm) high.
£125–150 *COT*

A West Country pine box settle, painted to simulate oak, 36in (91.5cm) wide.
£1,200–1,500 *SWN*

A late Georgian spoon rack, with a salt box and spice drawers, with original grained finish, c1810, 18in (45.5cm) wide.
£400–500 *COT*

An early Victorian astragal glazed corner cabinet, with original grained paint, c1840, 30in (76.5cm) wide.
£400–450 *COT*

A set of 3 North Country spindle-backed chairs, with original paint, c1800, 18in (45.5cm) wide.
£700–800 *RYA*

A vinegar grained box, inscribed 'George Winchester – 12 years old – His Box', c1880, 11in (28cm) wide.
£90–110 *WaH*

A painted pine country shelf, c1920, 49½in (125cm) wide.
£300–400 *Ber*

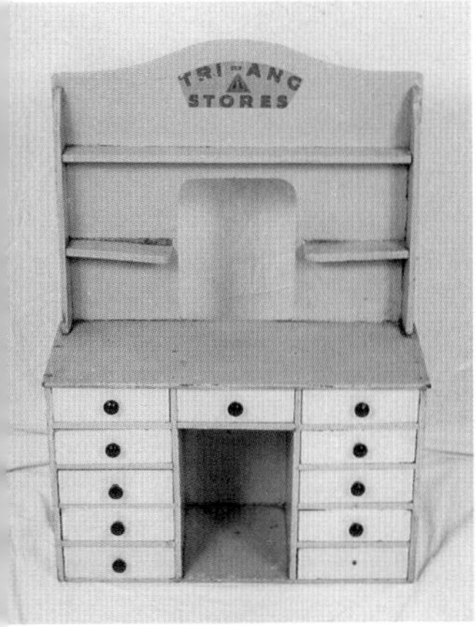

A pine 'Tri-ang Stores' toy shop, with original paint, 24in (61cm) wide.
£125–175 *COT*

A set of spice drawers, with porcelain knobs, c1880, 24in (61cm) high.
£50–75 *COT*

A painted chest of drawers, with 2 short and 2 long drawers, damaged, c1830, 35½in (91cm) wide.
£500–600 *WaH*

A painted pine chest of drawers, c1925, 35½in (90cm) wide.
£180–200 *BEL*

An Edwardian pine sewing box, with swag decoration, on cabriole legs, with original paint finish, c1900, 24in (61cm) wide.
£150–200 *COT*

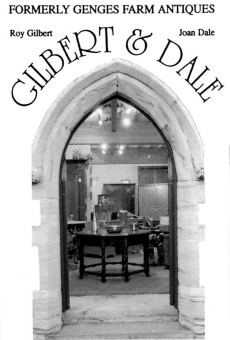

A Victorian dressing chest, painted to simulate burr-walnut, c1860, 38in (96.5cm) wide.
£400–500 *COT*

A Victorian pine painted dressing chest, c1880, 40in (101.5cm) wide.
£450–550 *COT*

A Regency pine washstand, with gallery back, original paint finish, c1830, 38in (96.5cm) wide.
£700–800 *COT*

A Georgian pine butler's cupboard, grain painted, blue painted interior, 2 brushing slides, mother-of-pearl roundels on ebony handles, c1800.
£2,200–2,600 *COT*

A pine plant stand, with painted legs, c1840, 32in (81.5cm) high.
£80–100 *Cou*

A grained pine cooking box, complete with tins, c1860.
£100–150 *COT*

A Georgian three-drawer dresser base, with original powder-blue paint, c1800, 69in (175cm) wide.
£1,800–2,200 *COT*

A mid-Victorian grain-painted child's toy crib, 20in (51cm) long.
£100–150 *COT*

A painted pine wardrobe, c1770, 71in (180cm) wide.
£2,000–2,500 *BEL*

An Austrian painted cupboard, c1830, base moulding replaced, 36in (91.5cm) wide.
£2,800–3,200 *RYA*

A Georgian corner cupboard, with original grained paint, c1780, 39in (99cm) wide.
£1,800–2,200 *COT*

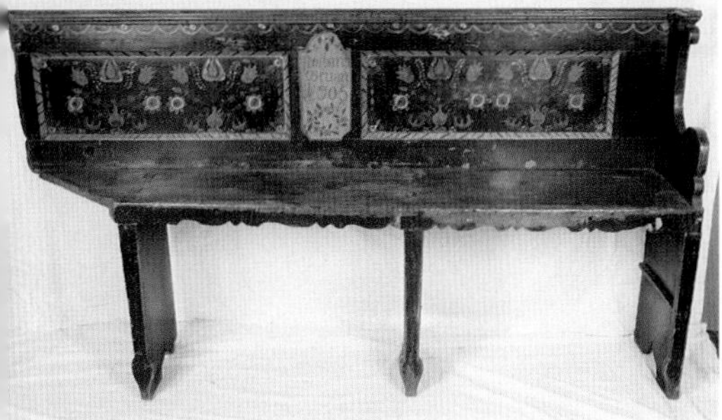

One half of an Austrian corner bench, 18thC, repainted in 1905, 74in (188cm) wide.
£750–900 *COT*

An early Victorian grain-painted chest of 3 drawers, with a gallery back, c1830, 28in (71cm) wide.
£500–600 *COT*

A dresser base, with 3 drawers above 2 panelled doors, 60in (152cm) wide, and a delft rack, with 3 shelves and fluted column ends, some original blue paint, c1780.
£3,800–4,800 *RYA*

An early Georgian pine lace or campaign chest, the hinged lid enclosing a small well above 2 drawers with original handles, original finish, c1740, 24in (61cm) wide.
£500–650 *COT*

An Orkney shepherd's chair, made from recycled timber, traces of old paint, c1840, 21½in (54cm) wide.
£1,000–1,300 *RYA*

A West Country painted pine dresser, with glazed cupboard doors above, c1770.
£14,000–18,000 *RYA*

An Austrian painted cupboard, c1830, base moulding replaced, 36in (91.5cm) wide.
£2,800–3,200 *RYA*

An Austrian painted bed, initialled and dated '1796'.
£4,000–4,500 *RYA*

An armoire, painted to simulate marble, with floral decoration, the central cartouche with initials 'IK' and dated '1793', 56in (142cm) wide.
£10,000–12,000 *RYA*

A painted floor-standing corner cupboard, with a carved mask, c1730.
£4,500–5,500 *RYA*

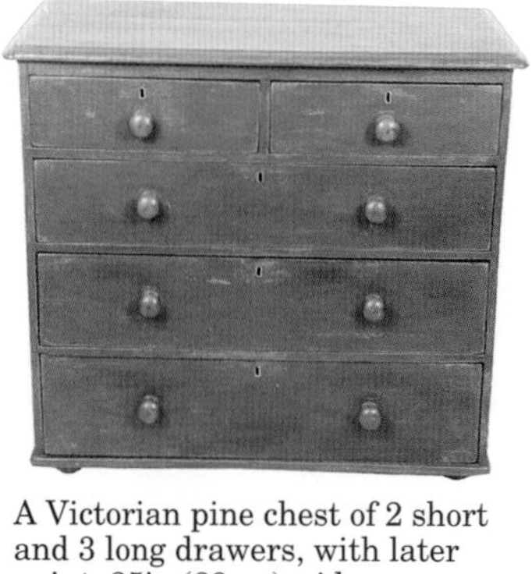

A Victorian pine chest of 2 short and 3 long drawers, with later paint, 35in (89cm) wide.
£250–300 *FOX*

A pine hand-painted armoire, decorated with folk art depicting horsemen, dated '1836', 48in (122cm) wide.
£5,500–6,500 *RYA*

An American rocking chair, the back panel painted with fruit decoration, c1830.
£500–600 *JBL*

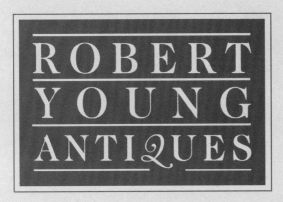

A Georgian pine clerk's table, with original varnish, c1780, 38in (96.5cm) wide.
£200–300 *COT*

A painted pine wall cupboard, 19thC, 18in (45.5cm) high.
£80–100 *Cou*

A late Georgian elm child's chair, c1820, 16in (40.5cm) wide.
£100–150 *COT*

A painted pine wardrobe, with one door, c1900, 41½in (105cm) wide.
£250–300 *BEL*

A grained pine cupboard, c1860, 30in (76cm) wide.
£300–350 *COT*

A painted pine wardrobe, with decoration on the 2 doors, c1840, 59in (150cm) wide.
£500–600 *BEL*

A painted pine coffer, c1890, 38½in (97cm) wide.
£350–450 *MCA*

A Victorian pine grain-painted blanket box, with 2 drawers inside, and a candle box, c1850, 48in (122cm) wide.
£200–250 *COT*

A Queen Anne painted pine dresser, in original condition, 60in (150cm) wide.
£10,000–12,000 *AP*

A Continental painted pine cupboard, mid-18thC, 29in (73cm) wide.
£2,500–3,000 *AP*

A French painted pine food cupboard, mid-18thC, 30½in (76cm) wide.
£2,200–2,800 *AP*

An East Anglian painted pine chest, in original condition, 18thC, 25in (63cm) wide.
£1,500–2,000 *AP*

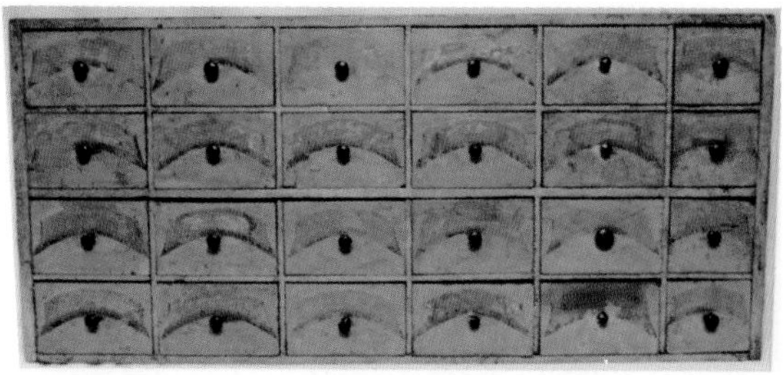

A painted pine flight of drawers, c1830, 44½in (112cm) wide.
£2,000–2,500 *AP*

r. A pine rack, for storing wooden spoons, c1850, 12in (30.5cm) wide.
£350–400 *AP*

l. A French painted pine hanging cupboard, containing a collection of children's plates, 18thC, 31in (78cm) wide.
£2,750–3,250 *AP*

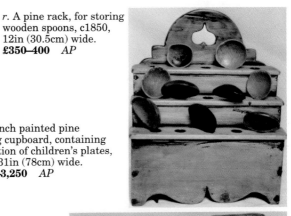

r. A pine box, decorated with paper, c1740, 16in (40cm) wide.
£400–500 *AP*

A miniature fruitwood spoon rack, with shaped cresting, containing bone spoons, c1760, 15in (38cm) high.
£750–800 *RYA*

A Scandinavian food box, 19thC.
£175–200 *SWN*

A Welsh stepped spoon rack, with a collection of old cawl spoons, paintwork original, early 19thC, 11in (28cm) high
£750–800 *RYA*

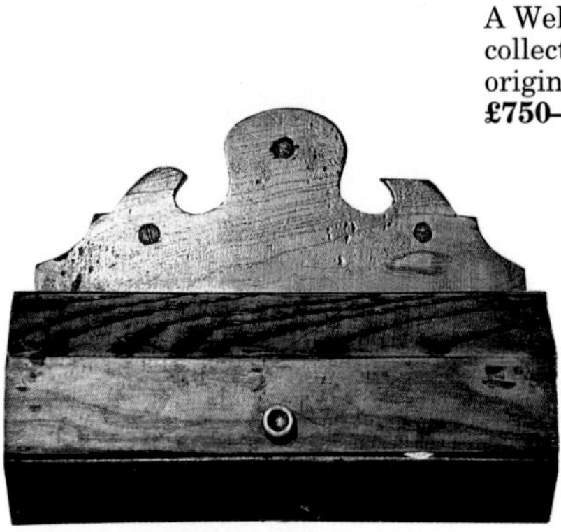

A hexagonal elm salt box, with shaped cresting, c1800, 11½in (29cm) wide.
£300–350 *RYA*

A wooden bucket, with a metal handle, c1900, 12in (30.5cm) high.
£40–50 *FOX*

A Northumbrian beehive riddle board, c1760, 16½in (42cm) wide.
£300–350 *RYA*

A Scandinavian food box, 19thC.
£125–150 *SWN*

A pine cutlery tray, 12in (30.5cm) long.
£25–30 *FOX*

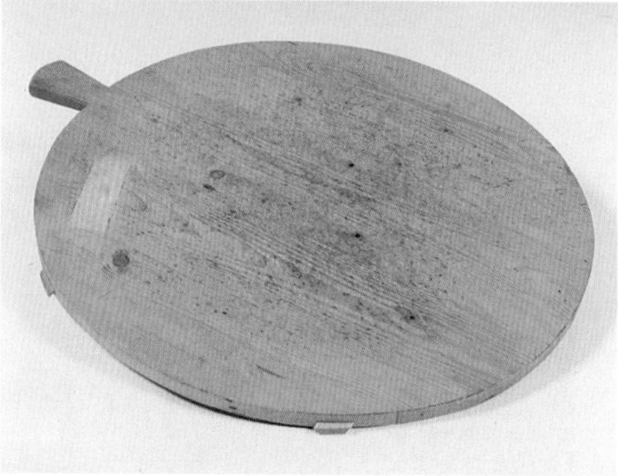

A pine cheeseboard, 19thC, 25in (63.5cm) long.
£25–30 *AnD*

An Eastern European wooden trough, 19thC, 31in (78.5cm) long.
£75–80 *AnD*

Two pine mashers, 1870s, 10in (25.5cm) high.
£30–40 each *CEMB*

A peck measure, 12in (30.5cm) diam.
£65–70 *MIL*

A pair of elm bellows, c1880, 21in (53cm) long.
£55–65 *MIL*

A housemaid's pine box, c1890, 14in (35.5cm) wide.
£65–75 *MIL*

A potato basket, 25in (63.5cm) wide.
£50–55 *MIL*

A French grape basket, 19in (48cm) long.
£35–40 *MIL*

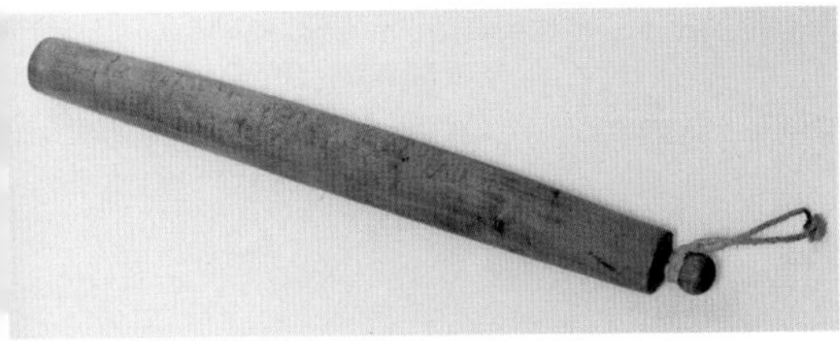

A Victorian wooden rolling pin, 16in (40.5cm) long.
£12–15 *TaB*

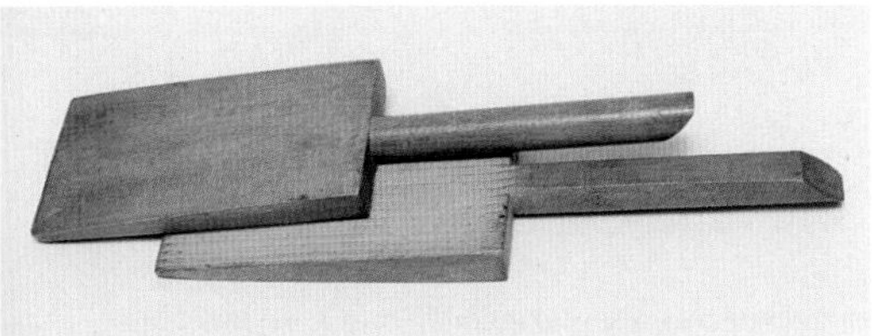

Two small wooden butter pats, 8in (20.5cm) long.
£10–15 *TaB*

A French wooden coffee grinder, c1920–30, 6½in (16cm) high.
£20–25 *CEMB*

A Romanian butter maker, c1870, 28in (71cm) high.
£90–100 *OPH*

A terracotta dairy pail, the inside glazed, with a wicker handle, 15in (38.5cm) high.
£70–80 *TaB*

An Eastern European pine stand, with a pine tray, stand 28in (71cm) high.
£100–120 *NWE*

A small Victorian range, 26in (6cm) wide.
£400–450 *WaH*

An enamel cereal bin, c1920, 14in (35.5cm) high.
£22–25 *OPH*

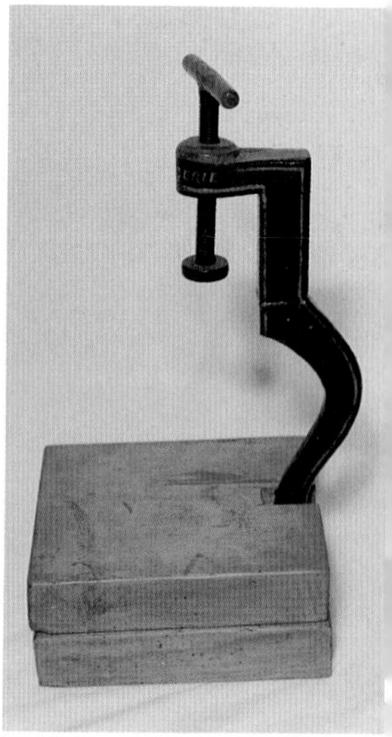

A French cheese press, c1920, 17in (43.5cm) high.
£55–65 *OPH*

An enamel washing boiler, c1920, 11in (28cm) high.
£40–50 *OPH*

Two wicker baskets, largest 27in (69cm) long.
£15–18 each *NWE*

Two copper saucepans, with lids, c1860, largest 9in (23cm) diam.
£230–280 *MIL*

A set of 3 tin and brass measures, largest 10in (25.5cm) high.
£100–120 *MIL*

A milk can, with brass handle, stamped with the name of the dairy, early 1900s, 7½in (19cm) high.
£80–90 *TaB*

A blue enamel Universal Ham Cooker, 15in (38cm) high.
£25–30 *TaB*

A tin and brass pint bottling measure, 9in (23cm) high.
£40–45 *MIL*

A tin cream bowl, with handles on each side, c1880, 20in (51cm) diam.
£30–35 *MIL*

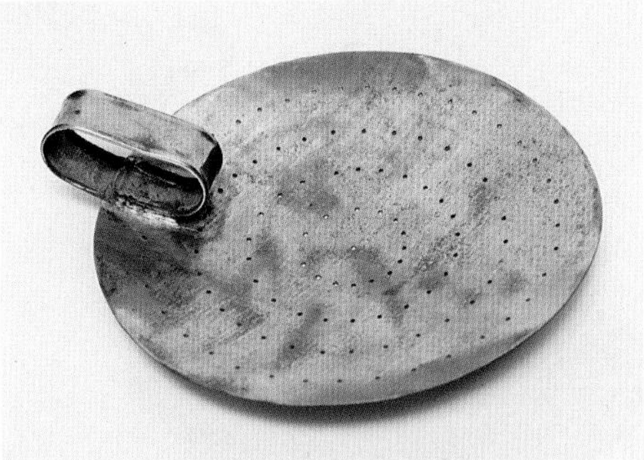

A metal cream skimmer, 8in (20.5cm) diam.
£12–15 *TaB*

Four tin and brass cream cans, one gill to 2 pints, largest 4½in (11.5cm) high.
£400–420 *MIL*

An iron skillet, with spout, c1850, 14in (35.5cm) diam.
£40–45 *MIL*

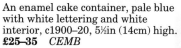

An enamel cake container, pale blue with white lettering and white interior, c1900–20, 5½in (14cm) high.
£25–35 *CEMB*

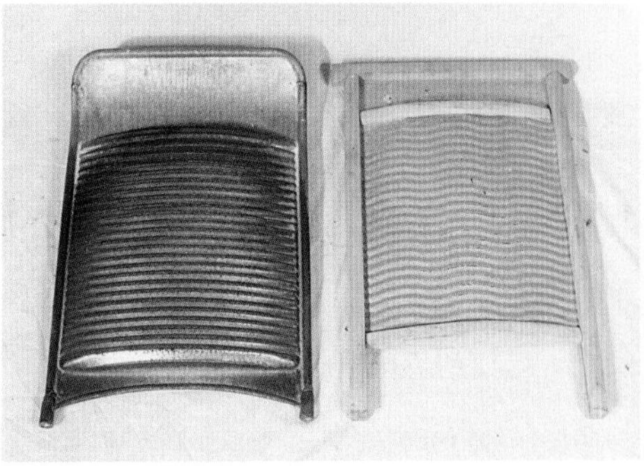

Two German galvanized wash boards, c1920, largest 22in (56cm) wide.
£10–15 each *NWE*

A metal egg whisk, with original pottery basin, c1930s, 10½in (26.5cm) high.
£20–22 *TaB*

A metal cream can, with a brass screw stopper, 5in (13cm) high.
£40–45 *MIL*

A pewter pillar ice-cream mould, c1868, 6½in (16cm) high.
£150–200 *CEMB*

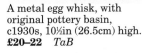

l. A copper fish kettle, c1860, 20in (51cm) wide.
£250–300 *MIL*

A set of Salter household scales, with a cast-iron body with tin pan, c1930, 10½in (27cm) high.
£20–25 *CEMB*

A metal cream can, 9in (23cm) high.
£50–60 *MIL*

A tin and brass two-gallon milk can, 13in (33cm) high.
£75–85 *MIL*

An Eastern European painted pine blanket box, with candle box, lock and key missing, 22in (56cm) wide.
£250–300 *HGN*

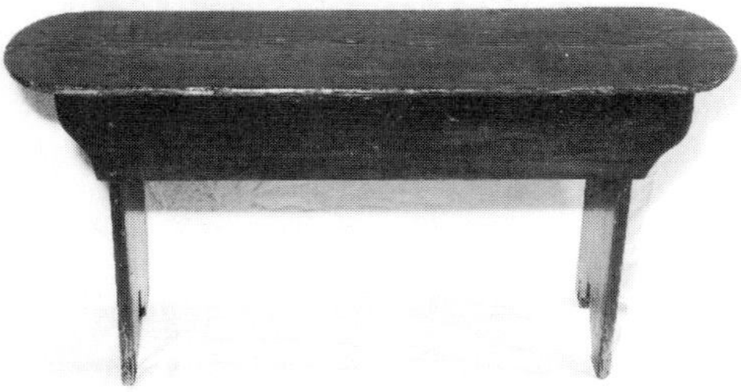

A pine stool, c1870, 38in (96.5cm) long.
£100–150 *PEN*

A painted pine estate desk, with internal drawers, c1800, 23in (59cm) wide.
£425–475 *PEN*

A painted pine occasional table, 17½in (44.5cm) wide.
£400–450 *PEN*

A pine cricket table, with painted base, original paint, c1840, 28½in (71cm) diam.
£600–650 *PEN*

A French painted pine folding table, c1850, 35in (89cm) diam.
£350–400 *PEN*

l. A Regency glazed pine hanging cupboard, c1810, 31in (79cm) wide.
£500–600 *PEN*

A Regency painted pine simulated rosewood occasional table, 18in (45.5cm) wide.
£400–500 *PEN*

A Georgian pine sideboard, 38in (96.5cm) wide.
£450–500 *PEN*

A Welsh painted sycamore stool, original paint, 13½in (34cm) high.
£40–50 *PEN*

A set of painted pine library steps, c1840, 27in (69cm) high.
£300–350 *PEN*

A green painted stool, c1850, 15in (38cm) wide.
£40–50 *PEN*

A northern French chestnut armoire, with terracotta wash, c1785, 51in (129.5cm) wide.
£1,500–1,800 *PEN*

A painted simulated bamboo chest of drawers, original paint, c1880, 42½in (107cm) wide.
£650–800 *PEN*

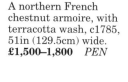

r. A painted pine box, c1850, 28in (71cm) wide.
£65–80 *PEN*

l. A Scandanavian painted pine cupboard, with single door, dated '1804', 47in (119cm) wide.
£1,200–1,500 *GD*

r. A painted pine cupboard, with shelves, 36in (91.5cm) wide.
£500–600 *PEN*

A child's black painted Windsor armchair, with shaped fan-back above 7 spindles and flat-shaped set back arms over a saddle seat, on splayed baluster turned legs jointed by a bulbous turned H-stretcher, 19thC.
£800–1,000 *CNY*

A Scandanavian painted beech spinning wheel, c1860, 37in (94cm) high.
£200–250 *RK*

A German painted and decorated pine marriage bedstead, the shaped headboard painted with a lady and a gentleman standing in a landscape, with floral and leaf motifs in polychrome, inscribed 'Johann and Maria Katharina' and the date '1824', with turned footposts, the tester panel overhead painted with bucolic landscapes within medallions in polychrome, 50½in (128cm) wide.
£4,000–4,500 *S(NY)*

A pine chest of drawers, with simulated bamboo decoration, 40in (101cm) wide.
£850–1,000 *PH*

A Victorian painted pine box/chest, with original decoration, 37in (94cm) wide.
£170–200 *AL*

A German painted pine box, c1850s, 24½in (62cm) wide.
£250–300 *WHA*

A painted pine marble-topped washstand, with original paintwork and handles, c1860, 36in (92cm) wide.
£350–400 *AL*

An original painted pine washstand, c1870, 36½in (93cm) high.
£250–300 *AL*

A painted pine box, with original lock and key, dated '1868', 44in (112cm) wide.
£425–475 *CHA*

A painted pine wedding chest, possibly Scandanavian, 30in (76cm) wide.
£400–500 *PH*

A Scandanavian painted pine coffer, original paint, dated '1808', 46in (117cm) wide.
£420–480 *GD*

A Scandanavian original painted pine coffer, 18thC, 50in (127cm) wide.
£420–480 *GD*

l. A paint-decorated poplar blanket box, painted black with red and amber mottling and amber faux marble veining, minor imperfections, New Jersey, early 19thC, 32in (81.5cm) wide.
£650–800 *SK(B)*

A red-painted high-post bedstead, with shaped headboard with scalloped crest above a row of spindles, the footposts similarly chamfered, on square tapering legs, Texas, mid-19thC, 52½in (133.5cm) wide.
£4,000–4,500 *CNY*

A French buffet, with block fronted doors, repainted, 1870s, 51in (129cm) wide.
£580–650 *GD*

A joined panelled and painted chest, the pine top above an oak six-board chest with fielded side pine panels, and a single drawer, the painted panels and drawer outlined with black applied mouldings, Boston or Coastal Massachusetts, c1800, 42in (106.5cm) wide.
£3,500–4,000 *SK(B)*

A painted blanket box, with applied mouldings, original red paint, New England, 18thC, 43in (109cm) wide.
£850–1,000 *SK(B)*

l. A pine chest, New England, with applied half-round moulding, lidded till and early stained brown surface, early 19thC, 44½in (112cm) wide.
£2,500–3,000 *SK(B)*

A Bavarian pine coffer, with panelled top and boarded sides, with iron carrying handles, the plinth base with name and date '1793', 18thC, 58in (147cm) wide.
£1,200–1,800 *S(S)*

A Victorian original painted pine bookcase, Cumbrian, c1850, 83in (210.5cm) high.
£1,400–1,800 *BH*

A blue-painted bowfront chest of drawers, c1820, 41½in (105cm) high.
£800–1,000 *RP*

A painted pine linen chest, c1830, 43in (109cm) wide.
£1,800–2,200 *RP*

A blue-painted kitchen chest of drawers, with brass knobs, late 19thC, 61in (155cm) wide.
£800–1,200 *PCh*

A painted pine chest of drawers, c1840, 42in (106.5cm) wide.
£500–600 *RP*

r. A painted pine chest of drawers, c1830, 36½in (92cm) high.
£500–600 *RP*

An original painted pine chest of drawers, c1850, 41in (104cm) wide.
£850–1,000 *AP*

A painted pine chest of drawers, 40in (101.5cm) wide.
£600–750 *AL*

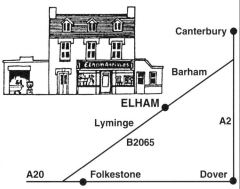

An oak and pine jointed chest with drawer, Massachusetts, old finish, c1700, 43in (109cm) wide.
£3,500–4,500 *SK(B)*

An American carved and painted pine blanket chest, Berks Country, Pennsylvania, dated '1788', the moulded hinged top opening to a deep well with till, 2 drawers below, 18thC.
£21,000–24,000 *B*

A oak and pine carved jointed chest of drawers, the centre panel with initials 'S.K.' above two drawers, old refinish, Connecticut Valley, probably Hadley area, c1700, 41in (104cm) wide.
£18,000–22,000 *SK(B)*

r. A Continental painted oak chest, the panelled doors painted with flowering plants flanking florally painted central panel above scalloped apron and block feet painted with trees, possibly Austrian, 54in (137cm) wide.
£3,000–3,500 *LHA*

A paint-decorated pine child's blanket chest, signed 'Jonathan Maitz', dated '1871', Pennsylvania, 27in (69cm) wide.
£15,000–18,000 *S(NY)*

A fan-back Windsor side chair, old black paint, New England, c1780.
£2,000–2,200 *SK(B)*

A George III oak and painted comb-back armchair, with solid seat and splayed legs, late 18thC.
£1,750–2,000 *S(S)*

l. A sack-back Windsor armchair, painted black, New England, c1780.
£2,200–2,600 *SK(B)*

r. A fan-back Windsor armchair, old black paint, imperfections, New England, c1780.
£2,000–2,200 *SK(B)*

A Windsor armchair, old black paint, probably Rhode Island, c1780.
£2,200–2,600 *SK(B)*

A pine corner cupboard, with painted dome, c1760, 50in (127cm) wide.
£4,000–5,000 *PH*

A Federal pine corner cupboard, with blue-painted interior, plate grooves, scallop surround, reeded lower section with hinged door opening to a shelf, early 19thC, edges of shelves scalloped at later date, 52in (132cm) wide.
£6,500–8,000 *S(NY)*

An Austrian painted armoire, c1807, 73in (185cm) high.
£7,500–8,500 *CHA*

l. A Swedish painted pine marriage chest, 18thC, 43in (109cm) wide.
£650–800 *DN*

A painted pine bowfront corner cupboard, with panelled doors, original paint, 19thC, 46in (117cm) wide.
£1,200–1,500 *BEL*

A painted pine armoire, with arched top, 48in (122cm) wide.
£400–500 *LAM*

A Napoleon III pine and simulated bamboo tall chest, with 6 drawers, c1860, 28in (71cm) wide.
£850–1,000 *S(S)*

A German painted pine box, c1854, 45in (114cm) wide.
£750–800 *CHA*

A chest of drawers, recently painted, no handles or knobs, 1860–80.
£240–270 *PIN*

A Scandanavian painted pine secrétaire, with fitted interior, c1845, 36in (93cm) wide.
£1,200–1,500 *BEL*

A pair of French cream-painted pine console tables, with cloven hoof feet tied by a curved stretcher surmounted by a figure of a putto playing a harp, originally gilt, 18thC, 36in (92cm) wide.
£3,500–4,500 *KEY*

A Belgian painted armoire, c1820, 72in (182.5cm) high.
£1,000–1,500 *UP*

A Scandanavian pine bench, painted with flowers on a brown and green ground, 19thC, 51in (130cm) wide.
£1,000–1,200 *DN*

A painted pine glazed hanging cupboard, c1840, 42in (106.5cm) wide.
£350–450 *KEY*

A French pine and faux bamboo escritoire, 39in (99cm) wide.
£400–450 *MCA*

A German painted pine cobbler's cupboard, 27in (68.5cm) wide.
£170–200 *CHA*

A German painted pine armoire, c1840, 55in (139cm) wide.
£650–800 *BEL*

A painted and decorated chest of drawers, the top with a ship within a painted oval reserve above 2 short drawers over 3 long drawers, on compressed ball feet, the entire surface painted brown and embellished with yellow highlights, the drawer fronts inscribed '1871/The Liberty/800 Tons/Falmouth', 39in (99cm) wide.
£850–1,000 *CNY*

A painted housekeeper's cupboard, Galway 18/19thC.
£4,000–5,000 *B*

A red painted pine cupboard, Texas, the projecting cornice above a pair of recessed panelled cupboard doors opening to an interior fitted with 3 shelves over a scalloped apron, on square tapering legs, mid-19thC, 50in (127cm) wide.
£2,000–2,500 *CNY*

A Victorian chiffonier, with original stain, 36in (91.5cm) wide.
£270–300 *CCP*

An American Empire painted slant front desk, the fall-front opening to reveal a fitted interior, the base with single drawer, on turned legs, lid inscribed 'The Flower and the Fern', c1840.
£450–550 *MMG*

A Romanian pine presser, original finish, c1850s, 37½in (95cm) wide.
£500–600 *OPH*

A Victorian table, with original finish, c1860, 27in (69cm) wide.
£350–400 *COT*

r. A Queen Anne brown-painted yellow pine architectural cupboard, Virginia, one side unfinished, late 18thC, 31in (79cm) wide.
£4,000–5,000 *S(NY)*

l. An American painted pine architectural corner cupboard, with moulded fluted cornice above a pair of arched glazed mullioned hinged doors opening to a painted shelved interior, the hinged panelled doors below opening to a shelf, c1780, 55in (139.5cm) wide.
£3,500–4,500 *S(NY)*

A painted pine low dresser, c1700, 60in (152cm) wide.
£3,500–4,000 *OSc*

A pair of painted chairs, 17in (43cm) wide.
£500–600 *PH*

A painted pine corner cupboard, with original glazing, 46in (117cm) wide.
£3,000–3,500 *PH*

A painted ship's box, c1880, paint restored, 17in (43cm) wide.
£150–180 *MCA*

A painted sycamore cupboard, East German or Polish border, c1818, 24in (61cm) wide.
£550–650 *CHA*

A Scandanavian painted pine chest of drawers, 37in (94cm) wide.
£375–425 *BEL*

A painted pine dressing table, 18thC, 42in (106.5cm) wide.
£1,400–1,600 *AP*

A late Victorian painted chest, with graduated drawers and compartment, a painting of birds on top, 15in (38cm) wide.
£250–300 *W*

A painted arched top dresser, 19thC, 98in (249cm) wide.
£4,000–5,000 *RK*

A Scandanavian painted pine chest of drawers, recently painted, c1890, 38in (96.5cm) wide.
£400–450 *BEL*

l. A German painted pine chest, 19½in (49cm) wide.
£275–325 *CHA*

A Victorian grey painted pine bookcase, in the Gothic taste, the upper section with a moulded cornice, the base with panelled cupboard doors, on a plinth, slightly reduced in length, late 19thC.
£35,000–45,000 *Bon*

A Queen Anne painted table, with original blue-green paint, early turned pull handle, minor repairs, New England, 18thC, 43in ((109cm) wide.
£14,000–18,000 *SK(B)*

r. A Victorian table, with single drawer, original colour wash, c1860, 40in (101.6cm) wide.
£350–400 *COT*

An early Victorian lyre-ended side table, with 2 frieze drawers, gallery back, original painted decoration, c1840, 44in (112cm) wide.
£400–500 *COT*

A painted pine 8-day clock, c1848.
£1,000–1,200 *BEL*

A late Federal painted washstand, with splashback, painted yellow and with black highlights and trailing fruit vines, New England, c1810, 28in (71cm) wide.
£1,000–1,200 *CNY*

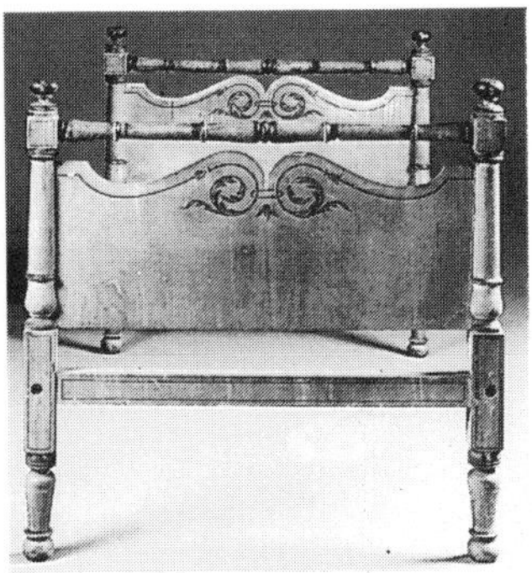

A pair of green and tan-painted headboards, each with ring turned baluster toprail flanked by turned finials, the waved board painted with foliate arabesques, on ring turned tapering legs, lacking side rails 47in (119.5cm) wide.
£800–1,000 *C*

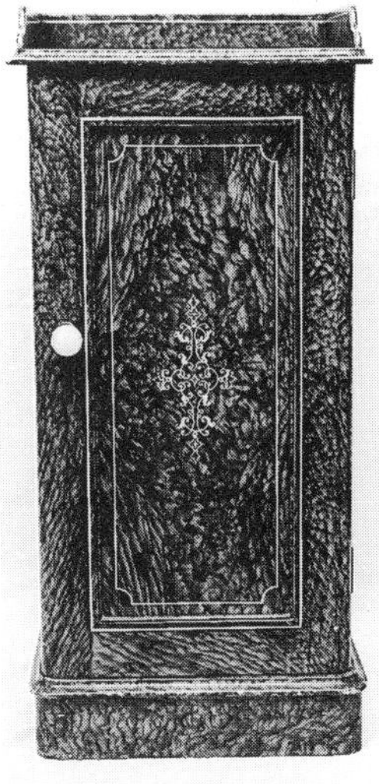

A painted pine pot cabinet, with gallery back, c1870, 32in (81.5cm) high.
£150–200 *ASP*

A wooden cradle, painted in red, yellow and black with geometric patterns, 19thC, 33in (83.8cm) wode.
£220–280 *EL*

l. A doll's house front, early 19thC, 28in (71cm) high.
£300–400 *SWN*

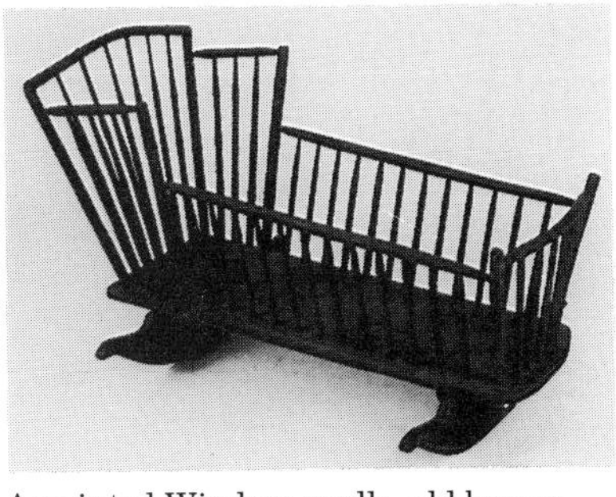

A painted Windsor cradle, old brown paint over blue-green, some damage, New England, c1810, 38in (96.5cm) long.
£2,500–3,000 *SK(B)*

l. A Georgian mule chest, with original paint, on bracket feet, moulding on top replaced, c1820, 39½in (100.5cm) wide.
£200–300 *POT*

r. A pine cot, hand painted using buttermilk paints, c1920, 30in (76cm) wide.
£100–125 *POT*

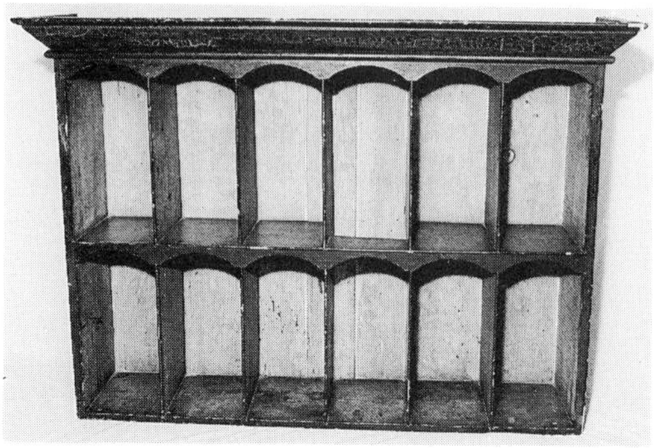

A hanging shelf unit, with numerous arches and original paint, c1830, 51½in (130.8cm) wide.
£350–400 *POT*

A pine box, with original paint and unusual hinge, c1820, 31in (78.5cm) wide.
£150–185 *POT*

A painted pine hanging corner cupboard, with fielded panels, c1750, 31½in (80cm) wide.
£500–600 *POT*

A French painted ash farmhouse ladderback chair, with rush seat.
£120–150 *AF*

A George III pine dresser, the associated raised back with moulded cornice above a painted frieze and open shelves, the base with 3 central drawers flanked by a pair of fielded panel cupboard doors, on stile feet, cornice partially lacking, 63in (160cm) wide.
£2,500–3,000 *S(S)*

An Austrian painted pine cupboard, with one bottom drawer, original lock and key, c1770, 78in (198cm) high
£2,500–3,000 *AF*

r. A Bohemian pine box, with original paint, dated '1771', 45½in (115.5cm) wide.
£500–600 *AF*

A Georgian Dutch-style box, painted in Pennsylvania, with original hinges and candle slide inside, on bracket feet, 48in (122cm) wide.
£750–1,000 *AF*

r. A European pine box, original paint, 38in (96.5cm) wide.
£250–300 *AF*

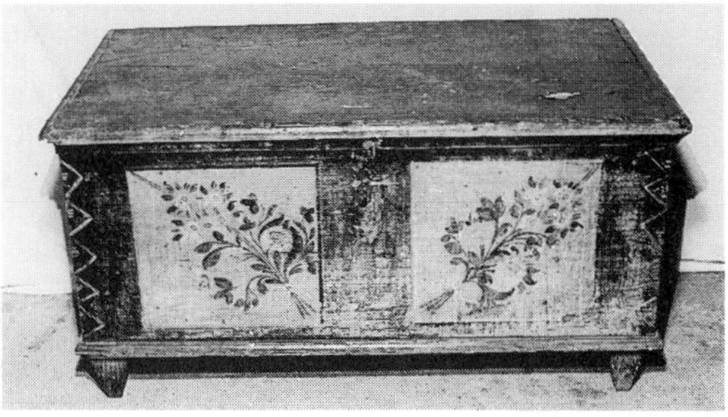

An Eastern European painted pine box, dated '1889', 58in (147.5cm) wide.
£250–300 *OCP*

An Austrian painted pine mule chest, with carved owl corbels, two false drawers and one bottom drawer, 47in (119.5cm) wide.
£700–800 *AF*

r. A European pine mule chest, with single drawer, original paint, 44in (112cm) wide.
£450–500 *AF*

An Irish painted settle table, 18thC, 65½in (166.5cm) long.
£800–900 *AF*

A Georgian painted pine corner cupboard, with carved cornice, astragel glazed door, bracket feet, original paint, c1800, 78in (198cm) high.
£900–1,100 *AF*

A Georgian Irish pine alcove cupboard, repainted, c1780, 84in (213.5cm)
£800–1,000 *AF*

An Irish pine country chair, original paint, 34in (86.5cm) high.
£60–75 *AF*

A painted pine captain's chair, c1890.
£120–150 *DFA*

A captain's chair, c1890.
£120–150 *DFA*

An Irish painted pine dresser, County Galway, c1860, 50½in (127cm) wide.
£1,000–1,200 *DFA*

A painted pine davenport, c1860, 22in (56cm) wide.
£750–900 *DFA*

An Irish painted pine dresser, c1860, 49in (124.5cm) wide.
£800–1,000 *DFA*

l. A painted pine desk, on tapered legs, c1880, 48in (122cm) wide.
£350–400 *DFA*

A painted pine drop-leaf table, c1880, 48in (122cm) long.
£170–200 *DFA*

A late Georgian Irish painted pine food cupboard, c1820, 48in (121.9cm) wide.
£1,000–1,200 *DFA*

An original painted dressing table, with drawer and cupboard, mirror and towel rail, turned legs, c1860, 37in (94cm) wide.
£350–400 *DMc*

A painted pine dresser, c1880, 51in (129.5cm) wide.
£650–800 *DFA*

A painted pine food cupboard, with panelled sides, on bracket feet, c1800, 55in (139.5cm) wide.
£650–800 *DFA*

A pine dressing chest and chest of drawers, each with 3 deep drawers, glass handles, original paint, c1860, 41in (104.1cm) wide.
£1,400–1,700 *AL*

A painted pine box, with original blue paint, c1880, 18½in (47cm) wide.
£75–90 *AL*

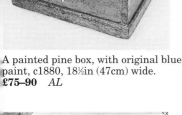

A painted pine trunk, original paint, c1880, 29in (73.5cm) wide.
£160–200 *AL*

l. An Irish painted pine writing table, with a drawer, on turned legs, c1880, 47in (119.5cm) wide.
£150–180 *HON*

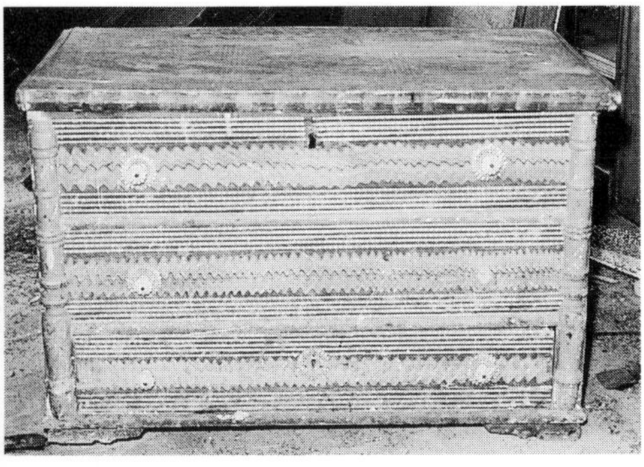

A painted pine linen box, with false drawers, c1875, 45in (114.5cm) wide.
£120–150 *DFA*

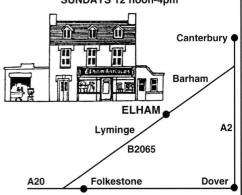

An Irish painted pine cottage dresser, with fretwork top and panelled doors, c1870, 47in (119.5cm) wide.
£900–1,100 *HON*

An Irish painted pine chiffonier, the carved back with original mirror, the base with 2 drawers and 2 cupboards, c1880, 46in (117cm) wide.
£275–325 *HON*

An Irish painted pine dresser, with 2 drawers and open base, c1860, 58in (148cm) wide.
£450–550 *SA*

An Austrian painted pine box, 29in (73.5cm) wide.
£250–270 *Byl*

An Austrian painted pine box, with candle box inside, c1870, 42in (106.5cm) wide.
£350–400 *Byl*

An Austrian painted pine blanket box, original paint, with candle box, c1870, 48in (122cm) wide.
£350–420 *Byl*

An Austrian painted pine box, c1850, 43in (109cm) wide.
£325–375 *Byl*

A Georgian carved and stained pine cradle, c1750, 22in (56cm) wide.
£420–480 *SA*

r. An Irish painted pine dresser, with 2 drawers and 2 cupboard doors to base, c1880, 56in (142cm) wide.
£650–800 *SA*

Old Court Pine

(Alain & Alicia Chawner)

Old Court • Collon • Co. Louth • S. Ireland

Tel: 041-26270
Fax: 041-26455
International Code: 00-353-41

Irish Dower Chest C1860

Glazed Book case C1880

Cottage Sideboard C1890

Original Cut Open Top Dresser C1880

Armoire C1890

Bed Press C1880

North Antrim Cupboard C1840

Coffee Table C1885

Gallery Back Washstand

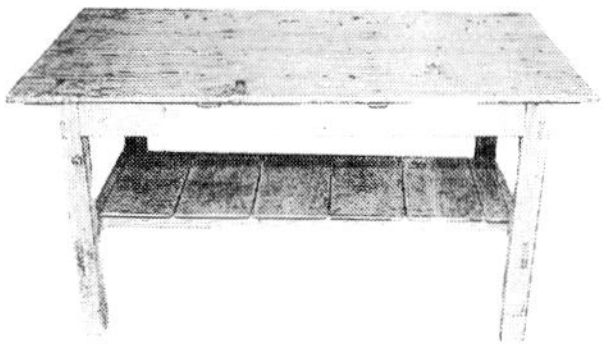

Pot board Farmhouse Table C1860

Up to 1000 pieces of Irish Country Pine at wholesale prices

50 minutes from Dublin Airport -
we can meet you.
Packing and containerisation on the premises.
Fax or ring us in advance.

KITCHENWARE

The kitchen has been the centre of domestic life for generations of women. While traditional pieces of kitchen furniture, such as dressers and tables, have long been desirable, the wide range of kitchen utensils and equipment has, until recently, largely been overlooked as a collecting area. The enormous success of the auction of Elizabeth David's Kitchen in London in 1993 played a major part in raising the status of kitchenware, reflecting its established popularity with many collectors and introducing it to a wider audience. In the full glare of the media, cooks and kitchenware enthusiasts from around the world gathered at Phillips auction house for the chance to buy an item from the kitchenware collection of Elizabeth David, one of the century's most important cookery writers.

Elizabeth David's interest in kitchenware is easy to understand as it is a fascinating and diverse field, appealing to a wide range of interests and pockets. Remarkably, it is still possible to find some early pieces of kitchenware from the 18th to the mid-19th century. These pieces offer a fascinating glimpse into pre-industrial society and range from high-quality tea caddies made by craftsmen to simple homemade griddles and herb and spice choppers. Beautiful copper moulds in a wealth of different shapes and sizes were produced from the 1830s onwards and were originally used in the kitchens of wealthy homes. Particularly popular with collectors today, they generally command the highest prices of all kitchenware.

Fortunately, collecting this field can also be easily affordable. The past few years have seen an explosion in popularity of items produced from the 1880s to the 1950s, arguably the most interesting period in the development of kitchenware. The 19th century saw the introduction of many designs that were to remain unchanged until today, such as the balloon whisk and the pastry crimper. In the 20th century, mass production led to the development of kitchenware as a huge international industry, with British makers such as Tala and Nutbrown leading the field.

Although many designs have not altered since the 19th century, different materials have come in and out of fashion. For instance, cast iron was commonly used for pots and pans, along with steel and vitreous enamel. By the early 20th century aluminium, a lighter and more versatile material, was favoured, especially in North America. From the 1920s onwards, stainless steel became the most popular metal for making cutlery.

Collectors today have an enormous range from which to choose. Favourite subjects include storage jars, wooden spoons and pie funnels, while other popular items are whisks, pudding basins, waffle makers and rolling pins. Some collectors prefer to concentrate on a specific type of material, such as wirework or enamel. Wirework has recently come back into fashion and items must always be examined carefully to make sure they are not modern reproductions. Early pieces will be of far higher quality and the wire will be twisted rather than soldered.

Whatever you choose to collect, most of these implements and utensils are still easy to find today, often for only a few pounds, and much enjoyment can be had from tracking them down in car boot sales, auctions, specialist kitchenware shops, markets or even junk shops. Prices reflect the diversity of these sources and vary according to geographical location, the availability of particular items and the overheads of the dealer. However, one of the joys of kitchenware is owning a collection of pie funnels that would cost tens of pounds can be as enjoyable as having a set of enamelled storage jars that could set you back over £100.

Perhaps the best and most inexpensive source of kitchenware is direct from your mother or grandmother, who can explain first-hand how a particular item was used in her kitchen. However, as kitchenware has grown in popularity, items that at one time were readily available are now not appearing on the market, with families keeping what would once have been discarded. At the same time, collectors are becoming more discerning and appreciate the craftsmanship and quality of older kitchenware items.

Finally, make the most of your kitchenware by, where possible, using an item for its original purpose. Remember, though, that older items will need more looking after than new ones, so take extra care with washing and drying up, and always store kitchenware safely in a dry place to prevent rust damage.

Christina Bishop

A rub-a-tub, 16½in (42cm) diam.
£35–40 *AL*

A wooden trough, 18in (45.5cm) wide.
£15–20
A meat cleaver.
£10–15
A wooden butterpat.
£5–10 *LAM*

A meat tenderizer.
£10–15 *AL*

l. A pair of scales, for weighing babies, 15in (38cm) high.
£40–50 *AL*

An enamel candlestick.
£12–15 *AL*

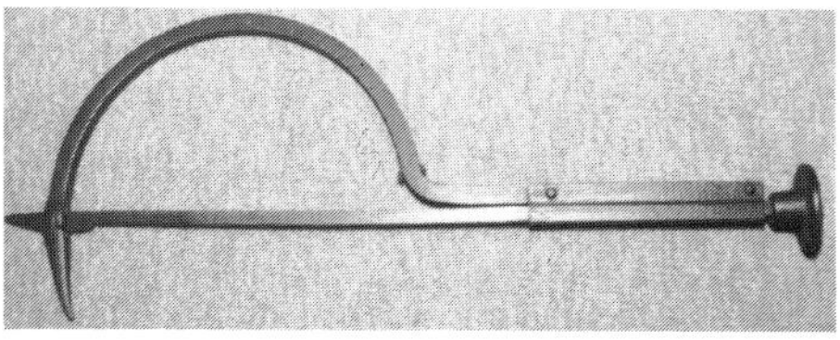

A thatcher's wrought-iron needle, 19thC.
£30–35 *PCA*

A chemist's ball, 21in (53.5cm) high.
£550–650 *JeB*

A metal-bound oak tub, 19thC, 14in (35.5cm) high.
£12–15 *PCA*

An oak costrel, with glass ends, 19thC, 10½in (26.5cm) high.
£80–100 *PCA*

r. A lacemaker's lamp, with hollow baluster stem and plain moulded foot, c1880, 10½in (26.5cm) high.
£100–150 *P*

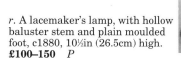

An oak silk thrower, 18thC, 25½in (65cm) long.
£80–100 *PCA*

A Victorian butcher's scales table, with brass plaque marked 'Chayney & Co, Ramsgate', 36in (91.5cm) wide.
£350–400 *WaH*

A selection of cutlery trays, c1900, largest 14in (35.5cm) long.
£15–20 each *ASP*

r. A pine butter churn, c1890, 17in (43cm) high.
£100–150 *ASP*

A corn ladle, old staple repair, late 19thC, 15in (38cm) long.
£65–80 *COT*

A pine salting trough, c1870, 31in (78.5cm) long.
£60–70 *ASP*

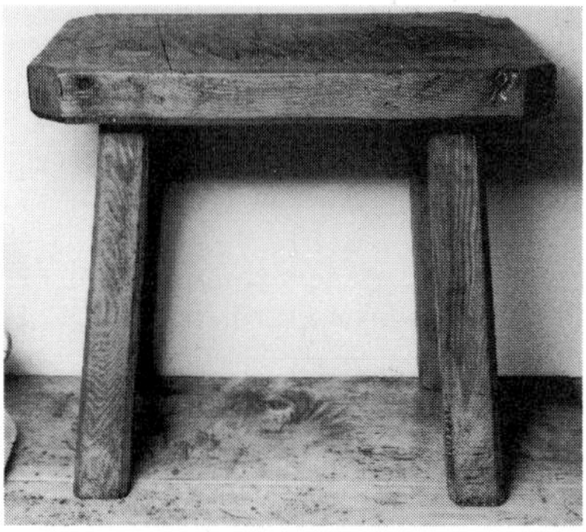

An oak butcher's block, late 19thC, 30in (76cm) wide.
£200–225 *PEN*

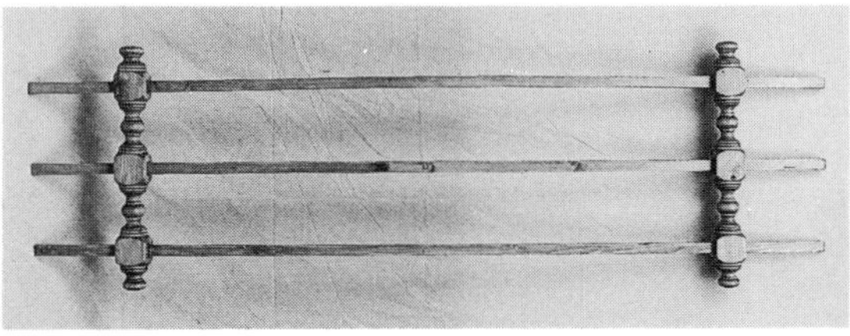

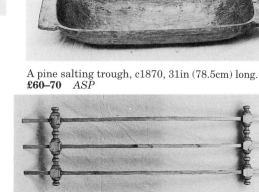

A pine hanging rack, c1880, 21in (53.5cm) wide.
£150–200 *ASP*

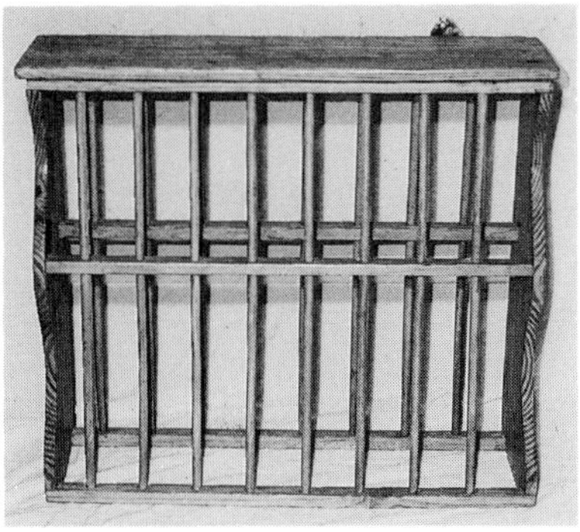

A pine plate rack, c1890, 29in (73.5cm) wide.
£200–220 *DFA*

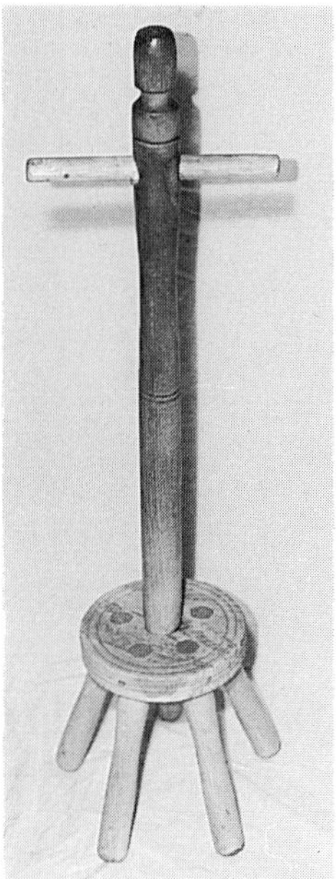

r. A wash dolly, c1880, 36in (91.5cm) high.
£30–40 *DFA*

A beech and maple butcher's block, on a 19thC pitch pine stand, c1890–1900, 24in (61cm) wide.
£200–220 *HNG*

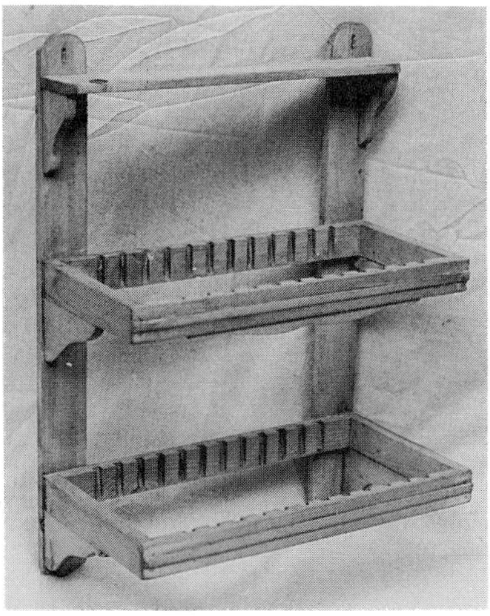

A pine dish rack, c1880,
24in (61cm) high.
£100–120 *ASP*

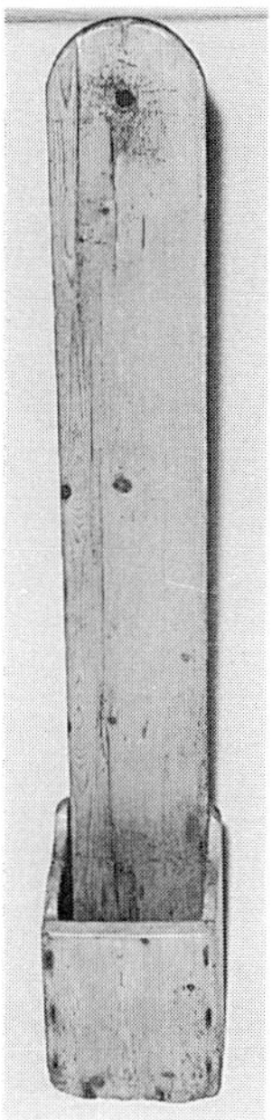

A brick holder, c1830,
40in (101.5cm) high.
£80–100 *DMe*

An elm chopping block, c1820,
30in (76cm) wide.
£100–150 *GD*

A pine salting trough,
36in (91.5cm) wide,
on a modern wrought-iron stand,
32½in (82.5cm) high.
£125–150 *ASP*

An Irish pine separator, for extracting the buttermilk from butter, c1870, 39in (99cm) long.
£150–200 *HON*

A willow banded bucket, c1900,
13in (33cm) diam.
£100–110 *WAC*

An Irish pine open wall rack, with drawer, c1870, 39in (99cm) high.
£125–150 *ASP*

A Continental pine apple barrel, c1880.
£90–110 *ASP*

Locate the source

The source of each illustration in *Miller's Pine & Country Buyer's Guide* can be found by checking the code letters at the end of each caption with the Key to Illustrations located at the front of the book.

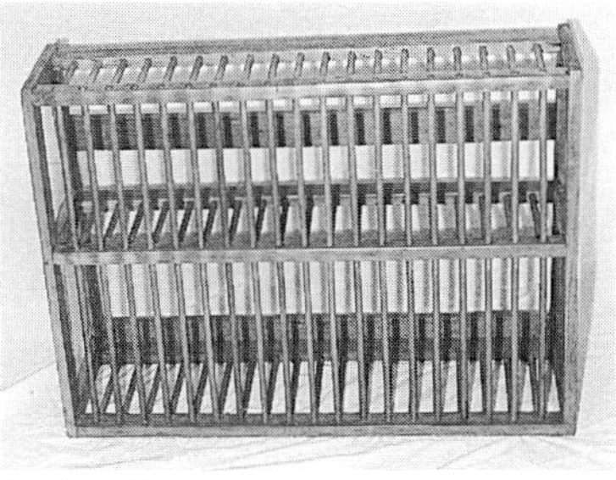

A pine plate rack, c1880,
36in (91.5cm) wide.
£250–300 *DFA*

A wooden wall egg rack, 15in (38cm) high.
£40–50
Two china eggs.
£8–10 each *AL*

A wooden bread slicer.
£65–80 *LAM*

An Edwardian marmalade slicer.
£30–40 *LAM*

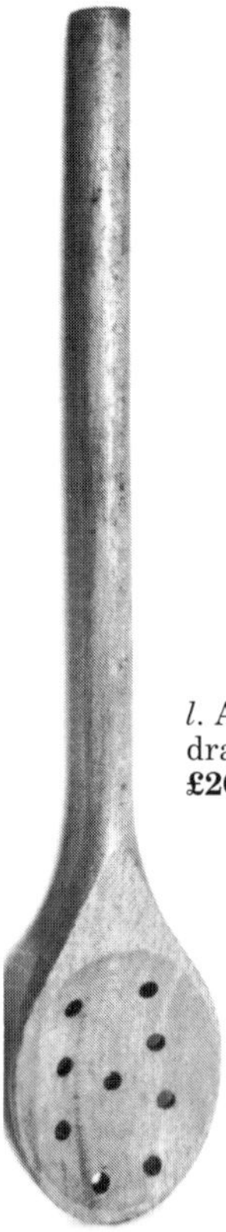

A wooden egg rack.
£20–25 *LAM*

l. A wooden draining spoon.
£20–25 *LAM*

A Spong miniature knife sharpener and cleaner.
£30–35 *LAM*

A grater/slicer.
£30–35 *LAM*

A pine sleeve board.
£25–30 *LAM*

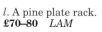

l. A pine plate rack.
£70–80 *LAM*

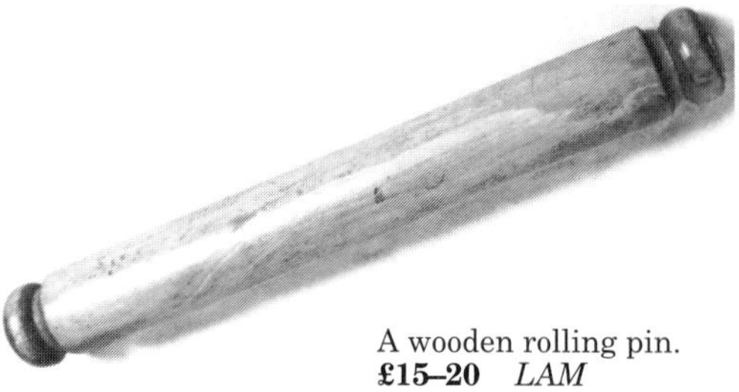

A wooden rolling pin.
£15–20 *LAM*

A pine spice rack,
28in (71cm) wide.
£150–200 *LAM*

A miniature chest
of spice drawers, c1890,
18in (46cm) high.
£250–30 *AL*

A pine lead-lined double trough,
46in (116.5cm) wide.
£400–500 *PH*

A pine spice cabinet, with
oak drawers, 18thC,
16in (40.5cm) wide.
£200–250 *AL*

An oak spice cupboard, with
rosewood inlay, c1690,
12in (30.5cm) square.
£650–750 *OSc*

A pine dough bin, 19thC,
34in (86.5cm) wide.
£500–550 *FF*

A wooden dough bin, 19thC,
32in (81.5cm) wide.
£75–100 *WHA*

A pine box, with 2 drawers,
14½in (36.5cm) wide.
£100–120 *AL*

A fitted pine wine cellaret,
c1850, 20in (51cm) wide.
£200–250 *AL*

A pine specimen chest,
15in (38cm) wide.
£80–100 *AL*

A pine salt box, carved
'Home Sweet Home' and 'W. J.
Bothwell', 18in (45.5cm) high.
£80–100 *AL*

A pine cutlery box, c1850,
7½in (19cm) wide.
£45–50 *W*

A pine butcher's block, c1880, 72in (182.5cm) wide.
£500–600 *UP*

A pine plate rack,
22in (56cm) wide.
£250–300 *LAM*

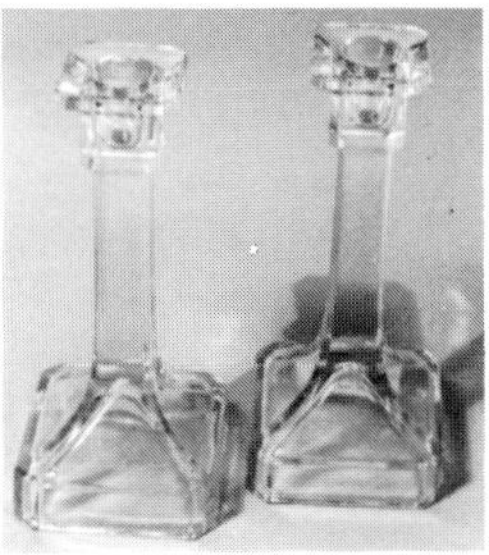

A pair of glass candlesticks, c1900, 7½in (19cm) high.
£15–25 *AL*

A green glass bottle, late 19thC, 18in (45.5cm) high.
£20–25 *AL*

A Victorian picnic set, 8in (20.5cm) wide.
£180–250 *AL*

A brown glazed pottery jug, chipped, late 19thC, 12in (30.5cm) high.
£7–8 *AL*

A pottery Alexandra Inhaler, glass tube missing, 19thC, 5in (12.5cm) high. **£35–45** *AL*

Three pottery Virol jars, late 19thC, largest 5in (12.5cm) high.
£10–15 each *AL*

A Brown & Polson's Blanc-Mange mould, late 19thC, 5in (12.5cm) diam.
£60–70 *AL*

l. A brown pottery drainer, 19thC.
£30–40 *AL*

Two pottery jugs, early 20thC, 8in (20.5cm) high.
£15–20 each *AL*

Various jugs, 20thC. **£15–20 each** *AL*

Two pestles and mortars, late 19thC.
£25–30 *AL*

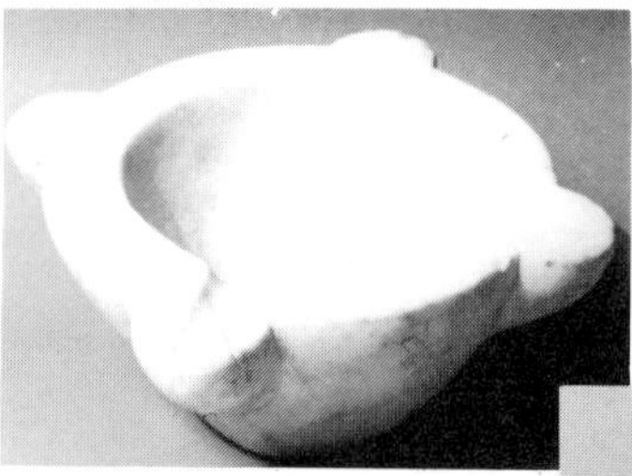

A marble mortar, mid-19thC, 5½in (14cm) wide.
£65–80 *AL*

Two pieces of Cornishware, early 20thC.
£25–30 each *AL*

A brown transfer-printed pottery jug, mid-19thC, 8in (20.5cm) high.
£25–30 *AL*

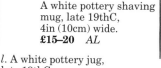

A white pottery shaving mug, late 19thC, 4in (10cm) wide.
£15–20 *AL*

l. A two-handled pottery jug, 19thC, 8½in (21cm) high.
£16–20 *AL*

l. A white pottery jug, late 19thC.
£16–20 *AL*

An Irish plate rail dresser, c1800, 61in (155cm) wide.
£900–1,100 *UP*

A large dough bin, the scrubbed top used as a work surface, c1820, 34in (86.5cm) wide.
£500–600 *AL*

An Irish cheese press, with 4 doors and 2 drawers, c1850, 78in (198cm) high.
£800–900 *LC*

A pine meat safe, c1890, 24in (61cm) wide.
£80–100 *SPA*

An elm dough bin, with 2 compartments, slight woodworm, c1800, 43in (109cm) wide.
£650–800 *OB*

A pine plate rack, with drain hole in bottom, c1840, 36in (91.5cm) wide.
£300–350 *AL*

A primitive oak chopping block, 19thC.
£250–300 *ARK*

An elm dough bin, on a stand, late 18thC.
£1,000–1,100 *Max*

r. A pine bread rack, 28in (71cm) wide.
£250–300 *W*

A butcher's block with shelf, c1850, 48in (122cm) long.
£450–550 *AL*

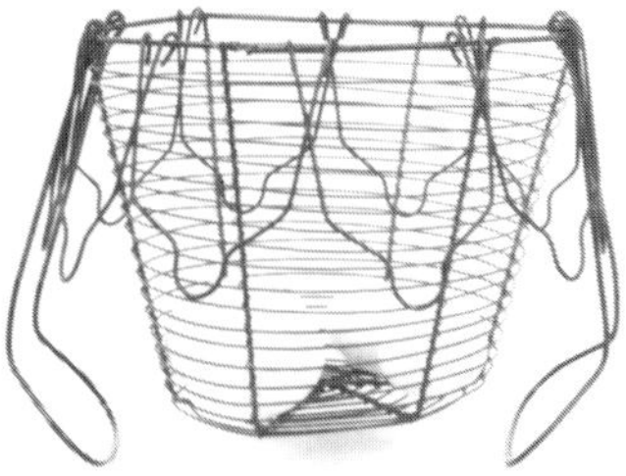

A Victorian egg basket, 6½in (16cm) high.
£30–40 *AL*

A stone hot water bottle, 12in (30.5cm) long.
£25–30 *AL*

A spot pattern jug, by T. G. Green & Co, 4in (10cm) high.
£30–40 *AL*

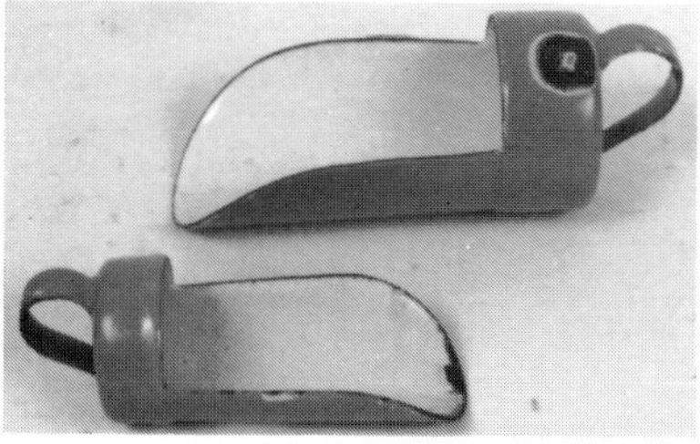

Two enamel scoops, largest 4½in (11.5cm) long.
£10–12 *AL*

A spot pattern plate, by T. G. Green & Co, 7in (18cm) diam.
£10–15 *AL*

A clothes dryer, 32in (81.5cm) hig
£40–50 *AL*

Two Cornish Kitchenware oval cups and saucers, by T. G. Green & Co.
£15–25 each *AL*

An Easimix bowl, with platform for easy mixing.
£14–17 *AL*

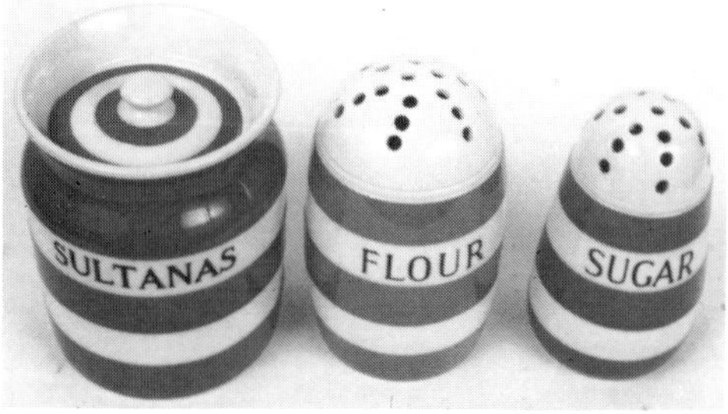

A selection of Cornish Kitchenware, by T. G. Green & Co, marked 'Sultanas' and 'Flour', 5in (12.5cm) high, 'Sugar' 4in (10cm) high.
£20–35 each *AL*

A wooden bee collection box, and comb, 18in (45.5cm) wide.
£55–65 *AL*

r. Two wooden flour barrels, largest 10in (25.5cm) high.
£80–100 each *AL*

Three milk cans, tin with brass rims, largest 8in (20.5cm) high.
£60–70 each *AL*

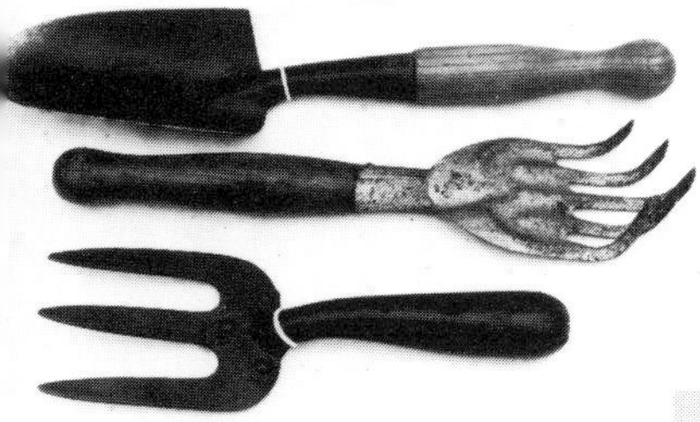

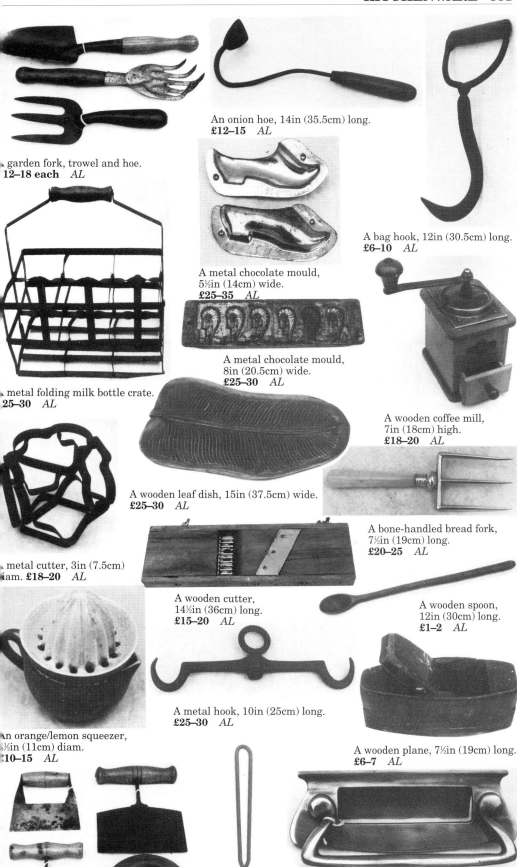

. garden fork, trowel and hoe.
12–18 each *AL*

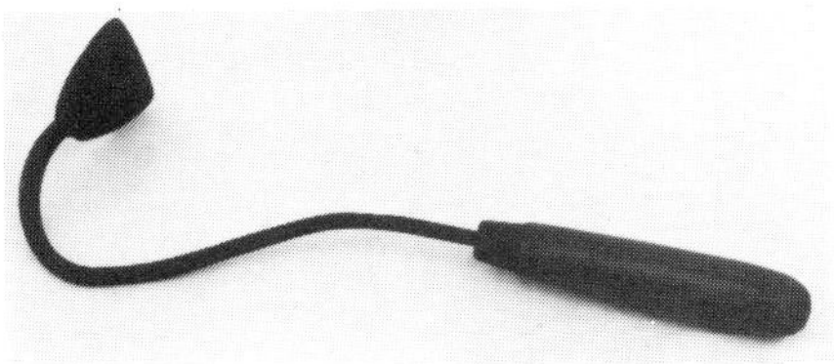

An onion hoe, 14in (35.5cm) long.
£12–15 *AL*

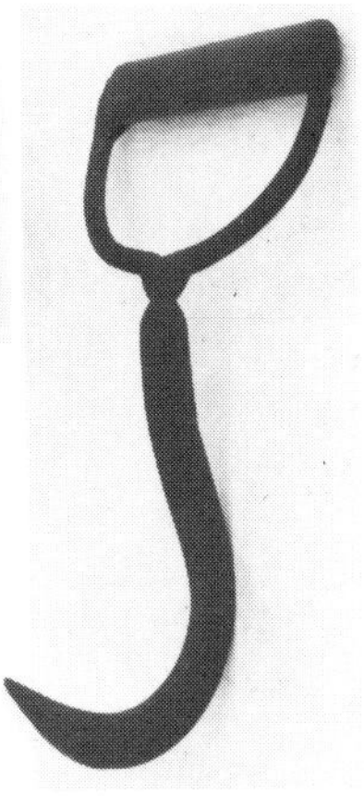

A bag hook, 12in (30.5cm) long.
£6–10 *AL*

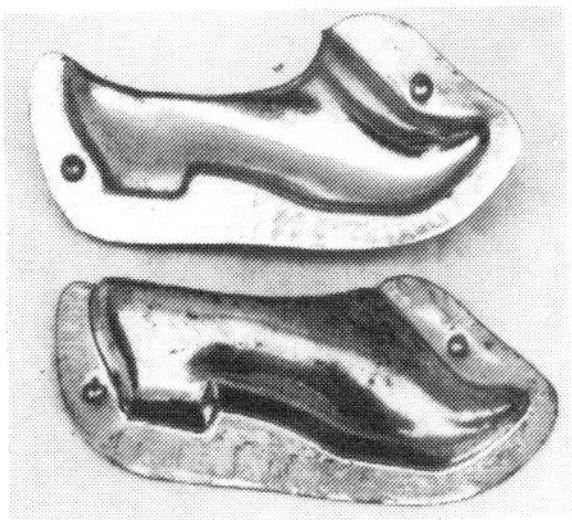

A metal chocolate mould, 5½in (14cm) wide.
£25–35 *AL*

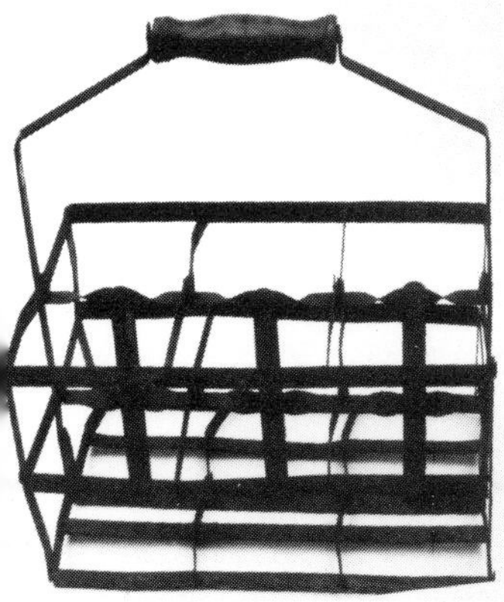

. metal folding milk bottle crate.
25–30 *AL*

A wooden coffee mill, 7in (18cm) high.
£18–20 *AL*

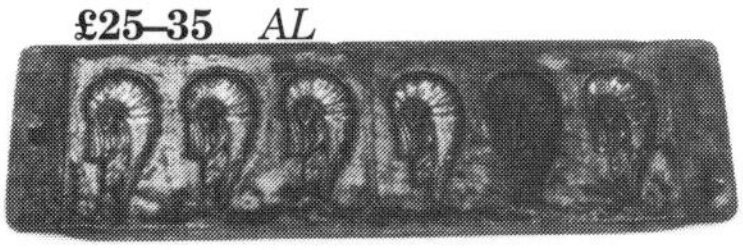

A metal chocolate mould, 8in (20.5cm) wide.
£25–30 *AL*

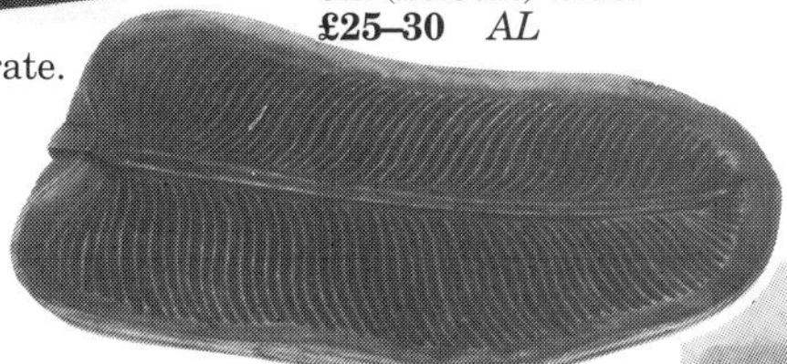

A wooden leaf dish, 15in (37.5cm) wide.
£25–30 *AL*

. metal cutter, 3in (7.5cm) iam. **£18–20** *AL*

A bone-handled bread fork, 7½in (19cm) long.
£20–25 *AL*

A wooden cutter, 14½in (36cm) long.
£15–20 *AL*

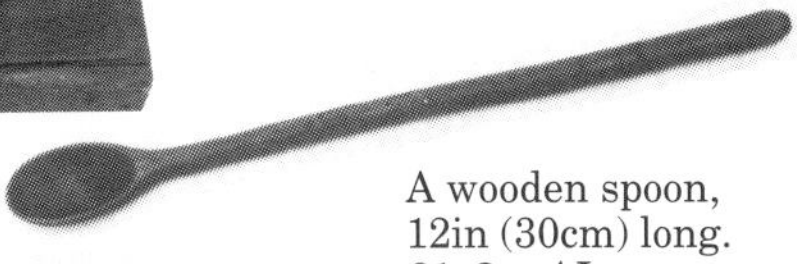

A wooden spoon, 12in (30cm) long.
£1–2 *AL*

n orange/lemon squeezer, ½in (11cm) diam.
10–15 *AL*

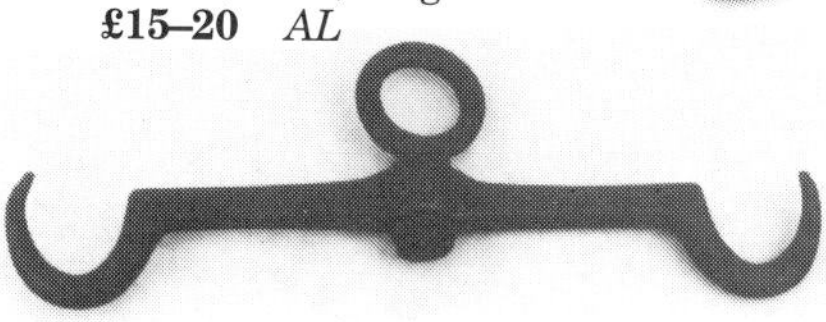

A metal hook, 10in (25cm) long.
£25–30 *AL*

A wooden plane, 7½in (19cm) long.
£6–7 *AL*

hopping blades. **£12–20 each** *AL*

A brass letterbox, 8½in (21cm) wide.
£30–40 *AL*

l. A wooden roller, 8in (20.5cm) long.
£8–12 *AL*

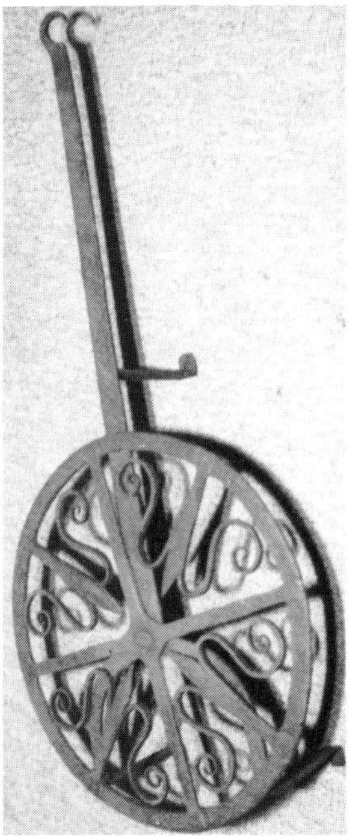

A wrought-iron revolving grill, early 19thC.
£250–300 *PCA*

An oak candle box, 18thC, 17½in (44cm) high.
£100–150 *PCA*

A rhubarb forcer, 28in (71cm) high
£75–100 *WRe*

A set of ceramic feet, for standing a dresser on stone floors.
£65–80 *AL*

A selection of Mauchline ware napkin rings, with transfer picture of the Isle of Wight and Beachy Head.
£10–25 each *DEL*

A bell-shaped tin chocolate mould, 5½in (14cm) high.
£25–30 *AL*

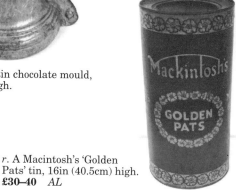

r. A Macintosh's 'Golden Pats' tin, 16in (40.5cm) high.
£30–40 *AL*

A copper saucepan, stamped 'H. E. Cars'.
£30–40 *ONS*

Three toffee hammers:
top: Sharps, 4in (10cm) long.
£8–10
centre: Blue Bird, 4in (10cm) long.
£8–10
bottom: with bone handle, 5in (12.5cm) long.
£15–20 *AL*

A selection of tin scoops, largest 12in (30.5cm) long.
£12–15 each *AL*

A pair of brass and iron fire dogs, 19thC, 7in (18cm) wide.
£45–50 *AL*

A selection of tin scoops, 19thC.
£20–25 *AL*

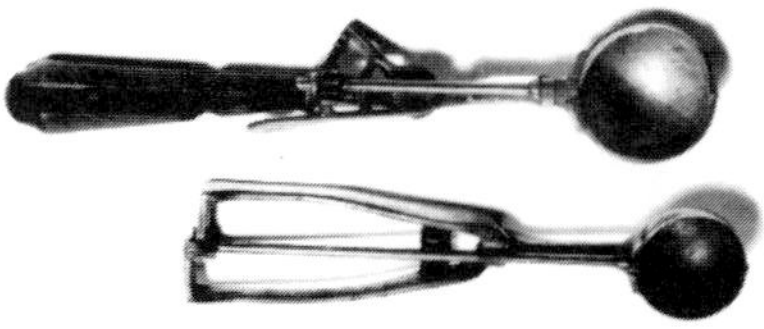

Two plated brass ice cream scoops, early 20thC.
£15–20 each *AL*

A pair of brass candlesticks, mid-19thC, 10in (25.5cm) high.
£65–80 *AL*

An iron foot last, 19thC.
£10–12 *AL*

A pine and glass egg timer, 7in (18cm) high, 19thC.
£25–30 *AL*

A selection of knives, late 19thC.
from top to bottom:
A butter knife, 8in (20.5cm) long. **£12–15**
A bread knife, 16in (40.5cm) long. **£16–20**
A bread knife, 15in (38cm) long. **£16–20**
A bread knife, with ivory handle, 15in (38cm) long. **£20–25** *AL*

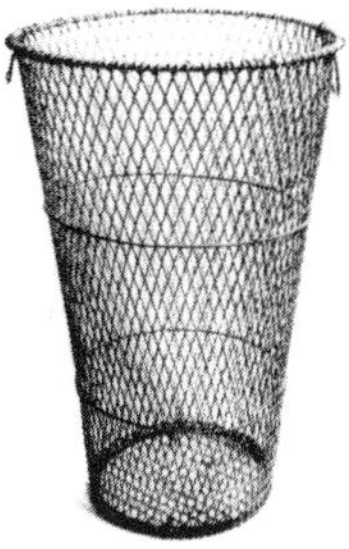

A wire waste paper basket, 23in (58.5cm) high.
£15–25 *AL*

r. An oak and iron-bound pump action butter churn, c1880.
£200–250 *CGC*

A wicker basket, early 20thC, 18in (46cm) wide.
£10–12 *AL*

A Cadbury's tin display stand, early 20thC, 13in (33cm) wide.
£30–40 *AL*

A pine tub, early 20thC, 16in (40.5cm) high.
£15–20 *AL*

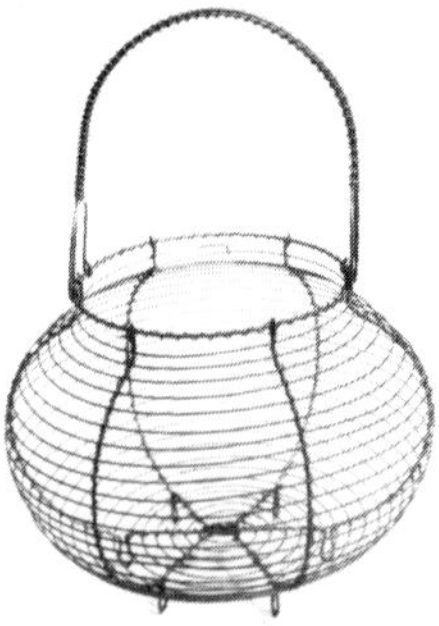

A wire egg basket, 19thC, 14in (36cm) high.
£20–25 *AL*

A housemaid's black and red painted tin box, 19thC, 12in (30.5cm) high.
£55–70 *AL*

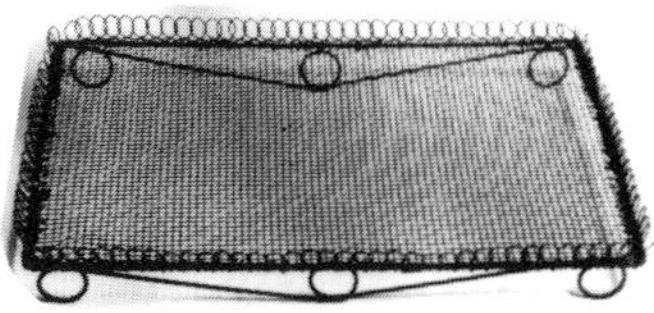

A wire cake stand, 14in (36cm) wide.
£25–30 *AL*

A brass and iron fireguard, early 20thC, 19in (48cm) wide.
£65–80 *AL*

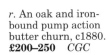

A Sussex trug, early 20thC, 21in (53cm) wide.
£25–35 *AL*

A wicker basket, early 20thC, 14in (35.5cm) wide.
£12–16 *AL*

A wicker basket, early 20thC, 16in (41cm) wide
£12–16 *AL*

A pine flour barrel, 19thC, 7in (18cm) high. **£60–70** *AL*

A wood and hair sieve, 19thC, 8in (20.5cm) diam.
£15–20 *AL*

Three wood and wire garden sieves, late 19thC, largest 22in (56cm) diam.
£12–15 each *AL*

A basket shopping trolley, c1920. **£25–35** *AL*

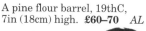

Three elm grain measures, early 20thC.
£25–35 each *AL*

l. A pine York County Hospital money box, 19thC, 9in (22.5cm) wide.
£25–30 *AL*

r. An elm and pine flax crusher, c1850, 34in (86cm) wide.
£60–70 *AL*

A mahogany knife box, mid-19thC, 18½in (59cm) wide.
£50–60 *AL*

A pine shoe cleaning box, 19thC, 12in (30.5cm) wide.
£25–35 *AL*

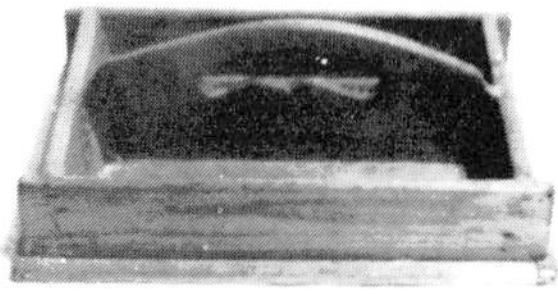

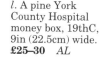

A pine knife box, 19thC, 14in (36cm) wide.
£20–25 *AL*

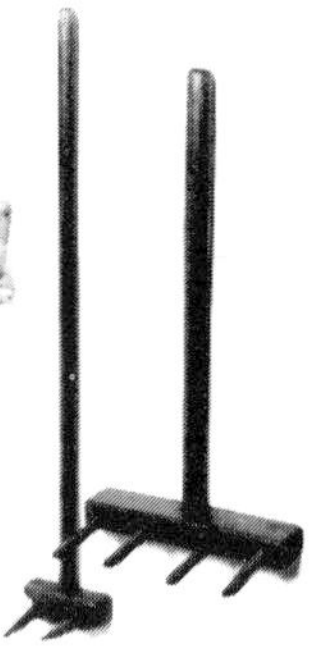

Two small wooden rakes.
£15–20 each *AL*

A pine letter rack, 19thC, 14in (36cm). **£30–40** *AL*

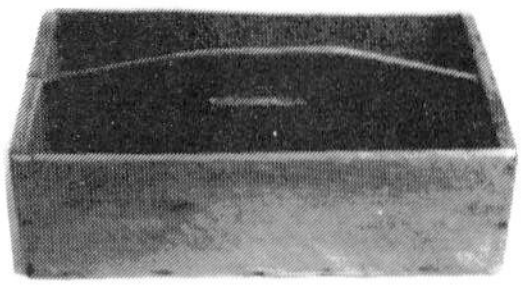

A pine knife box, 19thC, 13in (33cm) wide.
£25–35 *AL*

A sycamore bowl, early 19thC, 13in (33cm) diam. **£100–120** *AL*

A sycamore bowl, 14½in (37cm) diam.
£70–80 *AL*

A pine duck board, with copper nails, 19thC, 26in (66cm) long.
£20–25 *AL*

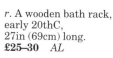

r. A wooden bath rack, early 20thC, 27in (69cm) long.
£25–30 *AL*

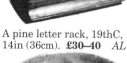

A sycamore bowl, early 19thC, 18½in (47cm) diam.
£90–120 *AL*

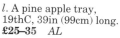

l. A pine apple tray, 19thC, 39in (99cm) long.
£25–35 *AL*

A brown and pale green crock, mid-19thC, 11in (28cm) wide. **£20–30** *AL*

A brown-glazed crock, mid-19thC, 12in (30.5cm) diam. **£30–40** *AL*

A crock, mid-19thC, 10in (25.5cm) high. **£25–30** *AL*

A bread crock, 10in (25.5cm) high. **£90–100** *AL*

A Zero Cool butter cooler, early 20thC, 11in (28cm) long. **£10–15** *AL*

Two brown pottery jelly moulds, 19thC, 4in (10cm) diam. **£20–25 each** *AL*

A glazed jug and basin, early 20thC, 17in (43cm) diam. **£35–40** *AL*

A brown and cream pottery casserole, 8in (20.5cm) diam. **£10–15** *AL*

A candle lamp, late-19thC, 10in (25cm) high. **£12–15** *AL*

A crock, c1850, 14in (36cm) high. **£40–50** *AL*

A set of iron balance scales and weights, late 19thC, 22in (56cm) high. **£75–100** *AL*

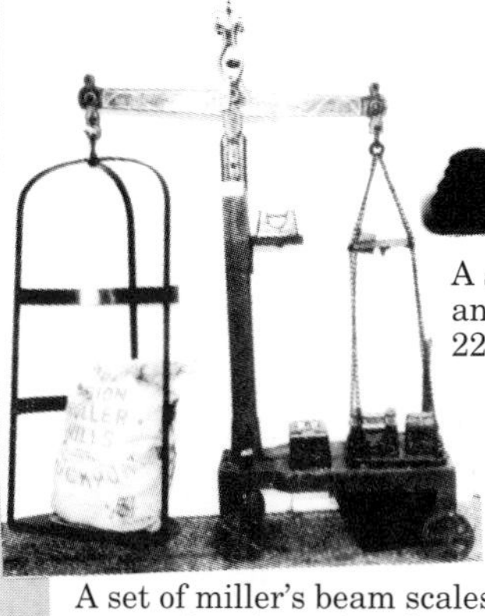

A set of miller's beam scales, restored and repainted, with weights. **£500–550** *CGC/FRM*

A hurricane lamp, early 20thC, 16in (40.5cm) high. **£10–15** *AL*

A set of platform scales, by W. & T. Avery, for butter and cheese, with brass weights. **£250–300** *BHW*

A Kenrick brass and iron coffee mill, 19thC, 6in (15cm) diam. **£100–120** *AL*

An iron kettle, 19thC, 13in (33cm) wide. **£40–50** *AL*

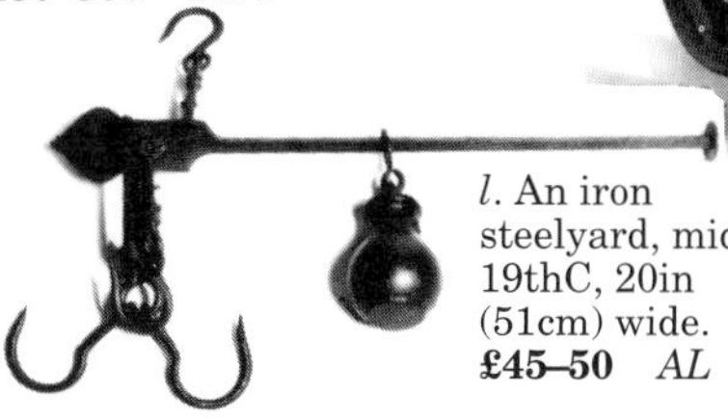

l. An iron steelyard, mid-19thC, 20in (51cm) wide. **£45–50** *AL*

l. Brass spring scales, early 20thC, 17in (43cm) long. **£25–30** *AL*

A brass kettle on stand, 19thC, 13in (33cm) wide. **£60–70** *AL*

l. A brass blow-lamp, early 20thC, 12in (30.5cm) long. **£11–13** *AL*

l. A tin coffee pot, late 19thC, 8in (20.5cm) high. **£25–30** *AL*

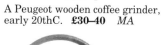

Two Victorian copper jelly moulds.
£12–15 each *AL*

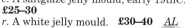

l. A pair of sugar nips, mid-19thC.
£50–55
c. A saltglaze jelly mould, early 19thC.
£25–30
r. A white jelly mould. **£30–40** *AL*

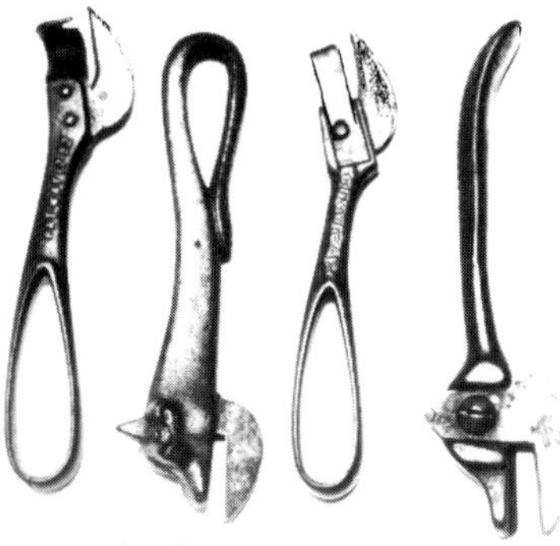

A selection of tin openers, 19thC.
£15–20 *MA*

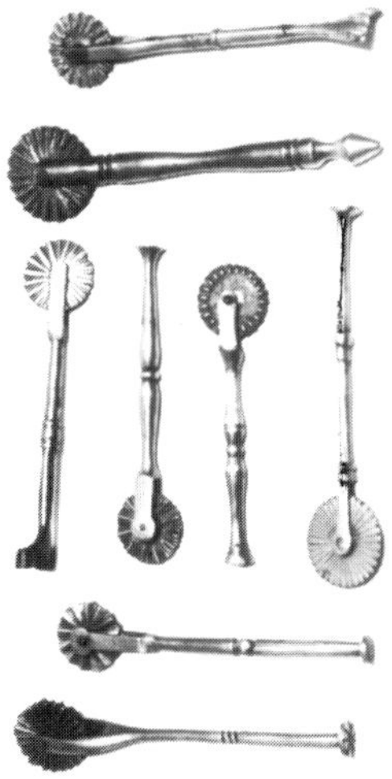

A selection of brass pastry jiggers, 19thC.
£30–35 *MA*

A pair of butter stamps,
2in (5cm) and 3in (7.6cm) long.
£40–70 each *AL*

A Victorian nutmeg grater, with compartment for spare nutmeg in the handle, 7½in (19cm) long.
£70–85 *AL*

A Peugeot wooden coffee grinder, early 20thC. **£30–40** *MA*

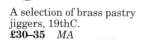

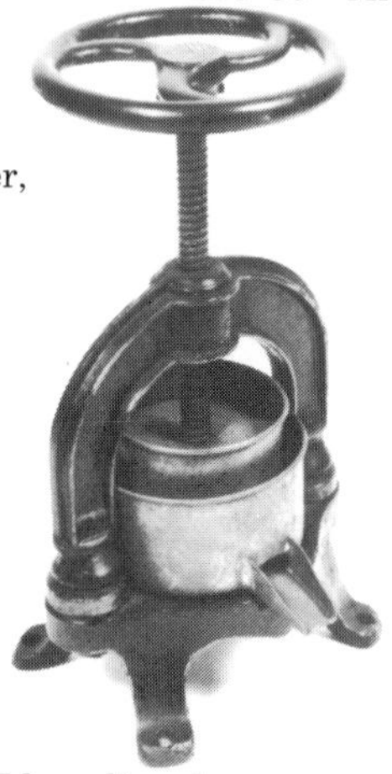

An Edwardian cheese press,
12in (30.5cm) high.
£75–100 *AL*

Three wooden pastry/butter rolling moulds, 19thC.
£40–70 each *Bon*

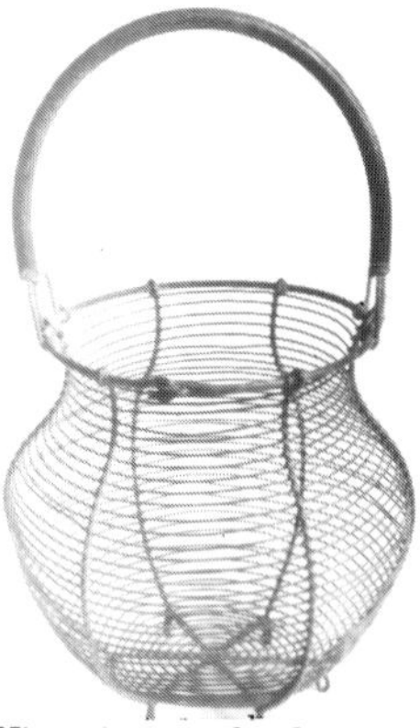

A Victorian egg basket,
10in (25.5cm) diam.
£10–12 *AL*

A Victorian wicker egg basket, 8in (20.5cm) diam.
£15–20 *AL*

A Regency cane basket,
11in (28cm) long.
£25–35 *AL*

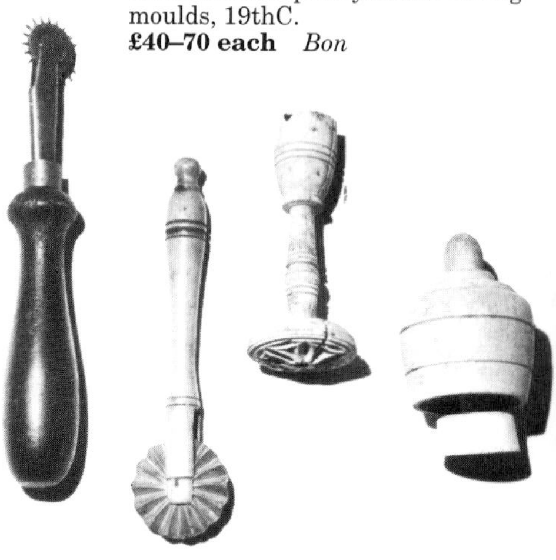

left to right:
A leather pricker, late 19thC. **£8–10**
A pastry marker, late 19thC. **£12–15**
Two butter prints. **£10–12 each** *LAC*

A set of Victorian black-glazed pottery food weights, largest 10in (25.5cm) diam.
£25–30 *AL*

A pine spoon rack, 19thC.
£200–250 *MAT*

A Victorian miniature pine chest of 2 drawers, 12½in (32cm) wide.
£30–40 *AL*

A Victorian small pine chest of drawers, 17in (43cm) wide.
£175–225 *AL*

l. A Victorian pine cat box, 11in (28cm) wide.
£65–80 *AL*

A Guernsey cream can and cover, made of tin, the bottom impressed 'De La Rue, maker Guernsey', c1880, 8in (20.5cm) high.
£25–35 *AL*

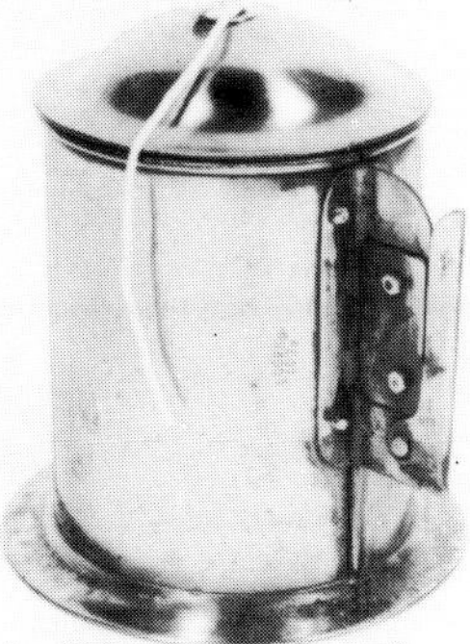

An Edwardian tin string container, with cutter at side, 7in (18cm) high.
£10–15 *AL*

An Edwardian string holder, Sandows patent, 6½in (16.5cm) wide.
£10–15 *AL*

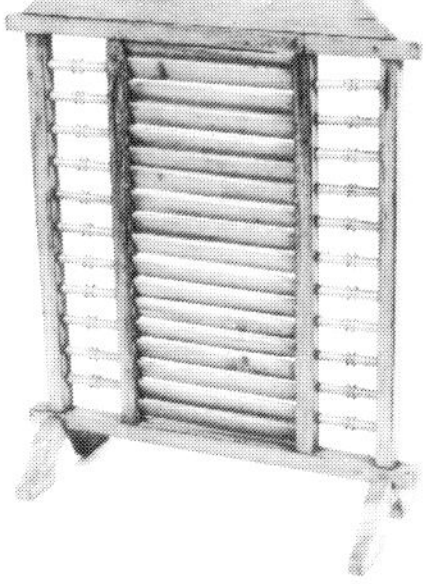

A Victorian pine fire screen, 18in (45.5cm) wide.
£50–60 *AL*

A George V wooden gallon measure, with duty mark, woodwork in base, 5in (12.5cm) high.
£50–60 *AL*

An Edwardian tea tin, 13in (33cm) high.
£45–60 *AL*

An Edwardian green painted tea tin, 15½in (39.5cm) high.
£75–100 *AL*

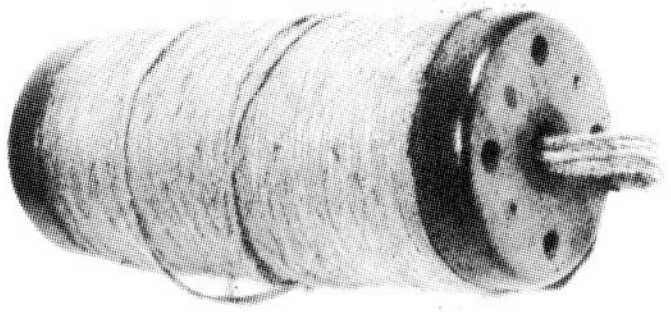

An Edwardian string holder, 12½in (32cm) wide.
£15–20 *AL*

A Victorian miniature pine cupboard.
£45–50 *AL*

Irons

It was not until the 16thC that Europeans used a heated tool to smooth clothes. Earlier they used a mangle, or rubbing devices, to flatten cloth while it was damp.

It is not clear whether the idea of using a hot iron arose spontaneously in the west, or whether it was introduced from the Orient. The Dutch probably introduced ironing to add to the white woman's burden. And what a burden! So that the iron should retain its heat as long as possible it was made as heavy as a woman could handle – often weighing 6lbs or more.

At first there were two kinds of iron: the sad iron, heated on the stove, and the box iron, hollow and kept hot by a pair of solid iron 'slugs' heated in the fire and inserted alternately into its body. The box iron was the aristocrat – often made of brass and elaborately embossed. The sad iron, made of iron, was a functional, blacksmith-made affair, heavy, practical and ponderous – in fact, the true middle-English meaning of the word 'sad'.

As use of the iron spread during the 17th and 18thC, the need for a self-heating iron became obvious. In the 19thC designs appeared that allowed for a charcoal fire to burn inside the iron. These mainly originated in America and were immediately popular. The Bless & Drake foundry produced 100,000 of them in 1865 alone! Then came all sorts of variations, including improvements in draught control so that charcoal or coke would burn more evenly. Then there were methods of burning gas, paraffin, vegetable oil, petrol and methylated spirits.

In 1870, a Mrs Potts of Iowa, USA, fed up with her old sad iron, decided to improve it. First, she designed one that was pointed at both ends for ironing into corners. Then she patented one with a detachable handle and two soles that were heated on the stove and the handle attached alternately to each so that it never got too hot.

Electricity came in the 1880s. The old-timers fought on well into the 20thC, but now a flex trails where once wafted smoke and fumes.

A tailor's iron, by Levine & Sons, 35 Greenfield Street, London W1, 19thC, 8in (20.5cm) long.
£45–50 *FA*

A lace iron, late 19thC, 4in (10.2cm) long.
£30–35 *FA*

A cap iron, late 19thC, 5in (12.5cm) long.
£25–30 *FA*

A French flat iron No. 5, c1900, 6in (15cm) long.
£15–20 *FA*

A Belgian flat iron No. 4, late 19thC, 6½in (16.5cm) long.
£20–25 *FA*

A Kenrick No. 3 smoothing iron, 5in (12.5cm) long.
£30–40 *FA*

r. A straight chimney charcoal iron, made in Hong Kong at the end of WW1 for the eastern market, 8in (20.5cm) high.
£30–40 *FA*

A Vulcan chimney iron, with vulcan head damper, late 19thC, 7in (18cm) long.
£50–60 *FA*

A Victorian plaited rush basket, 13in (33cm) wide.
£15–20 *AL*

A Victorian heavy wicker egg basket, 13in (33cm) diam.
£25–30 *AL*

A Victorian willow and wicker basket, 9in (23cm) diam.
£15–20 *AL*

A wicker eel trap, 19thC, 31in (78.5cm) high.
£25–30 *AL*

A Victorian wicker and rush egg basket, 13in (33cm) wide.
£15–20 *AL*

A Victorian wicker bread basket, 13in (33cm) diam.
£30–35 *AL*

A Victorian wicker basket, 14in (35.5cm) wide.
£10–15 *AL*

A Victorian wicker basket, 13in (33cm) wide.
£15–20 *AL*

A wicker basket, early 20thC, 18in (45.5cm) long.
£15–20 *AL*

A Victorian wicker and plaited rush basket, 10in (25.5cm) diam.
£15–20 *AL*

A Victorian wicker shopping basket, 15in (38cm) wide.
£10–15 *AL*

A Victorian willow basket, 10½in (26.5cm) diam.
£15–20 *AL*

A wicker basket, early 20thC, 14in (35.6cm) wide.
£12–16 *AL*

A pine bread board, carved with wheatears, early 19thC, 11½in (29cm) diam.
£15–20 *AL*

A pair of Victorian bellows, 32in (81.5cm) wide.
£80–90 *OA*

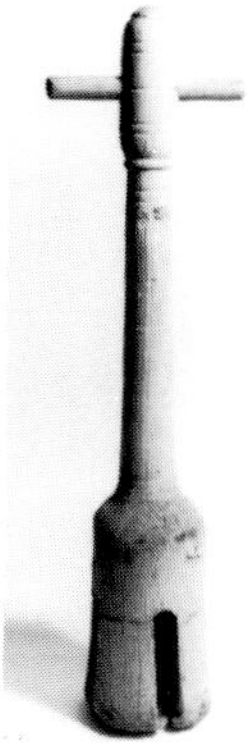

A wooden chump dolly, 34in (86.5cm) high.
£50–60 *EM*

A wooden poss stick, 46in (117cm) high.
£50–60 *EM*

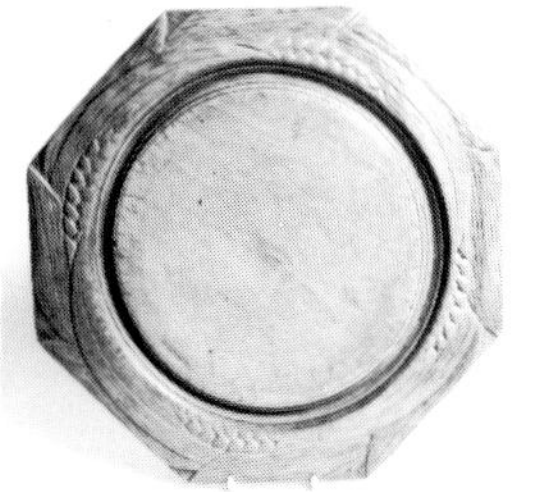

A pine bread board, carved with wheatears, 12in (30.5cm) diam.
£30–35 *AL*

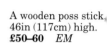

Two poss sticks, with copper bases, largest 21in (53.5cm) long.
£15–25 each *EM*

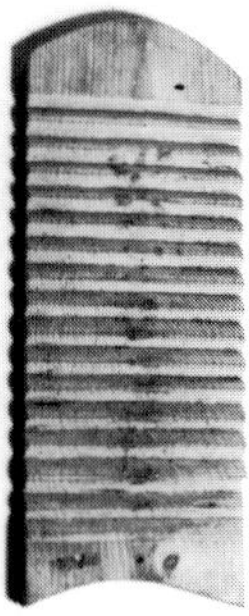

l. A Victorian pine washboard, 24in (61cm) high.
£30-40 *EM*

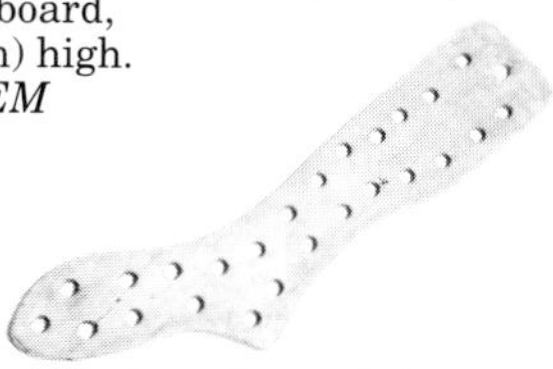

A pair of wooden sock driers, 23in (59cm) long. **£40–50** *EM*

A Victorian pine bread board, carved with 'Our Daily Bread', 12in (30.5cm) diam. **£60–65** *AL*

A copper posser, with valve, by Paul Birkett, 23in (58.4cm) high.
£25–30 *EM*

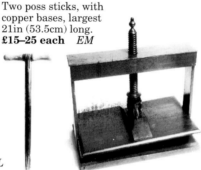

A wooden napkin press, 15in (38cm) long. **£200–250** *EM*

A fruitwood linen press, 24in (61cm) wide. **£65–80** *EM*

A metal washboard, in a wooden frame, 22in (56cm) high.
£12–15 *EM*

A wooden hanging soap container, 12½in (31.8cm) high.
£30–35 *EM*

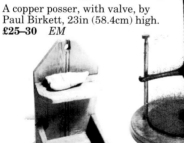

A Victorian metal and brass cheese press, on a wooden base, 10in (25.5cm) long.
£25–30 *AL*

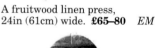

A Victorian oak, pine and poplar metal-bound cheese press, 10in (25.5cm) diam.
£25–35 *OA*

A mahogany coal box, fitted with brass handles, with a scoop in the drawer, c1900, 15in (38cm) high.
£200–250 *BB*

A cheese vat, 20in (51cm) diam.
£175–225 *MPA*

A wooden 'Hudson's' Extract of Soap' box, 16in (40.5cm) wide.
£30–40 *EM*

A wooden ladle, 18thC, 11in (28cm) long.
£20–25 *OA*

A pine egg rack, c1890, 21in (53.3cm) wide.
£60–65 *AL*

An Edwardian inlaid oak coal box, with metal liner and fitted scoop, 18in (45.5cm) wide.
£100–150 *Ph*

A pair of Victorian boxwood butter pats, 11in (28cm) long.
£8–12 *OA*

A stone pestle, with a wooden handle, 19thC, 13in (33cm) long.
£10–12 *OA*

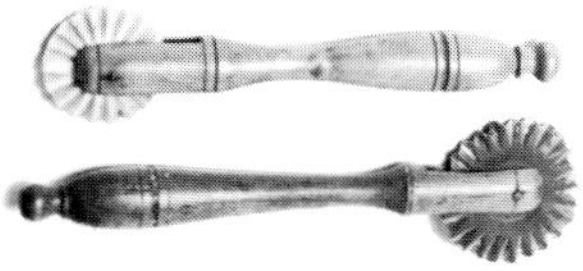

Two Victorian pastry cutters, 5½in (14cm) long.
£20–25 *OA*

A wire sieve and mortar, 19thC, 8in (20.5cm) wide.
£9–11 *AL*

An iron raisin pipper, dated '7th October 1897', 12in (30.5cm) wide.
£30–40 *AL*

A Victorian earthenware colander, 9in (23cm) diam.
£30–40 *AL*

A mahogany knife box, c1840, 16½in (42cm) wide.
£65–75 *AL*

An iron trivet, 19thC, 7in (18cm) wide.
£15–20 *AL*

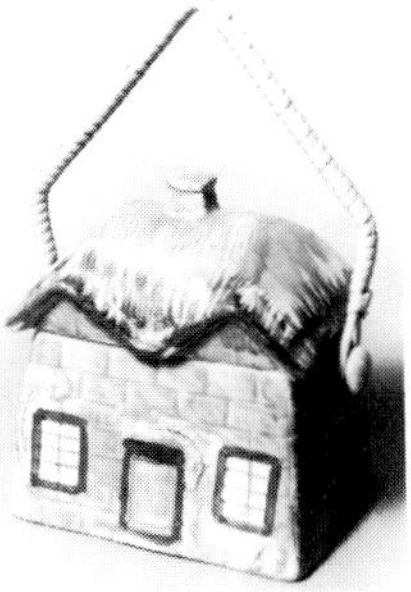

A cottage biscuit barrel, by Price Bros, c1930, 7½in (19cm) high.
£30–40 *GWe*

An earthenware butter tub, with glass liner, 1920s, 6in (15cm) diam.
£10–12 *AL*

A Victorian stoneware double walled butter tub, 6in (15cm) diam.
£15–20 *OA*

l. A stoneware jar, with moulded decoration, 6in (15cm) high.
£20–25 *OA*

A Scottish earthenware bread crock, 19in (48.3cm) wide.
£150–175 *MPA*

A stoneware storage jar, 10in (25.5cm) high.
£18–20 *OA*

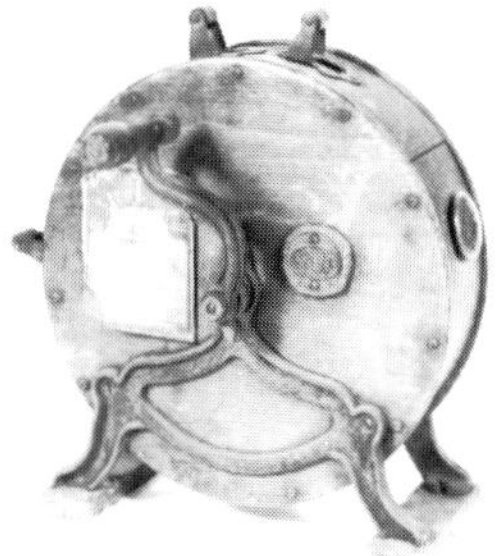

A Spong knife polisher,
c1910, 17in (43cm) high.
£100–120 *Ph*

A Victorian Beranger wooden box counter weighing machine, 16in (40.5cm) wide.
£100–120 *EEW*

A Royal mangle, with rubber rollers, pressure adjustment and fixing clamps,
17in (43cm) wide.
£20–25 *EM*

A cork press, by Townson & Mercer Ltd, late 19thC.
£60–70 *Be*

A galvanized metal automatic washer, with brass tap at the base, c1910, marked 'The Dream', 19in (48.5cm) high.
£35–45 *EM*

r. A set of tinplate scales, c1890,
10½in (26.5cm) high.
£25–30 *AL*

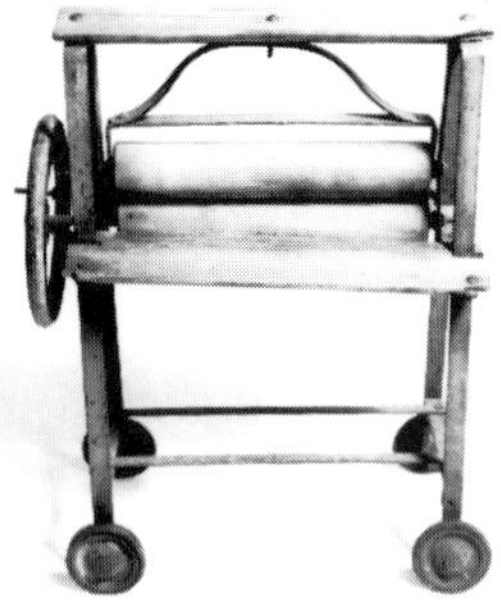

A Victorian child's wooden mangle, metal frame, on rubber tyred wheels,
20in (51cm) high.
£30–35 *EM*

An orange slicer, early 20thC,
16in (40.5cm) long.
£15–20 *BHW*

An American tin 'No. 4 Three Minute Bread Mixer', awarded Gold Medal at St. Louis Exposition, 1904,
12in (30.5cm) high.
£90–100 *AL*

A set of cast-iron household scales, marked 'British Made', c1890, 12½in (32cm) high.
£30–35 *AL*

An iron single beam sweet scale, with brass pans, c1850, 16in (40.6cm) wide.
£100–120 *EEW*

A hand-operated child's washing machine and mangle, with a wooden lid, 27in (68.5cm) high.
£40–50 *EM*

A set of cast-iron and brass vegetable scales, by Morgan & Sons, c1900, 23in (58.5cm) wide.
£65–80 *AL*

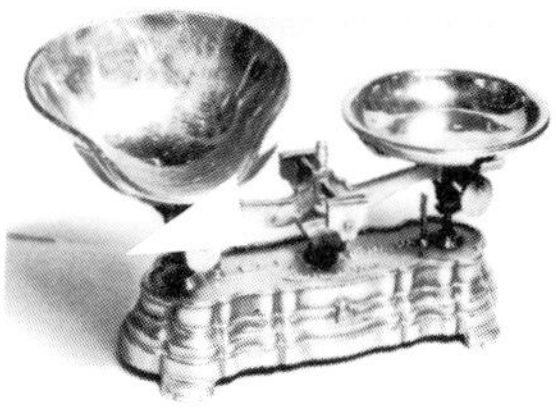

A set of brass and cast-iron scales, c1900, 9in (23cm) long.
£120–140 *BB*

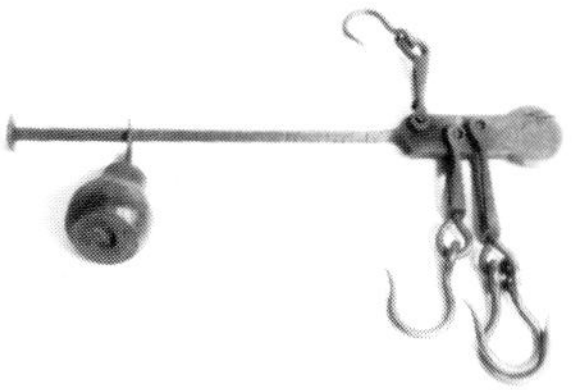

A cast iron steelyard, 19thC,
18in (45.7cm) long.
£45–50 *AL*

A tin watering can, early 20thC, 16in (40.5cm) high.
£15–25 *AL*

A tin urn, with brass tap, 19thC, 12in (30.5cm) high.
£15–20 *AL*

A tin watering can, early 20thC, 15in (38cm) high.
£15–25 *AL*

A tin milk can, c1900, 18½in (47cm) high.
£12–15 *AL*

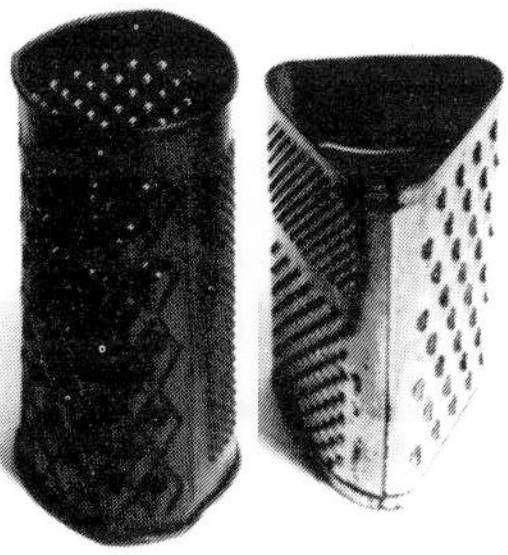

Two tin cheese graters, early 20thC, largest 8in (20.5cm) high.
£4–8 each *AL*

A blue enamel mug, early 20thC, 3in (7.5cm) high.
£8–10 *AL*

A selection of wooden and iron chopping utensils, late 19thC, 16in (40.5cm) wide.
£12–20 each *AL*

A blue enamel mug, late 19thC, 3½in (9cm) high.
£12–15 *AL*

A brass bowl, early 19thC, 12in (30.5cm) diam.
£40–45 *AL*

A two-handled chopping knife, with boxwood handles, steel blade, late 19thC, 13in (33cm) long.
£20–25 *AL*

An iron and wood marmalade chopper, late 19thC, 16in (40.5cm) wide.
£15–20 *AL*

Two iron string holders, 19thC, 8in (20.5cm) wide.
£10–12 each *AL*

A red and white enamelled iron mincer, late 19thC, 12in (30.5cm) high.
£8–10 *AL*

An iron and blue enamel tongue press, 19thC, 10in (25.5cm) high.
£30–35 *AL*

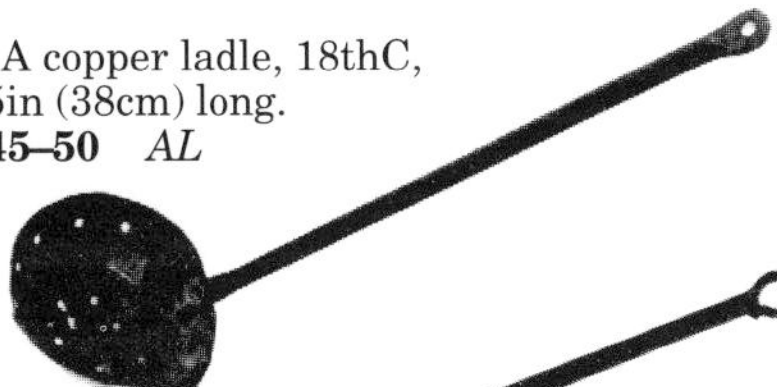

r. A copper ladle, 18thC, 15in (38cm) long.
£45–50 *AL*

An iron keel, 19thC, 21in (53.5cm) long.
£40–50 *AL*

A wood and iron wallpaper roller, 19thC, 8in (20.5cm) long.
£5–10 *AL*

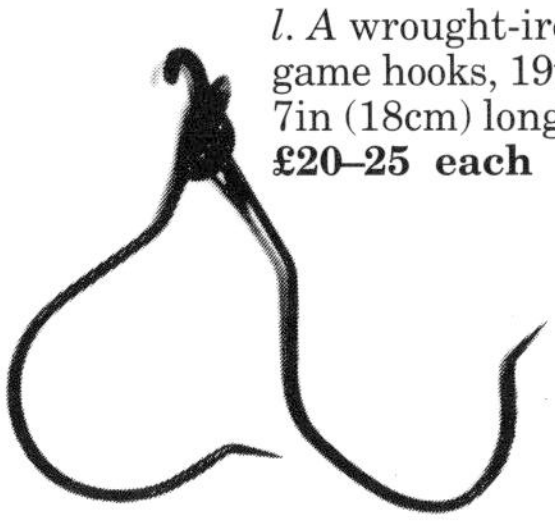

l. A wrought-iron game hooks, 19thC, 7in (18cm) long.
£20–25 each *AL*

GLOSSARY

Acanthus A leaf motif used in carved and inlaid decoration.
Apron The shaped skirt of wood that runs beneath the legs of a table or feet of a chest.
Armoire The Continental term for a large tall cupboard originally used for storing armour.
Astragal A small semi-circular moulding in architecture, and in furniture a term often applied to the glazing bars of cabinets and bookcases. Astragals are sometimes in brass.
Backboard The unpolished back of wall furniture.
Bacon settle Long, backed seat with boxed base, or on legs, with a storage press in the back.
Baluster The shaped turning, or slender pillar with a bulbous base, used on the legs and pedestals of tables.
Banding Decorative veneer used around the edges of tables and drawers.
Barley twist The spiral shape much favoured for turned legs of the second half of the 17thC.
Bevel The decorative angled edge of a mirror.
Bow front The outward curved front found on chests of drawers from the late 18thC.
Bracket foot A squared foot, the most commonly found foot on 18thC cabinet furniture.
Breakfront The term for a piece of furniture with a protruding central section.
Brushing slide The pull-out slide found above the drawer of some small 18thC chests.
Bun foot A flattened version of the ball foot.
Bureau A writing desk with a fall front, enclosing a fitted interior, with drawers below.
Bureau bookcase A bureau with a bookcase above.
Cabriole leg A gently curving S-shaped leg found on tables and chairs of the late 17th and 18thC.
Cellaret 18thC term for wine coolers and containers, and the drawer in some sideboards designed for storing wine.
Chamfer An angled corner.
Chest on stand A two-part tall chest of drawers, also known as a tallboy or highboy.
Cheval mirror A tall dressing mirror, supported by two uprights.
Chiffonier A side cabinet with or without a drawer and with one or more shelves above.
Children's furniture Usually small scale furniture for children's usage.
Coffer A joined and panelled low chest with handles but without feet, made for travelling, usually of oak, with a lid.
Commode A highly decorated chest of drawers or cabinet, often of bombé shape, with applied mounts.
Corbel Projecting bracket found on the frieze of cabinet furniture.
Cornice The projecting moulding at the top of tall furniture.
Country/Provincial furniture The functional furniture made away from the major cities and main centres of production.
Cross banding A veneered edge to table tops and drawer fronts, at right angles to the main veneer.
Dentils Small rectangular blocks applied at regular intervals to the cornices of much 18thC furniture.
Dished table top A hollowed out solid top, associated with tripod tables with pie-crust edges.
Drop-leaf Any table with a fixed central section and hinged flaps.
Dummy drawer A decorative false drawer, complete with handle.
Escritoire A cabinet with a hinged front, which provides a writing surface, and a fitted interior.
Escutcheon Brass plate surrounding and protecting the edges of a keyhole – sometimes with a cap or cover on a pivot.
Etagère A small work table consisting of shelves or trays one above the other.
Fall front The flap of a bureau or secrétaire that pulls forward to provide a writing surface.
Fielded panel A raised panel with a bevelled or chamfered edge that fits into a framework.
Finial A decorative turned knob applied to the top of fine bureau bookcases etc.
Fluting Decorative concave, parallel grooves running down the legs of tables and chairs.
Foliate carving Carved flower and leaf motifs.
Fretwork Fine pierced decoration.
Frieze The framework immediately below a table top.
Gadroon A decorative border, carved or moulded, comprising a series of short flutes or reeds.
Gallery A wood or metal border around the top edge of a table or washstand.
Harlequin A set of chairs that are similar but do not match.
Intaglio An incised design, as opposed to a design in relief.
Joined Method of furniture construction from 15thC until the end of the 17thC using mortice and tenon joints secured by pegs or dowels, without glue.
Joined stool A stool, usually in oak, of joined construction.
Lowboy A small side table on cabriole legs, from the early 18thC.
Married The term used for an item that has been made up from two or more pieces of furniture, usually of the same period.
Mule chest A coffer with a single row of drawers in the base.
Ogee A double curve of slender S-shape.
Ormolu A mount or article that is gilded or gold coloured.
Patina The build-up of wax and dirt that gives old furniture a soft mellow look.
Pedestal desk A flat desk, usually with a leathered top, that stands on two banks of drawers.
Pediment The gabled structure that surmounts a cornice.
Platform base Three or four-cornered flat bases of tables supporting a central pedestal above and standing on scrolled or paw feet.
Plinth base A solid base, not raised on feet.
Potboard The bottom shelf of a dresser or court cupboard, often just above the floor.
Reeding Parallel strips of convex flutes found on the legs of chairs and tables.
Secrétaire A writing cabinet with a mock drawer front that lets down to provide a writing surface, revealing recessed pigeon holes.
Secrétaire bookcase A secrétaire with a bookcase fitted above.
Serpentine Undulating front for a case piece – convex in the centre and concave at the ends. Used for cabinets, chests, sideboard and so on, late 18thC.
Settle The earliest form of chair to seat two or more people.
Spandrel A decorative corner bracket, usually pierced and found at the tops of legs.
Splat The central upright in a chair back; loosely applied to all members in a chair back.
Stiles The vertical parts of a framework, usually associated with early furniture.
Stretchers The horizontal bars that unite and strengthen the legs of chairs and other furniture.
Tester The canopy or ceiling over a bed.
Tripod table A small table with a round top supported by a three-legged pillar.
Whatnot A mobile stand with open shelves.
Windsor chair A type of wooden chair with a spindle back.

DIRECTORY OF SPECIALISTS

If you would like to contact any of the following dealers, we would advise readers to telephone before a visit, therefore avoiding a wasted journey.

OAK & COUNTRY

Cambridgeshire
Simon & Penny Rumble,
Causeway End Farm
House,
Chittering,
CB5 9PW
Tel: 01223 861831

Cumbria
Anvil Antiques,
Cartmel,
Grange-over-Sands,
LA11 6QA
Tel: 015395 36362

Hampshire
Cedar Antiques Ltd,
High Street,
Hartley Wintney,
RG27 8NY
Tel: 01252 843252

Kent
Berry Antiques,
11–13 Stone Street,
Cranbrook,
TN17 3HF
Tel: 01580 712345

Douglas Bryan Antiques,
The Old Bakery,
St Davids Bridge,
Cranbrook,
TN17 3HN
Tel: 01580 713103

Flower House Antiques,
90 High Street,
Tenterden,
TN30 6HT
Tel: 01580 763764

Sutton Valence
Antiques,
North Street,
Sutton Valence
ME17 3AP
Tel: 01622 675332

Swan Antiques,
Stone Street,
Cranbrook,
TN17 3HF
Tel: 01580 712720

London
Robert Young Antiques,
68 Battersea Bridge Rd,
SW11 3AG
Tel: 020 7228 7847

Middlesex
Robert Phelps Ltd,
133–135 St Margaret's Rd,
East Twickenham,
TW1 1RG
Tel: 020 8892 1778/7129

Northamptonshire
Paul Hopwell,
30 High Street,
West Haddon,
NN6 7AP
Tel: 01788 510636

Shropshire
John & Anne Clegg,
12 Old Street,
Ludlow, SY8 1NP
Tel: 01584 873176

Somerset
Pennard House Antiques,
3–4 Piccadilly,
London Road,
Bath, BA1 6PL
Tel: 01225 313791/
01749 860260

Westville House Antiques,
Littleton,
Nr Somerton,
TA11 6NP
Tel: 01458 273376

East Sussex
The Old Mint House,
High Street,
Pevensey, BN24 5LF
Tel: 01323 762337
E-mail:
minthouse@mistral.co.uk

Wales
Country Antiques
(Wales),
Castle Mill, Kidwelly,
Carmarthenshire,
SA17 4UU
Tel: 01554 890534

West Midlands
L. P. Furniture,
(The Old Brewery),
Short Acre Street,
Walsall, WS2 8HW
Tel: 01922 746764

Wiltshire
Combe Cottage Antiques,
Castle Combe,
Chippenham,
SN14 7HU
Tel: 01249 782250

Crudwell Furniture
Strippers,
The Workshop,
Oddpenny Farm,
Crudwell, SN16 9SJ
Tel: 01285 770970

PINE & PAINTED

Buckinghamshire
For Pine,
340 Berkhampstead Rd,
Chesham, HP5 3HF
Tel: 01494 776119

Cheshire
Richmond Galleries,
Watergate Building,
New Crane Street,
Chester, CH1 4JE
Tel: 01244 317602

Cumbria
Ben Eggleston Antiques,
The Dovecote,
Long Marton,
Appleby, CA16 6BJ
Tel: 01768 361849

Utopia Antiques Ltd,
Yew Tree Barn, (on A590),
Newton-in-Cartmel,
Grange-over-Sands,
LA11 6JP
Tel: 015395 30065

Devon
Cullompton,
Old Tannery Antiques,
The Old Tannery,
Exeter Road,
Cullompton, EX15 1DT
Tel: 01884 38476/266429

Fagins Antiques,
The Old Whiteways
Cider Factory,
Hele, Exeter,
EX5 4PW
Tel: 01392 882062

Fine Pine,
Woodland Road,
Habertonford,
Nr Totnes, TQ9 7SU
Tel: 01803 732465

Essex
English Rose Antiques,
7 Church Street,
Coggeshall, CO6 1TU
Tel: 01376 562683
Mobile: 07770 880790

Gloucestershire
Bed of Roses,
12 Prestbury Road,
Cheltenham,
GL52 2PW
Tel: 01242 231918

Country Homes,
61 Long Street,
Tetbury,
GL8 8AA
Tel: 01666 502342

Hampshire
Pine Cellars,
39 Jewry Street,
Winchester,
SO23 8RY
Tel: 01962 777546/
867014

Humberside
Bell Antiques,
68A Harold Street,
Grimsby,
DN35 0HH
Tel: 01472 695110

Kent
Antique & Design,
The Old Oast,
Hollow Lane,
Canterbury,
CT1 3SA
Tel: 01227 762871

Penny Lampard,
28 High Street,
Headcorn,
TN27 9NE
Tel: 01622 890682

David Masters Antiques,
Elm Tree Farm,
High Halden,
Ashford,
TN26 3BP
Tel: 01233 850551

Old English Pine,
100 Sandgate High St,
Sandgate,
Folkestone,
CT20 3BY
Tel: 01303 248560

Up Country,
The Old Corn Stores,
68 St John's Road,
Tunbridge Wells,
TN4 9PE
Tel: 01892 523341

The Warehouse,
29–30 Queens Gardens,
Worthington Street,
Dover, CT17 9AH
Tel: 01304 242006

Lancashire
Enloc Antiques,
96 Keighley Road,
Colne,
BB8 OPH
Tel: 01282 867101

Leicestershire
Richard Kimbell,
Riverside,
Market Harborough,
LE16 7PT
Tel: 01858 433444

London
Robert Young Antiques,
68 Battersea Bridge Rd,
SW11 3AG
Tel: 020 7228 7847

Northern Ireland
Albert Forsythe,
The Old Rectory,
24 Carnteel Road,
Aughmacloy,
Co Tyrone, BT69 2DU
Tel: 01662 557522

Nottinghamshire
Jack Spratt Antiques,
Unit 5 George Street,
Newark, NG24 1LU
Tel: 01636 707714

Republic of Ireland
Bygones of Ireland Ltd,
Lodge Road,
Westport, Co Mayo
Tel: (098) 26132/25701

Delvin Farm Antiques,
Gormonston,
Co Meath
Tel: 00 353 1 841 2285

Honan's Antiques,
Crowe Street,
Gort,
Co Galway
Tel: 00 353 916 31407

Ireland's Own Antiques,
Alpine House,
Carlow Road,
Abbeyleix, Co Laois
Tel: 00 353 502 31348

Scotland
Times Past Antiques,
Broadfold Farm,
Auchterarder,
Perthshire, PH3 1DR
Tel: 01764 663166

Somerset
Gilbert & Dale Antiques,
The Old Chapel,
Church Street,
Ilchester,
Nr Yeovil,
BA22 8ZA
Tel: 01935 840464

Walcot Reclamations,
108 Walcot Street,
Bath,
BA1 5BG
Tel: 01225 444404

Wells Reclamation & Co,
Coxley,
Nr Wells,
BA5 1RQ
Tel: 01749 677087

Westville House
Antiques,
Littleton,
Nr Somerton,
TA11 6NP
Tel: 01458 273376

Staffordshire
Johnson's,
120 Mill Street,
Leek,
ST13 8HA
Tel: 01538 386745

Surrey
Cherub Antiques
of Carshalton,
Spring House,
Benhill Road,
Sutton,
SM1 3RN
Tel: 020 8661 7427/
020 8643 0028

East Sussex
Bob Hoare Antiques,
Unit Q Phoenix Place,
North Street,
Lewes,
BN7 2DQ
Tel: 01273 480557

Ann Lingard,
Ropewalk Antiques,
Ropewalk,
Rye,
TN31 7NA
Tel: 01797 223486

Graham Price Antiques
Ltd,
Apple Store,
Chaucer Industrial
Estate,
Dittons Road,
Polegate,
BN26 6JF
Tel: 01323 487167

The Netherlands
Jacques Van Der Tol,
Antennestraat 34,
1322 A E Almere-Stad
Tel: 00 31 3653 62050

Wales
Heritage Restorations,
Maes Y Glydfa,
Llanfair Caereinion,
Welshpool,
Powys,
SY21 0HD
Tel: 1938 810384
Website:
www.heritagerestorations
.co.uk

The Pot Board,
30 King Street,
Carmarthen,
SA31 1BS
Tel: 01834 842699
01267 236623
Email:
Gill@potboard.co.uk
Website:
www.potboard.co.uk

Warwickshire
The Old Pine House,
16 Warwick Street,
Royal Leamington Spa,
CV32 5LL
Tel: 01926 470477

Christopher Peters
Antiques,
19 Broad Street,
Brinklow,
Nr Rugby,
CV23 0LS
Tel: 01788 832673

Wiltshire
Crudwell Furniture
Strippers,
The Workshop,
Oddpenny Farm,
Crudwell,
SN16 9SJ
Tel: 01285 770970

North Wiltshire
Exporters,
Farm Hill House,
Brinkworth,
Nr Chippenham,
SN15 5AJ
Tel: 01666 510876

Yorkshire
Simon Byrne Antiques,
Unit 16
Eastburn Mills,
Eastburn,
Keighley,
BD20 7SJ
Tel: 01535 656297

KITCHENWARE

Berkshire
Below Stairs,
103 High Street,
Hungerford,
RG17 0NB
Tel: 01488 682317

Cheshire
Maria Hopwood
Antiques,
Hulgrave Hall,
Tiverton,
Tarporley,
CW6 9UQ
Tel: 01829 733313

Gloucestershire
Judi Bland,
Durham House
Antique Centre,
Sheep Street,
Stow-on-the-Wold,
GL54 1AA
Tel: 01451 870404/
01276 857576

Kent
Penny Lampard,
28 High Street,
Headcorn,
TN27 9NE
Tel: 01622 890682

Lancashire
The Old Bakery,
36 Inglewhite Road,
Longridge,
Preston,
PR3 3JS
Tel: 01772 785411

London
Christina Bishop,
Viewing by
appointment only
Tel: 020 7221 4688

Suffolk
Tartan Bow,
Tel: 01379 783057
(open Fridays 10-5pm,
other days by appt)

East Sussex
Ann Lingard,
Ropewalk Antiques,
Ropewalk,
Rye,
TN31 7NA
Tel: 01797 223486

West Midlands
The Dog House,
309 Bloxwich Road,
Walsall,
WS2 7BD
Tel: 01922 30829

INDEX TO ADVERTISERS

An unusual Austrian pine kneehole desk, with leather top, centre section pulls out, on turned feet, late 19thC, 49in (124.5cm) wide.
£1,200–1,300 *HeR*

A Scandinavian pine settle, with corner cupboard, c1820, 124in (315cm) wide.
£525–575 *BEL*